THE ELGAR COMPANION TO DECENTRALIZED FINANCE, DIGITAL ASSETS, AND BLOCKCHAIN TECHNOLOGIES

It is with profound sadness that we acknowledge the passing of Philipp Sandner, a distinguished scholar and cherished colleague. His intellectual rigor, dedication, and collaborative spirit greatly enriched this work and inspired all who had the privilege of working with him.

We extend our heartfelt condolences to Philipp Sandner's family, friends, and colleagues. His legacy of excellence and his commitment to advancing knowledge will endure through his contributions to this book and beyond. Philipp's presence will be sorely missed, but his influence will continue to be felt by all who engage with his work.

The Elgar Companion to Decentralized Finance, Digital Assets, and Blockchain Technologies

Edited by

Henrik Cronqvist

The George L. Argyros School of Business and Economics, Chapman University, USA

Desiree-Jessica Pely

Institute for Capital Markets and Corporate Finance, Ludwig-Maximilians-Universität München, Germany

Edward Elgar PUBLISHING

Cheltenham, UK • Northampton, MA, USA

Published by
Edward Elgar Publishing Limited
The Lypiatts
15 Lansdown Road
Cheltenham
Glos GL50 2JA
UK

Edward Elgar Publishing, Inc.
William Pratt House
9 Dewey Court
Northampton
Massachusetts 01060
USA

A catalogue record for this book
is available from the British Library

Library of Congress Control Number: 2024934167

This book is available electronically in the **Elgar**online
Economics subject collection
http://dx.doi.org/10.4337/9781035307760

Printed on elemental chlorine free (ECF)
recycled paper containing 30% Post-Consumer Waste

ISBN 978 1 0353 0775 3 (cased)
ISBN 978 1 0353 0776 0 (eBook)

Printed and bound in the USA

Contents

Contributors

Mario Bernardi, Chicago Global, Pyth Network, United States.

Alexander Brauneis, Nottingham Trent University Business School Institute of Finance, United Kingdom.

Dirk Bullmann, European Central Bank; Adviser to the Chief Services Officer / Innovation Coordinator, European Union (Germany).

Mariana Carmona, Instituto Tecnológico Autónomo de México, Mexico.

Ben Charoenwong, National University of Singapore Business School, Singapore.

Gordon Clarke, Monetics, a Singapore-based payments consulting firm, Singapore.

Henrik Cronqvist, The George L. Argyros School of Business and Economics, Chapman University, USA.

Michele Fabi, IP Paris, Ecole Polytechnique, CREST, France.

Marco Fama, Università degli Studi di Bergamo, Italy.

David Florysiak, IU International University of Applied Sciences in Germany and University of Southern Denmark.

Hans Gersbach, CER-ETH – Center of Economic Research at ETH Zurich, Switzerland.

Lucio Gobbi, Università di Trento, Italy.

Paz Gomez, Instituto Tecnológico Autónomo de México, Mexico.

Felix Hoops, Technical University of Munich, Germany.

Emir Hrnjic, NUS Business School and Asian Institute of Digital Finance National University of Singapore.

Felix Irresberger, Durham University, United Kingdom.

Kose John, New York University, United States.

Marcel Kaiser, Frankfurt School Blockchain Center, Germany.

Myriam Kassoul, IP Paris, Ecole Polytechnique, CREST, France.

Anies Khan, Frankfurt School Blockchain Center, Germany.

Stefano Lucarelli, Università degli Studi di Bergamo, Italy.

Mieszko Mazur, ESSCA School of Management, France.

Roland Mestel, University of Graz Institute of Banking, Austria.

Eva Meyer, TUM School of Management, Munich, Germany.

Fernando Molina, J.P. Morgan, School of Business, Torcuato Di Tella University (UTDT), Argentina.

Burak Öz, Technical University of Munich, Germany.

Desiree-Jessica Pely, Institute for Capital Markets and Corporate Finance, Ludwig-Maximilians-Universität München, Germany.

Efstathios Polyzos, Zayed University, College of Business, United Arab Emirates.

Mathias Ponte, TUM School of Management, Munich, Germany.

Julien Prat, CNRS, IP Paris, Ecole Polytechnique, CREST, France.

Martin Rauch, Finance, University of Graz, Austria.

Pablo Roccatagliata, J.P. Morgan, School of Business, Torcuato Di Tella University (UTDT), Argentina.

Fahad Saleh, Wake Forest University, United States.

Philipp Sandner, Frankfurt School Blockchain Center, Germany.

Andrew Urquhart, ICMA Centre, Henley Business School, University of Reading, United Kingdom

Roger Wattenhofer, CEPR, Distributed Computing Group ETH Zurich, Switzerland.

Isabell Welpe, TUM School of Management, Munich, Germany.

Introduction to *The Elgar Companion to Decentralized Finance, Digital Assets, and Blockchain Technologies*

Henrik Cronqvist and Desiree-Jessica Pely

For as long as wealth has existed, human beings have always dedicated their lives to pursuing a higher standard of life personally and socially. For example, land hoarding dates back to ancient Egypt, capital allocation to the Industrial Revolution (Allen 2009), and the Roaring Twenties saw stock prices more than quadruple (White 1990). To this day, all aforementioned assets had one common characteristic: a centralized form of wealth. The government plays a crucial role to reinforce such ownership and land, and without a state, capital would have little to no value (Hardin 1968). An individual's wealth is typically held by an institution, usually a bank, which facilitates its movement to and from relevant parties.

This changed in January 2009, when Bitcoin (BTC), the world's first cryptocurrency, was created by Satoshi Nakamoto, a pseudonym used by the original inventor(s) (Chohan 2017). Bitcoin operates on a fundamentally different level compared to traditional assets. For example, the cryptocurrency has no physical form and its movement is tracked using a digital ledger known as a Blockchain. While Bitcoin's initial uptake was limited—its first real-world transaction was the purchase of two large pizzas in Jacksonville, Florida, for 10,000 BTC (Yermack 2015)—its value increased steadily throughout the 2010s. In April 2011, it took parity with the US dollar, before its peak at $1242 on November 29, 2013. Bitcoin recessed for the next four years before reaching new heights in 2017. Four years later, on October 20, 2021, Bitcoin tripled, and the value of the two pizzas was worth close to $670 million.

This type of growth has made cryptocurrencies some of the most relevant financial instruments on the market. But, while many perceive the space as a "get rich quick" scheme for the TikTok generation, others believe that it has the potential to be so much more.

Cryptocurrencies allow moving away from centralized finance into decentralized finance (DeFi). DeFi removes the need for banks and other financial institutions using blockchain and similar online ledgers. Anyone with an internet connection can get access, holding funds in online wallets, and transferring assets quickly and privately—without the involvement of government or financial institutions (Schar 2020). But is this rational?

When we consider behavior within an economic context as wealth accumulation represents, we often assume that all agents act "rationally," that is, individuals making choices to maximize their utility after carefully considering all details and taking into account any other options they may or may not have. However, this is nearly impossible as decision-makers do not have the "perfect" set of information to make rational decisions. In fact, when humans make decisions, they are subject to different biases that make those choices easier. The theory of these biases and other psychological determinants of choices is known as behavioral economics. We distinguish between behavioral states, traits, and actions as suggested by Cronqvist and Pely (2019).

One bias that can influence our behavior is rooted in our traits, which are shaped by factors such as our upbringing, environment, historical events, and life experiences. For instance, individuals who grew up during the Great Depression may exhibit more risk-averse tendencies compared to those who came of age during a period of economic prosperity (Malmendier and Nagel 2011; Schoar and Zuo 2016).

In addition, our moods and emotions can significantly influence the decisions we make, representing behavioral states where impulses drive temporary choices. For example, individuals may indulge in short-sighted purchases following positive news or avoid strategic risks when feeling anxious about the future (Mannor et al. 2016). Past decisions also impact future choices, leading us to seek shortcuts by replicating previous actions.

Lastly, social and cultural norms play a crucial role in decision-making, also referred to as behavioral actions. This phenomenon can be observed in herding effects, where positive sentiment or topical relevance surrounding an asset can influence others to invest as well. Recent studies suggest that crypto markets are particularly susceptible to herding effects, especially in times of uncertainty (Bouri et al. 2019). These influences have a heightened impact on decisions related to assets in DeFi. Unlike traditional economic decisions, assessing the value of cryptocurrencies lacks the same level of objectivity, making it challenging to determine where to begin.

The abstract nature of crypto markets, paired with the extreme volatility of assets, meme coins, and rug pulls, make them significantly more vulnerable to behavioral biases than other centralized assets. For this reason, we decided to edit a Companion with chapters discussing the future of decentralization in finance.

We start with an overview of the status quo and the impact of DeFi on existing financial systems, illustrated by Khan and Sandner (Chapter 1), and a deep dive into decentralized lending, led by Irresberger, John, and Salehm (Chapter 2), ahead of Bullman's (Chapter 3) prediction of the role that crypto will play in the future of payments.

Next, we cover a discussion surrounding regulation and the role of the central bank. Fama, Gobbi, and Lucarelli (Chapter 4) analyze crypto's interaction with monetary policy, followed by Clarke and Hrnic (Chapter 5) addressing the concern over crypto destabilizing currencies in emerging economies. MiCAR (Markets in Crypto Assets Regulation) and the growing number of utility coins are covered by Florysiak (Chapter 6), preceding Gersbach and Wattenhofer's (Chapter 7) blueprint for an eFranc. Regulation is needed as crypto thefts occur on a regular basis. Charoenwong and Bernardi (Chapter 8) take us through cryptocurrency thefts that occurred over the past decade.

After that, we present the functionality and design of digital assets, outlining their theoretical and empirical foundations. Brauneis, Mestel, and Rauch (Chapter 9) start with a deep dive into the operating principal of automated market makers built on top of smart contract blockchains, replacing central authorities or third-party middlemen, before Fabi, Kassoul, and Prat (Chapter 10) provide an extensive theoretical and empirical literature review on market makers. Molina and Roccatagliata (Chapter 11) cover mechanism design and changes to ETH (Ethereum) gas prices, before Öz and Hoops (Chapter 12) consider how maximum extractable value may change the trajectory of the tokenized assets. Kaiser (Chapter 13) considers the impact that scale will have on cross-chain infrastructure among different assets. Lastly, Mazur and Polyzos (Chapter 14) provide an overview on non-fungible tokens (NFTs), an alternative digital asset instrument.

To conclude, we look at DeFi through the lens of sustainability. Urquhart (Chapter 15) evaluates the environmental, social, and governance (ESG) implications of Bitcoin. In contrast, Meyer, Welpe, Sandner, and Ponte (Chapter 16) argue that the societal benefit of regenerative finance could contribute in years to come. Finally, Carmona and Gomez (Chapter 17) study the impact of DeFi on global financial inclusion.

REFERENCES

Allen, R.C. (2009). "Engels' pause: Technical change, capital accumulation, and inequality in the British Industrial Revolution," *Explorations in Economic History*, 46(4), 418–435.

Bouri, E., Gupta, R., and Roubaud, D. (2019). "Herding behavior in cryptocurrencies," *Finance Research Letters*, 29, 216–221.

Chohan, U.W. (2017). "A history of Bitcoin," available at SSRN: https://papers.ssrn.com/sol3/papers.cfm?abstract_id=3047875.

Cronqvist, H., and Pély, D.-J. (2019), "Behavioral and Social Corporate Finance," *Oxford Research Encyclopedia of Economics and Finance*, https://doi.org/10.1093/acrefore/9780190625979.013.427

Hardin, G. (1968). "The Tragedy of the Commons," *Science*, 162(3859), 1243–1248.

Malmendier, U., and Nagel, S. (2011). "Depression babies: Do macroeconomic experiences affect risk-taking," *Quarterly Journal of Economics*, 126(1), 373–416.

Mannor, M.J., Wowak, A.J., and Bartkus, V.O. (2016). "Heavy lies the crown? How job anxiety affects top executive decision-making in gain and loss contexts," *Strategic Management Journal*, 37, 1968–1989.

Schar, F. (2020). "Decentralized finance: On Blockchain- and smart contract-based financial markets," available at SSRN: https://papers.ssrn.com/sol3/papers.cfm?abstract_id=3571335.

Schoar, A., and Zuo, L. (2016). "Does the market value CEO styles?," *American Economic Review: Papers and Proceedings*, 106(5), 262–266.

White, E.N. (1990). "The Stock Market Boom and Crash of 1929 Revisited," *Journal of Economic Perspectives*, 4(2), 67–83.

Yermac, D. (2015). "Is Bitcoin a real currency? An economic appraisal," available at SSRN: https://papers.ssrn.com/sol3/papers.cfm?abstract_id=2361599.

1. DeFi: an overview of use cases and a status quo analysis of the ecosystem

Anies Khan and Philipp Sandner

INTRODUCTION

Decentralized finance (DeFi) refers to an emerging alternative or complementary financial infrastructure to the existing centralized financial system, built on public blockchains (Schär 2020). It uses smart contracts to replicate existing financial services in a more open, inclusive, transparent, and efficient manner, as well as to create entirely new financial services enabled by the underlying blockchain technology such as autonomous liquidity pools, decentralized stablecoins, and flash loans (Schär 2020). Existing literature suggests that DeFi may offer solutions to some of the key problems inherent in the centralized financial system: centralized control, limited access, inefficiency, lack of interoperability, and opacity (Harvey et al. 2020). Furthermore, there are risks to consider such as fraud, volatility, usability, and regulatory uncertainty leading to barriers to widespread adoption of the DeFi applications (Chen and Bellavitis 2020).

As the DeFi applications increasingly attract funds, a comprehensive overview is needed for the affected parties to understand the concepts and implications. To evaluate the current state and potential future impact, the following research questions were derived: What is the current state of the DeFi ecosystem in terms of existing use cases and adoption? What are the benefits and risks of DeFi in its current state? What is the potential impact on the existing financial system? Which obstacles is DeFi facing regarding its widespread adoption?

THEORETICAL BACKGROUND

The Traditional Financial System

In this chapter, we briefly outline the problems of the existing financial system referred to as the traditional financial system or the centralized financial system (CeFi) with its main features and issues. On a high level, a financial system connects financial market participants, such as depositors and investors in need of funds, with financial institutions acting as intermediaries to exchange funds (Chen and Bellavitis 2020; Gurusamy 2009).

In general, financial institutions can exclude anyone from using their services at their discretion. The limited access also refers to the unbanked population who do not have access to any financial services. Furthermore, most people who have access to financial services do not receive the most competitive pricing and most favorable terms, reserving those for players with much wealth, such as large institutions (Harvey et al. 2020).

In the traditional financial system, there is often an opacity of rules by which financial products operate. There are often private agreements, back-deals, and centralization that enhance the system's opacity (Qin et al. 2021b).

The control of the financial system is exerted by governments and large institutions that hold near-monopolies over the money supply, the inflation rate, and access to investment opportunities. Asset owners and traders must rely on these centralized institutions to manage their funds and make transactions (Harvey et al. 2020; Stepanova and Eriņš 2021).

The lack of interoperability in traditional finance refers to the fact that the products are difficult or impossible to integrate, as different financial institutions must maintain their own ledgers. If integration is possible, it generally requires at least a wire transfer, which can be time-consuming and costly for the customer (Chen and Bellavitis 2020; Harvey et al. 2020).

Smart Contracts

Smart contracts are a key component of the DeFi ecosystem; therefore, their essential features and functionalities are explained in this section. Smart contracts are computerized transaction protocols that automatically execute, control, or record the legally relevant events and actions according to the predefined terms of a contract or agreement (Fries and Paal 2019; Savelyev 2017; Tapscott and Tapscott 2016). The main objective of a smart contract is to eliminate the need for trusted intermediaries to ensure that the terms in the contract are met, while reducing arbitrations, enforcement costs, and fraud losses (Fries and Paal 2019).

This theoretical concept was first introduced by Nick Szabo in the 1990s, but for a technical implementation, a tamper-resistant underlying infrastructure was required (Lauslahti et al. 2017). Szabo used vending machines as the primitive ancestor of smart contracts to illustrate their general concept. The machine takes in coins and dispenses change and the product according to the displayed price. The vending machine can be described as the bearer of the contract, allowing anyone with coins to be able to participate in an exchange, while the lockbox of the machine securely stores the coins (Szabo 1997).

The emergence of Ethereum made it possible to realize Szabo's vision of a contract that can be fully computerized and without the intervention of intermediaries in a transparent manner. Using the Ethereum blockchain as the infrastructure layer prevents the execution of the contracts from being stopped by a single party unless this possibility has been specifically built into the code (Fries and Paal 2019). This characteristic made it possible to move from automated contracts as described in the vending machine example to truly autonomous smart contracts, which are capable of self-execution and self-enforcement (Lauslahti et al. 2017).

Therefore, in the context of blockchain, smart contracts can be redefined as small applications stored on a blockchain and executed in parallel by a large set of validators or nodes (Schär 2020). Given that multiple blockchain nodes execute smart contract code, it is not controlled by, and cannot be stopped by, any single party, which distinguishes smart contracts on the public and permissionless blockchain from if-then relationships in other computer systems that are controlled by individual parties (Fries and Paal 2019).

A simple example for an application of a smart contract could be an escrow agreement which is based on the occurrence of certain conditions or predefined terms to release funds. The advantages of smart contracts arise when multiple parties who wish to engage in some form of an agreement or contract do not trust each other, as they can reduce transaction costs such as the costs of coming to an agreement, formalization, and enforcement (Voshmgir 2020). Furthermore, smart contracts allow automation and autonomy, as no external authority can overrule the predefined terms of the smart contract (Ferreira 2021).

Despite the huge potential smart contracts offer, there are also some challenges. Perceived as one of the main advantages of smart contracts, their irreversibility can also be viewed as a challenge: if all the involved parties in a smart contract agree to change terms, the changes might not be possible if potential future changes to the agreed terms were not accounted for by the time of writing the initial code (von Haller Gronbaek 2016). From a technical perspective, smart contracts can be subject to bugs, as faulty written code and cannot be adjusted once the contract is running, which can be exploited by malicious actors. If the relevant data for the execution of the contract is coming from off-chain sources called oracles, the reliability of the data can pose a security concern (Voshmgir 2020). Lastly, there are transactional privacy concerns, as even on pseudonymous public blockchains the identities of the contractual parties might be traceable through transactional graph analysis methods and software (Ferreira 2021).

Decentralized Autonomous Organizations

Furthermore, smart contracts allow for the governance of a larger group of people who share the same interests or goals, such as in an organization or club, without the need for a formalized traditional centralized organization. These forms of organizations are called decentralized autonomous organizations (DAOs). Unlike in traditional companies, organizations, or institutions where the rights and legal obligations are regulated through legal contracts and enforced by the legal system that encompasses the organization, a smart contract formalizes the governance rules of a DAO, such as bylaws and governing statutes by code, and replaces the legal enforcement of these rules with its code (Voshmgir 2020).

Oracles

Blockchain oracles refer to third-party services providing smart contracts with external information that can trigger the predefined actions of the smart contract, serving as a bridge between the blockchain and the outside world, as smart contracts cannot access any data that is outside of the blockchain network (Beniiche 2020; Mammadzada et al. 2020; Mou 2021).

For the execution of many contractual agreements, access to relevant information from the outside world (off-chain data) is essential. Without oracles, the smart contract's use cases would be limited to agreements that solely require data from within the network such as transactional data or account balance data (Beniiche 2020; Mou 2021).

The data transmitted by oracles to the blockchain comes in many forms. Examples include exchange rate data, political events, or the successful completion of payment. The oracle itself is not the source of the data, but rather the external data agent that requests, verifies, authenticates the off-chain data sources, and then transmits the data to a smart contract (Beniiche 2020; Mammadzada et al. 2020).

While oracles widely extend the use cases of smart contracts, they also introduce risks known as the oracle problem, which consists of two parts. The first is that smart contracts running on a public blockchain on their own cannot access external data. By using oracles to access off-chain data, the advantages of the "trustlessness," achieved by using a public blockchain, might be compromised (Mou 2021). The second is that third-party oracles themselves could potentially provide false data or no data at all, reintroducing a single point of failure. Even trusted oracles can be subject to "man-in-the-middle attacks," where malicious actors modify or falsify the data that oracles feed into smart contracts (Mou 2021). The oracle problem remains a mostly unsolved issue, but decentralized oracles such as Chainlink can resolve some of these concerns and provide smart contracts with external data that requires little trust between parties (Beniiche 2020; Mou 2021).

Decentralized Applications

Decentralized apps (dApps) are software applications that have their backend, which consists of sets of interacting smart contracts running on a public blockchain (Abdulhakeem and Hu 2021; Metcalfe 2020; Ozcan 2021).

Their centralized counterparts, centralized software applications, typically include a user interface, such as a mobile app, a website, or a desktop application that is installed on a computer. The data is provided by a single entity, stored, and processed either on the provider's servers or on the user's computer. DApps are similar to centralized software applications in terms of their user interface, as they are typically accessible from a website or a mobile app (Metcalfe 2020). The key differences of dApps include their use of the blockchain for data storage and processing and independence: no single server or entity controls them; decisions are made by nodes in the network (Bareis 2019; Metcalfe 2020). This leads to certain advantages compared to centralized software applications: dApps are permissionless and censorship-resistant, no user can be excluded from using them, and no one can alter the code once the dApp is deployed.

Because they consist of smart contracts running on a blockchain, anyone is able to inspect the code and understand how the dApps function, increasing transparency compared to centralized software applications (Antonopoulos and Wood 2018; Harvey et al. 2020).

Smart Contract Platforms

Smart contract platforms are blockchain networks that allow the creation of smart contracts. They are often referred to as the second generation of blockchains, supporting programmable transactions and smart contracts that enable the use of the underlying blockchain technology for more advanced use cases than digital payment systems with integrated cryptocurrencies (Bareis 2019; Srivastava et al. 2018).

Ethereum

Ethereum was the first smart contract platform, remaining the largest and most widely used when comparing relevant metrics such as market capitalization of the native token, the total number of dApps, daily active users, daily transaction volume, and the number of smart contracts (CoinMarketCap 2021b; Kolb et al. 2020; State of the DApps 2021). Therefore, this chapter focuses on Ethereum to illustrate the key concepts.

Vitalik Buterin's intention was to build a blockchain with an integrated Turing-complete programming language, Solidity, that allows users to write powerful smart contracts that have "their own arbitrary rules for ownership, transaction formats and state transition functions" (Buterin 2014: 12).

The Ethereum network follows the same general logic as the Bitcoin network, using the blockchain as a distributed ledger storing account balances and their movements. Because Ethereum also enables smart contracts, the Ethereum blockchain needs to additionally hold the collective memory of all smart contracts deployed and running on the Ethereum Virtual Machine[1] Together with the accounts and balances, this is called the complete state of Ethereum. Every finalized block in the blockchain has only one state, which is agreed upon by all nodes in the network. That state is changed and updated with each new block that is added. An example of a state change could be a simple Ether transaction from one account to another, or the deployment of a smart contract (Ethereum Foundation 2021b; Ichiba Hotchkiss 2019).

To come to a consensus regarding the state, Ethereum uses a proof-of-work algorithm but currently plans a proof-of-stake mechanism as at the time of writing in September 2021. Nodes in the Ethereum network refer to computers that run an Ethereum client, such as Geth, on their computer. Because each node executes all smart contract codes on the Ethereum virtual machine (EVM), the Ethereum network is often referred to as a global, decentralized supercomputer.

Ethereum features two types of accounts: externally owned accounts (EOAs), controlled by humans with their private keys, and smart contract accounts, controlled by their smart contract code. Both types of accounts can hold, send, and receive Ether[2] and interact with deployed smart contracts (Buterin 2014). The key differences are that smart contract accounts have no private key controlling them and are controlled by the code within the account and a set of predefined triggers within that code. Transactions in the Ethereum network generally refer to transferring value between accounts, creating new smart contracts, or triggering smart contracts (Ethereum Foundation, 2021a).

When Ether is used to transfer value between accounts or to create or use smart contracts, the user or creator of the transaction is required to pay a fee in Ether called gas. Gas refers to the unit that measures the amount of resources[3] required to execute a specific operation on the Ethereum network (Ethereum Foundation 2021c). Each line of code in a smart contract that needs to be executed will take a certain amount of gas, making more complex smart contracts more costly. The overall transaction fees depend on the resources required by the transaction and on the supply and demand between the network's miners and users. The gas must be provided prior to the execution of the smart contract, and if the contract runs out of gas, it will stop running.

Tokens and Cryptocurrencies

In general, tokens can represent any form of economic value or access rights. Tokens existed before blockchain technology emerged. Examples of tokens include casino chips which represent money, airline tickets that grant the owner access to a certain flight, or paper money and coins. Usually, tokens include some measures against counterfeiting to ensure their validity and security (Voshmgir 2020).

Cryptographic tokens represent programmable assets or access rights that are managed (by a smart contract) on an underlying blockchain. The tokens do not represent a digital file that is stored locally; instead, the token refers to an asset or access right collectively managed by the blockchain network. They can only be accessed or transferred by the person owning the private key for the blockchain address that the tokens are assigned to. Validity and security for cryptographic tokens are managed by the smart contract that created them and the consensus mechanism of the underlying blockchain (Voshmgir 2020).

The first type of tokens were native protocol tokens or cryptocurrencies of public and permissionless blockchains, which are issued directly by the blockchain protocol on which they run, such as Bitcoin on the Bitcoin network or Ether on the Ethereum network (Nakamoto 2008; Yermack 2015). In the respective blockchain networks, the tokens typically serve as an incentive to keep their decentral infrastructure secure and stable.

Smart contracts platforms such as Ethereum allow for the creation of individual tokens called second-layer tokens, which can be further distinguished by how they were formed. Those created by smart contracts are called application tokens. Second-layer tokens can also be created through sidechains (Voshmgir 2020).

The smart contracts creating tokens are referred to as token contracts. They specify the properties of the tokens, how they are managed, and the rights of the token holders. The main difference from native protocol tokens is that second-layer tokens are managed by smart contracts running on top of another blockchain instead of having their own blockchain, and that they can have any function or property. They can be used to represent virtually anything, ranging from any digital or physical asset, access rights, or the right to perform an action in the network or real world. They are also frequently used as a governance mechanism, allowing the holders to vote on things such as protocol upgrades (Cryptopedia Staff 2021; Voshmgir 2020). Ethereum has implemented standardized token contracts to create tokens, such as the ERC-20 standard for fungible tokens and the ERC-721 standard for non-fungible tokens (NFTs). NFTs can be used to represent tokens with differing properties that can be distinguished from each other, for example, to represent unique art pieces or anything that uniquely identifies a person, such as any type of ID. These second-layer tokens play a crucial role in the DeFi ecosystem as most of the DeFi protocols use them.

While this basic technical classification into native protocol tokens and second-layer tokens is mostly agreed upon, many other dimensions that tokens can be classified by exist, with no clear consensus so far.

Decentralized Finance

In a broad sense, decentralized finance can be defined as an ecosystem of financial services or applications built on top of public smart contracts platforms or open blockchain-based protocols (Birch 2020; Sandner and von Wachter 2019; Schär 2020).

This broad definition would also classify first-generation blockchain protocols that aimed to replicate financial services such as Bitcoin into DeFi. This chapter focuses on a narrower definition of DeFi, only including DeFi services built on smart contract platforms. Specifically, the majority of DeFi applications are built on Ethereum at the time of writing in September 2021 (Consensys n.d.; DeFi Pulse 2021; Schär 2020).

An important aspect distinguishing "true" DeFi applications from centralized finance (CeFi) applications, or services in the blockchain or digital asset space such as traditional crypto exchanges such as Binance or Coinbase, lies in DeFi applications' characteristic as non-custodial, meaning that the private keys to the users' wallets remain with the users, giving them full control over their funds at any time (Dain et al. 2020; Werner et al. 2021).

Properties of DeFi

An additional important aspect characterizing DeFi is that it is decentral, as it is based on decentral public smart contract platforms, leading to little or no need for intermediaries or centralized institutions, such as clearinghouses or custodians whose role will be taken over by the smart contracts (Katona 2021; Sandner and von Wachter 2019; Schär 2020). The governance of DeFi is also decentral, as most DeFi protocols occur as DAOs that are governed by governance token holders, which anyone can acquire (Amler et al. 2021).

Because the DeFi ecosystem is based on public or permissionless blockchains, it is open for anyone to use DeFi services, and no party can be excluded (Amler et al. 2021; Chen and Bellavitis 2020). In contrast to the traditional financial system, it is also open in the sense that anyone can take over the role of the financial institutions themselves: by becoming a miner or validator, anyone can help to provide the infrastructure for the ecosystem. If the governance structure is a DAO, it is possible to suggest and vote for changes in a DeFi protocol or the underlying smart contract platform or even directly contribute to the development of the underlying smart contract platform (Jameson 2021).

The DeFi ecosystem is transparent in multiple dimensions. All transactions on a public blockchain are publicly available, although only pseudonymously, as the users behind the transactions cannot be directly linked to their public keys. Therefore, all the usage and stored funds are publicly visible at any time (Amler et al. 2021). DeFi applications are mainly developed using open-source code, allowing any party to inspect and audit the code of the application at any time (Stepanova and Eriņš 2021; Werner et al. 2021).

When DeFi is defined, the goal often consists of recreating and replacing existing centralized financial services (John 2020; Popescu 2020). The underlying blockchain technology additionally enables the development of entirely new financial products such as flash loans that were not possible or feasible in centralized finance (Qin et al. 2021b).

The DeFi ecosystem is often described as interoperable and composable. Interoperability can be distinguished into functional interoperability and technical interoperability. Functional interoperability refers to the ability of different applications to interact because they exist on the same platform. Technical interoperability refers to the ability of two different platforms to interact. The DeFi ecosystem is functionally interoperable, as smart contracts of different DeFi applications can interact with each other if they run on the same blockchain. This allows users to interact with different DeFi applications within the same transaction and seamlessly move their funds from one protocol to another (Chen and Bellavitis 2020; Meegan and Koens 2021).

Composability refers to the fact that DeFi applications not only can interact with each other but also can be combined to build entirely new applications with complex architectures or to optimize the transaction output (John 2020; Werner et al. 2021).

Blockchain transactions allow sequential transactions, which allow combining multiple financial operations into one transaction. Atomic enforcement of these transactions means that either the entire transaction is executed with all operations, or the transaction fails if one more single operation fails (Qin et al. 2021b).

The DeFi infrastructure

The DeFi ecosystem consists of a multilayered infrastructure, with each layer having its distinct purpose. The different layers build on each other, creating an open and composable infrastructure (Schär 2020). Schär (2020) suggests the following conceptual framework to analyze these layers.

The settlement layer (layer 1) consists of the blockchain and its native protocol token. It includes the basic operating rules of the ecosystem, and transactions are executed on this layer. Its purpose is to store ownership information securely and to build the foundation for trustless transaction executions.

The application layer (layer 2) consists of all assets that are issued on top of the settlement layer, including the native protocol tokens and second-layer tokens, such as ERC-20 tokens.

The protocol layer (layer 3) consists of DeFi protocols which can have different use cases such as decentralized exchanges, on-chain asset management, and more. The protocols are implemented as a set of smart contracts that can be accessed by any user or any DeFi application, making them highly interoperable. The protocol layer mainly refers to the backend of these protocols consisting of the smart contracts that define how the protocols function and are governed.

The application layer (layer 4) consists of user-facing dApps that connect to the single protocols. The user interface between the users and the smart contracts on the protocol layer is usually a web-based front-end, offering a better user experience (UX) than the protocol layer.

The aggregation layer (layer 5) can be viewed as an extension of the application layer where aggregators create user-facing platforms that connect different protocols and dApps. Usually, the aggregation layer consists of platforms that compare and rate different dApps and protocols according to the rates and services they offer (LongHash Ventures 2021; Schär 2020).

The layers are hierarchical; each layer cannot exist and function without the layer below. The implementations of different DeFi applications are a result of the interactions and transactions of the different layers with each other. The level of decentralization, scalability, and security of each layer depends on the layers below and, therefore, ultimately on the settlement layer (Hay 2020; Schär 2020).

METHODOLOGY

To gain insights regarding the current state of DeFi and its potential impact on the traditional financial system, expert interviews were conducted as an efficient and concentrated method of gathering qualitative data. The additional rationale for choosing expert interviews was to understand the relevant parties' perception of the DeFi ecosystem at its current development stage and its future impact on the existing financial system.

According to Flick (2014), expert interviews are a specific form of semi-structured interviews. While structured interviews use a predetermined set of questions with the same wording asked in the same order, semi-structured interviews are less rigid regarding the structure, content, and wording of the questions, allowing additional

Table 1.1 Overview of the interviewed experts

Interview	Position	Nature of Business
Expert 1	Chief Digital Officer	Private bank
Expert 2	Senior Advisor	Financial supervisory authority
Expert 3	Software Engineer	Infrastructure and dApp development
Expert 4	Senior Manager Digitalization and Innovation	State-owned development bank
Expert 5	Managing Director New Digital Markets	Stock exchange
Expert 6	Head of Cloud and DLT Division	Retail bank
Expert 7	Venture Developer	DeFi startup
Expert 8	CEO	DeFi startup
Expert 9	Product Manager	FinTech in crypto custody
Expert 10	CEO	DeFi startup
Expert 11	CFO and COO	FinTech in asset tokenization
Expert 12	CEO	DeFi startup

in-depth or prompt questions that are not part of the interview schedule, at the discretion of the interviewer (Cassell 2015; Kumar 2010; Mayer 2008).

Considering the heterogeneity of the experts, the semi-structured interview approach was chosen, allowing slightly differing interview schedules for the different groups of experts. In total, there were three versions of the interview schedule consisting of open-ended questions with sub-questions.

In the scope of this chapter, "expert" generally describes an individual who deals with blockchain and DeFi-related topics in their professional activities and acts as one of the key responsible people within their organization regarding these topics. Table 1.1 gives and overview of the interviewed experts.

The summarizing qualitative content analyses suggested by Mayring (2016) comprised the methodical procedure mainly used to analyze the interviews. To briefly describe the method: through omissions, paraphrasing, generalization, construction, integration, selection, and bundling, the text material is reduced while the important content is preserved. In this approach, the material is gradually generalized, and the material abundance is diminished (Mayring 2016).

To give an overview of the existing DeFi applications and draw a comparison between DeFi and CeFi, the existing applications were described using primary sources such as the protocols' white papers, and secondary sources such as academic literature to supplement the findings.

RESULTS AND DISCUSSION

Overview of Decentralized Finance Use Cases and Applications

Stablecoins

A major problem of cryptocurrencies lies in their excessive price volatility, frequently mentioned by scholars and practitioners as the main reason why they cannot function as a currency. The volatility hinders them in satisfying the three functions of money: unit of account, store of value, and medium of exchange (Yermack 2015).

Due to this circumstance, an entire sub-category of cryptographic tokens called stablecoins emerged, intending to reduce volatility and designed to maintain a stable market price through different mechanisms (Harvey et al. 2020; Popescu 2020; Voshmgir 2020).

Stablecoins with off-chain collateral

Stablecoins with off-chain collateral can be backed by a fiat currency or any other asset class such as precious metals, which are stored by a custodian such as a bank. Holding stablecoins may be equivalent to holding a claim to the collateral (Schär 2020). Popular examples are the USDT and USDC, which are US dollar (USD)-backed stablecoins and run as ERC-20 tokens on the Ethereum blockchain.

These stablecoins can be used to hedge against volatility as the price changes are minimal. However, they introduce counterparty risks because a centralized organization issues the stablecoins (Ethereum Foundation 2021e; Schär 2020).

Stablecoins with on-chain collateral

Stablecoins with on-chain collateral are collateralized with cryptographic tokens, usually with the native protocol token, which is locked into a smart contract. Because of the volatility of this collateral, the stablecoins need to be overcollateralized in order to keep the stablecoin at the desired stable value (Schär 2020). To illustrate the main concepts used by stablecoins with on-chain collateral to achieve a stable price, we outline the mechanisms of MakerDAO's DAI stablecoin.

DAI is an ERC-20 token designed to maintain a value of US$1. Any user can create DAI by locking ETH into the smart contract Maker collateral vault. To create US$1 worth of DAI, one must lock at least US$1.50 worth of ETH into the Maker collateral vault; therefore, it must be overcollateralized by 150 percent. The locked collateral can be recovered at any time by returning the DAI to the collateral vault plus interest which accrues, called the stability fee (Maker Team 2020).

There are three scenarios regarding the value of the underlying collateral: (1) if the USD value of the locked collateral increases, the user can create new DAI up to the overcollateralization ratio; (2) if the value of the collateral drops below the overcollateralization ratio, the user can return the DAI or deposit more collateral; and (3) if the USD value drops below a certain threshold called liquidation ratio, the position is liquidated. The collateral is then actioned off to keepers, which are independent external actors, usually bots, that are incentivized by arbitrage opportunities. They help to maintain the target price by buying DAI when the market price is below the target price, and vice versa (Maker Team 2020).

The price peg of DAI is achieved through the overcollateralization and mechanisms that influence its supply and demand. Liquidation events put positive price pressure on DAI, as they increase the demand for DAI, counteracting the negative price effect that would be caused if the DAIs in circulation were undercollateralized (Harvey et al. 2020). The stability fee can be adjusted to incentivize the generation or repayment of DAI and therefore directly influencing the supply of DAI. Additionally, DAI can be locked into a DAI Savings Rate (DSR) contract to earn interest. By adjusting the DSR, the demand for DAI can be influenced. The DSR is financed through the proceeds from the stability fee (Maker Team 2020). There is also a total debt ceiling in the Maker Protocol limiting the number of DAI that can be created for each type of collateral, and therefore limiting the total supply (Maker Team 2020).

The advantages of stablecoins backed with on-chain collateral are the full transparency regarding the processes maintaining the peg and full decentralization of the issuer. Compared to stablecoins with off-chain collateral, there is no external custodian involved, mitigating the need for trust. Drawbacks include a less precise price peg and the constant need to monitor the collateral value to avoid costly liquidations (Ethereum Foundation 2021e).

Stablecoins without collateral

Stablecoins without collateral typically use an algorithm encoded in a smart contract to adjust the supply to peg the price to that of the desired asset, usually the US dollar, therefore also being referred to as algorithmic stablecoins (Berentsen and Schär 2019).

The basic stability mechanism behind them consists of expanding the supply when the market price is above the target price, and taking measures to decrease the supply when the market price is below the target price (Moin et al. 2020). Increasing the supply can simply be performed by the issuance of additional stablecoins. Decreasing the supply can be performed by withdrawing stablecoins from circulation financed through the reserves that the protocol has accumulated, for example, through the initial sale of the stablecoins or collected transaction fees. The protocol or smart contract therefore acts similarly to a central bank with an algorithmic monetary policy that is fully transparent and predictable (Bullmann et al. 2019). Changing this monetary policy typically requires some form of a consensus process, for example a voting process through a governance token (Huber 2021).

The clear advantages of algorithmic stablecoins rest on strict and observable policy. In comparison to central banks, they only have one specific price target, which is clearly defined (Bullmann et al. 2019). This also increases their degree of decentralization compared to stablecoins with off-chain collateral. Additionally, being independent of a collateral asset decouples them from potential volatility of the collateral and mitigates scalability issues as well as the capital inefficiency that (over) collateralization introduces (Bithumb Global 2021; Catalini and de Gortari 2021).

The fixed rules of the strict policy also include drawbacks, as the smart contract might not have suitable measures for unordinary situations such as a crash of the crypto market. Changing the algorithm through a voting process might prevent the protocol from reacting in a timely manner, and would require that all stakeholders understand the implications of changing the algorithm in a certain way (Bullmann et al. 2019). The price peg relies on the reliability of the issuing mechanism and the user's expectations. Once the user's expectation changes, due to either an observed flaw with the algorithm or an unjustified reason, there is nothing to maintain the peg and the price typically drops significantly (Moin et al. 2020).

Decentralized Exchange Protocols

Decentralized exchanges (DEX) refer to DeFi protocols that allow users to trade cryptographic tokens without the need for a trusted third party as an intermediary for the trade or as a custodian. Depending on the implementation, a smart contract takes over the role of the custodian and escrow service, executing the transaction of the token exchange atomically once the exchange conditions agreed upon by the users are met (Harvey et al. 2020; Schär 2020). The rules and regulations of trades are encoded in the smart contract code of the protocol and users interact with the contract to trade assets (Amler et al. 2021; Lin et al. 2019).

In contrast to their counterpart – that is, central cryptocurrency exchanges – decentralized exchanges are non-custodial, mitigating the counterparty and security risks these centralized exchanges pose to the user by storing their private keys (Schär 2020). In the past, there have been many examples of hacks or dishonest behavior in centralized crypto exchanges. Prominent examples include the hack of the crypto exchanges Mt Gox in 2014, and its successor Bitfinex in 2016, which resulted in 850 000 and 119 755 Bitcoins stolen, respectively (Knight and Takemoto 2014). Due to the irreversible nature of blockchain transactions, there is usually little to no chance of retrieving stolen funds.

Decentralized order book exchanges

Earlier implementations of decentralized exchanges use an order book[4] as the mechanism for discovering a counterparty similar to traditional stock exchanges and centralized crypto exchanges (Schär 2020). Market makers provide liquidity to the exchanges by broadcasting their buy and sell orders, and can remove or update the orders if market conditions change. Market takers can fill these orders if they agree on the rates and amounts provided (Harvey et al. 2020). The process of the order book matching between takers and makers can be inefficient because it always requires the existence of at least two parties that are willing to engage in a trade and that have to agree on an exchange rate (Harvey et al. 2020).

On-chain order book exchanges

In on-chain order book exchanges, the order book is directly placed in a smart contract on the blockchain and confirmed by the network participants, allowing anyone to access and submit orders to the order book (Lin et al. 2019). On-chain order book exchanges enjoy the benefits of the decentralized nature of the blockchain: the order book is independent and censorship-resistant as it cannot be shut down by a single party and requires little trust in centralized off-chain actors. But the order book's cost, performance, and security depend on the underlying blockchain. Every order book update is a transaction on the blockchain that requires a transaction cost. To update an order, a user must wait for the network to reach a consensus regarding that order, therefore leading to a latency of the order book. If the security of the blockchain is compromised, the order book is also compromised (Lin et al. 2019).

Off-chain order book exchanges
In off-chain order book exchanges, the order books are hosted and updated off-chain by centralized third parties, called relayers. The relayers receive orders from makers and provide this information (quotes) to the takers. They may charge a fee for this service. The relayers' power is limited as they never control the funds or execute orders. In certain protocols, the relayers can restrict the access to submitting or viewing the order book (Lin et al. 2019; Schär 2020). The key differences to on-chain order books are that the makers signal their orders off-chain to relayers, which then aggregate them in their order books, from which the takers can choose suitable orders to fill. The actual trade is then executed as a transaction on the blockchain (Lin et al. 2019).

In the 0x protocol, makers directly submit their signed buy and sell orders off-chain to a relayer who aggregates them into his order book. Takers can then view the order books to find a suitable order to fill and submit it to the 0x protocol. The exchange will then be executed on the 0x exchange contract running on the Ethereum blockchain (Warren and Bandeali 2017).

Better performance signifies one of the key benefits of off-chain order books. Makers can submit and update their orders without waiting for a block to be confirmed. Because submitting and updating orders happens off-chain, the makers do not need to pay costly transaction fees. This also leads to less conjunction of the network as the overall number of on-chain transactions for each trade is reduced. Because the order books are hosted off-chain, there are fewer blockchain-originated vulnerabilities, such as the risk of a 51 percent attack and front-running[5] (Lin et al. 2019; Warren and Bandeali 2017).

A disadvantage of off-chain hosted order books is that it requires a higher degree of trust in the relayers to accurately display and update orders. Additionally, off-chain order books may be subject to greater legal and regulatory requirements, which may be costly and compromise some of the DeFi properties such as decentralization and openness (Lin et al. 2019).

Automated market makers
Automated market makers (AMM) or constant function market makers (CFMM) use smart contracts to hold liquidity pools of at least two tokens, allowing anyone to deposit tokens of one type and withdraw tokens of the other type. A pricing function

in the smart contract determines the exchange rate based on the reserves available in the liquidity pool (Harvey et al. 2020; Schär 2020).

The pricing function, also referred to as the constant product formula, in a simple form can be expressed as $xy = k$, where k is the invariant that remains constant for a given level of liquidity. x and y represent the pool's token reserves of the trading pair (Schär 2020; Zinsmeister et al. 2020). When someone executes a trade, they will deposit one type of token (x) and withdraw the other type (y). This will change the token reserves x and y of the liquidity pool; therefore, the pricing function can be expressed as $(x + \Delta x)*(y + \Delta y) = k$. Because k remains constant and Δx represents the number of tokens deposited, Δy is the only unknown which can be expressed as $\Delta y = \frac{k}{x + \Delta x}$-y by rearranging $(x + \Delta x)*(y + \Delta y) = k$ (Schär 2020).

The reserves of the pool cannot be fully depleted as the price of each token rises to infinity relative to the other when its reserves in the pool approach zero (Schär 2020). Because the exchange rate is determined by the price function instead of an oracle, the AMMs require arbitrageurs to level the price with other markets. Whenever there is a price difference between a liquidity pool in an AMM protocol and other markets, arbitrageurs will exploit this by withdrawing or depositing the tokens with the relative price difference to other markets. As this process influences the reserves of the tokens in the liquidity pool, it will affect the relative price of the token pair within the contract. Arbitrageurs continue to withdraw or deposit the token with the relative price difference until the price in the pool is equal to the market price (Pourpouneh et al. 2020).

Liquidity providers are users that deposit equal values of both tokens of a trading pair, increasing the overall liquidity in the pool without an impact on the exchange rate (Angeris and Chitra 2020). The liquidity of the pool can be directly measured by the invariant k (Harvey et al. 2020). Liquidity providers are incentivized to provide liquidity by receiving compensation, typically in the form of liquidity tokens or pool tokens (Angeris and Chitra 2020). AMM protocols charge a fee for each trade using the proceeds to compensate the liquidity providers or to increase the pool's reserves (Amler et al. 2021). The liquidity providers earn trading fees pro rata based on their contribution to the liquidity pool. After depositing tokens, liquidity providers own a percentage share in the pool, depending on their contribution to the overall pool size. Upon withdrawal, they are entitled to that percentage of the total tokens in the pool, which can result in a different allocation of x and y tokens than they initially deposited (Harvey et al. 2020).

The main advantage of AMMs is that they eliminate the need for the existence of buyers and sellers at the same time to facilitate a trade, as well as the need for order books and pricing oracles (Pourpouneh et al. 2020). The constant product formula eliminates the need for order books and pricing oracles.

A general problem in AMM is the impermanent loss that liquidity providers are exposed to. Impermanent loss refers to the opportunity costs between depositing a trading pair of tokens into a liquidity pool compared to holding on to the tokens (Pourpouneh et al. 2020). When the trading pair in the pool experiences relative market price changes in any direction, the arbitrageurs will exploit this arbitrage opportunity until the pool's exchange rate is equal to the market rate, (Pourpouneh et al. 2020). External arbitrageurs exploit all the profit from these price differences at the expense of the liquidity providers who keep the platforms alive (Harvey et al. 2020). Therefore, the liquidity providers experience an opportunity cost of depositing the trading pair of tokens into a liquidity pool compared to holding on to them. The impermanent loss can only be reversed if the exchange rate reverts to the original level when the funds were deposited. It is only realized when assets are withdrawn from the liquidity pool, making the loss permanent (Caldarelli and Ellul 2021).

Smart contract-based reserve aggregators

Smart contract-based reserve aggregators allow liquidity providers to advertise their prices for specific trading pairs. A user who wants to exchange their tokens for other tokens can send a request to a smart contract of the protocol. The smart contract will then compare prices (aggregate) from all liquidity providers and choose the best offer on behalf of the user and execute the trade automatically. The key difference to AMMs is that the price is set by the liquidity providers upfront, and there is no pricing function within the smart contract to determine the price. When there are few or only one liquidity provider, this approach might lead to unfavorable prices for the user or even monopolistic price setting from the liquidity providers. To avoid this scenario, smart contract-based reserve aggregation protocols typically implement some form of price control mechanisms, such as maximum prices or a minimum amount of liquidity providers required for a trading pair. The drawback of those mechanisms is that they can reintroduce a certain degree of centralization, such as centralized pricing oracles. The most popular implementation of this concept is Kyber Network, although the protocol offers a wider range of features than only smart contract-based reserve aggregation (Luu and Velner 2017; Schär 2020).

Peer-to-peer exchange protocols

Peer-to-peer (P2P) or over-the-counter (OTC) exchange protocols utilize smart contracts to connect counterparties that are looking to trade a pair of tokens. Users can simply communicate the token pair that they are willing to trade to the smart contract, which then brings matching parties together. The exchange rate will then be negotiated off-chain by the two parties privately, and the trade will then be executed based on the agreed-upon exchange rate on-chain through a smart contract, mitigating the counterparty risk (Oved and Mosites 2017).

P2P protocols are not susceptible to front-running because the transaction only becomes public on the blockchain once executed, and no other party can interfere in the transaction prior by offering a better rate. P2P protocols offer high scalability and cost-effectiveness, as only the trade is performed on-chain, and negotiations take place off-chain, reducing the overall number of transactions and gas fees required (Oved and Mosites 2017).

Decentralized Lending Platforms

Decentralized lending platforms are currently the most popular DeFi platforms, with a total value locked of $38.88 billion on August 28, 2021 (DeFi Pulse 2021). They enable users to borrow and lend cryptographic tokens with smart contracts acting as the intermediary (Amler et al. 2021; Jensen et al. 2021). Compared to the centralized financial system, the novelty includes that anyone can engage in lending or borrowing through these platforms without any form of KYC practices. Especially for borrowers, it means that the concept of credit scores becomes irrelevant (Stepanova and Eriņš 2021). The absence of an intermediary and the pseudonymity of blockchain transactions complicate or even prevent enforcement of repayment of the loans, and the high volatility of cryptographic tokens as collateral can result in loans being insufficiently collateralized depending on the market conditions. Therefore, other mechanisms to protect lenders have emerged in DeFi lending: the loans are either overcollateralized or require an instant repayment (flash loans) (Jensen et al. 2021; Meegan and Koens 2021).

Overcollateralized loans

Overcollateralized loans are secured by on-chain collateral locked into a smart contract that exceeds the value of the loan, enabling borrowers to utilize their cryptographic tokens as collateral for a loan (Qin et al. 2021a; Ramos et al. 2020). The collateralization ratio is the ratio between the total value of the collateral and the total value of the debt: $collateralization\ ratio = \frac{value\ of\ collateral}{value\ of\ debt}$ and must be larger than 1 in overcollateralized loans (Qin et al. 2021a).

This might raise the question of why a borrower would use liquid tokens as collateral to take out a loan of a smaller value in the form of other tokens. There can be different rationales to obtain an overcollateralized loan. A borrower might want to hold on to the collateral tokens but needs instant liquidity. Reasons for keeping the collateral tokens could be the expectation of a price appreciation of the collateral token or tax benefits of holding tokens for a certain amount of time. Additionally, overcollateralized loans allow borrowers to create leveraged positions (Gudgeon et al. 2020).

In collateralized debt positions (CDPs), when the collateral is deposited into a smart contract, newly created tokens are issued for the loan, such as the DAI stablecoin in the Maker Protocol. CDPs do not require a counterparty or lender to create a loan (Schär 2020).

In collateralized debt markets, funds are provided by lenders, and this does not necessarily require the creation of a new token. The borrowers and lenders can be matched peer-to-peer, which requires the existence of both counterparties who need to agree on a fixed rate and time period for the loan (Schär 2020). The more common approach are protocols that use lending pools where the funds of all lenders are aggregated in a lending pool in a smart contract, which is the case in the Aave and Compound. The lenders can earn interest immediately upon depositing their funds, typically with variable interest rates based on the supply and demand in the pool. The maturity and size of the loan can typically be freely chosen by the borrower (Schär 2020).

When the market value of the collateral drops below the collateralization rate, at a certain predefined liquidation threshold a loan will be liquidated to protect the lenders. The liquidation process is performed by liquidators who are monitoring loans, seeking an opportunity to buy the collateral at a discount. This way, the protocol can retrieve the outstanding debt and interest. Usually, an additional penalty is charged, and the remaining collateral is returned to the borrower (Gudgeon et al. 2020). A liquidation can take the form of an auction, as in the case of Maker Protocol, or as a fixed spread liquidation, where the protocol offers the collateral at fixed discount to interested buyers (liquidators) such as in the case of Aave and Compound (Qin et al. 2021a). Usually there are additional pools in lending protocols with protocol reserves in place to cover losses if the liquidation does not raise enough funds to recover (Aave [2019] 2020).

Flash loans

The concept of flash loans was first implemented by the Aave protocol in 2020 and is a native concept of DeFi being non-existent in traditional finance (Aave 2019/2020; Wang et al. 2021; Zeller 2020). A flash loan is essentially a non-collateralized loan that must be borrowed and repaid, with interest within the same transaction block. The concept relies on the atomicity of the blockchain: if the flash loan is not repaid, including the interest within the same block, the transaction is collectively reverted and the flash loan never gets issued (Bartoletti et al. 2020; Qin et al. 2021c). To request a flash loan, a smart contract must be programmed specifying the request and the repayment of the principal and interest (Wang et al. 2021). This request is made possible by the EVM, which enables the programming of smart contracts with the capability to revert a transaction if a condition is not met during the execution (Qin et al. 2021c).

Flash loans allow anyone willing to pay the fees to obtain a flash loan of any size, given the protocol's liquidity. Because the transaction fails if a flash loan is not repaid, the lender is not exposed to debt default, unless there are smart contract and blockchain vulnerabilities (Meegan and Koens 2021; Qin et al. 2021c).

Flash loans can be used to exploit arbitrage opportunities between different decentralized exchanges running on the Ethereum blockchain without the need for upfront capital except for the gas fees to launch the transaction. If the arbitrage opportunity ceases to exist or is not profitable enough to repay the interest, the transaction will be reverted. Compared to arbitrage in traditional markets where the arbitrageur can potentially lose all their used assets, the arbitrageur only bears the risks of losing the gas fees in case of a failure in the transaction (Wang et al. 2021).

Flash loans can also be used to close overcollateralized loans and retrieve the locked collateral. For example, when a borrower cannot repay the CDP, they could take out a flash loan, repay the CDP thus releasing theircollateral, and use a proportion of their collateral to repay the flash loan. Flash loans can also be used to swap the collateral for another more stable collateral type such as a stablecoin if the market price of the original collateral decreases, to avoid a liquidation (Wang et al. 2021).

Flash loans allow traders to manipulate prices on decentralized exchanges without large amounts of capital as only the interest flash loans and gas fees must be paid. This is known as wash trading (Wang et al. 2021). The interest rate on flash loans on Aave is 0.09 percent at the time of writing in September 2021 (Aave 2021b).

On-Chain Asset Management

Asset management in traditional finance refers to "the practice of allocating financial assets such as to satisfy the long-term financial objectives of an institution or an individual" (Jensen et al. 2021: 51). Asset managers use investment funds consisting of baskets of different assets to diversify their client's portfolios. Different DeFi platforms offer on-chain funds that allow users to invest in a basket of crypto assets and employ different strategies through a smart contract (Schär 2020).

The basic mechanics consist of the following. The investors lock their assets into a smart contract and receive fund tokens representing their share of the total assets in the smart contract or fund. The funds in the smart contract are then collectively invested according to a predefined strategy encoded in the smart contract. The investors can withdraw their assets from the fund at any time by returning the fund tokens to the smart contract (Jensen et al. 2021; Schär 2020).

The type of funds can be distinguished into automated funds, which automatically execute a particular investment strategy encoded in the smart contract, and actively managed funds, where a fund manager invests the fund's assets. The fund manager's actions are limited to the predefined strategy written in the smart contract (Jensen et al. 2021; Schär 2020).

The smart contract additionally ensures that no principal–agent problems emerge between the fund manager and the investors as the rules the fund manager must follow and the actions he can take are enforced through the code. Furthermore, the funds do not require a custodian as the smart contract acts as one and allows anyone to start a fund (Schär 2020). Examples of on-chain fund protocols include Set Protocol, Enzyme Finance, and Yearn Vaults (Cronje 2021; Feng and Weickmann 2019; Trinkler and El Isa 2017).

Qualitative Comparison of CeFi and DeFi Services

Stablecoins

Stablecoins with on-chain collateral such as the DAI stablecoin or the Celo Dollar can fulfill the unit of account and store of value functions of money sufficiently, while satisfying the principals of DeFi in contrast to fiat backed stablecoins. The unit of account function is fulfilled due to their peg to a commonly used unit of account such as the US dollar. The store of value is fulfilled due to their price stability which is comparable to that of major currencies. The medium of exchange function is still limited to services that accept payments via ERC-20 tokens, which primarily are within the DeFi ecosystem, centralized crypto exchanges, and crypto banks.

Decentralized exchange protocols

Decentralized exchange protocols theoretically offer a suitable, decentralized alternative to centralized crypto exchanges at their current stage, mitigating counterparty risks that users are exposed to when using centralized crypto exchanges.

An additional advantage is the accessibility of decentralized exchange protocol allowing anyone to start trading or even start a new trading pair without the need of going through know your customer (KYC) procedures. The theoretically reduced transaction costs due to the absence of an intermediary is currently overshadowed by the peak in gas prices; a token swap on Uniswap costs on average 50 gwei, which is approximately $30 at the time of this writing (etherscan.io 2021).

Decentralized exchange protocols are limited in terms of the tradable assets to mainly ERC-20 tokens and can therefore not be compared to traditional (stock) exchanges at the moment. The trading volume of decentralized exchanges are currently rather small compared to centralized exchanges. This becomes evident when comparing the 24h (24-hour) trade volume of the largest centralized crypto exchange Binance of $92 billion to the 24h trade volume of the largest decentralized exchange protocol Uniswap of $1.53 billion (CoinMarketCap 2021a; Uniswap 2021).

Other limitations to consider are the absence of fiat on-ramps and that the user interfaces remain challenging for the average user, ultimately leading to the need for centralized crypto exchanges for most of the users.

Decentralized lending

Decentralized lending platforms mainly offer an opportunity to earn yields on crypto assets, utilize crypto assets as collateral for a loan and engage in arbitrage trading between decentralized exchanges without the need to deploy a large amount of capital. At the current stage of development, the decentralized lending platforms must rely on overcollateralization to protect lenders, highly limiting the use cases of these loans. As only rather liquid ERC-20 tokens can be used as collateral, a collateralized loan in the traditional sense where the borrower leaves an illiquid asset to get liquidity cannot be replicated by these platforms yet.

On-chain asset management

The on-chain asset management platforms offer a fully decentralized alternative to other types of centralized crypto funds, such as crypto ETFs, crypto index funds, private investment funds, or similar products that are based on returns of crypto assets. The absence of an intermediary reduces overall transaction costs here and lowers entry barriers in funds that require a minimal amount to start investing. Expert 15 drew a comparison between the costs of traditional funds compared to Enzyme vaults: "Setting up a traditional fund at least costs 100 000 euros but setting up an Ezyme Finance vault, an on-chain asset management platform, takes only two minutes and you pay 50 euros for gas currently."

It is important to mention that the on-chain asset management at its current state cannot replace traditional asset managers, as they are mainly limited to assets that are available on-chain and to strategies that can be encoded in a smart contract if the fund is automated. If a fund is actively managed by a fund manager, the rules in the smart contract according to which the fund manager must act must be tightly balanced between granting the fund manager the rights to optimize the returns of the fund, while limiting potential malicious behavior. Expert 15 highlighted the potential of on-chain asset management in the future if more assets become tokenized and available on chain: “It’s a giant use case: Pools with vintage cars, cars, stocks, with all kinds of tokenized assets inside.” Additionally, the regulatory uncertainty particularly limits institutional investors from taking advantage of on-chain funds.

Benefits and Opportunities of DeFi

Benefits

The decentralization property leads to an independence from large financial institutions, overall reducing the costs of transactions (Stepanova and Eriņš 2021). The decentralization can also enhance the overall trust in the system. Expert 12 highlighted that the increased efficiency and trust are the main benefits of DeFi: “The smart contracts hold the custody; no fund manager needs to be trusted. Oftentimes the trust was abused in the past.”

Therefore, the efficiency of transactions increases, which turns business models that were infeasible in a centralized finance into viable ones (Chen and Bellavitis 2020). DeFi substitutes CeFi’s trusted central counterparties with smart contracts that are theoretically capable of fulfilling central counterparty tasks, including as custody, escrow agents, and clearing and settlement. Theoretically, such methods provide a considerably reduced counterparty risk and make transactions more efficient overall (Katona 2021).

In the current environment of low interest rates, the different DeFi protocols offer comparably high yields, Aave for example offers a 6 percent deposit annual percentage yield (APY) for lenders of the DAI stablecoin (Aave 2021a). These yields are connected with higher risks as Expert 1 mentioned. The currently high yields for depositors are due to the high demand of liquidity in the protocols according to Expert 10.

Additionally, DeFi enables anyone to take various roles within the ecosystem such as providing liquidity to pools or participating in the governance of protocols, which is not possible in centralized finance. This opens the possibility to earn additional income.

Closely related to participating in the DeFi ecosystem with different potential roles, DeFi’s openness enables innovativeness through its open-source code base. “Without many restrictions you can develop a new financial service. You have an idea, and you can code it if you like, and you do not have to be a coder for yourself. You can combine certain parts and create your own smart contract and that smart contract serves as a financial service,” as summarized by Expert 2.

Risks of DeFi

Technical risks

Expert 3 highlights that the "code is law" paradigm of smart contracts can be viewed as an advantage as well as a risk of DeFi. The immutable code of smart contracts can always contain errors and bugs that may allow attackers to exploit these errors and steal funds. Additionally, Expert 5 stressed that, depending on the degree of DeFi adoption, "these bugs of exploits could become the new financial crashes." Compared to the traditional financial system, no party could fix or control these bugs.

Schär (2020) and Expert 12 highlight that the average user may not be able to understand the smart contract code and evaluate its security based on that. Coding smart contracts error-free is particularly difficult since the smart contract code cannot be changed once implemented. Therefore, future developments must be accounted for initially (Grigo et al. 2020).

In times of high demand for transactions, gas prices increase accordingly, leading to escalating gas prices and highly restricting the benefit of the low transaction costs in DeFi, favoring wealthy individuals. This also leads to transactions being delayed, resulting in market inefficiencies and information delays. The burdens of these increased gas prices are mainly carried by the users, who must closely observe the market in these times, as the inability to make transactions in a timely manner may lead to liquidations and the associated fees (Jensen et al. 2021).

Expert 8 also sees "the current inefficiency in latency of networks" as one of the significant disadvantages of DeFi. "Ethereum is not yet scalable. It is still quite slow compared to more traditional kinds of financial networks." However, he stressed that these "are just interim problems as we move on"; suggesting that this will not hold DeFi back permanently. Expert 2 states that these high transaction costs also act as a stopper to widespread adoption in all payment-related areas due to the limited practicability for daily payments.

Regulatory risks

Regulatory risk was the most prominent risk mentioned by the literature and by all experts interviewed. The lack of a legal framework and standards seems to be one of the primary sources of risks. Some of the major aspects of DeFi, such as the borderless, pseudonymity, decentralized governance structures, result in regulatory challenges: national regulations may not apply or cannot be enforced, leading to a situation where responsibility and accountability may be unclear (Financial Stability Board 2019).

As DeFi acts according to the "code is law" paradigm, there is no responsible entity to contact if a smart contract code is faulty (Stepanova and Eriņš 2021). According to Expert 9, DeFi assets are "very hard to regulate, and regulators are going to look for two things: anti-money-laundering and also protection of customer funds." Expert 10 mentioned that the currently unregulated space naturally attracts players that would abuse it and expects regulation to enter the space, leading to a situation with an unregulated market and a completely regulated market.

Usability risks and risks related to human error

At the current stage, the leading DeFi protocols are still rather user-unfriendly for users without knowledge regarding information technology, finance, and crypto, making the handling of non-custodial wallets such as MetaMask and private keys a major challenge. Paired with the finality of transactions, this leads to a risk of losing one's funds.

Expert 1 mentioned that higher user-friendliness is required by DeFi to become really mainstream, and it may require some centralized elements to give unsophisticated users the level of security they need. Expert 10 viewed the loss of seed keys as a major problem in non-custodial DeFi that needs to be addressed, and suggested a "form of a keyless recovery of accounts" as a potential solution. Nicely illustrating this point, regulated FinTech startups are currently emerging that build user-friendly interfaces for the DeFi protocols, mainly in the area of lending. They offer a similar user interface as traditional banking apps and some even offer deposit insurance.

Infrastructural risks

The interconnectedness and composability of the DeFi applications also introduce new risk factors such as dependencies. An issue with the smart contract of one DeFi service could potentially affect all other DeFi applications using the compromised service or that share the same open-source code.

The "tightly coupled and complex liquidity systems can generate an excessive degree of financial integration, resulting in systemic dependencies between applications" (Jensen et al. 2021: 53). This may even introduce systemic risk, as a failure or exploitation of one application could spread quickly through the ecosystem.

Expert 10 mentioned the risk of rehypothecation, which is the problem of not being diversified when investing in different protocols, as they are interconnected to each other. This could lead to a domino effect when one protocol fails, leading to other protocols failing as well.

Expert 9 considered the interconnectedness to be a risk that currently remains within the DeFi ecosystem: "So, I do think DeFi proposes a risk to traditional finance in a sense, but it has to permeate the real economy first."

Centralization risks

The decentralization property of DeFi seems to be more an architectural than a political one at the current stage, reintroducing the risk of centralization. Most protocols are still partially centrally governed by their developer teams or investors holding admin keys for upgrades or emergency shutdowns, or holding on to the majority of the governance tokens (Financial Stability Board 2019; Popescu 2020). An additional factor contributing to the risk of centralization is the dependency on oracles.

Impact on Centralized Finance

Overall, the impact on the centralized financial system was not viewed by the experts as an immediate threat of replacing the existing system. DeFi protocols are expected to gain a share of the traditional market in certain areas and potentially introduce a decentralized infrastructure to the traditional players. Expert 11 concluded that traditional finance will not disappear, but "margins will get smaller and more competitive because there will be a split," and that DeFi will exist "next to the traditional market." In contrast, Expert 9 believes that "yields will disappear, and DeFi will gradually transition into traditional finance."

There were two main ideas regarding the impact on centralized finance: a hybrid model in which DeFi coexists with centralized finance, as most experts expect; and a model in which DeFi slowly transitions into centralized finance with proper regulation, but losing some of its core principles such as decentralization, becoming rather an infrastructure layer for centralized finance. Expert 2 highlighted the infrastructural impact of DeFi: the financial service industry could see the benefits of having "one infrastructure layer where there is no debate what data is correct" as a lot of time is spent "to reconcile their books and look which bank's books are correct." Expert 11 expected DeFi to potentially split into an unregulated market and a completely regulated market.

It is important to note that the interviewed experts from the centralized finance group (Expert 1, 4, 5, 6, 9, and 11) concluded that they do not view DeFi as a threat to their business, but rather as an opportunity.

Opportunities for collaboration

Potential areas of collaboration mentioned by the experts were in providing liquidity to DeFi protocols and building user-friendly interfaces and fiat on-ramps into DeFi.

Expert 1, 3, 6, and 8 saw the main potential for collaboration between CeFi and DeFi to be in providing liquidity to DeFi protocols, as their institutions are the ones with access to liquidity. Expert 2 noted that a large source of liquidity can be institutional money which would require proper regulation to provide liquidity, and without this it would be "very hard at the current stage or the stage in the next one or two years for concrete collaborations between centralized finance services and DeFi services." Expert 9 noted that while providing liquidity to DeFi protocols offers high yields, currently the main responsibility for CeFi institutions lies in protecting their customer funds from the risks associated with these yields. Expert 12 believed that CeFi will play a key role in connecting DeFi to the users in a user-friendly way.

Expert 10 suggested that CeFi institutions could provide credit scores to DeFi to overcome the problem of overcollateralization and form some sort of partnership. Similar to Experts 1, 6, and 8, he saw the potential of collaboration in the form of building fiat on-ramps into DeFi to provide liquidity.

In contrast to the other experts, Expert 7 did not see a potential for collaboration, as he believed that "the cultural barrier is very underestimated." Expert 5 expects collaboration to take place only "if there's regulation in the sense of regulated operators but on a decentralized network," supporting the views of Expert 7.

Participation in the DeFi ecosystem

Experts 1, 4, 5, 9, and 11 from the centralized finance group, which included a private bank, a state-owned development bank, a stock exchange, and two FinTechs, stated that their organizations do not participate nor have immediate plans to participate in the DeFi ecosystem directly at the moment. Expert 6, who represented a retail bank, could not disclose any information regarding their organization's participation.

Obstacles Regarding Widespread DeFi Adoption

The main obstacles identified from the expert interviews regarding a widespread adoption of DeFi were the lack of regulation and KYC practices, the scalability issues of Ethereum, the lack of trust in DeFi protocols, and the lack of education of users and financial institutions regarding DeFi.

CONCLUSION

Overall, DeFi offers promising solutions to some of the problems that centralized finance raises, and has the potential to become one of the most important areas of blockchain if the technology is properly developed. It offers opportunities to replicate the existing financial services in a more transparent and open way without requiring as much trust between parties.

But at its current stage, there are still many challenges to overcome. The technical risks, scalability issues, and missing regulations are obstacles to widespread adoption. Additionally, education regarding the blockchain technology in general, and DeFi specifically, is required.

Regarding the current state of DeFi, it can be concluded that the existing DeFi services at their current stage are mainly limited to the on-chain world and do not have an immediate impact on the traditional part of the centralized financial system yet. This idea was also reflected in the expert interviews, as none of the centralized finance representatives expressed any plans to participate in DeFi at the moment. Potentials for future collaboration between CeFi and DeFi were discovered in the areas of providing liquidity, and acting as a gateway for their clients into DeFi.

Due to the limited scope of the chapter and their relatively recent emergence, the use cases of decentralized derivatives and decentralized insurance were omitted from this chapter.

NOTES

1. The Ethereum virtual machine (EVM) is the part of the Ethereum network that handles smart contract deployment and execution. Simple transactions such as value transfers between accounts do not affect the EVM, but more complex computations involve a computation by the EVM to update its state. In simple terms, the EVM can

be viewed as a "global decentralized computer containing millions of executable objects [smart contracts], each with its own permanent data store" that allows any participant of the network to request the execution of arbitrary code on it, which changes its state (*Chapter 13: The Ethereum Virtual Machine* n.d.; Ethereum Foundation 2021d).

2. Ether (ETH) is the native cryptocurrency of the Ethereum network.
3. Resources are the computational work and storage that a smart contract requires.
4. In traditional stock exchanges, the order book refers to an electronic list of buy and sell orders for a specific security or financial instrument organized by price level (Kenton 2021). In crypto exchanges, the order books consist of a list of buy and sell orders for a trading pair of cryptographic tokens.
5. Front-running generally refers to the behavior of capitalizing on early access to market information, such as upcoming transactions by a party with access to this information (Daian et al. 2019; Eskandari et al. 2019).

REFERENCES

Aave. ([2019] 2020). *Aave Protocol Whitepaper V1.0*. https://github.com/aave/aave-protocol/blob/4b4545fb583fd4f400507b10f3c3114f45b8a037/docs/Aave_Protocol_Whitepaper_v1_0.pdf.

Aave. (2021a). *Aave—Open Source DeFi Protocol*. https://aave.com/.

Aave. (2021b). *Flash Loans*. https://docs.aave.com/developers/guides/flash-loans.

Abdulhakeem, S.A., and Hu, Q. (2021). Powered by Blockchain Technology, DeFi (Decentralized Finance) Strives to Increase Financial Inclusion of the Unbanked by Reshaping the World Financial System. *Modern Economy*, 12(1), 1–16. https://doi.org/10.4236/me.2021.121001.

Amler, H., Eckey, L., Faust, S., Kaiser, M., Sandner, P., and Schlosser, D. (2021). *DeFi-ning DeFi: Challenges and Pathway*. http://arxiv.org/abs/2101.05589.

Angeris, G., and Chitra, T. (2020). Improved Price Oracles: Constant Function Market Makers. In *Proceedings of the 2nd ACM Conference on Advances in Financial Technologies* (pp. 80–91).

Antonopoulos, A.M., and Wood, G. (2018). *Mastering Ethereum: Building Smart Contracts and Dapps*. O'Reilly Media.

Bareis, M. (2019). Comparison of Ethereum and NEO as Smart Contract Platforms. *Business Informatics*, 109.

Bartoletti, M., Chiang, J.H., and Lluch-Lafuente, A. (2020). *SoK: Lending Pools in Decentralized Finance*. http://arxiv.org/abs/2012.13230.

Beniiche, A. (2020). A Study of Blockchain Oracles. *ArXiv:2004.07140 [Cs]*. http://arxiv.org/abs/2004.07140.

Berentsen, A., and Schär, F. (2019). *Stablecoins: The Quest for a Low-Volatility Cryptocurrency* (pp. 65–71).

Birch, J. (2020). *MakerDAO's Gustav Arentoft: Decentralization Is Not a Binary Choice*. Cointelegraph. https://cointelegraph.com/news/makerdaos-gustav-arentoft-decentralization-is-not-a-binary-choice.

Bithumb Global. (2021). *Algorithmic Stablecoins: A Beginner's Guide | Hacker Noon*. https://hackernoon.com/algorithmic-stablecoins-a-beginners-guide-pmh320t.

Bullmann, D., Klemm, J., and Pinna, A. (2019). *In Search for Stability in Crypto-Assets: Are Stablecoins the Solution?* ECB Occasional Paper, 230.

Buterin, V. (2014). A Next-Generation Smart Contract and Decentralized Application Platform. *White Paper*, 3(37).
Caldarelli, G., and Ellul, J. (2021). The Blockchain Oracle Problem in Decentralized Finance—A Multivocal Approach. *Applied Sciences*, 11(16), 7572.
Cassell, C. (2015). *Conducting Research Interviews for Business and Management Students*. SAGE Publications. https://books.google.de/books?id=JD5TBwAAQBAJ.
Catalini, C., and de Gortari, A. (2021). *On the Economic Design of Stablecoins*. Available at SSRN 3899499.
Chapter 13: The Ethereum Virtual Machine. (n.d.). Retrieved August 6, 2021, from https://cypherpunks-core.github.io/ethereumbook/13evm.html.
Chen, Y., and Bellavitis, C. (2020). Blockchain Disruption and Decentralized Finance: The Rise of Decentralized Business Models. *Journal of Business Venturing Insights*, 13. https://doi.org/10.1016/J.JBVI.2019.E00151.
CoinMarketCap. (2021a). *Binance Trade Volume and Market Listings*. CoinMarketCap. https://coinmarketcap.com/exchanges/binance/.
CoinMarketCap. (2021b). *Top Smart Contracts Tokens by Market Capitalization | CoinMarketCap*. https://coinmarketcap.com/view/smart-contracts/.
Consensys. (n.d.). *Blockchain for Decentralized Finance (DeFi)*. ConsenSys. Retrieved August 11, 2021, from https://consensys.net/blockchain-use-cases/decentralized-finance/.
Cronje, A. (2021). *Introduction to Yearn*. https://docs.yearn.finance/.
Cryptopedia Staff. (2021). *Cryptocurrencies vs. Tokens: Digital Assets*. Gemini. https://www.gemini.com/cryptopedia/cryptocurrencies-vs-tokens-difference.
Daian, P., Goldfeder, S., Kell, T., Li, Y., Zhao, X., Bentov, I., Breidenbach, L., and Juels, A. (2019). *Flash Boys 2.0: Frontrunning, Transaction Reordering, and Consensus Instability in Decentralized Exchanges*. https://arxiv.org/abs/1904.05234v1.
Dain, A., Hays, D., Yorke, B., and Rosenberg, H. (2020). *DeFI Adoption 2020: A Definitive Guide to Entering the Industry*. Cointelegraph Research paper. https://research.cointelegraph.com/reports/defi-adoption-2020-a-definitive-guide-to-entering-the-industry.
DeFi Pulse. (2021). *DeFi Pulse | The DeFi Leaderboard | Stats, Charts and Guides*. https://defipulse.com.
Eskandari, S., Moosavi, M., and Clark, J. (2019). *SoK: Transparent Dishonesty: Front-Running Attacks on Blockchain*. SSRN Scholarly Paper ID 3369236. Social Science Research Network. https://papers.ssrn.com/abstract=3369236.
Ethereum Foundation. (2021a). *Ethereum Accounts*. ethereum.org. https://ethereum.org/en/developers/docs/accounts/.
Ethereum Foundation. (2021b). *Ethereum Virtual Machine (EVM)*. ethereum.org. https://ethereum.org.
Ethereum Foundation. (2021c). *Gas and Fees*. ethereum.org. https://ethereum.org/en/developers/docs/gas/.
Ethereum Foundation. (2021d). *Intro to Ethereum*. ethereum.org. https://ethereum.org/en/developers/docs/intro-to-ethereum/.
Ethereum Foundation. (2021e). *Stablecoins*. ethereum.org. https://ethereum.org/en/stablecoins/.
etherscan.io. (2021). *Ethereum Gas Tracker | Etherscan*. Ethereum (ETH) Blockchain Explorer. http://etherscan.io/gastracker.
Feng, F., and Weickmann, B. (2019). *Set: A Protocol for Baskets of Tokenized Assets*. Whitepaper, 34.
Ferreira, A. (2021). Regulating smart contracts: Legal revolution or simply evolution? *Telecommunications Policy*, *45*(2), 102081. https://doi.org/10.1016/j.telpol.2020.102081.
Financial Stability Board. (2019). *Decentralised Financial Technologies: Report on Financial Stability, Regulatory and Governance Implications*. www.fsb.org/emailalert.
Flick, U. (2014). *An Introduction to Qualitative Research*. SAGE Publications.

Fries, M., and Paal, B.P. (2019). *Smart Contracts*. Mohr Siebeck.
Grigo, J., Hansen, P., Patz Anika, and von Wachter, V. (2020). *Decentralized Finance (DeFi)—A New Fintech Revolution?* www.bitkom.org.
Gudgeon, L., Werner, S.M., Perez, D., and Knottenbelt, W.J. (2020). DeFi Protocols for Loanable Funds: Interest Rates, Liquidity and Market Efficiency. *ArXiv:2006.13922 [Cs, q-Fin]*. http://arxiv.org/abs/2006.13922.
Gurusamy, S. (2009). *Financial Services and System*. Tata McGraw-Hill Education Private.
Harvey, C.R., Ramachandran, A., and Santoro, J. (2020). DeFi and the Future of Finance. *SSRN Electronic Journal*. https://doi.org/10.2139/ssrn.3711777.
Hay, A. (2020, September 13). *How Decentralized is "Decentralized Finance"?* Coinmonks. https://medium.com/coinmonks/how-decentralized-is-decentralized-finance-89aea3070e8f.
Huber, R. (2021, April 15). *Algorithmic Stablecoins*. Bitcoin Suisse. https://www.bitcoinsuisse.com/research/decrypt/algorithmic-stablecoins.
Ichiba Hotchkiss, G. (2019). *The 1.x Files: The State of Stateless Ethereum*. https://blog.ethereum.org/2019/12/30/eth1x-files-state-of-stateless-ethereum/.
Jameson, H. (2021). *Ethereum Improvement Proposals (EIPs)*. https://ethereum.org.
Jensen, J.R., von Wachter, V., and Ross, O. (2021). An Introduction to Decentralized Finance (DeFi). *Complex Systems Informatics and Modeling Quarterly*, 26, 46–54. https://doi.org/10.7250/csimq.2021-26.03.
John, J. (2020). *Decentralised Finance: Usecases and Risks for Mass Adoption*. https://uploads-ssl.webflow.com/60201c98c0783465694de095/602d76364a228a2f7c9d33a8_Decentralised%20Finance.pdf.
Katona, T. (2021). Decentralized Finance: The Possibilities of a Blockchain "Money Lego" System. *Financial and Economic Review*, 20(1), 74–102.
Kenton, W. (2021). *Order Book*. Investopedia. https://www.investopedia.com/terms/o/order-book.asp.
Knight, S., and Takemoto, Y. (2014, February 28). *Mt. Gox Files for Bankruptcy, Hit with Lawsuit*. Reuters. https://www.reuters.com/article/us-bitcoin-mtgox-bankruptcy-idUSBREA1R0FX20140228.
Kolb, J., Abdelbaky, M., Katz, R.H., and Culler, D.E. (2020). Core Concepts, Challenges, and Future Directions in Blockchain: A Centralized Tutorial. *ACM Computing Surveys*, 53(1). https://doi.org/10.1145/3366370.
Kumar, R. (2010). *Research Methodology: A Step-by-Step Guide for Beginners*. SAGE Publications. https://books.google.de/books?id=a3PwLukoFlMC.
Lauslahti, K., Mattila, J., and Seppala, T. (2017). Smart Contracts How Will Blockchain Technology Affect Contractual Practices? *SSRN Electronic Journal*. https://doi.org/10.2139/ssrn.3154043.
Lin, L. X., Budish, E., Cong, L. W., He, Z., Bergquist, J.H., Panesir, M.S., Kelly, J., Lauer, M., Prinster, R., and Zhang, S. (2019). Deconstructing Decentralized Exchanges. *Stanford Journal of Blockchain Law and Policy*, 2(1), 58–77.
LongHash Ventures. (2021, August 3). *The Aggregation Layer: A Key Catalyst for DeFi Adoption*. Medium. https://longhashsg.medium.com/the-aggregation-layer-a-key-catalyst-for-defi-adoption-3215b6b3684b.
Luu, Y.V.L., and Velner, Y. (2017). *Kybernetwork: A Trustless Decentralized Exchange and Payment Service*. Whitepaper. https://api-new.whitepaper.io/documents/pdf?id=HydX2IZRz.
Maker Team. (2020). *The Maker Protocol White Paper*. https://makerdao.com/en/whitepaper/.
Mammadzada, K., Iqbal, M., Milani, F., García-Bañuelos, L., and Matulevičius, R. (2020). Blockchain Oracles: A Framework for Blockchain-Based Applications. *International Conference on Business Process Management*, 19–34.

Mayer, H.O. (2008). *Interview und schriftliche Befragung: Entwicklung, Durchführung und Auswertung*. Oldenbourg. https://books.google.de/books?id=rV1NvgAACAAJ.
Mayring, P. (2016). *Einführung in die qualitative Sozialforschung: Eine Anleitung zu qualitativem Denken* (6., überarbeitete Auflage). Beltz.
Meegan, X., and Koens, T. (2021). *Lessons Learned from Decentralised Finance (DeFi)*. https://www.ingwb.com/binaries/content/assets/insights/themes/distributed-ledger-technology/defi_white_paper_v2.0.pdf.
Metcalfe, W. (2020). Ethereum, Smart Contracts, DApps. In *Blockchain and Crypt Currency* (pp. 77–93). Springer.
Moin, A., Sekniqi, K., and Sirer, E.G. (2020). SoK: A Classification Framework for Stablecoin Designs. *International Conference on Financial Cryptography and Data Security*, 174–197.
Mou, V. (2021). *Blockchain Oracles Explained*. Binance Academy. https://academy.binance.com/en/articles/blockchain-oracles-explained.
Nakamoto, S. (2008). Bitcoin: A Peer-to-Peer Electronic Cash System. *Decentralized Business Review*, 21260.
Oved, M., and Mosites, D. (2017). Swap: A Peer-to-Peer Protocol for Trading Ethereum Tokens. *Whitepaper Database*, 21.
Ozcan, R. (2021). *Decentralized Finance* (pp. 57–75). https://doi.org/10.1007/978-3-030-72624-9_4.
Popescu, A.-D. (2020). Decentralized Finance (DeFi)—The Lego of Finance. *Social Sciences and Education Research Review*, 7(1), 321–348.
Pourpouneh, M., Nielsen, K., and Ross, O. (2020). *Automated Market Makers*. IFRO Working Paper No. 2020/08. https://www.econstor.eu/handle/10419/222424.
Qin, K., Zhou, L., Gamito, P., Jovanovic, P., and Gervais, A. (2021a). An Empirical Study of DeFi Liquidations: Incentives, Risks, and Instabilities. *ArXiv:2106.06389 [Cs, q-Fin]*. http://arxiv.org/abs/2106.06389.
Qin, K., Zhou, L., and Gervais, A. (2021b). CeFi vs. DeFi—Comparing Centralized to Decentralized Finance; CeFi vs. DeFi—Comparing Centralized to Decentralized Finance. In *Proceedings of ACM Conference (Conference'17)* (Vol. 1).
Qin, K., Zhou, L., Livshits, B., and Gervais, A. (2021c). Attacking the DeFi Ecosystem with Flash Loans for Fun and Profit. In *International Conference on Financial Cryptography and Data Security* (pp. 3–32). Springer.
Ramos, D., Zanko, G., and Bogotá, M. (2020). *A Review of the Current State of Decentralized Finance as a Subsector of the Cryptocurrency Market*. MobileyourLife. https://www.mobileyourlife.com/research.
Sandner, P., and von Wachter, V. (2019). *Decentralized Finance (DeFi): What Do You Need To Know? | by Philipp Sandner | Medium*. https://philippsandner.medium.com/decentralized-finance-defi-what-do-you-need-to-know-9cd5e8c2a48.
Savelyev, A. (2017). Contract Law 2.0: 'Smart' Contracts as the Beginning of the End of Classic Contract Law. *Information and Communications Technology Law*, *26*(2), 116–134. https://doi.org/10.1080/13600834.2017.1301036.
Schär, F. (2020). Decentralized Finance: On Blockchain- and Smart Contract-based Financial Markets. *SSRN Electronic Journal*. https://doi.org/10.2139/ssrn.3571335.
Srivastava, A., Bhattacharya, P., Singh, A., and Mathur, A. (2018). *A Systematic Review on Evolution of Blockchain Generations*, 7, 1–8.
State of the DApps. (2021). *State of the DApps—DApp Statistics*. https://www.stateofthedapps.com/stats/platform/ethereum#new.
Stepanova, V., and Eriņš, I. (2021). Review of Decentralized Finance Applications and Their Total Value Locked. *TEM Journal*, 10(1), 327–333. https://doi.org/10.18421/TEM101-41.
Szabo, N. (1997). *Formalizing and Securing Relationships on Public Networks*. First Monday.
Tapscott, D., and Tapscott, A. (2016). *Blockchain Revolution: How the Technology Behind Bitcoin and Other Cryptocurrencies is Changing the World*. Penguin UK.

Trinkler, R., and El Isa, M. (2017). *Melon Protocol: A Blockchain Protocol for Digital Asset Management*. Whitepaper.
Uniswap. (2021). *Uniswap Info*. https://info.uniswap.org/#/.
von Haller Gronbaek, M. (2016). Blockchain 2.0, Smart Contracts and Challenges. *Comput. Law, SCL Mag*, 1–5.
Voshmgir, S. (2020). *Token Economy: How the Web3 Reinvents the Internet* (Vol. 2). Token Kitchen.
Wang, D., Wu, S., Lin, Z., Wu, L., Yuan, X., Zhou, Y., Wang, H., and Ren, K. (2021). Towards a First Step to Understand Flash Loan and Its Applications in DeFi Ecosystem. *Proceedings of the Ninth International Workshop on Security in Blockchain and Cloud Computing*, 23–28. https://doi.org/10.1145/3457977.3460301.
Warren, W., and Bandeali, A. (2017). *0x: An Open Protocol for Decentralized Exchange on the Ethereum Blockchain*. https://Github.Com/0xProject/Whitepaper, 04–18.
Werner, S.M., Perez, D., Gudgeon, L., Klages-Mundt, A., Harz, D., and Knottenbelt, W.J. (2021). SoK: Decentralized Finance (DeFi). *Papers*. https://ideas.repec.org/p/arx/papers/2101.08778.html.
Yermack, D. (2015). Chapter 2—Is Bitcoin a Real Currency? An Economic Appraisal. In D. Lee Kuo Chuen (ed.), *Handbook of Digital Currency* (pp. 31–43). Academic Press. https://doi.org/10.1016/B978-0-12-802117-0.00002-3.
Zeller, M. (2020). *Sneak peek at Flash Loans. Aave protocol launched a bit less than... | by Marc Zeller | Aave Blog | Medium*. https://medium.com/aave/sneak-peek-at-flash-loans-f2b28a394d62.
Zinsmeister, N., Robinson, D., and Adams, Hayden. (2020). *Uniswap v2 Core*. 10.

2. Decentralized lending

Felix Irresberger, Kose John, and Fahad Saleh

INTRODUCTION: WHAT IS DECENTRALIZED LENDING?

Borrowing and lending of cash and other assets is an important function in any financial system. Households require mortgages and personal loans to fund purchases of real estate or cars and other personal items for consumption; businesses require long-term financing for investment purposes or credit lines to cover operating costs when needed; financial and other institutions engage in very short-term money markets to be able to meet payments and gain (from) liquidity for trading purposes. The common attribute in these situations is that on the one hand there are those that seek funding, the borrowers, and on the other hand those that supply liquidity, the lenders. Typically only one or at most a handful of central financial intermediaries are involved in facilitating the matching of the two types of agents. Decentralized finance (DeFi) is a new type of financial market infrastructure based on distributed ledger technologies, such as blockchains, to implement automated financial protocols that require neither the involvement of such centralized financial intermediation, nor the institutions to provide respective infrastructure and coordinate the interactions between its users (for example, via liquidity provision). These blockchains allow anyone to upload and execute computer code, "smart contracts," to automate and make contingent transactions that resemble straightforward interactions such as money markets, which represent the basis for many DeFi applications. With the emergence of the term "DeFi," activities by traditional financial institutions and within centralized markets are now often referred to as centralized finance (CeFi), which DeFi aims to disintermediate. As a major part of this DeFi ecosystem, decentralized lending protocols have emerged, which aim to resemble traditional debt contracts without incurring the costs and issues stemming from CeFi institutions and markets.

What is a Decentralized Lending Protocol?

Decentralized lending (DL) refers to a very specific marketplace for borrowing and lending of digital assets in which: (1) blockchains are used as settlement layers for interactions (transactions) between agents; (2) smart contracts are employed to implement lending protocols that govern interactions between borrowers and liquidity suppliers; (3) only cryptoassets such as Ether (ETH) or stablecoins such as Tether (USDT) are (currently) supported; (4) maintenance of the protocol (code) is performed by a community of governance token holders; and (5) liquidity supply and trust mediation is performed by a collective of market participants that benefit from and share the cost of decentralized liquidity provision. In essence, a DL protocol is a set of instructions encoded in a collection of smart contracts running on shared, blockchain-based computing infrastructure to create debt agreements between two or more parties. This setup comes with benefits and issues when compared to traditional lending. Having automated protocols based on standardized code can make the borrowing process more efficient and transparent from an operational point of view and thus lower the cost of entry to increase participation by many users. However, since all interactions need to be encoded in smart contracts that are "uploaded" to the shared ledger (blockchain) beforehand, DL protocols are much less flexible when it comes to customizing and adjusting risk parameters of the debt contract.

Where Does Decentralization in DeFi Lending Come From?

Decentralization is a key feature of DeFi lending protocols and enters the picture in various forms.

Transaction settlement layer

Settlement of transactions is performed upon public blockchains such as Ethereum, Tron, and BSC, which allow the creation, storage, and transfer of non-custodial, digital assets between two parties in a decentralized manner. These blockchains employ different consensus protocols that govern how network nodes collectively decide on the validity of a set of transactions on the ledger. Therefore, there is no need for a central infrastructure provider to initiate, record, or close debt agreements between multiple parties. The Ethereum blockchain has been dominantly used as settlement infrastructure for DeFi protocols (see Irresberger et al. 2022), in terms of both the number of DeFi related smart contracts and the number of active users of those applications, but other blockchains such as Tron, Binance Smart Chain, Avalanche, and Solana also host various DL protocols.

Smart contracts

Deploying and testing new smart lending contracts on shared blockchain infrastructure is relatively straightforward and inexpensive (for example, compared to opening over-the-counter debt markets for large institutions) and any user can create, audit, and use smart contracts. The low cost of entry and transparency enhances participation by many users and therefore results in a more decentralized and tested ecosystem underlying the DL protocols.

Decentralized assets

Many cryptoassets used in DL protocols are decentralized in the sense that there is no central issuing institution behind the creation of that asset (for example, ETH is created as part of the block creation in Ethereum). Furthermore, those digital assets are not held by financial intermediaries but are non-custodial and controlled by DL protocol users themselves (for example, held in their digital wallet with private keys known only to them), or are locked away in accounts (digital vaults) that are governed automatically via smart contract instructions.

Governance

Decisions on any changes to DL protocols, such as risk parameters or debt contract terms, are not made by a single entity, but by a collective of stakeholders that organize communities around the governance of a specific protocol. This decentralized governance is often facilitated by the existence of governance tokens attached to the DL protocol (another smart contract application) that give their holders voting rights on protocol updates and aligns incentives of governing users to sustainably maintain the DL protocol.

Liquidity provision

In the absence of a central liquidity provider (for example, banks taking deposits and then deciding on which loans to give out or money market funds offering repos), decentralized lending relies on liquidity provision by a collective of market participants. Such decentralized liquidity provision requires incentives to commit funds to a common liquidity pool, thereby avoiding market failures. For example, to resemble fractional reserve banking (that is, digital money creation or lending), without excessive collateralization, such liquidity pools would need to replace central banks as a mediator of trust.

How is DeFi Different from CeFi Lending?

Decentralized lending protocols rely on matching savers and borrowers by attracting each side with competitive interest rates. There is no credit risk assessment of anonymous users in a decentralized setting, so that DeFi lending protocols rely on adjustment of benchmark borrowing and savings rates to give incentives for users to add assets to liquidity pools that can be drawn upon by some users to borrow. In many DL protocols, encoded mathematical formulas set interest rates automatically, depending on the level of utilization of the liquidity pool (that is, how many assets in the pool are used for lending versus borrowing). In other protocols, interest rates may be voted on and set by governance token holders that make up a decentralized community of decision-makers. Furthermore, there are several mechanisms to facilitate decentralized loans. The two most common approaches are illustrated in Figure 2.1.

Popular DL protocols, such as Aave and Compound, resemble the functioning of a collateralized debt market (CDM) via pooling of assets by lenders to give to potential borrowers, whereas MakerDAO, for example, uses collateralized debt positions (CDPs), often called "vaults," to originate decentralized loans (see Schär 2021). The lending pool mechanism, illustrated on the left side of the figure, does not facilitate direct lending relationships between borrowers and lenders (as may be the case in peer-to-peer platforms), but relies on pooling of assets by investors and interaction of borrowers with that lending pool. However, instead of having a debt agreement between the borrower and an intermediary such as a bank, which pools liquidity from

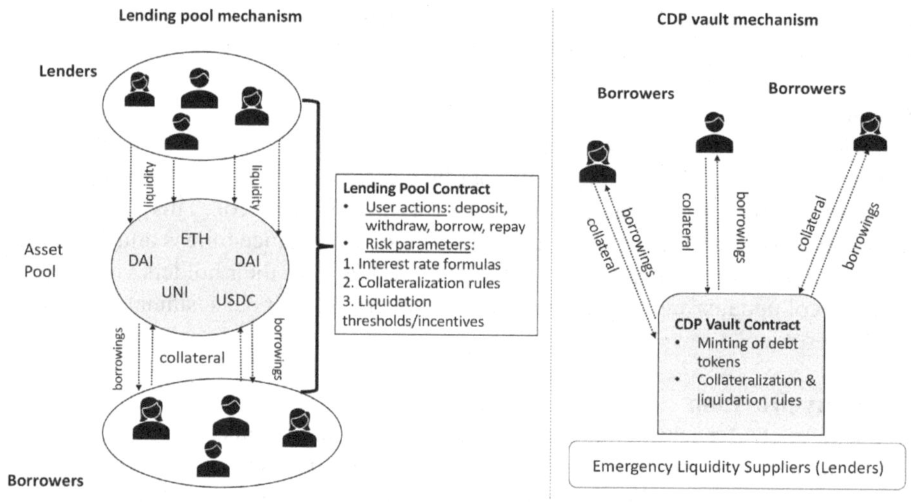

Figure 2.1 Decentralized lending protocol mechanisms

depositors without matching depositor and borrower directly, the agreement would be with the decentralized lending pool protocol itself. The lending pool has rules encoded in the corresponding smart contract that govern the interactions of lenders and borrowers with the pool, and the risk parameters put in place to encourage or discourage certain types of risk-taking behavior by users of the pool. For example, the smart contract contains instructions on how much leverage borrowers can take on by providing collateral, and at what point their debt position requires additional funds. It also describes mathematical functions that set interest rates algorithmically given current market prices.

The CDP vault mechanism is also based on borrower interaction with a smart contract, but there is no pooling of assets from other users. Borrowers may receive their debt from newly minted assets by the protocol itself, and the smart contract will describe risk parameters and auction mechanisms that are put in place to manage CDP vault liquidations. Compared to lending pools, debt is denominated only in the newly minted debt tokens (for example, DAI), which needs to be provided by emergency liquidity suppliers that can act as lenders of last resort, should the system need recapitalization after borrower defaults.

Lending and borrowing can occur in various forms within DeFi applications and are not strictly limited only to pure decentralized lending protocols. For example, there are DeFi applications that support (decentralized) margin trading and perpetual futures contracts on cryptoassets, which require lending of cryptoassets by other users that act as liquidity providers (rather than a centralized exchange filling that role), but these platforms are usually not classified as decentralized lending applications. In our high-level review, we will focus on protocols where decentralized loan facilitation is the main objective and that rely on either the lending pool or CDP vault mechanism.

For further illustration of the differences between CeFi lending and DL protocols, consider the case of a collateralized debt position. In a simple CDP contract, the borrower requires cash with short maturity that is borrowed from the lender (liquidity supplier) and provides risky collateral. The value of the collateral exceeds the value of the debt at the beginning of the contract. After maturity has been reached, the borrower decides to repay the debt with interest to retrieve the collateral, or to default on their obligation and lose the collateral to the lender, or to renew the debt agreement for another period, possibly at a new interest rate or with different collateral requirements. This decision likely depends on whether the value of the collateral has increased or decreased during that time period and whether the borrower is able to provide additional collateral if needed.

In CeFi this could correspond to a repurchase agreement, for example, where financial institutions such as investment banks provide highly liquid, risky collateral such as mortgage-backed securities or stocks to borrow cash (equivalents) for liquidity purposes; the lending counterparties could be large investors such as money market funds. Contracts are traded over the counter and interest rates charged could, in principle, depend on the credibility of the borrowing institution, their available inventory or market conditions, such as the rate levels of the interbank lending market. Borrowers will be known to lenders, which requires additional screening by the lender. Specific transactions and debt contracts may not be publicly viewable by other parties, and terms may differ case by case.

In DeFi, smart contract code that mimics collateralized debt positions would need simple instructions on what kind of assets are acceptable as collateral, the quantity of debt that can be borrowed and at what rate (given market prices of collateral assets), and the conditions under which the CDP would have to be liquidated to protect liquidity providers from defaulting borrowers. Once these instructions are designed and deployed to the blockchain via smart contract code, users can freely interact with the debt contract by following the clear set of instructions. Liquidity is provided either by the protocol itself (for example, there are encoded instructions on how many units of assets or tokens should be created by the protocol) or by market participants willing to lend their assets (for example, US dollar stablecoins) to a pool of assets that can subsequently be borrowed by other users. Since DL protocols operate on public blockchains, all debt and liquidity positions as well as interactions between users are transparent. On the flipside, users are pseudonymous, and thus it is not possible to perform any form of borrower screening that could influence the terms of the debt contract for individual users.

What are Common Use Cases for Decentralized Lending Protocols?

Decentralized lending protocols only allow cryptoassets that exist within the blockchain ecosystem. Therefore, most existing protocols resemble money markets facilitating short-term borrowing and lending of cryptoassets, but do not support other lending setups or loan products such as mortgages or business or personal loans that are customized to a particular financing need. Even more restricting, lending protocols have one set of rules that applies to every borrower and lender. Because of these practical restrictions, DL protocols are employed by its users for few, very specific use cases, such as the following.

Leveraged long trading

Assume a user possesses a risky cryptoasset, such as Ether (ETH), that they believe will appreciate in the future: that is, they would like to take a long position in this asset to profit from this expected value increase, without necessarily having to sell the cryptoasset. Figure 2.2 illustrates how the user can enter a leveraged long position using a decentralized lending pool to effectively bet on price appreciation of the risky (collateral) asset without the need to dispose of the asset owned. The first step is to deposit the risky collateral (ETH) to the lending pool and receive another asset, such as a USD stablecoin (for example, USDC), which can then in the second step be traded on a decentralized exchange (DEX) to buy more of the risky cryptoasset. The user then holds the risky cryptoasset acquired with the borrowings, and exchanges it back for more units of the initially borrowed stablecoin when it has appreciated in price. In the final step, debt principal and interest are paid back, and profits are retained by the user. The initially provided risky collateral is returned to the user from the lending pool.

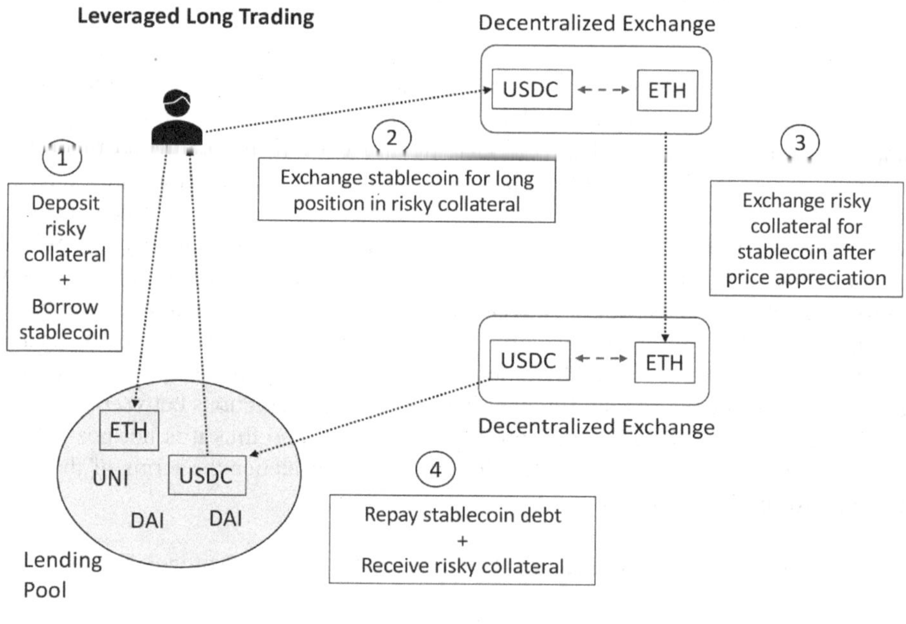

Figure 2.2 Illustration of leveraged long trading with lending pools and decentralized exchanges

Short-selling

Lending protocols may also be used to construct short-sales of cryptoassets. Assume that a user holds stablecoins and wishes to bet on falling prices of a risky cryptoasset. The user can do so by depositing and collateralizing the stablecoin to the lending pool and borrowing units of a risky cryptoasset, which is then exchanged for units of a stablecoin on a DEX (that is, sold). After the price of the risky cryptoasset has depreciated, the user will exchange back the stablecoins to units of the risky cryptoasset at a more favorable rate, and return the assets back to the lending pool with interest. Note that the user could also use the stablecoins obtained in the second step to lend out with interest in a DL protocol while waiting for the risky asset value to depreciate.

Flash loans and arbitrage

Traders can borrow from DL protocols to exploit differences in exchange rates of cryptoassets across two or more (decentralized) exchanges. While the steps to exercise these arbitrage opportunities can be carried out in separate, consecutive transactions to interact with respective DeFi protocols, there exists an innovation within some DL protocols that allow users to bundle these steps together. This smart contract (function) is called a flash loan and essentially consists of a set of instructions that execute borrowing and trading actions across protocols in one single transaction that is submitted and evaluated on the blockchain. The unique feature of a flash loan smart contract is that to borrow from a DL protocol (lending pool), no collateral is required to execute a particular trade as described before. That is, the DL protocol would allow the user to borrow units of a cryptoasset to execute a set of (trading) transactions with the condition that all the steps are valid transactions, and the borrowed units are returned with interest within the same transaction (block). As a consequence, flash loans are loans of zero duration and are either fully executed or dismissed (the transacting user would lose transaction fees associated with submitting the instructions to the smart contract platform). Flash loans allow users to take advantage of identified arbitrage opportunities without having to hold excessive collateral. Another common use case of flash loans is to swap collateral assets locked in decentralized lending protocols (for example, to mitigate potential price drops that lead to undercollateralized debt positions or exploit better investment opportunities). This swap is done with a flash loan that borrows units of the borrowed asset and repays the debt of the original position, and immediately opens a new debt position by depositing a new type of collateral. In this case, the collateral swap is executed without the need to acquire or forgo investment returns on units of the borrowed cryptoassets to repay the original debt.

AN OVERVIEW OF DECENTRALIZED LENDING PROTOCOLS

Decentralized loans can be originated and repaid at any time, are open-ended, and do not require approval or permission other than meeting pre-specified, transparent conditions. Loans have floating rates that are updated by block (unit of time) given market conditions and, most often, pre-specified interest rate formulas. Prices and interest rates from other DL markets are retrieved via oracle protocols (for example, Chainlink on the Ethereum blockchain) and used for benchmarking parameters and computing collateralization ratios. Before any user engages with a decentralized lending platform, they will perform market research: potential borrowers will assess the terms under which they can open a collateralized debt position using a DL protocol; that is, they will study current market conditions such as utilization of liquidity pools (supply levels) and corresponding dynamic interest rates and then decide on the amount and type of collateral asset that they can provide to take out a decentralized loan. Market research can be done via web-based dashboards created by developers and users of decentralized lending platforms, but can also be done by anyone able to retrieve publicly available data from the blockchain underlying the DL protocol. DeFi dashboards display metrics on the total amounts of assets supplied and borrowed to a particular protocol as well as current interest rates and market prices of assets used in the calculation of collateral and debt position values. We refrain from reporting current market capitalizations or interest rates on protocols as these are highly volatile and the dominance of specific protocols may be changing within short periods of time. Instead, we focus on providing a survey of multiple existing platforms and highlight commonalities and differences among them for further study. We first describe the workflow of a DL protocol relying on lending pools, followed by a discussion of the CDP vault mechanism to facilitate decentralized loans. In each case, we summarize the action set of specific types of users, including borrowers, lenders, and liquidators.

Lending Pool Mechanism

The core features of a lending pool-based mechanism are written into the smart contract code, which describes the action set of users as well as how system parameters such as (market) interest rates and collateral prices, liquidation thresholds, and liquidation incentives are set and updated over time. Many lending pool smart contracts have the following four functions that users can choose to use to interact with the lending pool: deposit, redeem, borrow, and repay. That is, users can: (1) deposit assets to the lending pool; (2) redeem claims on fractions of the assets in the pool (that is, withdraw their contribution plus interest accrued); (3) borrow from the lending pool after providing collateral; or (4) repay the borrowed debt. Each of those actions will change the state of the lending pool, for example the size of the asset pool and its utilization by borrowers, which in turn will have consequences for the interest given and charged by lenders and borrowers, respectively. For illustration, we consider the four core functions within a lending pool protocol which are used by both borrower and lender, and explain the consequences of their actions for utilization ratios and interest rates. For simplicity, we assume that there are existing lending pools for two cryptoassets, X and Y, with borrowing utilizations u(X) and u(Y), and corresponding borrowing and lending interest rates, respectively:

1. Deposit. Both the borrower and lender need to transfer assets to the lending pool, that is, they trigger the Deposit() function of a lending pool contract. To track the contributions of both users, they receive newly minted tokens that bear interest and represent their share of assets in the lending pool, which is and will remain proportional to the share of assets they provided overall. All else being equal, after a Deposit() transaction, because new assets are added to the pools for assets X and Y, utilization within each pool will decrease as the denominator of the utilization ratio—the total liquidity supplied to a pool—is increasing. This in turn will generally decrease the borrowing and lending rates for assets in respective pools.
2. Redeem. Lenders deposit assets to the pool to receive interest. Interest on liquidity provided accrues after every block, and is realized when users redeem the interest-bearing token for their deposited assets in the form of a better exchange rate between interest bearing token (receipt) and original assets deposited. Redeemed interest-bearing tokens are destroyed (burned) once they are sent back to the lending pool contract. Mechanically, if one unit of asset X was deposited and exchanged for 50 units of the interest-bearing token version of X (that is, an initial exchange rate of 1/50 = 0.02), and the annual lending interest rate was 5 percent, the exchange rate would rise accordingly so that we have 0.02*1.05 = 0.021, corresponding to a claim to 50*0.021 = 1.05 of X units after one year, assuming that rates were constant. That is, although the total amount of interest-bearing tokens has not changed, the total amount of units of asset X they can retrieve from exchanging those tokens has increased due to interest accrued. Using the Redeem() function to exchange the interest-bearing tokens for the original deposited (including accrued interest) will reduce the total amount of liquidity supplied to the asset pool, which increases the utilization rate of the pool, thereby increasing borrowing and lending rates.
3. Borrow. To take out a decentralized loan, the borrower triggers a Borrow() function of the lending pool contract which requires placement of an interest-bearing token from another asset pool as collateral. Note that the interest-bearing tokens can be transferred and used for other purposes outside the lending pool platform if they are not used as collateral. Using the above example, a borrower deposits units of Y to receive interest-bearing tokens representing shares in the Y asset pool; these tokens can then be used as collateral to borrow against and retrieve units of X as debt. The borrowing capacity of the user depends on the ratio of the value of collateral asset Y and the borrowed debt value in units of X, that is, the collateralization ratio. At decentralized loan origination, the protocol will retrieve market prices of X and Y from a price oracle (for example, DeFi data oracle

protocol or price feeds drawn from several exchanges) to compute the collateralization ratio. This ratio needs to exceed a liquidation threshold (for example, 150 percent collateral to debt value) to indicate that the debt position is sufficiently funded. These valuations may change over time so that the DL protocol regularly checks whether the liquidation threshold has been breached and a debt position is healthy or must be liquidated by force. Borrow() increases the utilization ratio of an asset pool by increasing the amount of borrowed assets (holding liquidity supplied constant). Higher utilization results in higher borrowing and lending rates.

4. Repay. Assuming collateralization requirements are met, borrowing interest due will accrue with every block added to the blockchain using similar mechanics as described above for lending interest: if 100 units of interest-bearing token corresponding to asset Y are used to borrow one unit of X and the annual interest rate is 7.5 percent, the borrower accrues debt of 1.075 units of X needed to repay to retrieve the same 100 units of the collateral placed. The pool of assets increases when the borrower repays the debt with interest in the unit of the borrowed cryptoasset. This creates a spread that allows the pay-out to lenders for depositing their assets to the lending pool in the first place. Borrowers can choose to repay in part or in full. Repay() can have a mixed effect on the utilization ratio and interest rate of the asset pool. This is because the asset pool size will increase with the added units of the borrowed asset from paying interest, but because the debt position is (partially) closed, the total amount of borrowed assets decreases and so does the utilization ratio.

Other than borrowers and lenders, there are two other important types of users operating within a lending pool-based protocol: liquidators and governors.

Liquidators can be, but are not necessarily, borrowers or lenders themselves. They perform a risk monitoring role and make use of a LiquidationCall() function, which serves as a risk management mechanism of the protocol in case debt positions are not sufficiently collateralized. The idea behind liquidation calls is to give other users the motivation and ability to monitor existing borrowers' debt and to call out undercollateralized positions, such as when the market price of the underlying collateral asset has decreased so that the set liquidation threshold of the collateralization ratio has been breached. To give incentive to users to act as monitoring liquidators, users who trigger the LiquidationCall() function may acquire the underlying collateral asset (interest-bearing token) at a discounted price. This is called the liquidation incentive (sometimes "penalty" or "bonus") and is a set parameter in many lending pool-based protocols. Because liquidators monitor collateralization ratios and are waiting to take advantage of the liquidation incentive, borrowers in turn have the incentive to ensure that their position is actively managed by, for example, adding further collateral assets to the position when the collateral value falls. In cases where borrowers may decide to default on their position, liquidators help the DL protocol to recapitalize by providing liquidity to the asset pool (in terms of units of the borrowed asset). For illustration of the liquidation process, consider Figure 2.3.

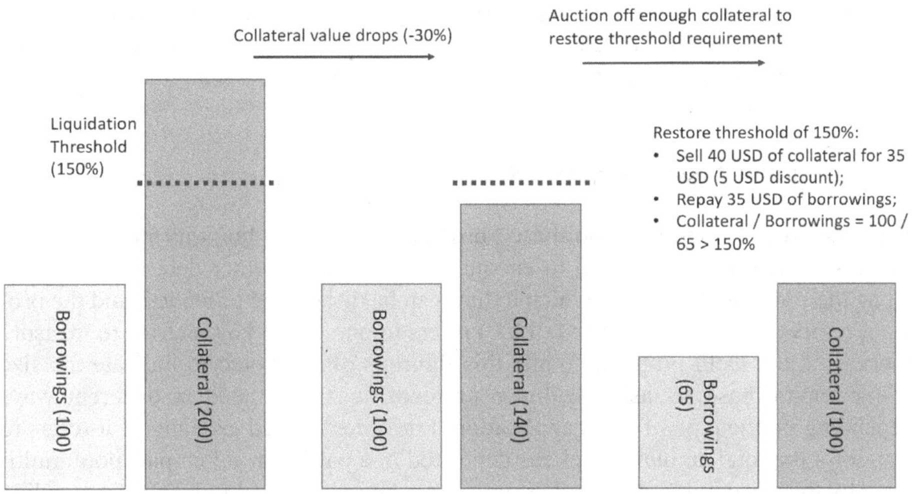

Figure 2.3 *Illustration of the lending pool liquidation process*

As a starting point, assume the decentralized loan is worth US$100 and the collateral pledged against it is worth US$200 and fulfills minimum loan-to-value (LTV) requirements at loan origination (for example, 60 percent LTV). The lending pool contract has set the liquidation threshold to 150 percent, which is met with a 200 percent collateralization ratio. In the next step, assume the collateral value decreases by 30 percent so that the collateralization ratio falls to 140 percent, that is, below the liquidation threshold. If the borrower decides not to repay or maintain the account beforehand, the position needs to be liquidated so that the collateral ratio is above the threshold again. This can be achieved if liquidators are willing to buy the collateral asset at a discounted price that settles part of the outstanding debt to restore a higher collateral ratio. Note that liquidations may either fully close the debt position or partially restore the collateralization ratio above the liquidation threshold, and thus the utilization ratio and interest rates of the asset pool may decrease. As an example, liquidators may buy US$40 worth of the collateral using the borrowings cryptoasset units worth US$35, that is, they would receive a discount of US$5 for providing the needed asset to repay part of the debt to the lending pool. After this sale, the collateral value lies at US$100 and the borrowings at US$65 so that the collateral ratio is slightly above the threshold at 100/65 = 153.8 percent.

Finally, "governors" are users that hold governance tokens of a specific DL protocol and thus are responsible for monitoring and improving the underlying design and functioning of lending pool-based markets. The value proposition of engaging in the governance process of a protocol is that the value of the governance token held by engaged users should appreciate in price when the protocol is running as intended, that is, users supply to and borrow from lending pools and repay their debt. Governors have rights to vote on proposals to introduce or change system parameters such as interest rate formulas, liquidation thresholds and penalties, permission of (collateral) assets, price oracles, and more. These decisions will have immediate consequences on user interactions and thus are regularly discussed publicly in online governance forums.

Setting Lending Pool Risk Parameters

The objective of a lending pool-based protocol is to attract liquidity in the form of assets supplied to the pool and to encourage borrowers to enter debt positions and repay their loan with interest, which in turn can be distributed to lenders and the protocol reserve. Total value locked (TVL) refers to one of the key metrics to measure success of any DeFi protocol. While this figure is often quoted to indicate the size of the capital base set aside within a protocol, it is calculated in different ways depending on the type of DeFi application. For decentralized exchanges, it refers to (roughly) the total amount of tokens deposited in a particular token pair pool multiplied by the price in US dollars (USD) (or alternatively quoted in ETH). For lending pools, TVL may refer to the total market capitalization (denominated in USD or other assets) of the assets that are pooled together using the Deposit() function minus the value of all borrowed assets. After deducting the total amount of borrowed assets (in USD), TVL is measured as all assets' value still available to be borrowed or used as collateral for borrowing. Higher TVL figures are beneficial to both borrowers and lenders, as both user types gain from having more capital deployed to lending pools as they make interest rates less volatile and less prone to runs on pooled assets. This is because a larger asset lending pool would require more capital to be withdrawn or added at the same time to significantly alter interest rates, as the utilization ratio of existing pools is harder to move. Thus, to reduce this liquidity risk, governors decide on system design parameters of the lending pool protocol that encourages or discourages risk-taking behavior by its users.

In the following, we discuss three major design choices and their economic implications: (1) liquidation thresholds and penalties; (2) collateralization rules; and (3) interest rate formulas. For each design choice, we provide details on their implementations for Aave, one of the first and largest lending pool-based protocols implemented upon multiple blockchains.

Liquidation thresholds and incentives

Overcollateralization is a necessary feature of DL protocols as there is no credit risk assessment or legal mechanism to enforce loan repayment by borrowers on these platforms. If the value of the collateral asset backing decentralized loans is volatile, the protocol faces collateral risk. Collateral risk refers to the possibility of collateral price changes that could result in the value of the collateral to be below the actual borrowings' value. In such a case, the debt contract would not be sufficiently backed, which would result in losses for the protocol (and lenders) as borrowers no longer have any incentive to repay their debt (with interest). Since collateral assets are locked up in the lending pool contract, collateralized assets can be seized if the borrower does not repay the debt owed and the position is liquidated; this serves as a risk mitigation mechanism against borrower (counterparty) default risk. However, this mechanism does not come without risk on its own: if liquidators (investors) believe that collateral values may further decrease in the near future, they may not be willing to buy the collateral even at discounted price levels, that is, the liquidation penalty (sometimes called liquidation bonus) in place to encourage liquidators to step in, is not high enough. Generally, assets that have high levels of liquidity in the open market will require lower liquidation penalties to attract liquidators (investors) to buy at the discounted price. Setting the liquidation penalty too high will make liquidations costlier for the stakeholders of the protocols (for example, lenders, governors) as they need to sell collateral assets at a higher discount, which can be risky when the collateral value is highly volatile, but may be necessary when the market liquidity of the asset is lower.

Governors are calibrating liquidation thresholds and liquidation penalties such that there is enough liquidation risk mitigation, using high liquidation thresholds and penalties, versus providing enough opportunity for borrowers to take risky positions, by using lower liquidation thresholds, and keeping liquidation penalties low enough to enhance the attractiveness of the lending pool to investors when interest is being repaid by borrowers, that is, increase TVL and protocol surplus (shares of the interest spread that may be collected in a reserve treasury of the lending pool contract, that is, not all profits from interest are distributed to lenders).

Collateralization rules

The community behind a DL protocol, whether run by an organization or by a collection of governance token holders, will set up their own risk governance framework that determines which kind of assets are permissible to use in the protocol and what risk parameters should be associated with those cryptoassets. Indeed, protocol governance will have risk frameworks that determine whether an asset is of a certain quality or has sufficient interest from borrowers and lenders. This classification of assets is often based on market risks, referring to their price return volatility and overall market capitalization, as well as on blockchain-related characteristics, such as on-chain transaction volume (as a form of liquidity) but can include more qualitative factors such as the degree of centralization behind a particular cryptoasset. For example, stablecoins issued by a company, such as Circle (USDC) or Tether (USDT), are considered to be more centralized and have the potential for a single point of failure and bear regulatory risk, which is risk that is considered by lending pool protocol designers when accepting and setting collateralization and liquidation risk parameters, but may perform well on other dimensions such as lower price volatility.

Aave V1 and V2 risk parameters

Table 2.1 lists selected cryptoassets that are permitted to be used as collateral and can be lent out via the Aave V1 and V2 protocols and reports a snapshot (October 2022) of risk parameters set by the protocol designers (governors): loan-to-value (collateralization) ratios at loan origination, liquidation thresholds (expressed as minimum ratio of collateral over debt value), and liquidation incentive.

Table 2.1 *Aave V1 and V2 risk parameters*

Aave V1 Snapshot (Oct 2022)				
Name	Symbol	LTV	Liquidation threshold	Liquidation incentive
Stablecoins				
DAI	DAI	75%	125%	5.00%
True USD	TUSD	75%	125%	5.00%
USDC	USDC	75%	125%	5.00%
Other risky cryptoassets				
Maker	MKR	50%	154%	10.00%
Uniswap	UNI	40%	154%	15.00%
Wrapped BTC	WBTC	60%	154%	15.00%
Wrapped ETH	WETH	75%	125%	5.00%
AAVE V2 Snapshot (Oct 2022)				
Name	Symbol	LTV	Liquidation threshold	Liquidation incentive
Stablecoins				
DAI	DAI	77%	125%	5.00%
True USD	TUSD	80%	120%	5.00%
USDC	USDC	86%	114%	5.00%
Other risky cryptoassets				
Maker	MKR	65%	143%	7.50%
Uniswap	UNI	60%	133%	9.00%
Wrapped BTC	WBTC	70%	133%	6.50%
Wrapped ETH	WETH	83%	118%	5.00%

Three of the most important cryptoassets permitted in lending pools are stablecoins, DAI, TUSD, and USDC; and many users tend to borrow (USD) stablecoins against risky collateral cryptoassets. In Aave V1, the three stablecoins DAI, TUSD, and USDC have the same LTV at 75 percent: that is, US$75 of cryptoasset debt needs to be backed by at least US$100 worth of another crypto collateral asset at decentralized loan origination (that is, corresponding to a collateralization ratio of 133 percent). Note that this is slightly above the collateralization ratio required at the liquidation threshold (125 percent) set for these stablecoins. This is because small price changes of a risky collateral would result in immediate liquidation, so this small difference between LTC and liquidation threshold acts as a buffer. In Aave V2, the LTV is slightly higher at 77 percent to 86 percent, which requires less collateral to be provided for loan origination, and is thus easier to achieve for potential borrowers. In both versions of the Aave protocol the liquidation incentive for stablecoins is set to 5 percent, which is the lowest among all selected assets shown in the table. Given that, in practice, stablecoin lending and borrowing (against other risky cryptoassets) is the most common use of lending pools, the liquidation incentive given to liquidators does not need to be excessively high to encourage liquidators to participate, as these are some of the most traded cryptoassets in existence and thus it is comparatively easier to provide liquidity in the form of stablecoins to repay debt when positions are liquidated. It is noteworthy that ETH, which is the cryptoasset native to the Ethereum blockchain ecosystem, exhibits similar risk parameters, indicating healthy performance with respect to the risk characteristics used for permission to be included as asset (collateral) in Aave lending pools (for example, high market value and trading volume, moderate volatility, low smart contract risk).

Comparing risk parameters of stablecoins and ETH to other risky cryptoassets such as MKR or UNI (governance tokens of other DeFi applications) and a tokenized version of Bitcoin's native cryptoasset tracking BTC price levels (WBTC), we observe that LTV ratios are significantly lower and liquidation thresholds are higher. That is, at origination, debt denominated in those assets would have to be collateralized more and remain high without risking early liquidation. Also, the difference in minimum collateralization level at origination versus liquidation is significantly larger for these riskier cryptoassets to avoid liquidation shortly after origination. These selected examples illustrate the principles behind (Aave's) lending pool risk governance framework, where risk parameters are set in line with expected market and operational risks of a particular cryptoasset. A quotation from the Aave developer documentation (October 2022) confirms this notion of risk governance as an integral part of decentralized lending pool protocols: "When market conditions change, risks change, and so we are continuously monitoring the assets integrated into the protocol which sometimes requires to quickly adapt the risk parameters" (https://docs.aave.com/risk/v/aave-v2/asset-risk/risk-parameters).

Interest rate formulas

Lending pools employ interest rate formulas to dynamically adjust rates to manage demand for borrowing and supply of liquidity to lend out. Intuitively, when demand for borrowing increases, that is, when a higher share of assets in the lending pool is utilized for borrowing by users, borrowing rates will automatically increase to raise the cost to the borrower, who in turn must either provide more collateral to the pool (add liquidity to the pool) or close their position voluntarily (repayment) or by force (liquidation). Similarly, if savings rates rise accordingly, more incentive exists for potential lenders to supply additional assets to the lending pool to earn interest on. In both cases, lending pool utilization would decrease following the increases in interest rates. Similarly, if utilization is lower due to less demand for borrowing or oversupply of liquidity, the fixed interest rate formulas would reduce borrowing cost and savings rates. Because of this mechanism, borrowers and lenders may be susceptible to large swings in interest rates, given changing demand and supply of liquidity.

Lending pool-based protocols employ a variety of interest rate functions that mechanically map the level of utilization to borrowing and lending rates, with the common feature that higher utilization corresponds to higher interest rates. However, they do differ in the speed at which rates are adjusted, especially when it comes to higher levels of utilization. Figure 2.4 illustrates three different types of interest rate formulas that are employed by current implementations of lending pool protocols. Linear interest rate formulas are sometimes employed by lending pool protocols for established cryptoassets where the risk of falling short on willing liquidity providers is low, and the demand for borrowing may be relatively stable. Non-linear formulas are more desirable if overutilization needs to be strongly discouraged, and reduction of borrowing activities needs to be enforced swiftly. Otherwise, overutilization will become too costly to the lending pool platform; that is, lenders would have a high risk of not being able to withdraw their funds given full utilization if the borrowing cost is not adjusted quickly, or is too low to discourage other users to liquidate or repay their debt positions. The most common formula type consists of a kinked interest rate function: when utilization is below a chosen optimal utilization (for example, 80 percent utilization), borrowing rates will increase at a slower speed; but when this target is exceeded, the function will increase rates at a higher speed.

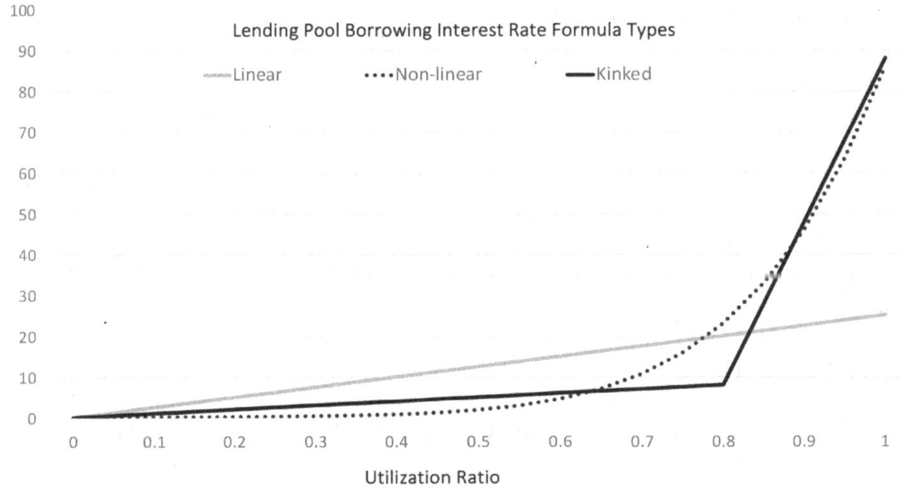

Figure 2.4 *Illustration of lending pool interest rate curves*

Note that function parameters, such as the slope of the curve or the function type, can differ within a lending pool by cryptoasset, depending on characteristics of the underlying asset. For example, in the Compound lending pool protocol, many of the assets will have a kinked interest rate formula, but some have linear functions (for example, for WETH) or could have piecewise non-linear functions instead of kinked formulas. Furthermore, a less liquidly traded cryptoasset may require a lower target utilization ratio (the point at which slopes will have to be higher to discourage additional, excessive borrowing) as investors will be less likely to step in to cover liquidated positions, but also to provide additional liquidity to the pool to counterbalance high utilization.

In our Aave example, variable borrowing interest rates are given by the following formula describing kinked interest rate functions of utilization: lending rates are derived from the borrowing rates by simply multiplying the borrowing rate by the utilization ratio and a reserve factor (that is, a fee charged by the protocol that is retained in the protocol's reserve treasury as capital buffer). Figure 2.5 plots borrowing rate formulas for five selected asset pools exhibiting different slopes and target utilization ratios. The highest can be found for the two stablecoins DAI and USDC at 80 percent and 90 percent, respectively. That is, only when borrowing capacity is over 80 percent, the interest rate formula increases borrowing costs at a higher rate to mitigate over-subscriptions of these asset pools. For more volatile but frequently traded cryptoassets such as wrapped ETH or BTC the slope of the curve changes at 70 percent and 65 percent, respectively, whereas UNI already switches at 45 percent utilization. Furthermore, the second slope is much higher for WBTC and UNI than for the other, less risky among the selected cryptoassets. This again reflects the risk assessment framework set up by Aave stakeholders that classifies cryptoassets by their likely liquidity or market risk for the protocol.

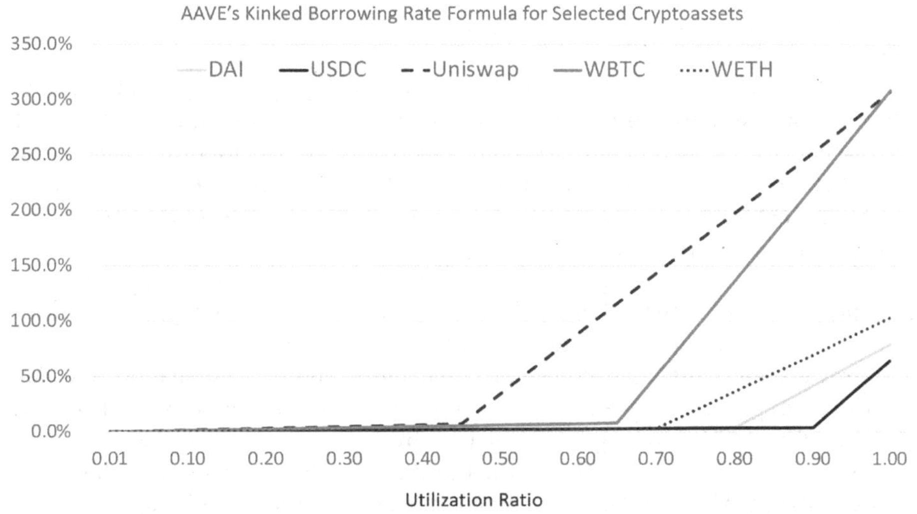

Figure 2.5 *Aave borrowing interest rates*

CDP Vault Mechanism

CDP vault lending protocols allow users to borrow newly minted stablecoins against collateral assets. This mechanism is most famously employed by the MakerDAO lending protocol, which will serve as our baseline case study, but also by others such as Liquity (Ethereum) or JustStables (Tron). A major difference to lending pool-based protocols is that there is only one kind of debt in the protocol: the system-generated debt stablecoin. Because of this, there is only one system-wide interest rate set by governance token holders of the protocol. Furthermore, there is no direct pool of liquidity supplied by lenders that borrowings are taken from; however, investors are encouraged to act as lenders of last resort when debt positions must be liquidated, and the system requires additional stablecoins to repay the debt. For illustration of CDP vault-based protocols, we will talk through some of the mechanics and economics underlying the MakerDAO protocol.

MakerDAO has three types of tokens: (1) a governance token, MKR, that allows users to participate in votes on system design and risk parameters and benefit from value appreciation of the token when the protocol is working well; (2) (risky) collateral assets that are used to create collateralized debt positions (vaults); and (3) the DAI stablecoin token with a soft USD peg, which is minted when CDP vaults are created, and burned when debt is repaid (with interest). DAI are held by the borrowers that request them from the protocol, but also by investors that have acquired DAI in markets existing outside the protocol.

CDP vaults are created by sending collateral assets to the respective contract address and then DAI stablecoins are created and sent to the borrowing user. Users create one vault for each collateral asset type they borrow against, and each vault accumulates interest on the number of DAI borrowed. DAI loans from a Maker vault are open-ended with a floating borrowing interest rate set by the governance token holders. Demand for borrowing, and therefore supply of DAI, is managed by adjusting interest rates and by setting risk parameters such as liquidation thresholds and discounts, or debt ceilings (maximum borrowing capacity) for different collateral asset vault types accordingly. In addition to DAI supply, governors can influence demand for DAI stablecoins by giving incentives to investors to acquire existing DAI on external markets (exchanges). DAI demand can be influenced via the protocol's monetary policy by adjusting the DAI Savings Rate (DSR) at which investors can earn interest on their DAI holdings within the protocol. Higher savings rates increase demand for DAI, while lower rates should result in the opposite.

Borrowers must maintain collateralization ratios above a liquidation threshold (for example, post new collateral if the market price of the asset drops). If borrowers repay the DAI borrowings with interest, by sending it back to the vault smart contract, their collateral asset is returned to them. Whenever a vault is closed, the corresponding DAI debt tokens are burned to reduce the stablecoin's supply. A CDP vault is liquidated when the borrower abandons the account and the collateralization ratio falls below the required threshold, in which case the collateral asset is auctioned off in the open market. As for lending pools, investors can monitor debt positions, trigger liquidations, and then bid for the collateral asset at a discount. However, MakerDAO has a slight difference in that it requires respective investors to have previously deposited DAI holdings into a savings smart contract that earns them interest (the DAI Savings Rate, DSR). While users that deposit into the DSR contract can withdraw their fund at any point in time, they are required to have deposited their DAI holdings at the time of a liquidation in order to participate in the auction of the collateral asset.

Setting CDP Vault Risk Parameters

CDP vaults are slightly simpler than lending pools, since less immediate interaction occurs between lenders and borrowers so that risk parameters and interest rates are set to minimize borrower liquidation risk and reduce the likelihood of negative net debt generated by the protocol. Some risk parameters in CDP vault-based protocols resemble those of lending pools. Liquidation thresholds and incentives are like those in lending pool protocols and may differ by the type of collateral asset permitted. For example, when price volatility of collateral assets increases, governors may want to increase liquidation penalties (bonuses) and savings rates to attract investors as DAI liquidity providers, or proactively set higher liquidation thresholds to encourage borrowers to either repay their position early or post additional collateral to mitigate excessive number of liquidations. Unlike lending pool-based protocols, interest rates are set by a collective of governance token holders that perform timely, but not automated, decentralized risk management to balance demand for borrowing with supply of liquidity.

As further risk control, MakerDAO enforces a debt ceiling for each vault (collateral) type which limits the total amount of DAI that can be minted as new debt by users. Risk parameter design decisions in MakerDAO require regular (weekly) governance board meetings where proposals on risk parameter or protocol design are discussed, evaluated, and voted on. This corresponds to so-called Maker Open Market Committee (MOMC) meetings. Governance token holders have a strong incentive to manage liquidation and liquidity supply risks accordingly, as the functioning of the protocol is tied to the valuation of their MKR token holdings, as described in the following.

On the positive side, the MakerDAO protocol charges interest to borrowers with open vaults and pays DAI interest to investors willing to act as lenders of last resort and vault monitors that trigger and benefit from liquidation. The spread between interest income and expense is then stored as a system surplus (reserve) that benefits governance token holders when the surplus has exceeded a safety buffer threshold, in which the stored DAI are sold on the open market against MKR tokens, which in turn are burned after the sale. A reduction in the supply of MKR benefits governance token holders through value appreciation. On the negative side, CDP vaults are exposed to market risk because collateral asset prices tend to be more volatile, and thus there is a risk that the vault must be liquidated. When a liquidation of a CDP vault occurs, the collateral is sold on the open market in an auction, which may or may not be successful, depending on the incentives given to investors as DAI liquidity providers (for example, liquidation penalty and savings rate). That is, there is an additional auction or liquidity supply risk that not enough DAI holders are willing to buy risky collateral at a discounted price. In such cases, additional MKR tokens are minted and sold to cover net debt created by the liquidated position, which increases MKR supply and dilutes its value. MKR holders benefit from the protocol running smoothly, which entails users opening and closing CDPs by repaying their debt. In summary, MakerDAO governors try to mitigate excessive liquidations by adjusting risk parameters in reaction to collateral market price developments.

LITERATURE ON DECENTRALIZED LENDING

Academic literature on decentralized lending protocols is scarce, but has contributions from across disciplines such as financial cryptography (security and privacy), economics, and policy. In the following, we provide a brief overview of the themes studied in the literature and highlight recent research contributions. For a general overview of the DeFi ecosystem and additional terminology around lending protocols, we refer to Schär (2021) and Xu and Vadgama (2022). Bartoletti et al. (2021) provide a more formal summary of commonalities and differences of decentralized lending protocols (that is, lending pool versus vault-stablecoin mechanisms).

Most academic work on the security and functioning of decentralized lending protocols is empirical, where researchers consider block or transaction-level data on user interactions with respective lending protocols. Gudgeon et al. (2020b) were among the first to study the dynamics of interest rate formulas, liquidity supply, and demand for borrowing of decentralized lending pools. Given the plethora of detailed on-chain data, researchers can identify attacks on lending protocols, such as economic exploits or smart contract code vulnerabilities or trace and classify users' activities across multiple protocols. For example, statistical analyses of lending pool transaction types are given in Green et al. (2022), who provide evidence on the time passed between depositing assets to a lending pool in Aave, that is, Deposit(), and triggering a subsequent other function such as repaying or liquidating positions; as well as Saengchote (2022) who classify Compound lending pool users and study flow of funds. Sun (2022) highlights that some lending pool users can trigger liquidity issues for the entire protocol, as they control relatively high shares of both the liquidity supply and debt borrowed in terms of stablecoins. When it comes to security issues, Qin et al. (2020) and Gudgeon et al. (2020a) illustrate how users can exploit vulnerabilities of protocol designs without the need for excessive capital upfront, for example, using flash loans to borrow and employ assets.

Financial Risks and Liquidations

It is apparent that decentralized lending protocols do not come without risks, such as liquidations due to changes in collateral prices or due to rapid changes in demand for borrowing and supply of liquidity. These financial risks are studied in the existing literature, with a focus on quantifying liquidation risks (Perez et al. 2021; Kozhan and Viswanath-Natraj 2021, 2022), evaluating incentive mechanisms (Qin et al. 2021), or discussing implications for financial stability of the DeFi ecosystem.

Some papers argue that systemic risk exists, stemming from decentralized lending protocols, because they allow DeFi users to build up leverage. Such leverage exacerbates both positive and negative price movements, and thus if losses occur on one

DeFi platform and borrowers must liquidate their positions, this may spill over to the rest of the DeFi ecosystem if users interact with multiple applications. Lehar and Parlour (2022) provide empirical evidence which suggests that deleveraging of positions via liquidations on one decentralized lending protocol leads to immediate collateral price decreases on decentralized exchanges, and permanently shifts collateral return distribution to have heavier tails. This result has consequences for remaining collateralized loans upon decentralized lending platforms, and can lead to further liquidations. Thus, because of the connectedness of DeFi platforms via common collateral types, contagion effects exist that can be triggered by liquidations. Darlin et al. (2022) quantify the extent to which users of popular lending pools and vault protocols engage in debt positions, and how they subsequently use their borrowings on other DeFi platforms, such as for trading and/or lending. By tracing on-chain transactions of users engaging with these protocols, they reconstruct the total amount of debt created and find high degrees of interconnectedness between major DeFi lending platforms (Aave, Compound, MakerDAO) and a DEX (Uniswap). That is, interconnectedness of DeFi protocols not only stems from using the same type of collateral assets but also from users operating on multiple platforms to execute leveraged trades or search for yield using borrowed funds. This concept is echoed by Aramonte et al. (2021), who view DeFi (lending) markets from the perspective of a regulator.

CONCLUSION

Decentralized lending protocols offer lenders the opportunity to receive a higher proportion of the proceeds from the borrowings of their funds as compared to depositing funds at a traditional bank. In this way, decentralized lending serves as a method to counter market power in the traditional financial sector, where banks extract rents from their depositors by holding onto most of the proceeds from deposits. As we have discussed, decentralized lending protocols entail a variety of risks and thus are not yet direct competitors to the banking sector. Nonetheless, decentralized lending protocols are at an early stage and are regularly being improved. In turn, these protocols possess great potential to impact the future of finance.

REFERENCES

Aramonte, S., Huang, W., Schrimpf, A. (2021). "DeFi Risks and the Decentralisation Illusion" *BIS Quarterly Review*, December, pp. 21–36.

Bartoletti, M., Chiang, J., Lafuente, A. (2021). "SoK: Lending Pools in Decentralized Finance" *Financial Cryptography and Data Security (FC 2021)*.

Darlin, M., Palaiokrassas, G., Tassiulas, L. (2022). "Debt-Financed Collateral and Stability Risks in the DeFi Ecosystem" *2022 4th Conference on Blockchain Research & Applications for Innovative Networks and Services (BRAINS)*.

Green, A., Cammilleri, C., Erickson, J., Seneviratne, O., Bennett, K. (2022). "DeFi Survival Analysis: Insights into Risks and User Behaviors" in: Pardalos, P., Kotsireas, I., Guo, Y., Knottenbelt, W. (eds) *Mathematical Research for Blockchain Economy. MARBLE 2022. Lecture Notes in Operations Research.* Springer, Cham.https://doi.org/10.1007/978-3-031-18679-0_8.

Gudgeon, L., Perez, D., Harz, D., Livshits, B., Gervais, A. (2020a). "The Decentralized Financial Crisis" Crypto Valley Conference 2020.

Gudgeon, L., Werner, S., Perez, D., Knottenbelt, W. (2020b). "DeFi Protocols for Loanable Funds: Interest Rates, Liquidity and Market Efficiency" *AFT '20: Proceedings of the 2nd ACM Conference on Advances in Financial Technologies.*

Irresberger, F., John, K., Mueller, P., Saleh, F. (2022). "The Public Blockchain Ecosystem: An Empirical Analysis" SSRN Working Paper.

Kozhan, R., Viswanath-Natraj, G. (2021). "Fundamentals of the MakerDAO Governance Token" *3rd International Conference on Blockchain Economics, Security and Protocols (Tokenomics 2021)*, pp. 11:1–11:5.

Kozhan, R., Viswanath-Natraj, G. (2022). "Decentralized Stablecoins and Collateral Risk". WBS Finance Group Research Paper. https://papers.ssrn.com/sol3/papers.cfm?abstract_id=3866975.

Lehar, A., Parlour, C. (2022). "Systemic Fragility in Decentralized Markets". SSRN Working Paper. https://papers.ssrn.com/sol3/papers.cfm?abstract_id=4164833.

Perez, D., Werner, S.M., Xu, J., Livshits, B. (2021). "Liquidations: DeFi on a Knife-edge" *Financial Cryptography and Data Security: 25th International Conference, FC 2021*, pp. 457–476.

Qin, K., Zhou, L., Gamito, P., Jovanovic, P., Gervais, A. (2021). "An Empirical Study of DeFi Liquidations: Incentives, Risks, and Instabilities" *IMC '21: Proceedings of the 21st ACM Internet Measurement Conference.*

Qin, K., Zhou, L., Livshits, B., Gervais, A. (2020). "Attacking the DeFi Ecosystem with Flash Loans for Fun and Profit" *Financial Cryptography FC'21.*

Saengchote, K. (2022). "Decentralized Lending and Its Users: Insights from Compound" SSRN Working Paper. https://papers.ssrn.com/sol3/papers.cfm?abstract_id=3925344.

Schär, F. (2021) "Decentralized Finance: On Blockchain- and Smart Contract-Based Financial Markets" *Federal Reserve Bank of St. Louis Review*, Second Quarter 2021, pp. 153–174. https://doi.org/10.20955/r.103.153-74.

Sun, X. (2022). "Illiquidity Risks in Lending Protocols (LPs): Evidence from Aave Protocol" SSRN Working Paper. https://papers.ssrn.com/sol3/papers.cfm?abstract_id=3985105.

Xu, J., Vadgama, N. (2022). "From Banks to DeFi: the Evolution of the Lending Market" in: Vadgama, N., Xu, J., Tasca, P. (eds) *Enabling the Internet of Value. Future of Business and Finance.* Springer, Cham. https://doi.org/10.1007/978-3-030-78184-2_6.

3. Ready P(l)ayer One: how we will pay tomorrow and what role crypto may play

Dirk Bullmann[1]

INTRODUCTION: TODAY'S WORLD OF PAYMENTS

We rely on payments every day, from buying a coffee to paying our rent. At the same time, we normally do not pay much attention to the technicalities happening in the background, how payments actually travel from the payer to the payee. Beyond the payment initiation process actually lies a complex network of payment systems and services which involves central banks, commercial banks, and other payment providers. Behind the curtain, they take care of what has often been referred to as the "inglamourous plumbing"[2] and what is an integral part of the backbone of the financial system. Like water pipes in our homes, we trust in the smooth functioning of the payment processes, and only notice their existence when the liquidity flow is interrupted.

The world of payments has changed over the past years, both in the brick-and-mortar business and in online shops. Boosted by the COVID-19 pandemic, we increasingly rely on digital payment means. We pay more with our mobile phones and with cards.[3] Besides these more visible developments at the "front end," the underlying payment plumbing processes are put into question. Can blockchain form the basis of the next generation of payment pipes? Do we still need the involvement of traditional players such as banks? Can cryptoassets, stablecoins, or central bank digital currency be pumped through those pipes, potentially replacing more traditional money?

This chapter aims to offer answers to those questions. It first takes a closer look at blockchain infrastructures and crypto coins through the lens of payments. In a second step, it discusses current business and user requirements for making payments, ranging from safety to efficiency. On this basis, it examines how blockchain and crypto coins can meet these requirements as compared to traditional payment pipes. Subsequently, this chapter offers some crystal ball gazing and discusses upcoming payment trends.

MIND THE GAP: BLOCKCHAIN RAILS AND CRYPTO TRAINS

Over the years, multiple use cases for the blockchain have evolved, ranging from healthcare and real estate to supply chain and logistics. The first business case, however, was payments. The Bitcoin White Paper,[4] which was published in 2008 under the pseudonym "Satoshi Nakamoto," sketched on only nine pages a new form of payment transfers. It designs a cryptoasset (Bitcoin) which is defined through a chain of digital signatures (blockchain[5]).

In very abstract terms, today's payment systems can be described as a technical infrastructure which exchanges assets—a rail network on which money trains are operating, metaphorically speaking—or systems that transfer, for example, the euro, US dollar, or Japanese yen, and sometimes even exchange multiple currencies. Following this logic, in the following sections we take a separate look at making payments with blockchain rails and crypto trains.

Blockchain Infrastructure

Today's payment systems are in essence based on centralized ledgers for holding and transferring money. Those ledgers are governed and operated by trusted intermediaries, such as private sector banks and central banks, which ensure that any debit from one account will always be matched by a similar credit to another account. The blockchain idea is fundamentally different from such a centralized ledger concept. It follows a decentralized approach and does not rely on trusted intermediaries for maintaining the network and validating payment transactions. Instead, trust is embedded into the decentralized blockchain design.

In principle, blockchains are open networks which are accessible to everyone. Participants do not necessarily need to reveal their identity, as payments are sent and received under a visible pseudonym. Payments are grouped into blocks and attached to a chronologically ordered chain of previously verified blocks. The validation of payment transactions and the generation of new blocks occurs through consensus mechanisms that, for example, involve solving complex, computationally intensive formulas (such as the so-called proof of work consensus mechanism[6]), which is why blockchains are considered manipulation resistant. The information stored in the blockchain is replicated many times within the decentralized network, resulting in a high level of reliability which, however, also means that each participant can view the entire transaction history. As a result, what is written on the blockchain in principle cannot be manipulated and tampered with.

This design is often referred to as public (or permissionless) blockchain. For many, those public blockchains are regarded as a game changer for the financial ecosystem as we know it. The public blockchain holds the promise of radically changing the current banking and financial system, which has been around for many centuries and has its roots in Renaissance Italy. The underlying argument is that if trust is a key ingredient of the blockchain, then the role of financial intermediaries is rendered superfluous.

What started with the Bitcoin blockchain in 2008 has over time evolved into a universe of different public blockchain platforms with multiple designs. One should therefore bear in mind that there is not "one chain to rule them all." Today, hundreds of different blockchains exist, of which around 30 to 40 are actively used and supported by their communities. It should also be noted that the level of decentralization, which is often mentioned as the blockchain's unique selling point, may vary from network to network. The Bitcoin blockchain is the first and maybe the purest of all blockchains when it comes to the level of decentralization, while most of its epigones cannot reach similar levels (for example, in terms of number of parties running the network and being involved in validation, maintenance, and decisions about the blockchain's future development). In a nutshell, there are many different types of public blockchain rails out there.

No contradiction in terms: private blockchains

It may or may not come as a surprise that precisely the players whose existence is put in question by the blockchain are exploring its potential. The blockchain is not regarded by them as a paradigm shift and a trigger for reshaping the financial system. On the contrary, incumbent market participants mainly regard the blockchain as a new technology that may bring benefits to the safety and efficiency of existing services, while largely leaving unchanged the current (centralized) governance arrangements and the existing wider ecosystem.

Against this background, the so-called private or permissioned blockchains have emerged. These are networks with limited user groups, whose participants are clearly identifiable and have clearly defined access rights. In private blockchains, trust in the integrity of the stored data does not have to be created using computationally intensive mechanisms. Rather, trust is already created through the identification of the participants when they are admitted to the blockchain network. This clearly mirrors arrangements in the traditional world. The design of private blockchains in fact conceptually deviates from the original blockchain idea of "Satoshi Nakamoto" in that they come with a clearly definable governance.[7]

At first glance, private blockchain arrangements and their largely centralized nature may appear to be an oxymoron, a contradiction in terms. However, the world of payments is very dynamic, and incumbent players need to constantly explore which technology is most suitable for meeting evolving business and user needs. Therefore, most big financial players have studied or are considering whether (private[8]) blockchains hold promise for their business and offer new opportunities, in the field of payments but also far beyond. While countless experiments, proofs of concept, and minimum viable products have been the result of those reflections, to date only a few blockchain payment services of limited scope and scale have gone live. For example, the global foreign exchange payment giant Continuous Linked Services (CLS), which settles over US$6.5 trillion of payments every day in 18 of the most actively traded currencies globally, already implemented a blockchain-based bilateral payment netting service tool in 2018, but does not consider moving its core payment settlement engine to the blockchain. At the time of this writing, no large-scale payment application is entirely based on blockchain architecture. The private blockchain rail network is overall still at its conception stage.

Payment Assets

Cryptic crypto: how to define and categorize cryptoassets

The cryptoasset phenomenon is multifaceted and therefore somewhat hard to categorize. What started with Bitcoin in 2008 has in the meantime expanded to a universe of approximately 10 000 cryptoassets[9] (either being a blockchain's native and exclusive token, or being hosted on existing blockchains). On average, 10 to 15 new cryptoassets come into existence every day,[10] most of which have very little economic relevance and are very small in size. The top ten cryptoassets represent around 90 percent of the overall market capitalization, with around two-thirds coming from the two largest coins: Bitcoin and Ethereum. To put things into perspective, the cryptoasset ecosystem currently represents around 1 percent of the global gross domestic product, but has been growing in recent years. As the figures suggest, the cryptoasset space is still a very dynamic (and volatile) environment which has seen peaks and valleys, crypto winters and crypto summers, but from a longer-term perspective is increasingly moving out of its niche.

Cryptoassets can serve different purposes and, similar to the underlying blockchain rails, can bear different features. Not all cryptoassets are equally suitable for making payments. Certain cryptoassets, for example, come in the form of a utility which allows access to certain services or products. Others are closer to what is considered a form of equity, for example having membership rights such as dividends. More recently, non-fungible tokens (NFTs) entered the crypto stage, representing ownership of real-world items such as art or music. The plethora of designs and business cases makes it challenging to arrive at a concrete definition of what constitutes a cryptoasset, all the more so when in the public debate terms such as "crypto coins," "cryptocurrencies," or "crypto tokens" are also used, sometimes synonymously and sometimes with slightly different meanings.[11] The European Union regulators,[12] for example, apply a broad definition in which a cryptoasset is considered to be "a digital representation of value or rights which may be transferred and stored electronically, using distributed ledger technology or similar technology." All this clearly illustrates that "cryptoasset" can only serve as an umbrella term.

Through the lens of the payments business, the key feature and common denominator of all cryptoassets is that, besides being recorded in digital form, there is no clearly identifiable issuer. In other words, cryptoassets do not represent a financial claim against a natural or legal person. Cryptoassets are not "scriptural money" which takes the form of deposit balances held on an account at a credit institution or a central bank. This makes them fundamentally different from money and currencies which are ultimately issued by the central bank of a jurisdiction.

The revolution's evolution: the advent of stablecoins

The specific design of cryptoassets, with the absence of an issuer who can also guarantee a certain degree of price stability, overall fuels their speculative dimension. For example, increases in cryptoasset prices often have self-reinforcing effects, such as in motivating investors to hop on board the crypto bandwagon. This effect is further amplified by the fact that crypto markets have less liquidity than traditional financial markets, and a smaller investor base. In fact, the historic volatility of cryptoassets ranges between 4 and 8 percent per day (with Bitcoin being at the lower end), and is substantially greater than that of traditional assets or currencies.

In order to curb the high volatility of cryptoassets, stablecoins emerged and became a fast-growing sub-segment of the cryptoasset market. The phenomenon of those "cryptoassets 2.0" started in 2014, but only gained visible traction in 2019, which broadly coincided with Facebook's (now dismantled) initiative for launching a global stablecoin and the increasing attention being given to the decentralized finance (DeFi) space. Moreover, stablecoins had initially served as a means to park cryptos, and as a bridge between traditional currencies and cryptoassets. Towards the end of 2022, stablecoins reached around 15 percent of the total value of the cryptoasset market. While there are roughly 200 different stablecoins in existence worldwide, around 90 percent of the market capitalization currently comes from two coins: Tether and USD Coin.

The stablecoin universe offers different concepts on how to minimize price fluctuations. In principle, four approaches can be distinguished with respect to the underlying stabilization mechanics:[13] (1) fund-backed stablecoins which are secured by claims held outside the blockchain, mainly in the form of funds in accounts of a central bank or commercial bank; (2) off-chain collateralized stablecoins backed by other traditional assets such as securities or commodities (for example, precious metals); (3) on-chain collateralized stablecoins which are directly backed by cryptoassets held on a blockchain; and (4) algorithmic stablecoins which do not rely on a risk mitigation based on collateral held off-chain or on-chain, but rather entail mechanisms to automatically balance supply and demand based on a peg to a traditional currency. In an algorithmic stablecoin, so-called oracles monitor the coin prices on crypto exchanges. If the market price increases, specific programs underlying the stablecoin (so-called smart contracts[14]) trigger the minting of new coins. Conversely, if the price falls, stablecoins are taken out of circulation. The coin supply is increased or decreased accordingly, in theory causing the price of an algorithmic stablecoin to move upwards or downwards, and thus bringing it back to the peg.

It can be argued that the level of innovation involved in the first two categories, fund-backed and off-chain collateralized stablecoins, is relatively low. In fact, these two asset types follow well-known collateralization approaches and rely on an identifiable entity for issuance and safe-keeping. While these stablecoin types are widely subsumed under the cryptoasset definition, strictly speaking they are not. They do not feature the most prominent characteristic of a cryptoasset, namely the absence of a financial claim on an identifiable entity. In contrast, in the two latter categories, namely on-chain collateralized and algorithmic stablecoins, the role of intermediaries is largely taken over by smart contract programs.

The million-crypto question is whether stablecoins actually live up to what they promise by name. Empirical evidence shows that the value of fund-backed and off-chain collateral stablecoins hovers relatively closely around the value of the reference asset. At the same time, anecdotal evidence shows that fluctuations can temporarily increase, for example if public doubts are cast on the existence of or the possibility to mobilize the underlying collateral. On-chain collateralized and algorithmic stablecoins bear higher volatility risks than the two other categories, as they rely on more volatile collateral (that is, cryptoassets, even with a high overcollateralization ratio serving as safety margin) or involve no collateral at all. Over the past years, there have been crashes of algorithmic stablecoins, which in turn also caused some turmoil in the whole stablecoin segment.

The future of money: GovCoins or central bank digital currencies

Central banks play a key role in the field of payments. For example, they operate systemically relevant "plumbing" systems themselves and are of course the ultimate source of money for banks (in the form of bank reserves held on accounts with central banks) and for the public at large (in the form of cash). Against this background, it is not surprising that several central banks around the globe in the mid-2010s started experiments on the usage of blockchain technology for payments.[15] These initiatives gained a lot of traction in the public debate and sparked broader reflections on whether the central banks themselves should or should not issue a digital currency. Today, more than 90 percent of the central banks[16] are conducting far-reaching research or running experiments, also in the form of joint initiatives across the central bank community.

"GovCoins" or central bank digital currency (CBDC) can be broadly defined as a "form of digital money, denominated in the national unit of account, which is a direct liability of the central bank."[17] CBDC is therefore fundamentally different from cryptoassets and stablecoins which, as discussed above, often have no identifiable issuer.

Today, consumers have no direct access to digital money backed by central banks. Only commercial banks have this privilege in the form of central bank reserves. Consumers rather have access to central bank money in the form of cash, and to commercial bank money held on accounts with credit institutions. Ultimately, the reflections of central banks around (retail[18]) CBDC therefore boils down to the question of why it should be issued to the public at large. From this, then, derive questions on the concrete CBDC design (for example, anonymous-like banknotes, interest-bearing to also serve as monetary policy tool) and how it should be technically implemented (for example, tiered structure with reliance on private sector banks for distribution, utilization of blockchain or traditional technology). Obviously, the first question around the motivation for issuing CBDC is the decisive factor, and this is the question that many central banks are currently grappling with.

In developed and larger economies, cash is increasingly in decline, a trend which has been accelerated by the COVID-19 pandemic.[19] At the same time, private sector payment solutions are gaining ground and, as described above, cryptoassets and stablecoins are *ante portas*. This dynamic raises the question of whether or not the increasing gap between public (central bank) and private (commercial bank) money should be filled with a CBDC. In such reflections, CBDC is mainly considered a complement to cash and an additional payment means which could contribute to the efficiency and safety of the existing payment arrangements. Thorough considerations are undertaken to ensure that CBDC does not disrupt the existing financial ecosystem and does not disintermediate traditional players such as private sector banks. Given the far-reaching potential implications, no central bank of a larger economy has yet fully embarked on a wide-scale CBDC.[20]

In emerging and smaller economies, other motivations such as financial inclusion (that is, banking the unbanked) might also prevail. Moreover, if the national market infrastructure is not well developed, or maybe even completely absent, the issuance of a CBDC arrangement may be desirable. These and other reasons have in the meantime led a small number of countries to develop and already go live with CBDC solutions.[21]

The Crypto Spectrum: Decentralization is Relative

The crypto space has an ocean of solutions, variants, and hybrid designs on offer. Categorizing them is a challenge that inevitably creates some sort of generalization, which in turn does not necessarily do justice to the design of individual blockchain networks and cryptoasset designs (Figure 3.1). The categorizations outlined in this chapter can therefore only serve as an orientational guide.

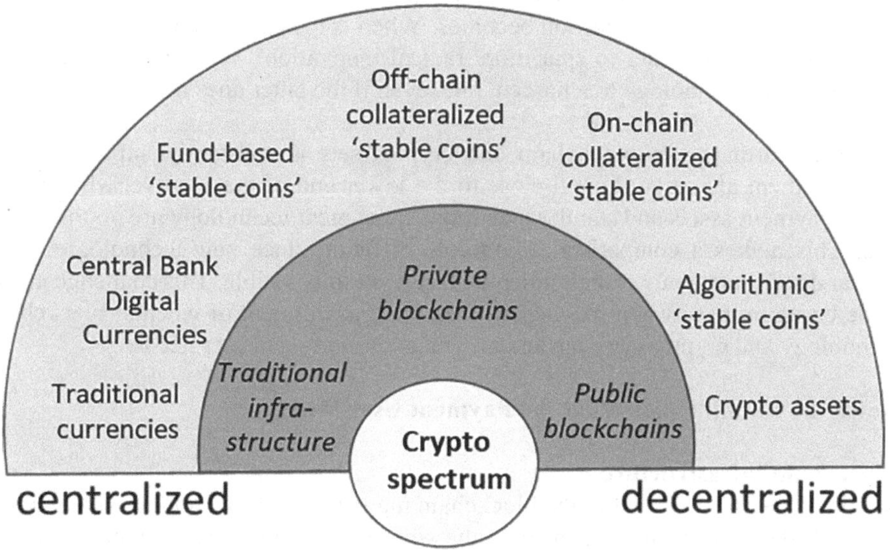

Figure 3.1 *The centralized and decentralized crypto spectrum*

Besides, the outlined categorization illustrates that the crypto space is not fully decentralized by default, and that the actual level of innovation varies from solution to solution; implying that not everything that sounds new actually is new, and that decentralization, which undoubtedly is one of the unique selling points of the crypto space, is more of a spectrum. In fact, as also discussed in this chapter, many blockchains and cryptoassets contain centralized elements which, in turn, bring them closer to currently existing and more traditional arrangements.

LOOKING UNDER THE HOOD: DEMANDS PLACED ON MODERN PAYMENT SYSTEMS

Jumping the Innovation S-Curve: Comparing Mature and Nascent Payment Technologies

One could certainly argue that blockchain and cryptoassets are still in their infant days; that this is nascent technology which cannot be easily compared with mature payment systems that have lready stood the test of time. There is certainly some truth to this (admittedly general) argument.

The innovation S-curve concept is a good way to illustrate the maturity dilemma which also applies to the crypto space. It stems from the 1980s and visualizes a technology's path of incremental innovation, starting with teething troubles and a linear curve progression, followed by increasing adoption with a steep course of the S-curve, and eventually ending with a flattening of the curve as a technology matures. The interesting question becomes: When is the best moment to jump down to another curve in order to spur more radical innovation? When should we move from a mature technology to a nascent one, even if the latter does not (yet) look very attractive?

The performance of blockchain and cryptoassets is constantly improving, but many of them are certainly still close to the lower end of the S-curve, while traditional payment assets and standard centralized payment technology are on the upper end. This makes a comparison admittedly difficult, since new technologies may appear disadvantageous as their potential is not yet fully visible. This challenge needs to be borne in mind when reading the following assessment of whether blockchain technology and cryptoassets can actually meet business and user needs.

Down the Rabbit Hole: What the Payment User Wants

Blockchain infrastructure

Moving a payment system to the blockchain may at first glance appear trivial, but it is not. Today's payment systems clog the wheels of the financial system and are of systemic relevance for the economy. Many of them have impressive turnovers. For example, the Eurosystem (which is composed of the European Central Bank and the European national central banks of the countries that have adopted the euro) operates the interbank payment system TARGET2, which processes a total value of around €2.2 trillion every day. In other words, TARGET2 settles the equivalent of the euro area gross domestic product in around six business days. Since a payment system's failure could have widespread knock-on effects and eventually create economic turmoil, strong public sector oversight and regulation exist.

One traditionally expects from a payment process that it be fast, reliable, confidential, and at the same time cheap. Moreover, cross-border payments require systems to be interoperable. These consequently form the benchmark that blockchain-based payment systems need to be able to meet.

The need for speed

In today's world, news, music, or videos can be accessed within a few seconds and around the clock. Payment processing must keep pace with this development, and as liquidity should not be tied up in one system for an unnecessarily long time, fast payments make a lot of sense from an efficiency perspective anyway. It should therefore not come as a surprise that the number of instant payment services around the globe is increasing at a rapid pace. Today, solutions exist in more than 60 jurisdictions,[22] facilitating payment transfers within seconds.

The speediness of blockchains has, over the years, been viewed critically, often using as an example the ten minutes average confirmation time for Bitcoin payments. Today's reality, however, looks different and many public blockchains can process payments within a few seconds. Private blockchains are by design easier to parameterize for speed anyway. Basically, everything is possible in terms of speed, bearing in mind that the velocity of a blockchain payment depends on many factors, including the size of the block, how the validation is done, how consistently the data is replicated within the network, and the size of the blockchain network itself.

The throughput of a payment system is also a decisive factor, as insufficient bandwidth can lead to congestion and eventually slow down processing. Large-value payment systems normally process less than 100 transactions per second, while the throughput in retail payment transactions can be 100 to 500 times higher, depending on the course of the day. In the blockchain space, various solutions have emerged (for example, the Lightning Network or sharding[23]) which help public blockchains to move towards a level playing field with incumbent payment solutions. At the time of this writing, several public blockchain solutions are already able to reach more than 50 000 transactions per second.

Never down

Payment systems nowadays can often represent a single point of failure. If one system component comes to a standstill, the whole system may stop operating. Centralized systems therefore need to have strong business continuity management in order to ensure the timely recovery of operations (normally within two hours) even in the event of a widescale or major disruption.[24] This includes the existence of secondary processing sites which can take over in case they are needed. If there is, for example, a power outage or a natural disaster in one geographic region, or a cyber-attack on the system, the secondary site (with a different risk profile) should be able to take over payment operations at short notice.

The decentralized network of a blockchain is touted as one of the greatest advantages in terms of availability and resilience, but the devil is in the detail. If all data is replicated within the network, this assumption makes perfect sense. In many cases, however, not all data can be found on the blockchain, mostly for reasons of confidentiality, or there is no complete mirroring within the blockchain network. Moreover, there may be certain central responsibilities in the blockchain (for example, in the form of a single participant certifying the payments) which, in case of failure, would stop the blockchain services from running. In other words, vulnerability in the form of a single point of failure may exist. Finally, it should also be borne in mind that the susceptibility to cyber-attacks increases with the size of the blockchain network and the associated larger attack surface.

Keeping the secret

In the financial sector at large, and for payment systems in particular, strong principles of confidentiality of personal data and data protection apply. While private blockchains by design can have features to ensure confidentiality, the data stored in public blockchain networks is in principle transparent and can be viewed by every participant. However, measures could be taken to strengthen confidentiality, for example by encrypting data, by storing sensitive data outside the blockchain, or by setting up clearly restricted read and write rights.

Furthermore, depending on their design, public blockchains may enable pseudonymous usage or offer special procedures that make it very difficult to trace payments (for example, by using so-called mixers or tumblers). Such features cannot be directly reconciled with the existing principles in the financial sector (for example, "know your customer," KYC). In conclusion, meeting existing privacy requirements may be faced with challenges, at least for specific public blockchain designs.

High quality at low price

The payments business is a network business in which an increase in the number of connected users directly increases the overall value for everyone connected. More users and more payment traffic should bring economies of scale and thus low transaction fees. Usually being a commodity, traditional payments are therefore comparably inexpensive. To give an indication, the instant retail payment system TIPS (TARGET Instant Payment System), run by the Eurosystem, currently charges €0.002 per transaction. It is also true, however, that payment fees can differ substantially at end user level, depending on which payment instrument and underlying process is used (for example, credit card, direct debits, credit transfers, mobile payments).[25]

Stark differences in fees can also be observed in blockchains,[26] albeit for different reasons. Transaction fees are typically engrained into the operating structure of a blockchain and range between zero and a two-digit amount. If the verification of payments is, for instance, based on the "proof of work" consensus mechanism, a busy blockchain network can lead to high fees; the reason being that transactions have an increased chance of being processed if high mining fees are paid. Some blockchain designs may therefore show undesirable volatility of fees, and come with transaction fees which make them unattractive for making transfers.

Connecting people

Cross-border payments continue to be on the rise and steadily increase by around 5 percent per year, currently standing above €150 trillion per annum,[27] Despite this increase, payment rails between countries are underdeveloped, making cross-border payments complex, slow, and expensive. The reasons are manifold, and range from differences in technical and business standards (including operating hours across time zones), to legal requirements (for example, anti-money laundering and countering the financing of terrorism). Moreover, there might be long payment transaction chains. For example, if the bank in the country of the sender and the bank in the country of the receiver do not have a business relationship, meaning no accounts with each other, then intermediaries are required, possibly also for the exchange of currencies if there are different denominations.

The pain points related to cross-border payments are long known and translated into a roadmap of the G20.[28] Interestingly, several building blocks of the G20 roadmap revolve around work that is still in its experimental stage (for example, by the Bank for International Settlements Innovation Hub), namely new multilateral, cross-border payment platforms and arrangements, CBDCs, and stablecoins with a global reach. In other words, blockchain and their payment assets are amongst the possible means to overcome current barriers in cross-border payments. At the same time, one should bear in mind that the existence of numerous blockchain rails already in itself poses challenges in terms of interoperability, irrespective of the cross-border dimension.

Ready or not: the blockchain trilemma

The above analysis shows that blockchain technology offers a huge variety of designs and parametrization, which should in principle allow for meeting the mentioned user requirements. For the sake of completeness, it should also be mentioned that, beyond the mere processing engine, many modern payment systems also offer sophisticated tools for optimizing system-internal payment flows, ranging from liquidity management over payment prioritization to queue management. Those add-on services could in principle be provided by smart contracts on the blockchain. Of course, the concrete suitability of a blockchain for a specific payment system requires more in-depth analysis. This would also need to involve wider reflection, for example on the legal and regulatory environment, which is not discussed in this chapter.

Finally, and coming back to the above conclusion that decentralization is a spectrum, in the design of a blockchain there is always the inherent trade-off between scalability, security, and decentralization. The founder of the Ethereum blockchain, Vitalik Buterin, has coined the term "blockchain trilemma" for this phenomenon. In a nutshell, it means that the more decentralized the blockchain design, the more secure but less scalable it becomes. In contrast, lowering the level of decentralization would bring higher scalability, but eventually come at the expense of security.

Payment assets

John Maynard Keynes once said that "[t]here is no subtler, no surer means of overturning the existing basis of society than to debauch the currency. The process engages all the hidden forces of economic law on the side of destruction, and does it in a manner which not one man in a million is able to diagnose." Maybe this view explains why in particular regulators and central banks are keeping a close eye on the developments around cryptoassets and stablecoins, and maybe this view also contributes to the motivation of central banks to explore the issuance of their own CBDC. In these reflections, the elephant in the room is whether cryptoassets and stablecoins could really take on the role of traditional money and currencies; whether they could not only complement, but one day even replace, money as we know it. In order to answer this question, it is worth looking at the three basic functions that money has to fulfill in our economies: a medium of exchange, a unit of account, and a store of value.

Ready to shop

Whether cryptoassets and stablecoins can serve as a medium of exchange, such as to buy goods or to grant credit and settle debts, on the one hand depends on the efficiency and safety of the underlying payment transfer rails, namely the blockchain (as discussed above). On the other hand, it hinges on their wider acceptance by consumers and companies.

There are numerous indications that the interconnections between the crypto space and the traditional financial sector are increasing. Online stores, for example, accept Bitcoin payments, and large private firms publicly announce their interest in cryptoassets for their cash management and as a means of payment for their products. The number of both institutional and retail cryptoasset investors is on the rise, and so is the number of investment products referenced to cryptoassets. Moreover, countries with comparably less stable currencies are considering granting cryptoassets legal tender status. One could derive from all these developments that acceptance is increasing, and that cryptoassets and stablecoins will no longer remain on the fringes of payments. Today, however, the crypto-based payment business is still rather small. On a daily basis, there are between 200 000 and 300 000 Bitcoin transactions on a global scale, while the number of retail payments in the euro area alone is around 1000 times higher.

The value of things

Measuring and comparing the prices of goods and services is the most visible role of a currency in our everyday life. Money serves as a unit of account, and this function is deeply engrained not only into our economies, but also in people's minds. Currencies such as the euro, US dollar, or yen represent the foundation of the respective financial market in that they serve as a standard of relative worth, also beyond their own territory of legal tender. Without them, we would be back to barter systems and would need to juggle with exchange ratios for every pair of goods; unimaginable in today's world.

Becoming an anchor unit of account certainly takes time. When the euro was introduced in the form of banknotes and coins in 2002, European citizens still converted in the back of their minds into the Deutsche Mark, Italian lira, or French franc. Some adapted faster than others, but it clearly did not happen overnight. Today, cryptoassets and stablecoins cannot sufficiently fulfill the unit of account function, mainly because they are not very widespread, as mentioned above. Moreover, their volatility prevents them from serving as a real unit of account.

Standing the test of time

Money needs to be durable and stable in value, and this is traditionally ensured by the issuing authority, or the central bank of a currency area, which takes all necessary measures to maintain their purchasing power and to limit and steer inflation. An effective store of value ensures that households can use stored money to buy goods and services in the future. As the former president of the European Central Bank, Mario Draghi, put it: "A euro today is a euro tomorrow."

As discussed above, cryptoassets are subject to wild fluctuations which make them a speculative rather than a stable asset. Also, stablecoins come with certain risks as regards to price stability, even if the underlying asset is a stable one. Volatility of cryptoassets and potential uncertainty on the soundness of stabilization mechanisms underlying stablecoins can potentially also impact the overall financial stability, originating from collapses of those assets, eventual market runs, and consequently spillover effects to the traditional financial system.

Since cryptoassets and stablecoins face challenges in meeting the three functions of money, central banks around the globe continue to stress that they are not money, and that labeling them as "currency" is a misnomer. They may have the ring of money, but they are not. In particular the absence of stability, both from a short- and a longer-term perspective, is the Achilles heel of the crypto space, at least when it comes to payments.

THE FUTURE HAS LANDED: WHAT IS NEXT IN PAYMENTS

From today's perspective, and through the lens of payment system users, the potential of blockchain technology can be viewed positively, while the volatility of cryptoassets, and to some extent also stablecoins, casts some doubts on their readiness. But user expectations are not cast in stone. As new payment trends emerge, the future suitability of blockchain-based and traditional payment systems needs to be reassessed. In the following, three developments are highlighted which are gaining traction and may impact the underlying payment services and systems.

Big in Small: The Rise of Micro and Nano Payments

There are developments on the horizon which may fuel the trend towards ever smaller payments, from micro to nano and maybe even beyond. While no agreed definition exists, there is a widespread view that micro payments are below €5 or $5, while nano payments are much tinier, possibly down to a fraction of a cent. The latter may be gaining ground quickly.

The Internet of Things (IoT) will most probably lead to a massive increase in the number of connected devices used for comparably small payments. This development is further amplified by the rapid expansion of the 5G network, but also by endeavors towards more frictionless payments, which happen in the background without conscious initiation (such as in walk-in/walk-out stores), driven for example by near-field communications and behavioral biometrics. At the beginning of 2019, there were around 8 to 10 billion IoT devices around the globe. By 2025, between 30 to 75 billion devices may exist, from cell phones and wearables to connected homes and cars. If that materializes as predicted, each of us would on average own up to eight connected things. These are striking numbers which open up a large variety of business cases which may happen fully autonomously. For example, sensors selling measured data to agents (about the weather or the traffic situation), or cars autonomously charging electricity per kilowatt hour. In such business cases, questions remain around digital identity, including the possibility of a fridge ordering food in the name of a household member.

The rise of micro and nano payments in the IoT space begs the question as to whether the existing payment infrastructure is fit for purpose. It is a twofold challenge, since the infrastructure needs to be able to process enormous volumes and also ensure that the processing is economically viable. The smaller the payment, the more pronounced the question of processing costs becomes. For the world of micro and nano payments, the traditional infrastructure may need an overhaul, or maybe the time has come for tailored blockchain infrastructures on a larger scale.

Going Green: Towards Payment Sustainability

The impact of climate change on our everyday lives has already changed from an abstract discussion on emission targets and limiting global temperature increases, to very concrete threats for humankind in the form of heatwaves, floods, and other natural disasters. Against this background, consumers are increasingly looking for sustainable products and solutions, and the market is adapting swiftly in order to deliver. It is a question of when, and not if, this development will reach the payments arena. While plastic card usage is a more obvious payment means where room for greener approaches clearly exist, the level of sustainability of the underlying and less visible plumbing infrastructure is admittedly more difficult to assess.

Central banks and global regulators have traditionally put more focus on the potential risk posed by climate change on the payment infrastructures. But they have increasingly started looking into the other direction: to what extent payments themselves contribute to climate change. Some central banks have already conducted studies on the ecological footprint of a payment means,[29] but a holistic and more systematic analysis of the end-to-end payment processes still remains to be established.

Even if there is no universal answer for all cases, it can be said that the decentralized nature of the blockchain with a reliance on a network of nodes does not necessarily appear superior to centralized solutions when it comes to energy consumption. The discussion on whether a blockchain can be run in a resource-conscious manner has so far been largely overshadowed by the energy-intensive "proof of work" consensus mechanism which has previously been used for the most relevant cryptoassets. However, the situation is changing, and after Ethereum moved from the proof of work to the "proof of stake"[30] method in the second half of 2022, only two out of the top ten cryptoassets (Bitcoin and Dogecoin) still rely on proof of work. Moreover, mining activities increasingly leverage green and renewable energy resources. These changes seem to show that the crypto players have understood the signs of the times and are moving towards greener solutions.

Beyond Regulation: The Emergence of Decentralized Finance

The inherent motivation behind the blockchain invention of "Satoshi Nakamoto" is the democratization of finance by creating a peer-to-peer payment flow. Decentralized finance (DeFi) exists in the same spirit in that it creates a financial ecosystem which allows business and resulting payments in a peer-to-peer manner and without involving traditional regulated custodians. In a decentralized set-up, it mimics services of the traditional financial sector, ranging from lending services, to trading and insurance services. The DeFi space is built on blockchain rails and relies on cryptoassets, typically in the form of stablecoins. The above assessment on the potential of blockchain infrastructures and payment assets can consequently be directly applied to payment flows around the DeFi services. This includes the tenet that decentralization is a spectrum. In fact, DeFi platforms often show some concentration of decision power, for example at the level of developer teams and early investors.

The size of the DeFi space is still relatively small, and ties to the traditional financial sector are limited. Its potential to grow depends on whether the DeFi business models allow for sustainable revenue streams below early adopter profits. The extent to which it needs to and can comply with regulatory requirements will certainly also play a role. In order to avoid regulatory arbitrage, the basic principle of "same risk, same rule" would need to apply to the DeFi space. However, the DeFi business contains not only risks similar to the traditional financial sector, but also new ones which directly derive from its decentralized nature (for example, lack of concrete governance).[31] In fact, since the absence of centralized entities is part of the very essence of the DeFi space, it is difficult to apply regulation as we know it.

CONCLUSION: THE FUTURE WORLD OF PAYMENTS

Already back in the 1960s, the American researcher and futurist Roy Almara believed that "we overestimate the impact of technology in the short-term and underestimate the effect in the long run." What has become known as Almara's law may also be applicable to blockchain and its payment assets. A lot has been said and written about their potential, but we do not see it fully materializing yet, at least not on a larger scale. Today's user needs in the field of payments can be met by today's centralized systems. Blockchain and its payment assets can maybe offer the same service level, but they are clearly not superior to the more traditional payment solutions out there.

The world of payment is changing at a very high speed. Fast-forwarding to the future, one could imagine a scenario where the technology around blockchain and its payment assets mature further, and where changes to business and user needs demand features for which traditional payment rails are no longer an obvious choice. Moreover, in addition to developments in the DeFi space, initiatives towards virtual reality economies under the headline of the Metaverse may create additional dynamics. Many companies are currently working on their own Metaverse solutions, but in order to allow for a Ready Player One-like common space, a decentralized concept based on a blockchain network with corresponding payment assets might be beneficial. Connected to this, ideas around the Web 3.0, which are geared towards the creation of a peer-to-peer version of the internet, are based on blockchain and digital assets. In conclusion, the crypto space remains vibrant, dynamic, and does not fall short of visions, neither in the real nor in the virtual world. Eventually, Amara's law may come true.

NOTES

1. European Central Bank; Adviser to the Chief Services Officer / Innovation Coordinator. The views and opinions expressed here are those of the author and do not necessarily reflect the official policy or position of the European Central Bank
2. The former President of the Federal Reserve Bank of New York, Gerald Corrigan, was one of the first to use the term "plumbing." It was subsequently referred to in speeches of Tomasso Padoa-Schioppa, the former executive board member of the European Central Bank, and used ever since for visualizing payment processing.
3. ECB (2022).
4. Nakamoto (2008).
5. The Bitcoin White Paper mentions the terms "block" and "chain" but the combined term "blockchain" only became mainstream around the year 2016.
6. Participants are given a complex task for creating a new block, and whoever manages to solve it first can attach it to the blockchain and receive a reward. This process is also often referred to as mining.
7. Calling them "blockchains" is often misleading. The overarching term "distributed ledger technologies" (DLT) was established to capture both variants, but has not

become mainstream. Consequently, "blockchain" is often written when the technology may not include a blockchain.

8. It should be noted that hybrid solutions are also being considered, which combine elements of private and public blockchains (for example, central authority with permissionless elements).
9. There are estimates of around 20 000 cryptoassets, which include inactive and discontinued ones.
10. Source: Statistica.com
11. A "token" is often referred to when the cryptoasset is built on an existing blockchain through smart contracts, and is not the native asset of a blockchain.
12. Regulation of the European Parliament and of the Council on Markets in Crypto-Assets (MiCAR).
13. Bullmann et al. (2019).
14. Smart contracts are computer programs which are stored on and automatically executed by a blockchain.
15. For example, a series of blockchain experiments with a focus on interbank payments started in 2016 by the Bank of Canada (project Jasper), Monetary Authority of Singapore (Ubin), and European Central Bank and Bank of Japan (Stella); followed in 2018 by the South African Reserve Bank (Khokha) and Bank of Thailand (Inthanon). De Nederlandsche Bank (with a blockchain-based coin called Dukaton) in 2015, and the Hong Kong Monetary Authority (LionRock, with a focus on retail CBDC) in 2017, also ran experiments. Over time, several of the afore-mentioned central banks joined forces. Regarding retail CBDC, the People's Bank of China started analysis back in 2014 (e-CNY), and Sveriges Riksbank in 2017 (e-krona).
16. Kosse and Mattei (2022).
17. Group of Central Banks (2020).
18. One can distinguish between retail CBDC (intended for use by the general public) and wholesale CBDC (for utilization in the interbank sphere). This section focuses on retail CBDC. Reflections around wholesale CBDC are mainly focused on the necessity to overcome inefficiencies in cross-border payment processing.
19. Committee on Payments and Market Infrastructures (2021a) Covid-19 accelerated the digitalization of payments.
20. The digital renminbi of the People's Bank of China, however, has been undergoing public testing since 2021.
21. Between 2020 and 2022, CBDCs were issued by Central Bank of the Bahamas (Sand Dollar), Eastern Caribbean Central Bank (DCash pilot), Bank of Nigeria (eNaira), and Bank of Jamaica (Jam-Dex).
22. Committee on Payments and Market Infrastructures (2021b).
23. The Lightning Network provides time-locked, off-chain payment channels for users. "Sharding" involves breaking down a blockchain into smaller blockchains to allow more transactions to be processed.
24. Committee on Payments and Market Infrastructures and International Organization of Securities Commissions (2012).
25. Junius et al. (2022).
26. Source: Bitinfocharts.com.
27. Source: Statistica.
28. Financial Stability Board (2020).
29. Hanegraaf et al. (2018) and Tiberi (2021).

30. A weighted random selection of participants is used, with the weights of the participants being based on the duration of participation and/or wealth (the “stake”).
31. OECD (2022).

REFERENCES

Bullmann, D., Klemm, J., Pinna, A. (2019). In search for stability in crypto-assets: are stablecoins the solution? https://papers.ssrn.com/sol3/papers.cfm?abstract_id=3444847.
Committee on Payments and Market Infrastructures (2021a). Covid-19 accelerated the digitalisation of payments.
Committee on Payments and Market Infrastructures (2021b). Developments in retail fast payments and implications for RTGS systems.
Committee on Payments and Market Infrastructures and International Organization of Securities Commissions (2012). Principles for financial market infrastructures.
ECB (2022). Study on the payment attitudes of consumers in the euro area (SPACE).
Financial Stability Board (2020). Enhancing cross-border payments—Stage 3 roadmap.
Group of Central Banks (2020). Central bank digital currencies: foundational principles and core features.
Hanegraaf, R., Jonker, N., Mandley, S., Miedema, J. (2018). Life cycle assessment of cash. DNB Working Paper 610.
Junius, K., Devigne, L., Honkkila, J., et al. (2022). Costs of retail payments—an overview of recent national studies in Europe. ECB Occasional Paper Series.
Kosse, A., Mattei, I. (2022). Gaining momentum—results of the 2021 BIS survey on central bank digital currency. BIS Papers No 125.
Nakamoto, S. (2008). Bitcoin: a peer-to-peer electronic cash system.
OECD (2022). Why decentralised finance (DeFi) matters and the policy implications.
Tiberi, P. (2021). The carbon footprint of the Target Instant Payment Settlement (TIPS) system: a comparative analysis with Bitcoin and other infrastructures.

4. Economic policy, regulation, and cryptocurrencies

Marco Fama, Lucio Gobbi, and Stefano Lucarelli

INTRODUCTION

Following the great financial crisis of 2007–2008, the financial system ended up in the dock. Different causes of this crisis have been identified, including the large-scale manifestation of information asymmetries in the financial asset generation process, the lack of adequate micro- and macro-prudential regulation, and the uncontrolled growth of liquidity within increasingly speculative markets. Cryptocurrencies were born in this context of growing skepticism toward mainstream financial intermediaries and the ability of monetary policies to rapidly revitalize the economy.

The pioneering experiences were rooted in a cultural milieu holding two different perspectives (May 1994): the so-called hacker ethic (Roio 2013) and the anti-statist libertarian political philosophy (Swartz 2018). The declared objective was to overcome the financial and monetary system in the name of a new paradigm based on the decentralization offered by blockchain. In this perspective, cryptocurrency represented a first opportunity to challenge the banks' monopoly on value transactions.

Bitcoin, the first cryptocurrency known on a large scale and still a benchmark for the entire sector, was launched in 2008 with the aim of creating a peer-to-peer anonymous payment system "without the need for a trusted third party" (Nakamoto 2008: 1). As the most recent research shows, crypto-consumers prefer Bitcoin to all other currencies, despite higher fees and longer blockchain processing times: 79 percent of them claim to own Bitcoin, 54.5 percent Ethereum, and 31.7 percent Litecoin (Cabuk and Silenzi 2021). Crypto consumers mainly purchase digital goods, including mobile phone top-ups, game credits, mobile phone applications, and digital entertainment services.[1] Despite the ambition of its inventor, the use of Bitcoin for transactional purposes has remained rather limited (Kharif 2018). It should be noted, however, that among all cryptocurrencies monitored by Chainalysis, the total transaction volume grew to $15.8 trillion in 2021, a 567 percent increase over the 2020 total. More cybercriminals are using cryptocurrencies: illicit addresses received US$14 billion during 2021, compared to US$7.8 billion in 2020. Yet the legitimate use of cryptocurrencies seems to far outpace the growth in criminal usage (Chainanalysis 2022). Demand for cryptocurrencies would still seem to be dominated by the speculative motive, although there is a not insignificant number of cryptocurrency holders who use them to purchase goods and services. Many analysts, however, consider the spread of cryptocurrencies with a transactions motive to be still far from the expectations of those who believed they would be the currency of the future.

To a large extent, this seems to be due to the excessive volatility that characterizes cryptocurrency, an issue that—as we discuss in this chapter—directly calls into question the rigidity of the monetary rules embedded in its own protocol (Amato and Fantacci 2020; Corbet et al. 2018; Huber and Sornette 2022).

Empirical evidence suggests that, at the moment, Bitcoin is mainly used and perceived as a highly speculative asset (Auer and Tercero-Lucas 2021; Fama et al. 2019; Baur and Dimpfl 2018; Baur et al. 2017), and there is still an intense debate about its concrete potential to act as an effective means of payment alternative to official money. Nevertheless, there is little doubt that the blockchain technology and the other innovations introduced by Bitcoin will play an increasingly important role within the existing economic and monetary system.

Furthermore, the Bitcoin experiment has inspired the creation of many other cryptocurrencies with different specificities, scope, and application possibilities. As of October 2022, the market capitalization of existing cryptocurrencies was approximately \$1 trillion, after having reached a peak of about \$3 trillion in 2021. Much of the existing experiences are based on fully decentralized systems, where users place their trust in the reliability of the underlying algorithms, the alleged neutrality of the cryptographic procedures, and the fact that the issuing rules are fixed and predetermined.

In response to the high volatility of the pioneering experiments, since 2014 new models have arisen—such as Tether, TrueUSD, and USD Coin—that are designed to preserve stability by pegging their value to a reference asset (a financial asset, a currency, a commodity, or a combination of assets). Stablecoins are more accessible and show high potential as private means of payment for e-commerce. However, compared to the first generation of cryptocurrencies, they present even more serious regulation problems (Financial Stability Board 2020; Schwarcz 2022).

In this chapter, we aim to show how the attitude of regulators, in particular the monetary authorities, towards cryptocurrencies has changed over time. It must be stressed that monetary authorities initially underestimated the relevance of cryptocurrencies, despite their growing popularity, as we will argue. From 2018 onwards, however, regulators started to pay close attention to the phenomenon, taking more seriously the possible threats for the stability of the financial system that could derive from an uncontrolled proliferation of cryptocurrencies, but also exploring alternative uses of their underlying technology, to the point of considering the possibility to create digital currencies directly issued by the central banks: central bank digital currencies (CBDCs).

Upon closer inspection, the approaches adopted by central bankers and the views of the major international monetary institutions—International Monetary Fund (IMF), Bank for International Settlements (BIS), Financial Stability Board (FSB)—differ widely, and there is no political consensus on the interventions that should be made with respect to cryptocurrencies (Mancini Griffoli et al. 2022; Auer and Classens 2018; Boar and Wehrli 2021; Financial Stability Board 2020). The same applies within the academic debate, where it is possible, however, to identify a consolidated stream of literature which considers cryptocurrencies as financial instruments that should be subject to specific regulations, in order to avoid speculative excesses and elusive or tax-evasive behaviors; a stance that, as we will discuss, does not necessarily coincide with the central bankers' perspective.

In the course of this chapter, we put forward the following hypothesis: CBDCs are a first step towards a monetary policy that can affect cryptocurrency flows. We then focus on the institutional dimension of cryptocurrencies and seek to understand how effectively this disruptive social innovation is shaping the history of monetary institutions. We conclude by arguing that CBDCs could be a way to endow the technological innovations introduced by Bitcoin with more lasting confidence, as well as an opportunity to improve the international monetary system.

CRYPTOCURRENCIES AND MONETARY AUTHORITIES

First generation cryptocurrencies, and Bitcoin in particular, were born with the ambition of disrupting the official monetary system (Amato and Fantacci 2020; Bower and Christensen 1995), replacing it with an electronic payment infrastructure that enables transactions "without the need for a trusted third party" (Nakamoto 2008: 1).

The lack of a central authority, as well as of other intermediaries, reflects the philosophy that inspired the creation of Bitcoin, in which libertarian philosophy and theories about the "denationalization of money" (Hayek 1976; Swartz 2018) are conflated with anti-state anarchist ideas, along with the hacker ethic, the cyberpunk movement, and crypto-anarchism (Himanen 2001; Roio 2013; May 1994). Activists who identify with the libertarian anti-statism close to the Austrian school of economics place great emphasis on the critique of debasement; that is, the artificial reduction of the value of money, which has characterized the monetary policy of central banks and, indirectly, of governments in different historical periods.

Accordingly, the way Bitcoin is designed leaves no room for the possibility of implementing a real monetary policy. In fact, the supply of the cryptocurrency is inscribed in the underlying algorithm and cannot be changed, no matter what happens in the real and financial markets (Nakamoto 2008).

In the absence of a central bank,[2] the issuing procedures are entrusted to "miners," who provide the computing power needed to solve the algorithm used to validate each transaction. In exchange, miners are rewarded with a transaction fee and a portion of new Bitcoins that are issued during the validation process (block subsidy). As shown in Figure 4.1, the Bitcoin supply varies over time until the final number of 21 million Bitcoins is reached. The subsidy that the system provides to miners tends to halve every four years, following a scheme through which the growth rate of the money supply decreases over time until reaching zero in 2041. This makes Bitcoin a potentially deflationary tool, more similar to a commodity-based monetary system (Fantacci 2019).

Most importantly, since there is no possibility to adjust the monetary supply to economic shocks, the cryptocurrency is structurally exposed to the risk of high volatility (Amato and Fantacci 2020; Liu and Tsyvinski 2021; Huber and Sornette 2022),

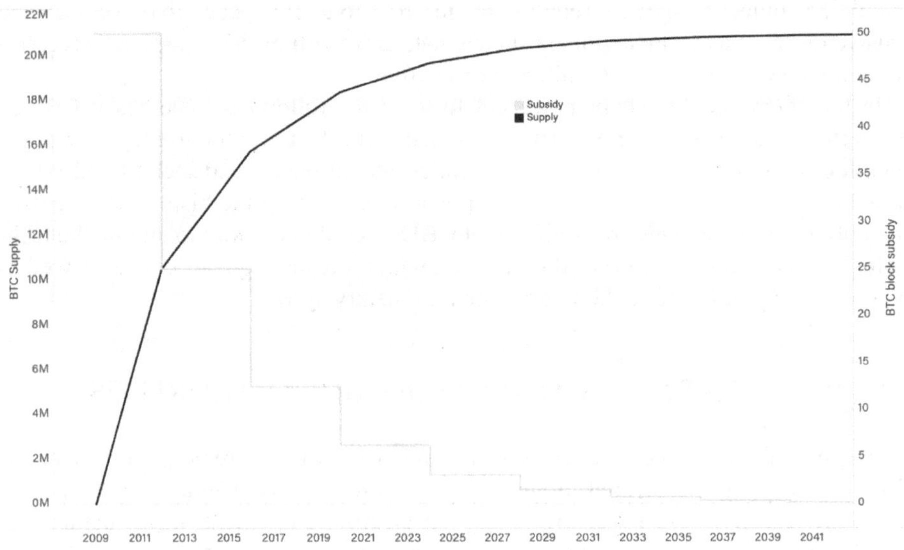

Source: CoinDesk Research.

Figure 4.1 *Bitcoin supply and block subsidy by year*

as illustrated in Figure 4.2. It is not a coincidence that Bitcoin is currently mostly perceived as a financial asset and is largely used for speculative ends (Fama et al. 2020; Baur and Dimpfl 2018; Baur et al. 2017).

There are several factors that are negatively affecting the possibility for Bitcoin to function as an effective means of payment. Some of these—such as the high transaction fees—are related to practical problems that can be overcome by adapting the underlying technological infrastructure, as has been the case with other cryptocurrencies. Yet, the main obstacle lies in the cryptocurrency's extreme volatility, provided that a fundamental property of money is that it works as a general equivalent enabling the facilitation of exchanges without suffering a loss in value (Boyer 2015).

This issue calls directly into question the existence of a central authority able to reinforce trust and to implement the actions needed to preserve the stability of a currency's value.[3] Considering the above, one should generally agree with the perspective of the European Central Bank (2015: 25), according to which cryptocurrencies do not fit the economic or legal definition of money, since they "do not have the nature of a highly liquid asset and have not reached the level of acceptance commonly associated with money." Yet, cryptocurrencies can be considered as a digital representation of value that, as stated by the same European Central Bank, "in some circumstances *can* be used as an alternative to money" (ibid.). This stance, which is fairly representative of the views of major monetary authorities, has probably contributed to the delay in cryptocurrency regulation that we are now witnessing.

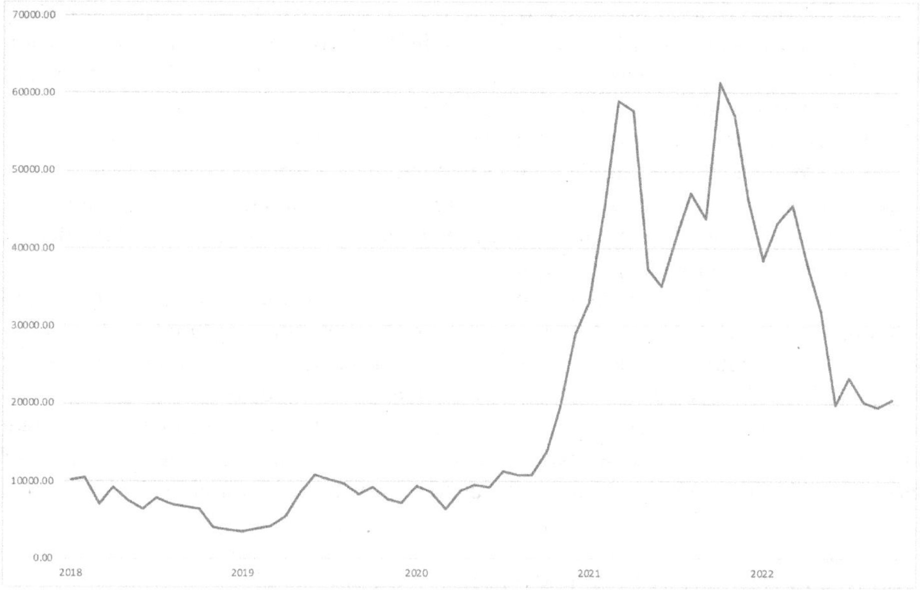

Source: Based on data from Coinmarketcap.com, https://coinmarketcap.com/currencies/bitcoin/historical-data/.

Figure 4.2 *Bitcoin market price , 2018–2022 (USD)*

The lack of a central authority is an issue that concerns not merely the stability of decentralized cryptocurrencies, but also the possibility of exerting political control over their distribution and the social purposes of their use. Just because they represent a possible, and less traceable, "alternative to money," cryptocurrencies have shown a certain tendency to be used for money laundering and other illicit purposes (Europol 2021). However, according to "The 2022 Crypto Crime Report" (Chainanalysis 2022), annual trends suggest that, with the exception of 2019—an anomalous year for cryptocurrency-based crime, largely due to the PlusToken Ponzi scheme—crime is becoming a smaller part of the cryptocurrency ecosystem.

Furthermore, looking at the Bitcoin experience, it is rather questionable that the cryptocurrency has enabled an effective redistribution of purchasing power, as was the intention of its inventors. Indeed, analyzing the concentration of production of Bitcoin, Makarov and Schoar (2021) found that at the end of 2021, the 0.1 percent of miners controlled 50 percent of the mining capacity, the top 10 percent controlled 90 percent, and the top 50 percent controlled 99 percent.[4] In addition, a relevant portion of all the Bitcoins in circulation is controlled by a few big players—the so-called whales—that can move the market at will (Khaosan 2018), with the risk of new processes of financial dispossession.

As shown in the empirical analysis by Fama et al. (2019), the dominant monetary policy instruments seem completely irrelevant in the explanation of Bitcoin volatility. At the same time, it must be recognized that, even within the official monetary system, central authorities have only a very indirect control over a relevant portion of the money supply, which is provided by private banks (Dow 2017) and financial investors in the form of loans or speculative activities.

This issue poses a broader set of questions related to the criticisms of our official monetary system and the same problems that led to the birth of cryptocurrencies. The issue of how to regulate existing cryptocurrencies hence intersects with the question of how we can look at them, and at the novelties they introduced, for reconsidering our economic and monetary policies.

As we will see in the next sections, monetary authorities have for many years relinquished the task of affecting the behavior of cryptocurrency holders. Instead, it has been state regulation that has sought to discourage the increase in cryptocurrency demand through specific normative interventions, mostly related to tax policy. This has been the prevailing scenario at least until the recent new phase that, in the wake of the Chinese project dating back to 2014, now seems to place the possibility of issuing one's own cryptocurrency at the center of the monetary authorities' attention.

HOW TO REGULATE CRYPTOCURRENCIES?

The cryptocurrencies sector is still largely unregulated. Ongoing debate about this topic proceeds unevenly, with new calls for regulation arising every time there is a collapse in the price of major cryptocurrencies. In general, central banks seem to share the concern that a rapid and wide spread of cryptocurrencies could compromise the stability of the financial system, due to the interdependence of regulated and unregulated participants, as well as to the lack of controls and instruments able to mitigate the effects of unfavorable events.

More specifically, there are three main problems that are usually evoked (Carney 2018): the extreme market price volatility; the recurring episodes of crisis due to fraud, computer incidents, or underlying faults, which also recently caused huge losses for users and operators; and the overall opacity of cryptocurrencies, the underlying trading mechanisms, and the ownership structures behind them.

However, as has already been pointed out by Sauce (2022), the crypto industry still navigates in an ambiguous and uncertain regulatory environment. As Auer and Claessens (2018: 52–53) observe:

> Many of the concerns raised would also apply to other asset classes and emergent technologies. But what sets cryptocurrencies apart is that they can function without institutional backing and are intrinsically borderless. This raises the question of whether one can expect regulation—in particular national regulation—to be effective ... The goals of regulating cryptocurrencies are largely similar to those for other financial assets and services and can be classified into three categories: combating the use of funds for illicit activities; protecting consumers and investors against fraud and other abuses; and ensuring the integrity of markets and payment systems and overall financial stability.

Analyzing the content produced by the Reuters News Agency between January 2015 and June 2018, the authors identified 151 articles related to cryptocurrency regulation. The articles referred to speeches and statements made by authorities and officials from Australia, China, Korea, Japan, Gibraltar, Hong Kong, India, Indonesia, Israel, the Philippines, the United Kingdom (UK), Singapore, the United States (US), Switzerland, and Chinese Taipei, as well as the European Union and its member states and major international institutions, groups, and regulatory bodies: euro area institutions, the BIS, the International Organization of Securities Commissions (IOSCO), FSB and the G20.

Auer and Claessens's analysis shows that after the general warnings, the most recurring news items were focused on the interoperability of cryptocurrencies with regulated financial entities, such as commercial banks, credit card companies, and exchange platforms. Most of the news comes from China, Japan, India, the UK, and the US. The number of news items has increased over time, indicating an increase in regulatory attempts related to cryptocurrencies.

Cryptocurrencies are not bound to territorial entities and have no borders. Yet the empirical analysis conducted by Auer and Claessens for the Bank of International Settlement shows that regulatory actions as well as news of potential interventions can strongly affect cryptocurrency prices and transaction volumes. However, this environment requires clarity on cryptocurrency activities from a legal perspective, and from the perspective of securities markets, as well as on the boundaries of national regulations. Indeed, as the cryptocurrency market continues to evolve, and the number of banks and funds engaging in cross-border arbitrage transactions continues to increase, regulation and enforcement in one jurisdiction could result in activity migrating to other jurisdictions with less stringent approaches. The adoption of internationally consistent approaches for cryptocurrencies is not something that can be taken for granted.

It may be useful to review the different forms of regulation related to cryptocurrencies that are currently being implemented around the world. We are faced with a very diverse landscape: we go from one extreme represented by El Salvador, which in September 2021 adopted Bitcoin as its current currency, to the opposite extreme represented by the People's Republic of China where, from September 2021, the People's Bank of China banned all cryptocurrency transactions.

As stressed in the last Thomson Reuters Report on cryptocurrency regulations (Hammond and Ehret 2022), much of the regulatory framework is still developing, and regulations diversify depending on uses such as payments, investments, derivatives, and tax status. Most countries have generally found ways to tax gains or income derived from cryptocurrencies. Considering the most recent annual crypto tax ranking edited by Coincub (2022), the highest taxation for residents is applied in Belgium, where capital gains on speculative transactions of cryptoassets are regarded as professional income and come under progressive taxation rates up to 50 percent. Other countries that set high rates for capital gains are Iceland, Israel, the Philippines, and Japan.

Recent contributions on the impact of regulation in the cryptocurrency market show that events which increase the probability of regulation adoption have a negative effect on cryptocurrency stock returns, both in the short and the longer term. The results are not surprising if we consider that the cryptocurrency market attracted investors because it was established in a decentralized manner, away from the supervision of any regulating institutions (Chokor and Alfieri 2021). It should also be specified that investors can take advantage of regulatory loopholes and dodge rigorous rules because—as we have already argued—there is currently no international consensus on basic regulatory criteria, and even on the classification of cryptoassets.

However, the spread of cryptocurrencies has caused a significant change in the institutional structure of the monetary and financial markets. It is in this context that the technological platforms that offer cryptocurrency custody, management, and conversion services are now entering into competition with traditional banks and financial intermediaries.

There are two main questions that monetary authorities should ask themselves, faced with a situation in which regulators do not seem particularly able to correct the distortions that a massive increase in the use of cryptocurrencies would cause: Can a monetary system in which privately issued cryptocurrencies circulate as media of exchange work? Is such a system stable? To answer these questions, Fernandes-Villaverde and Sanches (2018) propose a theoretical model of competition among privately issued fiat currencies. The stable coexistence of privately issued cryptocurrencies and central bank money depends on monetary policy. Particularly if the central bank does not guarantee price stability, privately issued currencies would be used, but they would lose their significance as a medium of exchange once the central bank legitimately guaranteed the real worth of money balances. Consequently, central banks can prevent cryptocurrencies from being used as a means of exchange by selecting a particular style of monetary policy. According to this viewpoint, the co-existence of fiat currency and cryptocurrencies can be beneficial by acting as a check on central banks rather than being a threat (Claeys et al. 2018: 8). However, from a more pragmatic perspective, the rise of cryptocurrencies as a viable means of exchange with dependable purchasing power poses some challenges to central banks. The success of monetary policy will firstly depend on how much money and bank deposits are replaced with cryptocurrencies by economic agents. Because the amount of broad money in the economy would decrease as a result of widespread substitution of bank deposits, there would be less control over the monetary environment. At its most extreme, base money creation and the associated impact on interest rates would be ineffectual. As Savona (2021) pointed out:

> The emergence of cryptos creates "out of thin air" a purchasing power in the hands of that part of households and businesses, especially financial ones, that "undermine" and "multiply" them through exchanges. While it is true that they have the characteristics of financial products, they are used as currency for exchanges; the fact that the authorities claim that they are not such does not correspond to the reality of the market. The result is ... a loss of effectiveness of monetary and fiscal policy; this is due to the fact that as a result of their dis-

> semination central banks lose their monopoly of money creation and control over interest rates, and the organs of democracy their power to fix the distribution of income they desire.

Against this background, one should not underestimate the fact that, with the creation of virtual currencies, the market would be in a position to interfere in the decisions of the monetary authorities, to the point of neutralizing their stabilizing effects.

The final threat relates to the appeal of cryptocurrencies as investment assets, which renders them susceptible to speculative bubbles. The stability of the financial institutions which central banks control would then be at risk, first from the possible unregulation of the cryptocurrency debt markets, and second from the impact of deleveraging and defaulting by economic agents on the real economy (Claeys et al. 2018: 9).

In recent years, the competition between cryptocurrencies and official currencies has taken the form of a confrontation between stablecoins and CBDCs. In the next section, we investigate this issue.

STABLECOINS, CENTRAL BANK DIGITAL CURRENCIES, AND MONETARY POLICY

Stablecoins are private cryptocurrencies, such as Tether, Binance USD, and USD Coin, that have arisen since 2014 in response to the extreme volatility that characterizes first generation cryptocurrencies (Fama et al. 2019; Huber and Sornette 2022). Unlike the first generation cryptocurrencies, stablecoins are not inspired by the ambition of replacing central banks and the existing financial system. In fact, their statutory objective is to maintain a fixed "exchange rate" with a selected currency, a feature that somehow indicates their subalternity to the official monetary system.

To date, stablecoins represent a share of only about 10 percent of the entire cryptocurrency market, although their growth rate is increasing. Table 4.1 shows the market capitalization, the price of a unit of cryptocurrency, and the volumes traded in a day of the top ten stablecoins. The top nine aim to maintain their exchange rate with the dollar at 1, the tenth seeks to replicate the price trend of gold per ounce. It can be noticed that the target was reached for all currencies on October 10, 2022. However, market capitalization and daily traded volumes are still relatively small. The stability of the value is given by the type of asset backing the currency (for example, currencies, gold, securities).

Figure 4.3 illustrates the composition of the assets used as reserves by the three main stablecoins. It is important to note that the composition of reserves consists exclusively of monetary and banking instruments for USD Coin and Binance USD, and that only Tether holds a share of its assets in market instruments, which usually are more risky.

Table 4.1 *Market capitalization, market prices, and volumes traded by stablecoins as of 22 October, 2022*

Stablecoin	Price	24h volume exchanged	Market capitalization
Tether (USDT)	$0.999189	$67.74b	$79.32b
USD Coin (USDC)		$48.57b	$4.43b
Binance USD (BUSD)	$0.999256	$21.05b	$3.02b
Multi-Collateral Dai (DAI)	$0.978142	$6.87b	$166.54m
Frax (FRAX)	$0.995002	$1.35b	$7.50m
Pax Dollar (USDP)		$946.09m	$2.74m
True USD (TUSD)	$0.999256	$878.74m	$51.38m
Neutrino USD (NUSD)	$0.978142	$665.40m	$678 284
Fei USD (FUSD)	$0.995002	$422.87m	$302 413
Tether Gold (XAUT)		$408.33m	$179 313

Source: Based on Coinmarketcap data, https://coinmarketcap.com/view/stablecoin/.

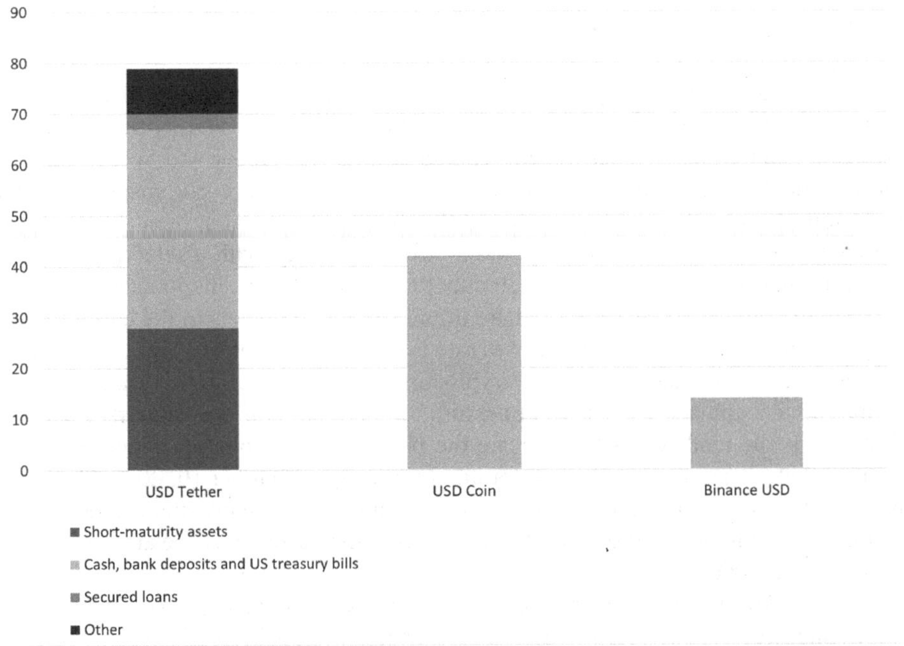

Source: Sveriges Riksbank (2022), https://www.riksbank.se/en-gb/press-and-published/publications/staff-memos/an-overview-of-fintech-and-cryptoassets/what-are-cryptoassets/stablecoins-are-intended-to-maintain-a-stable-price-over-time/.

Figure 4.3 *Reserve assets for USD Tether, USD Coin, and Binance USD (billion USD)*

The point we want to make here is that, notwithstanding their stability compared with other cryptocurrencies, stablecoins cannot be properly considered as money. As observed by Gorton and Zhang (2021: 911–912):

> While the technology changes, and the form of privately produced money changes, the issues with privately produced money do not change—namely, private money is a subpar medium of exchange and is subject to runs. To see this, one must recognize that money has several important properties, with the three most commonly stated ones being a store of value, a unit of account, and a medium of exchange. The property that's most obvious, yet not explicitly presented, is that money also must satisfy the no-questions-asked ("NQA") principle, which requires the money be accepted in a transaction without due diligence on its value. In other words, NQA means both parties to a transaction must agree that the money be accepted at par—a ten-dollar bill should be accepted as being worth ten dollars, not a penny less.

Moreover, the transaction costs for using stablecoins as a means of payment are even higher than those of payment circuits such as Visa or Mastercard (Mizrach 2023). Finally, it is important to note that the major stablecoins impose constraints on the redeemability of their investments.

Rather than money, indeed, stablecoins resemble money market mutual funds (MMMF); that is, mutual funds whose peculiarity lies in the fact that they invest exclusively in short-term money market instruments. In theory, stablecoins could be employed as a safe asset in the financial system. Safe assets play a very important function in the financial world, since they are used as highly rated collateral by financial operators. The quest for safe assets can be driven by the need to cope with financial regulation as well as to add low-risk components to portfolios created for risk-averse investors (Golec and Perotti 2017; Caballero et al. 2017; Amato et al. 2021).

As long as a proper diversification of reserves could minimize the risk of a stablecoin's failure, however, the financial history has shown that private financial assets have at best been considered as quasi-safe assets (Gorton et al. 2012; Krishnamurthy and Vissing-Jorgensen 2012). Indeed, despite their potential, stablecoins have raised regulatory problems and concerns about their stability much more seriously compared to first generation cryptocurrencies (G7 Working Group on Stablecoins 2019; Financial Stability Board 2020; Bains et al. 2022; Schwarcz 2022).

The most controversial issue concerns the ability of stablecoins to maintain their target value in adverse market conditions. Regulators' fears turned out to be real. In May 2022, the cryptocurrency market went through turmoil mainly due to global macroeconomic instability. Stablecoins did not withstand the shock. In particular, Tether had to temporarily break the peg with the dollar. Even more striking was the case of TerraUSD which abandoned the peg on May 9 and reduced its capitalization from €18 billion to €2 billion within a week (Adachi et al. 2022).

In sum, given the small size of the volumes traded, stablecoins do not appear to be a monetary instrument capable of compromising the stability of the financial system, or to function as an alternative to the official monetary system. Yet, being a bridge between the traditional financial system and the cryptocurrency one, the stablecoins market is a potential risk-spreader[5] which calls for more careful monitoring by monetary and regulatory authorities.

In response to the continuous development of cryptocurrencies and stablecoins, the leading central banks have begun to investigate the possibility of issuing their own digital currencies (CBDCs). From a technical point of view, CBDCs can be either token-based or account-based. Currently, there is not a clear tendency towards either of the two options. The Federal Reserve seems more inclined to opt for an account-based CBDC, the European Central Bank for a token-based one, and the People's Bank of China for a mixed form (Schwarcz 2022).

The design of a CBDC is very flexible and responds to the objectives of policy makers. There are two main aspects to be taken into account. The first concerns the fact that the CBDC is directly issued on current accounts that the central bank holds in the name of households and businesses. We call this case "retail CBDC." One way of issuing money that imposes a less radical change on the financial system is to involve financial intermediaries that already hold reserves at the central bank (Boar and Wehrli 2021). This case is referred to as "wholesale CBDC."

The second important aspect to consider in the analysis of a CBDC concerns whether the CBDC is interest bearing or not. This issue is directly connected with the function that policy makers want to entrust to a CBDC. A currency characterized by a positive yield can act as a safe asset entering into the portfolio choices of economic agents (Meaning et al. 2018). Instead, a non-interest bearing currency would act more as a means of payment competing with cash (Bordo and Levin 2017).

To date, the most relevant CBDC project is the one conceived by the Bank of China starting in 2014 for the implementation of the Digital Yuan. The aims of this project concern multiple objectives. The officially stated ones focus mainly on the efficiency of the payments system, the diversification of forms of cash, the endowment of a digital currency that favors the spread of international payments in Chinese currency, as well as in the endowment of an additional unconventional monetary policy instrument (Allen et al. 2022; Fantacci and Gobbi 2021). Figure 4.4 shows the geographic distribution of central banks that have activated monetary policy instruments classifiable as CBDCs, or are initiating pilot projects and studies in this regard (Soderberg et al. 2022).

When considering the possibility of creating an interest-bearing retail CBDC, one has to take into account the trade-off that it inevitably implies for the economic and financial system. First, since a CBDC is a safe asset that guarantees a positive return, the banking system will have to align the interest rate on sight deposits at least equal to the central bank's interest rate for the CBDC. If this were not the case, the banking system would suffer a substantial reduction in sight deposits, which are the main source of funding for commercial banks as well as potential bank runs. The predominant implication of this would be a higher cost of credit and potential reduction in investment (Keister and Sanches 2021; Cesaratto and Febrero 2022).

In this context, the central bank would gain more control over monetary aggregates than in the current system (Chen and Siklos 2022), where monetary aggregates

Source: Visualcapitalist, https://www.atlanticcouncil.org/cbdctracker/.

Figure 4.4 CBDC projects and studies

are mainly endogenously determined by the economic system (Graziani 2003). In oligopolistic banking environments, an interest-bearing CBDC can be used as a tool to lower the mark-up loaded on households and firms by effectively setting an upper bound (Chiu et al. 2019).

A non-interest-bearing CDBC tends to address the need to make the payment system more efficient by speeding it up and reducing transaction costs (Cecchetti and Schoenholtz 2021), creating a substitute for cash, while reducing tax evasion and illicit activities (Meaning et al. 2018; Cesaratto and Febrero 2022). In addition, a non-interest bearing CBDC can be used to implement unconventional monetary policies such as "helicopter money" (Reyes and Tenero 2022; Temperini et al. 2022). Helicopter money is a policy aimed at permanently increasing the monetary base. It was conceived by Milton Friedman (1969: 4–5), who presented the instrument in this way:

> Let us suppose now that one day a helicopter flies over this community and drops an additional $1,000 in bills from the sky, which is, of course, hastily collected by members of the community. Let us suppose further that everyone is convinced that this is a unique event which will never be repeated.

The main benefit of the proposal is to directly activate aggregate demand when the transmission channel of monetary policy is ineffective, or government debt levels are such that budget expansions are not possible. The introduction of a CBDC would allow the targeting of helicopter money operations to specific economic sectors (Temperini et al. 2022). Such a monetary policy instrument could prove crucial in times of severe economic crisis. However, the banking sector could be affected by the introduction of a CBDC, not only through a reduction in bank deposits, but also due to a decrease in demand for loans. More precisely, whenever the beneficiaries of the helicopter money policy are companies, the CBDC could be used by firms to reduce their indebtedness to the banking sector (Temperini et al. 2022).

The growing debate between economists and policy makers regarding the costs and benefits of introducing a CBDC signals the importance of the issue. This is correlated with the efforts of central banks to definitively absorb the innovations brought about by cryptocurrencies, as well as to mitigate their risk. Furthermore, the tensions on the stablecoins market and the inability of these tools to establish themselves as a means of payment show how difficult it is to undermine the institutional system of the state currency.

THE INSTITUTIONAL DIMENSION OF CRYPTOCURRENCIES

According to the vision which lies behind many cryptocurrencies, the lack of a central authority with the power of changing the rules at its own discretion should enhance stability; which, in any case, is supposed to be already ensured by the rigidity of the money supply, and the reliability of the blockchain technology used to validate the transactions and to issue the cryptocurrency. Empirically, however, this approach to monetary issues has shown all the problems that can derive from a poor understanding of what money is.

Here, a sociological perspective focused on the complexity of money as an institution hinged on a combination of inextricably merged social, economic, and technical factors can help us to achieve new insights on the limits and potentialities of cryptocurrencies, and to explore the role that the monetary authorities can play with respect to this phenomenon (Fama et al. 2020; Fama and Musolino 2020). A set of related questions that arise are: How should we consider cryptocurrencies, and which are the conditions required for their institutionalization? Do these instruments have the potential to challenge the existing notion of monetary sovereignty and to give rise to a new way of considering monetary policies? Which lessons can be learned from the pioneering experiments for the development of new digital currencies, including CBDC?

In seeking to address these questions, it is worth keeping in mind that money represents an example of what French anthropologist Marcel Mauss defined as a "total social fact" (Aglietta and Orléan 2002). As such, money is an institutional process binding individuals into social relations of interdependence and conflict; a process during which new shared meanings and forms of interaction between the economic and social spheres arise (Simmel 1978 [1907]).

In this respect, according to Luigi Doria (2020), an important novelty of Bitcoin is that, in seeking to remove uncertainty and to absolutize the economic agents' autonomy by means of disintermediation and decentralization, the cryptocurrency points to the creation of a "desocialized economic environment" in which individualist economic actors can somehow be "protected from the dangerous relationship with social relations and institutions." In this way, Bitcoin ends up embracing a techno-utopian vision that refuses to recognize that money is, above all, the result of a collective cognitive process that leads to the emergence of a common space of evaluation in which social bonds and values are translated into specific rules (Fumagalli and Lucarelli 2011: 200–201).

While financial intermediaries can technically be replaced, what defines the social legitimacy of a general equivalent that is accepted as a means of payment is the existence of a space of negotiation endowed with a coercive power. In other terms, for money to emerge, the existence of a community is necessary, as well as a process of social construction where trust, along with coercion, play an essential role (Ingham 2014).

More specifically, following the French Regulation's School approach (Aglietta et al. 2016), money needs three forms of trust, which are in different ways connected to the concept of sovereignty: ethical trust, which reflects the values of a community as they are embodied in political institutions and legal apparatus; hierarchical trust, that is incorporated in the public institution that produce the rules of the game, being responsible for the integrity of the payment system; and methodical trust, a procedural form of trust based on the routine use of payment methods and procedures that have proved effective.

In light of the above, how should we consider Bitcoin inventor's claim about having created a "cash system which does not need to rely on trust"? Upon closer inspection it seems that Bitcoin can be better described as an experiment pointing to an evolution of the forms of trust that back money, more than as a trustless monetary system. As a matter of fact, the blockchain can be seen as a sort of "technical institution" incorporating both methodical and hierarchical trust, which emerged from the ethical commitment of the core developers community toward the building of a stable peer-to-peer monetary system that would not rely on the state and bank intermediation (Malherbe et al. 2019).

Nevertheless, Bitcoin users do not belong to a well-defined community with clear territorial boundaries. They do not necessarily share the vision of the core developers and, most importantly, there is not a sovereign authority able to sustain the original ethical commitment by enforcing the rules and sanctioning any possible misconduct. The same mining process is based on a lucrative mechanism which subordinates the monetary rules—and the ethical trust they are supposed to incarnate—to the users' utilitarian propensities. The result is an unstable form of trust that, along with other practical and macroeconomic limits of Bitcoin, impedes a complete institutionalization of it.

The issue of trust hence intersects with the problems related to the deflationary approach that lies behind the cryptocurrency and the lack of a space for implementing monetary policies. The latter is necessary not only to preserve price stability and the value of money over time, but also to establish the condition and goals of economic production, as well as employment levels and other macroeconomic targets. This condition adds to the well-known environmental (Badea and Mungiu-Pupăzan 2021) and concentration (Khaosan 2018) problems connected to the mining process. Here, a paradox of Bitcoin emerges: provided that "to incentivize the mining process, the

Bitcoin supply has to be scarce to increase the relative value of the coin, but to be used as a means of payment and to sustain growth, the Bitcoin supply has to be sufficient to satisfy the demand for liquidity" (Malherbe et al. 2019: 141).

But the growing demand for cryptocurrencies for the transactional motive cannot be underestimated. We are therefore confronted with an evolution of the institutional framework of the cryptocurrency world that goes beyond the self-regulatory boundaries imagined by the inventors of Bitcoin, according to whom: "Bitcoin is not unregulated. It is regulated by algorithms instead of being regulated by government bureaucracies" (Antonopuolos 2013). Furthermore, the traditional institutions that are in charge of outlining the rules of international trade in real goods and financial assets are rethinking their spaces of intervention in response to the potential distortions that the spread of cryptocurrencies introduces into the international payments system.

CONCLUSION

First generation cryptocurrencies have indicated practical options for rethinking our monetary system and how to conceive monetary policies. Up until now, however, they have failed to build a concrete alternative to official money. Partly, this failure seems to be due to their decentralized nature, which implies the impossibility to implement monetary policies through which to reinforce trust and preserve price stability. Stablecoins, for their part, provide concrete solutions to deal with high volatility, but their transaction costs are still excessively high, in addition to entailing even greater regulatory problems compared to first generation cryptocurrencies.

At any rate, when exploring the institutional dimension of these experiments, and the reasons why cryptocurrencies are mainly used and perceived as speculative financial assets, practical problems about price stability and regulation must be considered, along with more general issues related to the nature of money, how this emerged, and why it is used, and the conditions needed for the establishment of new forms of monetary sovereignty.

The case of Bitcoin, in particular, suggests once again that money cannot be treated as a neutral instrument whose possible flaws are to be addressed on merely technical grounds. This is not to say that the technological innovations introduced by Bitcoin cannot play an important role in the creation of new monetary regimes, or that the same concept of monetary sovereignty cannot be revisited from new, including a-territorial, perspectives.

Nevertheless, while some of the technical limits of Bitcoin can be overcome, as has already happened in the case of other cryptocurrencies, the institutionalization of such experiences would require the establishment of more stable forms of trust sustained by some sort of central authority. In this sense, CBDCs might represent a way to equip the technological innovations introduced by Bitcoin with more durable trust, but also a solution to improve the effectiveness of our monetary system, thereby reinforcing its social acceptance. Ironically, this would imply a radical drift from the original mission of Bitcoin's inventor, to create a "decentralized payment system that does not need to rely on trust" (Nakamoto 2008: 1).

Finally, we must consider that the introduction of a CBDC could have very heterogeneous effects depending on its design. Generally speaking, CBDCs could change the monetary policy transmission mechanism, either by bypassing the banking system (retail CBDC) or by decreasing its degrees of freedom (wholesale CBDC). This change would help central banks to regain control over money supply, equipping them with new instruments for addressing economic crises. Yet, the costs and risks of such disintermediation should by no means be underestimated. Throughout the history of capitalism, banks have been crucial for dealing with the problems of information asymmetry and moral hazard in the credit market (Tamborini 2021). Certainly, regulators and policy makers will have to confront themselves with an arduous challenge, which requires analyzing the general economic equilibrium effects of the diverse options available, and carefully weighing all their potential costs and benefits.

NOTES

1. "The entire population of the survey exclusively consists of the registered users of the CryptoRefills website (www. cryptorefills.com). The population presumably consists of crypto-consumers, who are (i) actively using cryptocurrencies in shopping, (ii) have quit using cryptocurrencies in shopping for a while for any reason, or (iii) never tried but are eager to use cryptocurrencies in shopping in the future. The overall population size (N) is confirmed to be 4405 unique individuals." (Cabuk and Silenzi 2021: 47)
2. In theory, central banks have a monopoly over money supply. In practice, following circuitists and endogenous money theories, money creation is largely determined within the banking system according to the decisions made by the different economic actors (McLeay et al. 2014; Arestis and Sawyer 2006; Graziani 2003).
3. As we argue in the following sections, stablecoins seek to overcome this limit. Nevertheless, they have raised even more serious regulatory problems and concerns about their stability.
4. According to the Cambridge Center for Alternative Finance, the United States is the country where most bitcoins are generated (38 percent), followed by China (21 percent) and Kazakhstan (13 percent).
5. Regarding the literature on the contagion in the financial network, among others see Nier et al. (2007), Gai and Kapadia (2010), and Gaffeo et al. (2019).

REFERENCES

Adachi, M., Pereira Da Silva, P.B., Born, A., and Cappuccio, A. (2022). "Stablecoins' role in crypto and beyond: functions, risks and policy," *Macroprudential Bulletin*, July. European Central Bank. https://www.ecb.europa.eu/pub/financial-stability/macroprudential-bulletin/html/ecb.mpbu202207_2~836f682ed7.en.html.

Aglietta, M., and Orléan, A. (2002). *La monnaie entre violence et confiance.* [*Money between violence and confidence*], Paris: Odile Jacob.

Aglietta, M., Ould Ahmed, P., and Ponsot, J.-F. (2016). *Monnaie Entre Dettes et Souverainete [Currency: Between Debt and Sovereignty]*, Paris: Odile Jacob.

Allen, F., Gu, X., and Jagtiani, J. (2022). "Fintech, cryptocurrencies, and CBDC: financial structural transformation in China," *Journal of International Money and Finance*, vol. 124, 102625.

Amato, M., Belloni, E., Falbo, P., and Gobbi, L. (2021). "Europe, public debts, and safe assets: the scope for a European Debt Agency," *Economia Politica*, vol. 38, pp. 823–861.

Amato, M., and Fantacci, L. (2020). *A Fistful of Bitcoins: the Risks and Opportunities of Virtual Currencies*, Milano: Bocconi University Press.

Antonopoulos, A. (2013), "Bitcoin is not 'unregulated'." https://twitter.com/aantonop/status/413720314065846272.

Arestis, P., and Sawyer, M. (2006). "The nature and role of monetary policy when money is endogenous," *Cambridge Journal of Economics*, vol. 30(6), pp. 847–860.

Auer, R., and Claessens, S. (2018). "Regulating cryptocurrencies: assessing market reactions," *BIS Quarterly Review*, September, pp. 51–65.

Auer, R., and Tercero-Lucas, D. (2021). "Distrust or speculation? The socioeconomic drivers of U.S. cryptocurrency investments," BIS Working Papers 951, Bank for International Settlements.

Badea, L., and Mungiu-Pupăzan, M.C. (2021). "The economic and environmental impact of Bitcoin," *IEEE Access*, vol. 9, pp. 48091–48104.

Bains, P., Ismail, A., Melo, F., and Sugimoto, N. (2022). "Regulating the crypto ecosystem: the case of stablecoins and arrangements", *IMF Fintech Note* 2022/008, International Monetary Fund, Washington, DC. https://www.imf.org/en/Publications/fintech-notes/Issues/2022/09/26/Regulating-the-Crypto-Ecosystem-The-Case-of-Stablecoins-and-Arrangements-523724.

Baur, D.G., and Dimpfl, T. (2018). "Excess volatility as an impediment for a digital currency," *SSRN Electronic Journal*, March. https://ssrn.com/abstract=2949754.

Baur, D.G., Hong, K., and Lee, A.D. (2017). "Bitcoin: medium of exchange or speculative assets?" *SSRN Electronic Journal*, September. https://ssrn.com/abstract=2561183.

Boar, C., and Wehrli, A. (2021). "Ready, steady, go? Results of the third BIS survey on central bank digital currency," *BIS Papers from Bank for International Settlements*, n. 114. https://www.bis.org/publ/bppdf/bispap114.htm.

Bordo, M., and Levin, A.T. (2017). "Central bank digital currency and the future of monetary policy," *Economics Working Papers*, n. 17104, Hoover Institution, Stanford University. https://www.nber.org/papers/w23711.

Bower, J., and Christensen, C. (1995). "Disruptive technologies: catching the wave," *Harvard Business Review*, vol. 73, 43–53.

Boyer, R. (2015). *Economie politique des capitalismes* [*Political Economy of Capitalisms*], Paris: La Decouverte.

Caballero, R.J., Farhi, E., and Gourinchas, P.O. (2017). "The safe assets shortage conundrum," *Journal of Economic Perspective*, vol. 31, pp. 29–46.

Cabuk, U.C., and Silenzi, M. (2021). *Cryptocurrencies in Retail*, Consumer Adoption Report 2021, Amsterdam: CryptoReffils Labs.

Carney, M. (2018). "FSB Chair's letter to G20 finance ministers and central bank governors," March 13. https://www.fsb.org/2022/04/fsb-chairs-letter-to-g20-finance-ministers-and-central-bank-governors-april-2022/.

Cecchetti, S., and Schoenholtz, K. (2021). "Central bank digital currency: the battle for the soul of the financial system," VOX-EU—CEPR. https://voxeu.org/article/central-bank-digital-currency-battle-soul-financial-system.

Cesaratto, S., and Febrero, E. (2022). "Private and central bank digital currencies: a storm in a teacup? A Post-Keynesian appraisal," Working Paper, Universidad de Castiglia, 1/2022.
Chainanalysis (2022). *The 2022 Crypto Crime Report*, February. https://www.chainalysis.com/
Chen, H., and Siklos, P. (2022). "Central bank digital currency: a review and some macro-financial implications," *Journal of Financial Stability*, vol. 60. https://doi.org/10.1016/j.jfs.2022.100985.
Chiu, J., Davoodalhosseini, M., Jiang, J., and Zhu,Y. (2019). "Bank market power and central bank digital currency: theory and quantitative assessment," Bank of Canada Staff Working Paper, 2019-20, May.
Chokor, A., and Alfieri, E. (2021). "Long and-short-term impacts of regulation in the cryptocurrency market," *Quarterly Review of Economics and Finance*, vol. 81, pp. 157–173.
Claeys, G., Demertzis, M., and Efstathiou, K. (2018). "Cryptocurrencies and monetary policy," *Policy Contribution*, n. 10, June. https://www.bruegel.org/sites/default/files/wp_attachments/PC-10_2018_2.pdf.
Coincub (2022). "Coincub annual crypto tax ranking 2022." https://coincub.com/ranking/coincub-annual-crypto-tax-ranking-2022/.
Corbet, S., Lucey, B., and Yarovaya, L. (2018). "Datestamping the Bitcoin and Ethereum bubbles," *Finance Research Letters*, vol. 26, pp. 81–88.
Doria, L. (2020). "The cybernetic ethos of cryptocurrencies," *PArtecipazione & COnflitto*, vol. 13, n. 1, pp. 384–408.
Dow, S. (2017). "Central banking in the twenty-first century," *Cambridge Journal of Economics* 41, no. 6: 1539–1557. doi:10.1093/cje/bex051.
European Central Bank (2015). *Virtual Currency Schemes—A Further Analysis*, February. https://www.ecb.europa.eu/pub/pdf/other/virtualcurrencyschemesen.pdf.
Europol (2021). *Cryptocurrencies: Tracing the Evolution of Criminal Finances*, Europol Spotlight Report series, Luxembourg: Publications Office of the European Union.
Fama, M., Fumagalli, A., and Lucarelli, S. (2019). "Cryptocurrencies, monetary policy, and new forms of monetary sovereignty," *International Journal of Political Economy*, vol. 48(2), pp. 174–194.
Fama, M., Lucarelli, S., and Orzi, R. (2020). "Rethinking money, rebuilding communities: a multidimensional analysis of crypto and complementary currencies," *PArtecipazione & COnflitto*, vol. 13(1), pp. 337–359.
Fama, M., and Musolino, E. (2020). "Complementary currencies as a socio-technical innovation. evidence from a local clearing union in Italy," *PArtecipazione & COnflitto*, vol. 13(1), pp. 462–486.
Fantacci, L. (2019). "Cryptocurrencies and the denationalization of money," *International Journal of Political Economy*, vol. 48(2), pp. 105–126.
Fantacci, L., and Gobbi, L. (2021). "Stablecoins, central bank digital currencies and US dollar hegemony: the geopolitical stake of innovations in money and payments," *Accounting, Economics, and Law: A Convivium*. https://doi.org/10.1515/ael-2020-0053.
Fernandes-Villaverde, J., and Sanches, D.R. (2018). "On the economics of digital currencies," Working Papers 18-7, Federal Reserve Bank of Philadelphia.
Friedman, M. (1969). *The Optimum Quantity of Money and Other Essays*, Chicago, IL: Aldine Press.
Financial Stability Board (2020). *Regulation, Supervision and Oversight of "Global Stablecoins" Arrangements*.
Fumagalli, A., and Lucarelli, S. (2011). "A financialized monetary economy of production," *International Journal of Political Economy*, vol. 40(1), pp. 48–68.
G7 Working Group on Stablecoins (2019). *Investigating the Impact of Global Stablecoins*, Joint group of BIS, CPMI, IMF, and G7. https://www.bis.org/cpmi/publ/d187.pdf.

Gaffeo, E., Gobbi, L., and Molinari, M. (2019). "The economics of netting in financial networks," *Journal of Economic Interaction and Coordination*, Society for Economic Science with Heterogeneous Interacting Agents, vol. 14(3), pp. 595–622.

Gai, P., and Kapadia, S. (2010). "Contagion in financial networks," Bank of England working papers 383, Bank of England.

Golec, P., and Perotti, E. (2017). "Safe asset: a review," ECB Working Paper, n. 2035. https://www.ecb.europa.eu/pub/pdf/scpwps/ecbwp2035.en.pdf.

Gorton, G.B., Lewellen, S., and Metrick, A. (2012). "The safe-asset share," *American Economic Review*, vol. 101, pp. 104–105.

Gorton, G.B., and Zhang J. (2021). "Taming wildcat stablecoins," *University of Chicago Law Review*, 90, 909–971.

Graziani, A. (2003). *The Monetary Theory of Production*, Cambridge: Cambridge University Press.

Hammond, S., and Ehret, T. (2022). *Cryptocurrency Regulations by Country*, Thomson Reuters. https://www.thomsonreuters.com/en-us/posts/wp-content/uploads/sites/20/2022/04/Cryptos-Report-Compendium-2022.pdf.

Hayek, F. (1976). *Denationalisation of Money: An Analysis of the Theory and Practice of Concurrent Currencies*, Hobart Paper Special 70, London: Institute of Economic Affairs.

Himanen, P. (2001). *The Hacker Ethic and the Spirit of Information Age*, London: Martin Secker & Warburg.

Huber, T.A., and Sornette, D. (2022). "Boom, bust, and Bitcoin: Bitcoin-bubbles as innovation accelerators," *Journal of Economic Issues*, vol. 56(1), pp. 113–136.

Ingham, G.K. (2014). *The Nature of Money*, Cambridge: Polity Press.

Keister, T., and Sanches, D.R. (2021). "Should central banks issue digital currency?,". Working Papers, n. 21-37, Federal Reserve Bank of Philadelphia. https://www.philadelphiafed.org/-/media/frbp/assets/working-papers/2021/wp21-37.pdf.

Khaosan, V. (2018). "What is a Bitcoin whale?" https://www.ccn.com/bitcoin-whale/.

Kharif, O. (2018). "Bitcoin's use in commerce keeps falling even as volatility eases," *Bloomberg Europe Edition*, August 18. https://www.bloomberg.com/news/articles/2018-08 01/bitcoin s use in commerce-keeps-falling-even-as-volatility-eases.

Krishnamurthy, A., and Vissing-Jorgensen, A. (2012). "The aggregate demand for treasury debt," *Journal of Political Economy*, vol. 120(2), pp. 233–267.

Liu, Y., and Tsyvinski, A. (2021). "Risks and returns of cryptocurrency," *Review of Financial Studies*, vol. 34(6), pp. 2689–2727.

Makarov, I., and Schoar, A. (2021). "Blockchain analysis of the Bitcoin market," NBER Working Paper, n. 29396, October. http://www.nber.org/papers/w29396.

Malherbe, L., Montalban, M., Bédu, N., and Granier, C. (2019). "Cryptocurrencies and blockchain: opportunities and limits of a new monetary regime," *International Journal of Political Economy*, vol. 48(2), pp. 127–152.

Mancini Griffoli, T., Sun, T., and Yoshinaga, A. (2022). "Behind the scenes of central bank digital currency: emerging trends, insights, and policy lessons," *FinTech Notes*, n. 2022/004. https://www.imf.org/en/Publications/fintech-notes/Issues/2022/02/07/Behind-the-Scenes-of-Central-Bank-Digital-Currency-512174.

May, T. (1994). *The Cyphernomicon*, originally appeared in Cypherpunks electronic mailing list, September 10. https://nakamotoinstitute.org/static/docs/cyphernomicon.txt.

McLeay, M., Radia, A., and Thomas, R. (2014). "Money in the modern economy: an introduction," *Quarterly Bulletin*, 2014 Q1, Bank of England.

Meaning, J., Dyson, B., Barker, J., and Clayton, E. (2018). "Broadening narrow money: monetary policy with a Central Bank digital currency," Staff Working Paper, n. 724, Bank of England. https://www.ijcb.org/journal/ijcb21q2a1.pdf

Mizrach, B. (2023). "Stablecoins: survivorship, transactions costs and exchange microstructure," February 17. Available at SSRN: https://ssrn.com/abstract=3835219 or http://dx.doi.org/10.2139/ssrn.3835219.

Nakamoto, S. (2008). *Bitcoin: A Peer-to-Peer Electronic Cash System.* https://bitcoin.org/bitcoin.pdf.

Nier, E., Yang, J., Yorulmazer, T., and Alentorn, A. (2007). "Network models and financial stability," *Journal of Economic Dynamics and Control*, vol. 31, 2033–2060.

Reyes, R., and Tenero, S. (2022). "Helicopter money: what is it and what does it do?," CEPR Discussion Paper 17180.

Roio, "Jaromil" D. (2013). *Bitcoin. The End of the Taboo on Money*, April. https://files.dyne.org/readers/Bitcoin_end_of_taboo_on_money.pdf.

Sauce, L. (2022). "The unintended consequences of the regulation of cryptocurrencies," *Cambridge Journal of Economics*, vol. 46, pp. 57–71.

Savona, P. (2021). "Lineamenti teorici e pratici di un'economia con le cryptocurrency," *Lectio Magistralis*, Dipartimento di Scienze Economiche e Aziendali, Università di Cagliari, Ottobre 1. https://www.consob.it/web/consob/novita/-/asset_publisher/xMXdfdeSuZFj/content/lectio-magistralis-savona-su-cryptocurrency-1-ottobre-2021-/10194.

Schwarcz, S.L. (2022). "Regulating digital currencies: towards an analytical framework," *Boston University Law Review*, vol. 102, pp. 1037–1081.

Simmel, G. (1978 [1907]), *The Philosophy of Money*, London: Routledge.

Soderberg, G., Bechara, M., Bossu, W., Che, N., Davidovic, N., Kiff, J., Lukonga, I., Griffoli Mancini, T., Sun, T., and Yoshinaga, A. (2022). "Behind the scenes of central bank digital currency: emerging trends, insights, and policy lessons," *FinTech Notes*, n. 2022/004. https://www.imf.org/en/Publications/fintech-notes/Issues/2022/02/07/Behind-the-Scenes-of-Central-Bank-Digital-Currency-512174.

Sveriges Riksbank (2022). "An overview of fintech and cryptoassets," Staff memo, May. https://www.riksbank.se/en-gb/press-and-published/publications/staff-memos/an-overview-of-fintech-and-crytoassets/

Swartz, L. (2018). "What was Bitcoin, what will it be? The techno-economic imaginaries of a new money technology," *Cultural Studies*, vol. 32, n. 4, pp. 623–650.

Tamborini, R. (2021). *Economia e finanza*, Milano: Wolters Kluwer.

Temperini, J., D'Ippoliti, C., and Gobbi, L. (2022). "A new tool for economic policy: central bank digital currencies," Paper presented at the 19th Annual Conference of the Italian Association for the History of Political Economy (STOREP), May 27, Università della Tuscia.

5. Central bank digital currencies in emerging economies: practical considerations[1]

Gordon Clarke and Emir Hrnjic

INTRODUCTION

Digital money has been around ever since the records of deposits and loans in bank accounts became computerized in the 1970s, but it took another 20 years for customers to be able to manage their own banking from their own personal computers via internet applications.

In 2001, Smart Money in the Philippines was the first service to enable account-to-account transfers initiated via mobile phones. This concept of a payment system driven by a mobile network operator collaborating with a small number of banks quickly spread to the African continent, where Vodafone launched the very successful M-Pesa service in Kenya, which met a consumer need for fast fund transfers across a large geographic area.[2] Banks soon began to collaborate on building their own mobile payment systems. By the time of the financial crisis, the idea of central banks implementing financial market infrastructures for instant payments was gaining traction. Note that these systems transfer commercial bank money—money in commercial banks' accounts that belongs to the customer—and not central bank money.

The global financial crisis of 2007–2008 triggered a deep recession and severely undermined trust in the banking system. At the height of the crisis in January 2009, a private digital currency called Bitcoin was launched, triggering a revolution in private digital money. Moreover, Bitcoin introduced the innovative blockchain technology that enabled direct transfer of bitcoins between two participants without a trusted intermediary.

As massive amounts of money poured into the crypto and digital asset markets, central banks recognized that privately issued currencies could potentially undermine the stability of sovereign currencies, especially in countries with high inflation and unstable banking systems. After realizing that they can no longer stand on the sidelines, central banks have started exploring the potential for central bank digital currencies (CBDCs).

In this chapter, we review some of the developments in CBDCs and analyze objectives and practical considerations of CBDCs in emerging economies. While a Bank for International Settlements (BIS) paper (Chen et al. 2022) provides an extensive survey of CBDCs in emerging economies,[3] we confine our discussion to situations with which we have more direct familiarity. Our general view is that there is still significant reluctance to commit to large-scale national deployment of CBDCs even among countries with the most pressing motives, which are the emerging economies.

DIVERGENCE BETWEEN DEVELOPED AND EMERGING ECONOMIES

A study by the BIS[4] conducted at the end of 2021 surveyed 25 central banks in advanced economies (AEs) and 56 central banks in emerging markets and developing economies (EMDEs). The study reported that 90 percent of the central banks surveyed have carried out serious studies of the potential benefits of CBDCs, while many have conducted practical experiments, proof of concept exercises, and pilot projects.

An Atlantic Council survey in May 2022 reported that 105 countries, representing over 95 percent of global gross domestic product (GDP), are exploring a CBDC, while 50 countries are in an advanced phase of exploration. As a comparison, only 35 countries were considering a CBDC in May 2020.[5] BIS reports have reviewed the situation for Latin American, Caribbean,[6] and African[7] central banks. The overall view is that central banks remain cautious, and that country-specific factors drive the approach to CBDCs.

At the time of writing this chapter in June 2023, only six countries have launched CBDCs, and all of them have a GDP per capita below US$30 000 (at purchasing power parity, PPP). These countries have a low take-up, with the exception of the digital yuan in China.

The motivation for CBDC development varies considerably across central banks. While the advanced economies worry about payment efficiencies, payment safety, and financial stability, emerging economies give greater weight to financial inclusion and monetary policy implementation. Emerging economies are also concerned about reduction in cash usage, which in more advanced nations has been achieved by the implementation of instant payment systems (IPSs) and widespread use of cards which have largely migrated to contactless protocols during the pandemic.

The different approaches and expectations of various countries were on display at a CBDC Conference in Frankfurt in August 2022, where central bank officials of 12 countries provided a description of CBDC pilot or live projects.[8] The overall impression among conference participants is that the developed economies are considering CBDCs only as a contingency measure, should the demand arise in the future.

For example, the Monetary Authority of Singapore (MAS) was among the first central banks to conduct detailed technical studies on cryptocurrencies with Project Ubin, starting in 2016, which explored domestic and cross-border clearing and settlement on blockchain.[9] However, in a Parliamentary answer in March 2022, Lawrence Wong, then Deputy chairman of MAS and Minister for Finance, stated that MAS believes "there is no pressing need for issuance of a CBDC because financial inclusion is not a significant problem in Singapore, electronic payments in Singapore are already pervasive, seamless, fast and cheap, and cross-border links of Real-time Payment Systems are becoming available."[10]

Similarly, in the United Kingdom (UK), where the Bank of England has conducted major studies involving widely distributed consultation documents, little enthusiasm exists among politicians or the public. Concerns focus on questions about financial stability, and the risk that the Bank of England could find itself embroiled in controversies regarding anonymity and privacy. The conclusion in a House of Lords debate was that the risks seem currently to outweigh the benefits, and any potential launch would not happen in the short term.

While developed countries' experimentation in CBDCs represent insurance against future risks, there are potential drivers that could push them to go forward with CBDCs. First, the Chinese digital yuan may begin to gain significant strength in international trade, which may force the United States (US) or the European Union to deploy a CBDC for similar purposes. Second, a strong increase in the use of private cryptocurrency may affect monetary sovereignty. Finally, a strong case may exist for CBDCs to reduce costs and increase speed and efficiency in cross-border payments, which is a current aim of G20 policy.

Hence, the focus of developed economies has shifted to cross-border payments, improvement of trade finance processes, and facilitation of international supply chains. For example, Project Dunbar, led by the BIS Innovation Hub in Singapore in a consortium with central banks from Australia, Malaysia, Singapore, and South Africa has explored how multiple CBDCs linked via a common platform could enable cheaper, faster, and safer cross-border payments.[11] A report based on another BIS initiative known as Project mBridge, with over 20 commercial banks as well as the central banks of Thailand, Hong Kong, China, and the UAE, showed technical success in live transfer of several million US dollars (USD).[12]

In contrast, emerging economies have different ambitions and problems which governmental officials believe CBDCs could help to solve, such as financial inclusion, cash reduction, and monetary policy implementation. Sixty-five percent of the banks surveyed by the BIS at the end of 2021, mainly from emerging economies, reported that they would launch a retail CBDC in the short to medium term.[13] Emerging economies have expressed considerable interest in the use of stablecoins as well, partly to improve remittance processes and to encourage local FinTech development. Central banks seem to prefer single-currency-backed stablecoins as the most favorable solution, followed by multi-currency-backed stablecoins, and finally, commodity-backed stablecoins. Not surprisingly, central banks are extremely wary of stablecoins backed by cryptoassets or algorithmically controlled coins, due to the numerous scandals in that space.

Emerging economies have led the way in CBDC issuance. In fact, representatives from emerging markets at the Frankfurt CBDC Conference identified common factors for a successful CBDC:

- Executive sponsorship at a high level in the central bank.
- Clear and measurable objectives.

- Early involvement of stakeholders.
- Adoption programs to assure public acceptance.
- Focus on policy (before technology).
- Need for trade-offs in deploying blockchain solutions.
- A balance between privacy and anonymity.

In contrast to developed economies, emerging economies focused on solving immediate issues such as financial inclusion, cash reduction, and improved transmission of monetary policy to the market. At the same time, most emerging markets do not consider cross-border trade finance, international supply chain facilitation, and securities industry applications as priority issues (other than to eliminate the costs and inconvenience of using intermediary currencies such as the US dollar in cross-border payment).

Even though central bank officials have widely experimented with and learned a great deal about CBDCs over the past several years, rolling out national programs remains a challenge, due to the difficulty of convincing the banks, customers, and governments, especially in countries where a strong instant payment system (IPS) has already reduced cash usage and encouraged financial inclusion. Even in China, with the most successful CBDC pilot program so far, a full national launch plan has yet to be published.

The developed nations worry about the potential disruption to the financial system caused by the rapid growth of the crypto asset markets and the disastrous failures that are endemic in poorly regulated industries. Many stablecoin issuers, for example, acting like unregulated banks, lend their incoming funds to crypto ventures, so that an instability in one part of the market can start a vicious cycle and lead to crashes in other parts, as in the recent FTX collapse.[14]

For example, the US Federal Reserve has conducted many research projects, and the current US administration has issued an executive order[15] to further study the regulation of digital assets and consider whether CBDC issue is desirable in the longer term. The European Central Bank (ECB) has conducted a 24-month project on retail CBDC, and has published various working papers analyzing privacy issues. The overall view is that risks outweigh benefits, and a potential launch would not happen in the short term.

In countries where instant payment systems have been implemented by central banks or bank consortia, there has generally been an improvement in financial inclusion, but this effect is weaker than a government focus on delivering salaries, pensions, and welfare benefits to bank accounts. Basic bank accounts to provide the receiving facilities for these kinds of payments are not very profitable for the banks, but have been mandated in some jurisdictions, and this has helped to kick-start a wider use of bank finance by households, which has spurred development and investment.[16] Commercial bank campaigns to build branches and establish agency arrangements, and specific government initiatives on financial literacy, have also been used to tackle financial inclusion. CBDCs, on the other hand, represent specific central bank initiatives, in which the central bank assumes the liabilities and much of the cost. It therefore puts the central bank, as a government agency, at the heart of the financial inclusion issue.

For example, a recent UK aid project in Nepal, the Sakchyam Access to Finance for the Poor Programme, sought to open access to finance to a range of communities, especially in the west of the country. The program was focussed on encouraging microfinance activity in rural communities without banking presence by bringing laptop-based mobile connectivity to these communities. The results exceeded expectations.[17]

Cash reduction is another motivator for CBDCs in emerging markets, especially due to the unfavorable economics of an IPS in smaller countries with a low level of financial inclusion. Reduction in cash usage can deliver lower cash servicing costs, reduced security risks, reduction in the "grey market," and potential reduction in cash-based corruption. For example, Singapore Senior Minister Tharman Shanmugaratnam estimated that the cost of processing cash is about S$2 billion a year in Singapore.[18] The ECB estimated that the total cost of cash in Europe is 1 percent of GDP,[19] while the annual cost of cash in the US is estimated at $200 billion.[20] Cash reduction and cost savings associated with management of cash are especially important for island nations, where the movement of cash is logistically difficult and expensive.

The benefits of CBDCs in helping to gather better monetary data, leading to the potential for better monetary policy decisions and much faster transmission of monetary policy to the market, have yet to be empirically supported, as existing CBDCs have yet to approach the volume of usage that would enable a meaningful test of those objectives. However, the theory is sound, and directed injections of cash into parts of the economy would be a much faster tool than central bank adjustments to interest rates, which can take up to four quarters to trickle down into the real economy. A research study by the Bank of England concluded that a CBDC might "strengthen the monetary transmission mechanism" to the real economy.[21]

The ability to obtain better monetary data in many smaller nations is valuable and useful for the respective central banks to deliver monetary policy, manage cash and interest rates, and to direct funds to particular territories in times of crisis. Using a CBDC to focus cash support on particular regions or sectors in need could be of value to all the emerging economies. In general, emerging economies have a much stronger case for CBDC deployment, since developed countries have more methods of controlling cash supply and may not be as highly incentivized to launch a radically new financial instrument for such a purpose. As with mobile money, we may find emerging economies in the lead on CBDCs in order to meet their specific market needs, but they will be taking the bigger risks.

OBJECTIVES OF EMERGING ECONOMIES

The main CBDC objectives for emerging economies include financial inclusion, better monetary policy management, as well as reduction in cash, grey market, and corruption. However, where the economics of instant payment systems are unfavorable, as in most small economies, improving the efficiency of the payment system at retail level may be a driver.[22]

Managing incoming and outgoing money flows is another objective for many emerging countries, especially those whose economies are dependent on tourism (for example, Fiji and the Maldives) or those with a large diaspora resulting in a large inflow of funds (for example, the Philippines and Bangladesh); or more developed nations with a large outflow of funds from foreign workers (for example, the UAE and Saudi Arabia).

Incoming remittances and tourism-based revenues are generally denominated in US dollars or other hard currencies, which tends to create dollarization risks. Managing down dollarization was a major objective for Cambodia, for example, in launching the Bakong CBDC. Incoming remittances could potentially be managed using a global stablecoin as the remittance currency, with an automatic conversion of the stablecoin into domestic currency using a smart wallet. This approach has already been explored in several countries.

Several countries have also considered enabling the use of a major CBDC onshore by tourists. This approach would not be much different from allowing the use of AliPay and WeChat Pay by Chinese tourists when in foreign countries, which is widely permitted in tourist economies. The objective would be to encourage mass tourism from the burgeoning middle class from countries such as China and India, and potentially the USA and the euro zone, enabling tourists to spend freely in their tourist destination without having the inconvenience and cost of currency exchange. We could envisage smaller nations wishing to encourage tourism by having a means for retailers to acquire these CBDCs, with a central bank or commercial bank promise to redeem the CBDCs for domestic currency. That would both limit dollarization and encourage tourism by removing the cost of exchanging money; an attractive proposition for small nations such as the Bahamas, the Maldives, and Fiji.

Limiting dollarization to protect monetary sovereignty is closely linked to incoming remittances and funds from tourism. This concept is certainly of importance in countries with high tourism levels such as the Maldives, the Bahamas, and Fiji. As tourism brings in foreign currency, an appropriately deployed CBDC could curb dollarization and preserve monetary sovereignty, especially if seen as a better, less expensive, and more convenient method of payment by tourists.

Other objectives that have been described as motivators in emerging economies include reducing costs of currency distribution, reducing financial crime, improving cross-border settlement methods, inclusivity, increasing competition and efficiency in payments, programmability of money, and technical experimentation. While developed countries focus on trade payment and international supply chains, emerging economies focus on incoming remittances. The ability to achieve inexpensive and real-time cross-border transfers signifies an important issue for emerging economies such as the Bahamas, Cambodia, and Nigeria.

A common cross-border CBDC platform, moreover, would help with one of the major trade problems for emerging economies: the use of the US dollar in trade. It is difficult for the banks of small countries to obtain correspondent bank relationships to manage transfer of US dollars, especially since the spate of "de-risking" by major international banks initiated because of the 2008 financial crisis. Project mBridge explored the use of multiple CBDCs across a common platform, which could provide a way for emerging economies to save substantial costs not only in exchange transactions but also in the use of intermediaries to assist in trade payments.[23]

Technical experimentation with innovative payment architectures is of importance to many of the emerging market countries experimenting with CBDCs, as identified in the BIS study and our experiences with smaller nations such as the Maldives, Fiji, the Bahamas, Haiti, and Cambodia. None of these countries want to be left behind as the CBDC landscape develops, nor does any central bank wish to see their sovereign currency compromised by increased use of private currencies for domestic payment, which remains a significant threat.[24]

CBDC VERSUS CASH VERSUS INSTANT PAYMENT SYSTEMS

Cash has been around for a long time, and the best option for an offline monetary instrument is still cash. Even though there has long been a trend towards reduced use of cash, the cashless society may not be a realistic aim. In fact, Sweden experienced substantial push-back by consumers after the amount of cash in circulation fell to 40 percent of its traditional level.

Furthermore, technology is never foolproof: handsets malfunction, software fails, telecoms can be patchy. Additionally, prolonged electricity outages have occurred even in major cities such as New York and Auckland. We witness very limited take-up of all currently available CBDCs (with the exception of China) and less than clear domination over cash even by highly successful instant payment systems such as SWISH in Sweden and PromptPay in Thailand. While the aim of cash reduction has already been (partially) achieved in many developed countries, most emerging economies still face the problems of low financial inclusion and predominant usage of cash for day-to-day transactions.

High cash usage is problematic because cash has security problems and cash management is expensive for financial institutions and retailers. The public, on the other hand, may view it differently. For example, recent ECB surveys have shown that privacy is one of the biggest issues holding back general adoption of digital payment.[25] Cash is anonymous.

In poorer economies, however, such as Brazil, people seem more willing to sacrifice an amount of privacy in order to gain convenience and security.[26] In general, trust in banks is not high, but ordinary people in some poorer countries may place their trust in the central bank, since the central bank typically keeps the commercial banks under control and gets involved with community projects.[27] Hence, people in these places may have higher confidence in a CBDC operated by the central bank than in instant payment systems run by the commercial banks.

The "grey economy" constitutes a further concern of many emerging market governments. Central banks are considered responsible for organizing the payment systems in such a way as to encourage cash reduction. "Grey economy" activity can greatly distort the financial statistics of countries, to the extent that governments may not observe much of the actual economic activity. It is not just a matter of tax collection, or of any form of surveillance, but of levelling the playing field for everyone, so that everyone contributes fairly to the public good, as well as receives their fair share of the benefits. This requires that the distribution of tax receipts be rigorously managed, which is difficult to achieve in emerging economies with less developed institutions. Theoretically, a blockchain-based CBDC performing a major role in currency management can get around some of the issues of trust in the financial systems and government actions.

It is important to note that many of the CBDC objectives for emerging economies that we have discussed, notably cash-related ones, can be met by a IPS using conventional financial market infrastructure (FMI) technology:

- Better financial inclusion.
- Reduction of the grey economy.
- Cash-like convenience for users.
- Reduction of the security risks of carrying cash.
- Prevention of counterfeiting.
- Reduced cash payment fraud and corruption.
- Lower cost of currency issue.
- Lower cash management cost.

However, commercial banks in small emerging economies may not consider instant payment systems as a profitable investment opportunity, as their main benefit is the savings from handling less cash. The cost of the application software and infrastructure is largely fixed, but that fixed cost has to be defrayed over a smaller number of users and transactions. Since most existing instant payment systems are free to consumers, the main benefits come from savings for the banks, and savings for the central bank in terms of issuing and managing the cash supply (which are smaller in smaller markets).

While it is by no means clear that implementing a CBDC is less expensive than implementing an IPS, the central banks have to provide features in CBDC service which a commercial IPS can sidestep, notably offline working to assure inclusivity. Broadly, more of the cost falls on the central bank and less on the commercial banks. Moreover, a CBDC service would likely be subsidized as a major part of national infrastructure, whereas commercial banking infrastructure can lead to an acrimonious battle between commercial banks and central banks about the cost-sharing arrangements.

As central banks must carry the financial burden of national CBDC services, they will be regarded as a piece of vital financial infrastructure and encourage less developed countries to transition towards a digital economy. Inclusiveness remains an issue, since it is acceptable for an instant payment system run by commercial banks to be available for online users only, but a CBDC system must extend to the whole society, including offline access due to spotty telecom coverage and significant electricity outages.

Concerning end users, there are two major differences between an instant payment system and a CDBC system: namely the offline use of CBDC to cope with electricity and weaknesses in telecommunications, as well as reduced risk of default of central banks compared to commercial banks. A CBDC is central bank money and therefore any failures or attacks that result in customer losses would be reimbursable as a claim on the central bank. This dynamic is certainly not the case with commercial bank failures.

The likely outcome is that IPSs and CBDCs will be competing, and in practice, many consumers may not even be aware of the difference between central bank money and commercial bank money.

STRATEGIC CHOICES FOR CBDC

Central banks in emerging markets often have less control over their constituency of commercial banks than those in more developed countries, which makes it more difficult to maintain control over a complex system implementation. Any CBDC project carries a number of strategic choices. The first dilemma is whether to focus on wholesale or retail CBDC (or both). While wholesale CBDCs present less risks than retail CBDCs, since far fewer parties are involved and the impact on financial stability can be readily controlled, many of the important benefits, such as better monetary usage data, will only arise when a CBDC is widely used by the public. The 2021 BIS survey reported that most of the central banks are particularly interested in retail CBDCs.[28] Some consider both retail and wholesale CBDCs, while others are only looking into wholesale ones, mainly for cross-border or securities settlement purposes. A BIS study in 2020 argued that "work on retail CBDCs is more advanced where the informal economy is larger,"[29] and noted that emerging economies tended to focus on retail CBDC activity, which is consistent with financial inclusion and cash reduction objectives.[30]

Furthermore, central banks need to decide between token-based and account-based solutions. While a token-based solution is more like cash and easier to promote with the public as it allows a higher level of anonymity, an account-based solution is easier to implement and can use similar delivery channels to a domestic instant payment system. Constant tension occurs between the desire for full anonymity and money laundering risk managed by the use of balance limits and velocity limits. In general, the public prefers anonymity,[31] but central banks wish to obtain information from the CBDC system and detect criminal behavior. The ability to gain aggregate information without compromising privacy creates difficult design decisions. This means that there must be an agreed privacy framework to ensure that all parties get what they need, and the acceptability of the privacy framework is likely to be a major factor in the adoption of CBDCs.

Finally, central banks have to decide on CBDC designs, ideally in consultation with stakeholders. Since it is vital that central banks do not appear to be disintermediating their own constituency of licensed banks and PSPs, they prefer two-tier designs whereby the central bank acts as digital currency issuer (and redeemer), and the commercial banks and PSPs act as distributors to the public. No central bank, in our experience, would have any intention of centralizing CBDC customer accounts at the same central bank. In effect, this centralization results in central bank issued currency tokens being held in e-wallet accounts managed by the commercial banks, so that the practical distinction between tokens and accounts ceases to be meaningful. Personally identifiable information (PII) will remain at the commercial bank level as it does now, and central banks will track the activity of the tokens, not individual customer accounts.

RISKS TO CENTRAL BANKS AND THE INDUSTRY

Can a CBDC be sufficiently easy to use and sufficiently attractive that the balance of benefits creates a strong incentive for people to migrate away from cash and other means of payment? Successful instant payment systems such as PayNow in Singapore and PromptPay in Thailand were able to sign up a large number of users via the banks, but it took four to five years to reach the expected levels of usage. If a CBDC cannot generate a critical mass of adoption, it cannot meet its objectives. Acceptance by stakeholders and the public is crucial. Otherwise, private cryptocurrencies (despite their risks) will continue to attract users in countries with weak currencies and undermine them further.

Developed and emerging countries tend to have similar risks of CBDCs, but the benefits vary according to national objectives. The risks to the central bank issuer include the fact that no CBDC has become widely used enough to reveal the impact on financial stability and monetary stability. Therefore, it is important for central banks to experiment with the new technologies to prepare for issue, should global cryptocurrencies become widely used or should a dominant CBDC emerge in global trade finance.

The privacy issue is crucial. Central banks must be careful not to be drawn into controversial debates on privacy and state surveillance. In fact, most central banks are not keen to engage in massive surveillance operations. The aim will generally be to keep PII out of sight of the central bank. A clear privacy framework will need to be set for each public launch of a CBDC. This step goes hand in hand with an explicit assurance that the central bank is not trying to disintermediate the commercial banks in any way, which would damage trust in the regulator. Privacy and trust seem to represent major reasons for the lack of enthusiasm for CBDCs, as mentioned above.

As we have seen, one of the potential advantages of a CBDC over instant payment systems is that the central banks will be under pressure to make it fully inclusive, while safeguarding the use of the currency against the risks of telecoms and electricity outages.

There is a significant risk that holding CBDC in e-wallets will be seen as competing with commercial banks' deposits, even if CBDC e-wallets are offered by commercial banks. This creates the risk that banks will lose a proportion of the funds they traditionally used to leverage and support their credit businesses. This scenario will be more of a problem in emerging economies, where banks tend to be more dependent on deposits for funding as they have limited access to deep and broad capital markets. The big international banks can manage a shift from M1 to M0 money more easily than less capitalized local banks.

The effect of a CBDC on the commercial banking sector is important to understand. Central banks recognize that the balance between M0 and M1 may change markedly as a result of CBDC introduction. Furthermore, runs on bank deposits in times of economic stress could happen in either direction—to or from CBDC—including consumers dumping digital currency if there is a differential in interest rates with physical currency bank deposits. This scenario would create financial instability which could undermine public trust in the CBDC.

From the central banks' point of view security risks in central systems—the minting and management systems for digital currency—are generally manageable, as in FMIs. The majority of frauds and cyberattacks are perpetrated on payment origination systems at commercial banks, merchants, and businesses since they are much easier targets than well-protected central bank systems. However, central bank security monitoring facilities in emerging markets are generally less sophisticated than those in developed countries, and thus more likely to be targeted.

The commercial banks will need to play their part in a CBDC ecosystem, but the effect on existing businesses, especially domestic transfers, cross-border remittance providers, and money changers could be more severe. Hence, financial sector and government stakeholders must be included at an early stage in a national CBDC project. The Saudi Arabian central bank, SAMA, for example, has involved commercial banks from the very beginning. Commercial banks are keen to hear about the results of experimentation by central banks, and wish to take part in them wherever possible. Even if a CBDC is eventually not launched, experimentation can help commercial banks to explore various beneficial applications of blockchain databases and other new technologies for their own purposes.

Regulators may prefer to place boundaries on FinTech companies and aspiring players' products in the financial markets. Hence, a "sandbox" regime is useful to help companies and regulators understand one another and refine the rules. Sandbox experimentation may lead to legal changes, further opportunities for FinTech development, and refinement of economic stimulation. Even for CBDC development itself, a regulatory sandbox approach with clear guidelines can help innovators to bring beneficial products to market, while helping the regulators and the innovators to understand each other's needs.

But the most crucial element in the success of a retail CBDC is widespread adoption. Only when public education campaigns are run effectively (as in Brazil and

Singapore) does usage of digital payment become widespread enough for objectives to be met. Several current retail CBDC schemes are struggling to grow usage (for example, Nigeria and the Bahamas) and are initiating major marketing campaigns. It is not only education that matters, but also getting into place the enabling technologies such as standard QR (quick-response code) and contactless payments that use near-field communication (NFC) technology at point of sale and for peer-to-peer payments.

Central banks have to weigh the benefits and risks. For central banks in emerging economies, these issues must be balanced against urgent needs for financial inclusion and cash reduction. Hence, emerging market central banks may have to be prepared to take bigger risks to gain these benefits. For many countries, support from the international agencies is likely to be vital in providing the resources to commission suppliers, conduct proof-of-concept exercises, set up pilot trails, and eventually launch a CBDC.

MONETARY POLICY IMPLICATIONS

Enthusiasm seems lacking for the potential monetary policy transmission benefits of CBDCs, but all leaders of central banks are clear that they need to experiment with digitalization technologies to be ready for future market changes. As the world goes digital, these leaders recognize that they must fully understand the policy implications and the technologies involved.

The ability to manipulate the domestic short-term interest rate represents a central bank's main lever of power. Moreover, the bank can influence long-term interest rates by buying or selling long-term government bonds via quantitative easing and quantitative tightening.

The adoption of a CBDC (such as in the Bahamas) or a private cryptocurrency (such as in El Salvador with Bitcoin) could partially or fully replace physical fiat currencies and influence the ability of central banks to conduct monetary policy. While private cryptocurrencies in general do not function well as a medium of exchange due to their excessive volatility, stablecoins can alleviate this volatility to a large extent. Yet, privately issued stablecoins may have other issues (as seen in the notorious Luna Terra collapse) and may prevent the central bank from having proper control over the money supply. For example, the G7 working group on stablecoins opined that "stablecoins that reach global scale could pose challenges and risks to monetary policy."[32]

A dominant stablecoin could eventually replace some sovereign currencies, especially in countries with high inflation and an unstable banking system. According to a BIS report, cryptocurrencies could "rapidly establish a dominant position in global finance and pose a potential threat to competition, stability, and social welfare."[33] The result would be increased dollarization as well as fiat currency depreciation and inflation.

On the other hand, a CBDC could assist the conduct of monetary policy. A research study by the Bank of England concluded that a central bank digital currency might "strengthen the monetary transmission mechanism" to the real economy.[34] Hence, the currency could help target money supply and enable real-time access to data regarding money demand. Furthermore, interbank settlement systems for CBDC transactions would be fast and transparent; but that is also true of the fast-developing IPS in many countries.

Today, the main monetary policy tool available to a central bank is manipulation of the bank's own short-term interest rate, since it has a direct effect on commercial banks' funding costs and, as a result, bank lending rates. However, commercial bank deposit rates are not very responsive to central bank interest rate changes. A CBDC would potentially change this dynamic and make commercial banks' rates more responsive to policy rate changes. More specifically, a CBDC payment system under central bank control would enable the fine tuning of policy implementation via collection of sector or region-focussed currency usage data, and likely increase competition. In addition, competitive pressures would increase the sensitivity of deposit rates to central banks' interest rates.

In summary, CBDCs are likely to strengthen the transmission of monetary policy and help to target money supply into particular sectors or regions, while combating the risk of dominant private cryptocurrencies which could severely undermine the effect of monetary policy and stimulate high inflation. Hence, the central bank needs to be fully in control of the issue and use of digital currencies in its territory to avoid these problems.

A 2022 BIS report on CBDCs in emerging markets suggests that CBDCs should "seek to improve payment system efficiency and steer away from serving as a store of value to avoid the risk of disintermediation and major monetary policy implications."[35] This implies that there should not be an interest rate attached to CBDCs. Hence, they face another difficult design compromise: limiting potential monetary policy impact against the attractiveness of the instrument for public take-up.

Nevertheless, there could be some important uses of privately issued stablecoins for cross-border payments and for managing the dollarization risks of remittances. Their use would have to be subject to effective control by central bank regulators.

CONCLUSION

Revolutions are frequent in the world of payment systems. In the last 30 years, we have witnessed the introduction of real-time gross settlement (RTGS) between banks which eliminated systemic settlement risk, the introduction of mobile and instant payment systems providing immediate customer control over transfers, and the birth of cryptocurrencies and CBDCs. As smartphones become ubiquitous and e-commerce becomes the norm, we are entering a new phase in the history of money. Moreover, the digital asset markets are going mainstream with the potential to transform financial markets.

Unregulated private cryptocurrencies cannot fill this need reliably, and CBDCs are probably the best alternative as easy-to-use, safe, and efficient digital money. As developed countries hesitate to deploy them, the emerging economies have been venturing first.

The short-term balance of risk versus cost and benefit seems to not be the main issue for the emerging economies. Deployment and marketing of the official digital currency is considered necessary to kick-start various aspects of development held back by low financial inclusion and the costs and risks of physical cash. Another urgent consideration for some countries lies in combating the growing domestic use of cryptocurrencies which can erode monetary sovereignty.

We have yet to learn about the impact of CBDCs on financial stability or the potential for monetary policy improvements. Nor do we know whether CBDCs will benefit financial inclusion and cash reduction more effectively than instant payment systems have. We have learned, however, that the banking industry must be involved early to ensure that there will be an adequate degree of acceptance by stakeholders, and that adoption will not grow unless there is a public education campaign and good marketing by the banks and FinTechs.

It is still too early to say whether adoption rates will improve sufficiently for the existing public CBDC services to reach their objectives. Likewise, we have yet to learn whether it will be domestic retail CBDCs that become widespread, or whether the market will find itself restricted largely to wholesale and cross-border uses. As new CBDCs are launched and existing ones achieve higher adoption, researchers will soon have enough data to empirically examine various conjectures put forward in this chapter.

Developed nations carefully observe the emerging economies which have taken the risk of launching a public CBDC service, especially the degree of adoption, the effectiveness of the privacy and trust mechanisms, and the impact on monetary and financial stability. At the same time, emerging economies can benefit from the experience of the developed countries in deep and broad experimentation, including the area of cross-border payment, which may be the most promising area for the general use of CBDCs.

Open questions remain in many areas. Is it best to focus on wholesale or retail CBDCs? Are the monetary policy benefits and risks sufficiently understood? What are the benefits and risks for the commercial banks? Who will pay for CBDC initiatives in the long term? Are blockchain solutions necessary to achieve benefits from CBDCs? As with mobile payments, the emerging economies may well be the ones who chart the course.

NOTES

1. The authors would like to thank Mark Waters for outstanding research assistance.
2. Jacob (2016).
3. Chen et al. (2022).

4. Kosse and Mattei (2022).
5. Atlantic Council (n.d.).
6. Alfonso et al. (2022).
7. Alberola and Mattei (2022).
8. The CBDC Conference started last year and attracted a large number of central banks and speakers from major CBDC projects including the Bahamas, Brazil, France, Ghana, Israel, Jamaica, Japan, Kazakhstan, Nigeria, Sweden, Thailand, and Zambia
9. Monetary Authority of Singapore (2022a).
10. Monetary Authority of Singapore (2022b).
11. Bank for International Settlements (2022).
12. Bank for International Settlements (n.d.).
13. Kosse and Mattei (2022).
14. Huigsloot (2022).
15. White House (2022).
16. See, for example, the positive impact of financial inclusion on investment by individuals in China: Xu and Sun (2022).
17. Devex (n.d.).
18. Monetary Authority of Singapore (2018).
19. Schmiedel et al. (2012).
20. See, for example, Chakravorti and Mazzotta (2013).
21. Meaning et al. (2018).
22. Chen et al. (2022).
23. Bank for International Settlements (n.d.).
24. Chen et al. (2022).
25. ECB (2022).
26. Brazil—Finthropology survey from Frankfurt CBDC Conference, August 2022.
27. Bank of Ghana presentation at Frankfurt CBDC Conference, August 2022.
28. Kosse and Mattei (2022).
29. Ibid.: 1.
30. Auer et al. (2020).
31. See, for example, European Central Bank (2021).
32. G7 Working Group on Stablecoins (2019).
33. Arner et al. (2020).
34. Meaning et al. (2018).
35. Chen et al. (2022: 15).

REFERENCES

Alberola, Enrique, and Ilaria Mattei (2022), "Central Bank Digital Currencies in Africa," BIS Paper, No 128, November, https://www.bis.org/publ/bppdf/bispap128.pdf.

Alfonso, Viviana, Steven Kamin, and Fabrizio Zampoll (2022), "Central Bank Digital Currencies (CBDCs) in Latin America and the Caribbean," BIS paper, No 989, January, https://www.bis.org/publ/work989.pdf.

Arner, Douglas, Raphael Auer, and Jon Frost (2020), "Stablecoins: Risks, Potential and Regulation," BIS Working Papers, No 905, Monetary and Economic Department, November, https://www.bis.org/publ/work905.pdf.

Atlantic Council (n.d.), "Central Bank Digital Currency Tracker," https://www.atlanticcouncil.org/cbdctracker/, accessed December 11, 2022.
Auer, Raphael, Giulio Cornelli, and Jon Frost (2020), "Rise of the central bank digital currencies: drivers, approaches and technologies," BIS Paper, No 880, August, https://www.bis.org/publ/work880.pdf.
Bank for International Settlements (n.d.), "Project mBridge: Connecting Economies Through CBDC," https://www.bis.org/about/bisih/topics/cbdc/mcbdc_bridge.htm, accessed December 11, 2022.
Bank for International Settlements (2022), "BIS Innovation Hub and Central Banks of Australia, Malaysia, Singapore and South Africa Develop Experimental Multi-CBDC Platform for International Settlements," https://www.bis.org/press/p220322.htm, accessed December 11, 2022.
Chakravorti, Bhaskar, and Benjamin D. Mazzotta (2013), "The Cost of Cash in the United States," Institute for Business in the Global Context, September, https://sites.tufts.edu/digitalplanet/files/2020/06/Cost-of-Cash-US.pdf, accessed December 11, 2022.
Chen, Sally, Tirupam Goel, Han Qiu, and Ilhyock Shim (2022), "CBDCs in Emerging Market Economies," BIS paper, No 123, April, https://www.bis.org/publ/bppdf/bispap123.htm, accessed December 11, 2022.
Devex (n.d.), "Sakchyam Access to Finance for the Poor Programme (Sakchyam)," https://www.devex.com/organizations/sakchyam-access-to-finance-for-the-poor-programme-sakchyam-122443, accessed December 11, 2022.
European Central Bank (2021), "Eurosystem Report on the Public Consultation on a Digital Euro," April, https://www.ecb.europa.eu/pub/pdf/other/Eurosystem_report_on_the_public_consultation_on_a_digital_euro~539fa8cd8d.en.pdf.
European Central Bank (2022), "Study on the Payment Attitudes of Consumers in the Euro Area (SPACE)," https://www.ecb.europa.eu/stats/ecb_surveys/space/html/index.en.html.
G7 Working Group on Stablecoins (2019), "Investigating the Impact of Global Stablecoins," October, https://www.bis.org/cpmi/publ/d187.pdf.
Huigsloot, Luke (2022), "Tremors from FTX's Collapse Reverberate through the Scientific Community," November 17, https://cointelegraph.com/news/tremors-from-ftx-s-collapse-reverberate-through-the-scientific-community, accessed December 11, 2022.
Jacob, Frank (2016), "The Role of M-Pesa in Kenya's Economic and Political Development," in: Koster, M.M., M.M. Kithinji, and J.P. Rotich (eds), *Kenya After 50. African Histories and Modernities*, Palgrave Macmillan, New York, https://doi.org/10.1057/9781137574633_6.
Kosse, Anneke, and Ilaria Mattei, "Gaining Momentum—Results of the 2021 BIS Survey on Central Bank Digital Currencies," BIS Papers, No 125, May 2022, https://www.bis.org/publ/bppdf/bispap125.pdf.
Meaning, Jack, Ben Dyson, James Barker, and Emily Clayton (2018), "Broadening Narrow Money: Monetary Policy with a Central Bank Digital Currency," Bank of England Staff Working Paper No. 724, May, https://www.bankofengland.co.uk/-/media/boe/files/working-paper/2018/broadening-narrow-money-monetary-policy-with-a-central-bank-digital-currency.pdf.
Monetary Authority of Singapore (2018), "Reply to Parliamentary Question on Singapore's Move Towards a Cashless Society," https://www.mas.gov.sg/news/parliamentary-replies/2018/reply-to-parliamentary-question-on-the-move-towards-a-cashless-society, accessed December 11, 2022.
Monetary Authority of Singapore (2022a), "Project Ubin: Central Bank Digital Money using Distributed Ledger Technology," https://www.mas.gov.sg/schemes-and-initiatives/Project-Ubin, accessed December 11, 2022.

Monetary Authority of Singapore (2022b), "Reply to COS Cut on Digital Sing Dollar," https://www.mas.gov.sg/news/parliamentary-replies/2022/reply-to-cos-cut-on-digital-sing-dollar, accessed December 11, 2022.

Schmiedel, Heiko, Gergana Kostova, and Wiebe Ruttenberg (2012), "The Social and Private Costs of Retail Payment Instruments: A European Perspective," No 137, Occasional Paper Series from European Central Bank, September, https://www.ecb.europa.eu/pub/pdf/scpops/ecbocp137.pdf, accessed December 11, 2022.

White House (2022), "Fact Sheet: White House Releases First-Ever Comprehensive Framework for Responsible Development of Digital Assets," https://www.whitehouse.gov/briefing-room/statements-releases/2022/09/16/fact-sheet-white-house-releases-first-ever-comprehensive-framework-for-responsible-development-of-digital-assets/, accessed December 11, 2022.

Xu, Q., and W. Sun (2022), "Does Financial Inclusion Promote Investment and Affect Residents' Happiness? Evidence from China," *Front. Psychol.*, 13:988312. doi: 10.3389/fpsyg.2022.98831, accessed December 11, 2022.

6. Utility tokens, markets in crypto assets regulation (MiCAR), and the costs of being public

David Florysiak

INTRODUCTION

Digital platforms that run on blockchain technologies which offer products and services use their own digital currency to settle transactions and rely on decentralized governance. Publicly offering such platform digital currency, also called utility tokens, to consumers and investors provides a way to finance the platform development. The market for utility tokens is still largely unregulated, and in many jurisdictions across the world, tokens can be publicly offered to investors and consumers with little to no regulatory oversight and subsequently be listed on centralized or decentralized crypto exchanges. This activity has spurred the growth of financing the development of digital platforms by publicly offering utility tokens at low costs. The lack of regulation, however, also attracts many potential fraudulent token issuers (Florysiak and Schandlbauer 2022), and gives rise to market manipulation (Lee et al. 2022).

Regulators across the world do see the necessity to regulate the market for utility tokens to protect consumers and investors. But regulation would not only offer protection for market participants, but also increase the cost of financing for platform development and in turn dampen platform development growth and innovation. In September 2022, the European Union (EU) published the final draft for its regulation of "Markets in Crypto assets" (MiCAR 2020), hereafter "the regulation," that covers the market for utility tokens. The regulation is expected to apply in 2024, 18 months after its expected formal adoption in early 2023. The regulation will then apply to all public utility token offerings and to all admissions of utility tokens in regulated trading platforms to be offered to market participants in the EU.

The regulation's objectives consist of providing legal certainty, supporting innovation, protecting consumers and investors, and ensuring financial stability. It tries to achieve this by setting strict rules on the public offering of utility tokens or the admission of tokens on a trading platform. Mandatory extensive information disclosure in the form of a white paper plays a central role in the regulation. Moreover, token issuers need to publish insider information in a way similar to issuers of financial instruments, and prevent insider dealing. High administrative sanctions are put on violations of the regulation and any market manipulation, again similar to the rules that apply to financial instruments.

I review the regulation with a focus on its rules for the public offering of utility tokens and the listing of utility tokens on a trading platform and the associated costs of regulatory compliance for being public in the EU. The expected resulting direct and indirect costs will be significant. They include drafting the white paper disclosure document for which most token issuers will depend on external financial and legal expertise in order to comply with the regulation, minimize litigation risk, and maximize offering success. Financial experts need to help in setting the offer price or assess mandatory disclosure of risk factors. Moreover, issuers of listed tokens need to have an internal system that allows them to assess the relevance of insider information and its publication if necessary. To prevent insider dealings, token issuers need a regulatory compliance system, including a whistleblowing system. Indirect costs are incurred through underpricing, or the "money left on the table" if the offer price is smaller than the first market price of the token. The token issuer, however, controls the underpricing by setting the offer price. On average, the costs of underpricing will likely be reduced by the regulation compared to previous unregulated offerings, as lower information asymmetry between token issuer and investors is, on average, associated with lower underpricing (Rock 1986).

I expect not many utility token issuers to go public due to the high costs of being public. Only a few larger issuers might be able to list their token on EU-regulated trading platforms. The likely consequences of the regulation for the market for utility tokens will be that smaller issuers will list in non-EU markets with lower regulatory costs; EU-regulated trading platforms will probably establish a market segmentation as seen in EU-regulated exchanges for financial instruments that allows tokens to be listed in exchange-regulated segments with less disclosure requirements. This change will reduce the costs of being public, but weaken consumer and investor protection at their own risk. Finally, smaller digital platforms are deprived of issuing tokens as a means of financing and thus have to divert to alternative forms of financing such as venture capital.

Will the regulation hamper innovation? First, without regulation there is a large risk that the market could fail completely. The fraction of fraudulent token issuers is undisputedly high. In accordance with the idea of Akerlof (1970), due to a large degree of asymmetric information between token issuers and investors, when issuers know the quality of their platform, and investors cannot distinguish between good and bad platforms, there are adverse effects on token prices. Investors will pay the expected value of the token given the proportions of good and bad issuers in the market. That expected value can be below the reservation price that some issuers of good platforms set, which then drives those issuers out of the market. When those issuers of good platforms exit the market, the proportion of bad issuers rises, which pushes the expected value down further, potentially falling below the reservation price of other issuers of good platforms. With a relatively continuous distribution of platform quality, such effects can cascade and drive out all issuers of good platforms from the market, leading to a total market failure. The regulation will reduce asymmetric information between token issuers and consumers and investors, and thus help to prevent market failure.

Second, the regulatory environment will likely cause a structural change and lead to larger platforms entering the market at the expense of crowding out smaller platforms. The regulation reduces information asymmetry through increasing transparency. This issue is related to the literature on problems associated with low transparency in markets for relatively small, opaque firms. Bushee and Leuz (2005) studied the implementation of new Securities and Exchange Commission (SEC) requirements for stocks on the The Over-The-Counter Bulletin Board (OTCBB) market in the United States, and found that some small firms were forced to delist because of the associated costs, but that already complying firms and newly complying ones experienced significant benefits.

Finally, my expectation is that, on average, the regulation will not hamper innovation but rather provide an environment that allows for a functioning market for innovation financing in the long term. The regulation will likely undergo several adjustments but maintain its main foundation.

This chapter proceeds by first describing digital platforms and associated utility tokens, and reviews related literature focusing on ICOs, token valuation, and the role of the white paper within the ICO process. Nest is a summary of the relevant rules for utility tokens from the Markets in Crypto Assets Regulation (MiCAR). The chapter then gathers the resulting costs associated with being public under the regulation, and discusses the main findings. The final section concludes.

PLATFORM TOKENIZATION AND UTILITY TOKENS

Digital platforms that run on blockchain technologies which offer products and services use their own digital currency to settle transactions and rely on decentralized governance. Issuing such platform digital currency, also called utility tokens, provides a way to finance the platform development without relying on equity investors (Chod et al. 2022). Chod et al. (2022) show that raising capital by issuing tokens rather than equity may have positive effects on the moral hazard frictions between founders, investors, and users of a platform. Mitigating effort underprovision and elimination of a potential hold-up of platform users is greatest for smaller, less capital-intensive ventures.

Token values reflect investors' expectations of both future productivity growth of the digital platform, and user adoption (Cong et al. 2021). In an efficient market, listed tokens reflect the value of tokens as a function of users' transaction needs, the number of users of the platform, and the platform's productivity.

Utility tokens have been issued in ICOs (initial coin offerings) in the past years. Many issued utility tokens have also been listed on centralized crypto exchanges. The market for utility tokens is still largely unregulated. Issuing utility tokens is simple, and provides easy-access financing without any regulatory burden. This environment has led to the growth of the market for utility tokens and their digital platforms. At the same time, the ICO market is characterized by high levels of information asymmetry between entrepreneurs and investors; that is, investors cannot easily separate high-quality and low-quality ICO issuers, nor identify fraudulent ICO issuers.

Many studies have empirically analyzed the ICO market and the behavior of listed tokens in the current unregulated settings. An extensive body of literature analyzes topics such as funding success, which refers to whether or how funding was secured in an ICO, underpricing of listed tokens, or post-ICO performance of listed tokens (e.g., Adhami et al. 2018; Amsden and Schweizer 2018; Howell et al. 2020; Momtaz 2020; Benedetti and Kostovetsky 2021; Bourveau et al. 2022; Lee et al. 2022; Lyandres et al. 2022). Most of the information used to test the corresponding hypotheses are based on the ICO's white paper, a voluntary disclosure of information regarding the development of the digital platform and the token sale, and price and volume information about listed tokens from centralized crypto exchanges. Some studies analyze market abuse through "pump and dump" (e.g., Lee et al. 2022) or how the token market is affected by potential fraudulent ICO issuers (e.g., Florysiak and Schandlbauer 2022).

The white paper plays a primary role in trying to reduce information asymmetries between the ICO issuer and potential investors. White papers are usually published on the ICO issuer's website. In addition to the white paper, many ICO issuers extensively use social media channels such as Telegram, Twitter, Reddit, Medium, LinkedIn, or BitcoinTalk to disclose information regarding the ICO. Often the white paper contains detailed information on the intended products and services offered on the digital platform, and typically includes information on a roadmap including key milestones, a technical description of the underlying technology, the intended use of proceeds, the team, and the token sale. At other times, white papers are short and do not disclose much information or have no informative content, which is a potential indicator of a bad or fraudulent ICO (Florysiak and Schandlbauer 2022).

There clearly is a need to regulate utility tokens due to the high degree of asymmetric information between ICO issuers and investors, and the potentially large number of fraudulent ICO issuers that do not face any barriers to enter the market. As utility tokens can be seen as some hybrid of a consumption and investment good, regulators face challenges in how to set regulatory rules that balance the trade-off between protecting consumers and investors, and enabling innovation. Existing regulatory attempts across the world treat utility tokens very differently. Benedetti et al. (2022) provide an overview of different approaches to regulation in selected countries, and argue that token issuers avoid jurisdictions that limit their network growth and prevent users and investors from participating. The most extensive regulation covering the issuance and trading of utility tokens is MiCAR for the EU.

MARKETS IN CRYPTO ASSETS REGULATION (MICAR)

Overview

In September 2020, the European Commission published a draft of "The Markets in Crypto Assets Regulation." The regulation sets rules for dealing with cryptoassets in the EU and it is expected to apply in 2024. It is binding for all cryptoassets that do not qualify as financial instruments, deposits, or structured deposits under the EU financial services legislation, and that will be offered to EU consumers and investors or traded on an EU trading platform for cryptoassets. The regulation is broad and covers the offerings and marketing of all cryptoassets including utility tokens, asset-referenced tokens, e-money tokens, and the authorization and operation of cryptoasset service providers.

The main objectives of the regulation are to:

- provide legal certainty;
- support innovation;
- protect consumers and investors; and
- ensure financial stability.

This section focuses on the relevant rules that apply for utility tokens as described in the previous section. This includes Title II of the regulation, which sets the rules for the public offering and marketing of utility tokens. Title VI covers prohibitions and requirements to prevent market abuse involving utility tokens. Title VII details the administrative sanctions and measures that can be imposed for violations of the regulation.

Utility Tokens

The regulation differentiates three sub-categories of cryptoassets, one of which defines utility tokens as cryptoassets that provide digital access to goods and services, available on distributed ledger technology (DLT), and that are only accepted by the issuer. Utility tokens are considered a specific type of cryptoasset that are assumed to have non-financial purposes and are only used for the operation of the associated digital platform. The goods and services and the digital platform do not need to exist yet.

Public Offering and Admission on a Trading Platform

Title II of the regulation sets the rules for the public offering of utility tokens or the admission of tokens on a trading platform. The regulation requires the issuer to be a legal entity. Figure 6.1 shows the process for a public offering or an admission on a trading platform. The cryptoasset white paper that contains all relevant information for token investors forms the central element in this process. The competent authority of the home member state needs to be informed at least 20 days before the white paper is intended to be published on the issuer's website. The notification needs to explain why the token is subject to this regulation and not a financial instrument, electronic money, a deposit, or structured deposit that is subject to a different EU regulation. Additionally, all EU states where tokens will be offered or traded, and the corresponding dates, need to be given. White papers need not be approved by the regulator prior to publication. However, the regulator may request that the issuer provide additional information and suspend or prohibit the offering or admission on a trading platform if the regulation has been infringed. Submitted white papers will be published on the European Securities and Markets Authority's (ESMA) website.

After the notification, the white paper must be published on the website of the issuer. It needs to be available at least from the starting date of the offer or the admission on a trading platform. The white paper should remain available on the issuer's website for as long as the tokens are held by the public. The content of the white paper needs to be identical to that of the one submitted with the notification. Changes to the white paper after notification or publication that may affect the decision to invest into the token or to trade the token must be made public and the regulator notified.

Figure 6.1 *Process for public offering or admission on a trading platform*

There are several exemptions from the requirement to publish a white paper. For example, issuers are exempted if tokens are offered for free, offered to less than 150 persons per member state, or the total offering amount does not exceed €1 million over a period of 12 months. Moreover, if the service is not yet in operation, the duration of the public offering shall not exceed 12 months.

White Paper

The regulation defines a white paper as an information document with mandatory disclosure requirements. It defines the content and form of the white paper in detail. The white paper plays a central role in the regulation.

Figure 6.2 shows the mandatory structure of the white paper and required key information that needs to be disclosed. The detailed full set of required information is laid out in Annex 1 of the regulation. The rule also requires that issuers clearly state in the white paper that tokens may lose their value in part or full if the project fails or

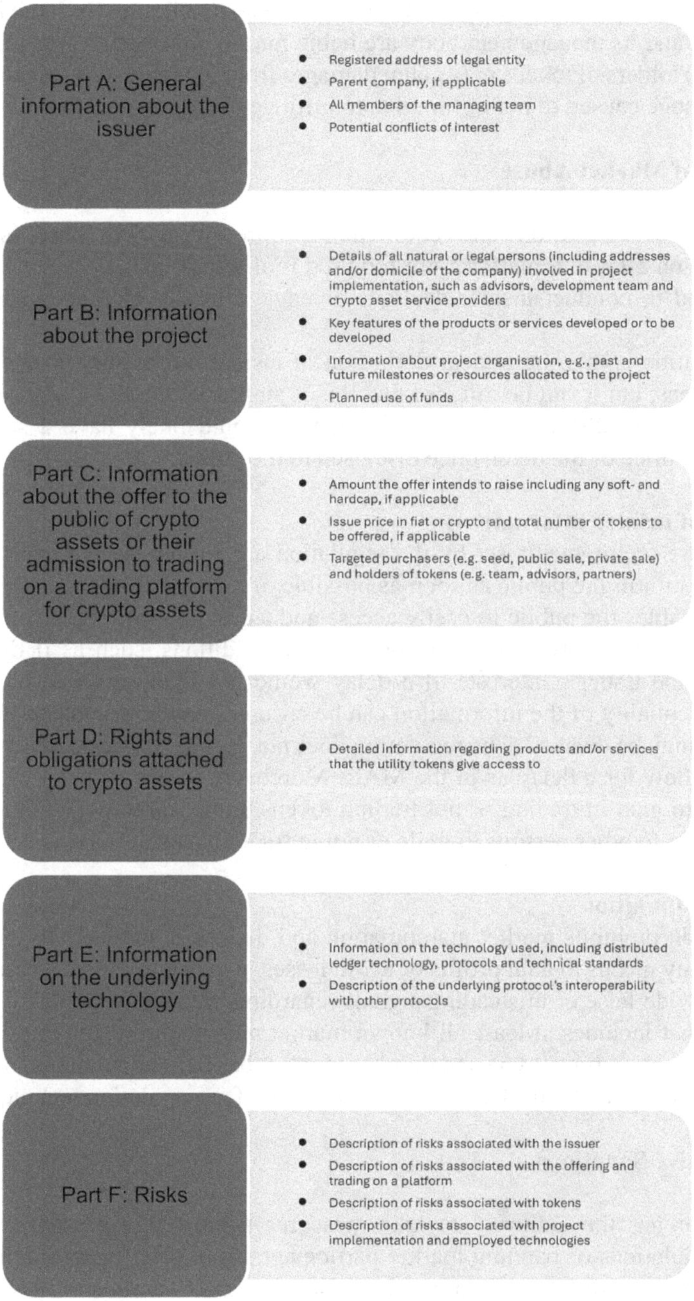

Figure 6.2 *Mandatory structure of the white paper and required key information*

is discontinued, may not always be transferable, or may be illiquid. Both the issuer as a legal entity and its management body are liable for the information provided in the white paper. Holders of tokens may claim damages from the issuer or its management body for damage caused to her or him due to infringement.

Prevention of Market Abuse

Title VI is about prohibitions and requirements to prevent market abuse. Issuers of tokens listed on a trading platform are required to disclose insider information and are prohibited to conduct insider dealings or engage in any market manipulation activities.

The regulation is missing a clear definition of insider information in the context of utility tokens, but it can be inferred that this is similar to the EU's Market Abuse Regulation (MAR) 2014, in that the information would likely have a significant impact on the price of the token once disclosed to the public.

Disclosure of insider information

The disclosure requirements set by the regulation are similar to that of the MAR. Issuers must inform the public as soon as possible of relevant insider information in a way that enables the public to easily access and assess the information in a complete, correct, and timely manner. Under certain conditions, such as if disclosure would harm the issuer's interests, if a delay would not likely mislead the public, and if confidentiality of the information can be ensured, public disclosure of insider information may be delayed. The regulation does not specify any legitimate interests that would allow for a delay as in the MAR. Moreover, no person shall use insider information to gain in trading or not trading tokens, either directly or indirectly by recommending to other persons to trade or not to trade tokens.

Market manipulation

The regulation prohibits market manipulation and defines it similarly to the MAR: essentially, any means to gain profits or avoid losses, which consists of any activities that may provide false or misleading signals regarding the supply, demand, or price of tokens. That includes at least all known market manipulation strategies in other asset classes such as runs (hype and dump), contract-based manipulations, or market power techniques (see Putniņš 2012 for a taxonomy of manipulation techniques).

Administrative Sanctions

The regulator has the authority to take measures against rule breakers, such as publishing violations or banning market participants from offering or trading cryptoassets. Moreover, the regulation provides for significant administrative sanctions to be levied on market participants. The administrative sanctions are similar to the regulation on prospectuses to be published when securities are offered to the public or admitted to trading on a regulated market (Prospectus 2014) and the regulation on market abuse (MAR).

Member states can set different maximum administrative sanction amounts for violations of the regulation. Table 6.1 summarizes the minimal maximum sanctions. The regulation differentiates between the type of violation, the legal form of market participant, and whether the amount of profits gained or losses avoided is determined. A violation of regulatory rules regarding token offerings or the admission of tokens on a trading platform receives a lesser sanction than a violation in disclosure of insider information and market manipulation. A legal person is sanctioned significantly more heavily than a natural person.

Table 6.1 *Maximum administrative sanction amounts for violations of the regulation*

Violation	Independent of amount of profits gained or losses avoided can be determined		Amount of profits gained or losses determined
	Natural person	Legal person	
Token offerings or the admission of tokens on a trading platform	up to €700 000	up to the maximum of €5 million and 3% of the last total annual turnover	two times the amount of profits gained or losses avoided
Disclosure of insider information and market manipulation	up to €5 million	up to the maximum of €15 million and 15% of the last total annual turnover	three times the amount of profits gained or losses avoided

THE COSTS OF BEING PUBLIC

The regulation, as outlined above, leads to several direct and indirect costs for participants in the market for utility tokens that sum up to the total expected cost of being public. In this section, I summarize the expected various cost components of compliance that allow a utility token to be offered to the public and traded on a trading platform.

Direct Costs

Public token offering and token listing

In an Initial Public Offering (IPO) for issuing securities, an underwriter serves as an intermediary between the issuer and investors. The underwriter assists in complying with the regulation by drafting the IPO prospectus and maximizing issuing success, which includes determining the amount to be raised in the public offering and the offer price. Moreover, the underwriter markets the offer to investors on a roadshow. For public utility offerings, there is no underwriter involved and thus there are no direct costs of underwriting. However, without an underwriter, the token issuer has costs for all functions that an underwriter would otherwise assist with.

It is costly to draft a white paper that complies with the regulation and minimizes litigation risk. Figure 6.2 contains the key information that must be provided in the white paper. All information needs to be carefully stated. For example, if any information provided or not provided, or falsely provided, might have an impact on the token price, investors could sue the issuer for any damage caused. Preparing all internal information on the issuer's side is time-consuming and thus costly. To make up for a missing underwriter in IPOs for equity offerings, most token issuers will depend on external financial and legal expertise to draft the offer document in order to comply with the regulation, minimize litigation risk, and maximize issuing success.

Financial experts will help to set the offer amount and offer price. This step requires a token valuation, which is derived from a digital platform valuation. However, a digital platform valuation depends on other factors beyond a valuation of financial assets that depends on cash flows. For example, Cong et al. (2021) propose a valuation model for digital platforms in which utility tokens derive their value from underlying economic activities such as network scale or user adoption on the platform.

Moreover, financial experts will help to identify and describe risk factors. The white paper requires an extensive description of risk factors, both systematic risks (token price, offer/trading venue, technology) and idiosyncratic risks (issuer-specific, project implementation):

- Token price risk or token returns are determined by systematic and idiosyncratic risk factors. A systematic risk factor is unpredictable over time and common to all tokens that are exposed to this risk. Idiosyncratic risk factors are specific to the issuer. Cong et al. (2022) developed a factor pricing model for tokens and find that market, size, momentum, value, and network factors can explain the cross-section of token returns.
- Offer/trading venue risk is associated with any factors that relate to cryptoasset service providers facilitating the offer of or trading of tokens, for example, custody and administration of tokens on behalf of third parties, or the operation of the trading platform itself. This risk might be any security issues that allow hacks and theft of tokens.
- Technology risk is associated with any factors that can have an impact on token prices and caused by the technology operating the digital platform, for example, a smart contract risk that allows hacks and theft of tokens.
- Issuer risk is associated with factors that are solely associated with the issuer but not any other issuer of tokens, for example, embezzlement of funds by management or internal personnel.
- Project implementation risk is associated with any factors that lead to the potential delay of, or failure to develop, the digital platform or any of its main features.

Marketing the token is costly, which includes preparation of marketing material that is also subject to regulation, such as the white paper. Moreover, additional costs are incurred by promotion of the token through digital channels such as social media or specialized platforms for token sale promotion to reach a broad set of investors.

Both the issuer as a legal entity and its management body are liable for the information provided in the white paper. The management body, however, is generally liable for their executive actions. Directors and officers incur direct costs for their liability insurance that covers litigation against the management board and pays for losses associated with lawsuits and legal defense fees. If not covered by insurance, the expected loss through this liability would increase the demanded compensation by the management body and decrease the profitability of the platform.

After setting up a legal entity with a registered address, recurring costs are incurred to produce audited financial statements for the legal entity. Further recurring costs include any listing costs that the cryptoasset service provider charges to facilitate the offer and the listing on the trading platform.

Mandatory disclosure

To prevent market abuse, the regulation requires mandatory disclosure of insider information. This rule requires issuers of listed tokens to have an internal system that allows them to determine whether specific insider information would affect the token price once made public, and subsequently, if necessary, to establish an appropriate disclosure channel that allows the public to easily access and assess the information in a complete, correct, and timely manner.

Prevention of insider dealing

To prevent insider dealing, the issuer should monitor and ideally publish any transactions in the tokens conducted by the management body. Moreover, the issuer needs a regulatory compliance system including a whistleblowing system.

Indirect Costs

Similar to IPOs, the literature on ICOs has shown that tokens are subject to underpricing, also called "money left on the table." Underpricing can be measured as the relation of the first token (market) price on the trading platform to its offer price. If the token price is larger than the offer price, the token offering is said to be underpriced. A higher offer price would have been feasible and thus more external funding could have been secured.

Benedetti and Kostovetsky (2021) document average underpricing of 179 percent. There could be several reasons why token offerings are underpriced. Models based on asymmetric information between investors and the issuer typically assume that low-quality issuers are willing to sell their shares at the average price (Akerlof 1970; Welch 1989). High-quality issuers, however, have an incentive to signal their type by selling shares at a price below their expected market valuation, thus creating underpricing, which deters low-quality types from imitation (Allen and Faulhaber

1989). Thus, this approach can be a potential way for high-quality issuers to signal their type. Florysiak and Schandlbauer (2022) show that high-quality issuers that signal their type by providing a white paper with informative content exhibit higher underpricing.

The token issuer controls the underpricing by setting the offer price. However, this ability requires the issuer to conduct a digital platform valuation and gather information about investor token demand and valuation. On average, the costs of underpricing will likely be reduced by the regulation as lower information asymmetry between token issuer and investors is, on average, associated with lower underpricing (Rock 1986).

DISCUSSION

The previous section summarizes all direct and indirect costs of issuing and listing utility tokens in the EU when the regulation comes into force. According to this regulation, utility tokens are heavily regulated, similarly to financial instruments in the EU.

The regulation will lead to significant direct costs of public token offerings compared to the status quo with almost no regulation. On the other hand, it will likely reduce indirect costs in the form of underpricing. For listed tokens, continuous mandatory disclosure requirements, such as the publication of insider information, puts a great regulatory burden on small and medium-sized platform issuers.

I expect not many utility token issuers to go public, due to the relatively high costs of being a publicly listed token. Only larger issuers might be able to list their token on EU-regulated trading platforms. Potential consequences of the regulation for the utility token market may include:

- Smaller issuers will list in non-EU markets with lower regulatory costs (regulatory arbitrage), and once large enough, subsequently list their tokens in the EU to access the EU market.
- EU-regulated trading platforms will probably establish a market segmentation, as seen in EU-regulated exchanges for financial instruments. For example, many stock exchanges in the region have primary boards where larger EU-regulated stocks subject to EU regulation are listed, while secondary boards allow issuing and listing stocks that are exchange-regulated and not subject to regulation, but to the rules, including disclosure requirements, set by the exchange (Vismara et al. 2012). This approach will reduce the costs of being public, but weaken consumer and investor protection at their own risk. Tokens listed on secondary boards may subsequently fail or upgrade to primary EU-regulated boards.
- The dependency on alternative financing such as venture capital for digital platforms will be strengthened, and issuing tokens as a means of financing will be reduced, especially for smaller platforms. Once large enough, tokens will be

issued on an EU-regulated trading platform and venture capitalists will exit their investment.

CONCLUSION

Will the regulation achieve its objectives concerning utility tokens? It will likely achieve a high degree in attaining legal certainty, protecting consumers and investors, and ensuring financial stability, but may lead to less support innovation. Furthermore, the regulation is very similar to that for EU-regulated markets in financial instruments and may thus be too costly for smaller digital platforms. But most digital platforms start small if not backed by external financing from venture capitalists. Thus, small digital platforms lose access to financing through token issuance in the EU and might divert to less regulated markets. These markets could emerge within the EU if trading platforms set up exchange-regulated boards that allow issuers to circumvent EU regulation.

The token market and existing secondary markets for stocks share many characteristics. While most secondary markets have very low listing and disclosure requirements (Vismara et al. 2012; Cumming and Johan 2014), Floros et al. (2018) analyzed a secondary exchange-regulated stock market segment at Frankfurt Stock Exchange that required no mandatory disclosure by listed firms, similar to the current situation of the token market without regulation. The authors show that this market eventually collapsed due to an ever-increasing influx of fraudulent firms until it was shut down by the regulator and the exchange. If exchange-regulated markets for tokens are to emerge, officials need to establish minimum disclosure requirements to prevent failure and to develop technologies to identify fraudulent tokens.

The MiCAR puts a tough and costly regulation on the offering and listing of utility tokens in the EU. However, it sounds worse than it is. In my evaluation, the regulation is a step in the right direction and establishes an environment that allows a functioning market for innovation financing in the long term. The notion that no regulation means no costs, and thus enables innovation, is wrong. A major advantage of the regulation is consumer and investor protection. Without the regulation, the market for utility tokens might fail completely due to a large fraction of fraudulent tokens.

REFERENCES

Adhami, S., Giudici, G., and Martinazzi, S. (2018). Why do businesses go crypto? An empirical analysis of initial coin offerings. *Journal of Economics and Business*, 100, 64–75.

Akerlof, G. (1970). The market for "lemons": quality uncertainty and the market mechanism. *Quarterly Journal of Economics*, 84, 488–500.

Allen, F., and Faulhaber, G.R. (1989). Signalling by underpricing in the IPO market. *Journal of Financial Economics*, 23, 303–323.

Amsden, R., and Schweizer, D. (2018). Are blockchain crowdsales the new "gold gush"? Success determinants of initial coin offerings. Working paper.
Benedetti, H., Abarzúa, L., and Caceres Fuentes, C. (2022). Utility tokens. Working paper.
Benedetti, H., and Kostovetsky, L. (2021). Digital tulips? Returns to investors in initial coin offerings. *Journal of Corporate Finance*, 66, 101786.
Bourveau, T., De George, E.T., Ellahie, A., and Macciocchi, D. (2022). The role of disclosure and information intermediaries in an unregulated capital market: evidence from initial coin offerings. *Journal of Accounting Research*, 60, 129–167.
Bushee, B.J., and Leuz, C. (2005). Economic consequences of SEC disclosure regulation: evidence from the OTC bulletin board. *Journal of Accounting and Economics*, 39, 233–264.
Chod, J., Trichakis, N., and Yang, S.A. (2022). Platform tokenization: financing, governance, and moral hazard. *Management Science*, 68, 6411–6433.
Cong, L.W., Karolyi, G.A., Tang, K., and Zhao, W. (2022). Value premium, network adoption, and factor pricing of crypto assets. Working paper.
Cong, L.W., Li, Y., and Wang, N. (2021). Tokenomics: dynamic adoption and valuation. *Review of Financial Studies*, 34, 1105–1155.
Cumming, D.J., and Johan, S.A. (2014). *Venture capital and private equity contracting: an international perspective*. Academic Press.
Floros, I.V., Florysiak, D., and Johnson, S.M. (2018). An autopsy of a total stock market failure. Working paper.
Florysiak, D., and Schandlbauer, A. (2022). Experts or charlatans? ICO analysts and white paper informativeness. *Journal of Banking and Finance*, 139, 106476.
Howell, S.T., Niessner, M., and Yermack, D. (2020). Initial coin offerings: financing growth with cryptocurrency token sales. *Review of Financial Studies*, 33, 3925–3974.
Lee, J., Li, T., and Shin, D. (2022). The wisdom of crowds in fintech: evidence from initial coin offerings. *Review of Corporate Finance Studies*, 11, 1–46.
Lyandres, E., Palazzo, B., and Rabetti, D. (2022). Initial coin offering (ICO) success and post-ICO performance. *Management Science*, 68(12), 8658–8679.
MAR (2014). Regulation of the European Parliament and of the Council on market abuse (market abuse regulation), https://eur-lex.europa.eu/legal-content/EN/TXT/?uri=celex%3A32014R0596.
MiCAR (2020). Regulation of the European Parliament and of the Council on Markets in Crypto-assets, and amending Directive (EU) 2019/1937. https://eur-lex.europa.eu/legal-content/EN/TXT/?uri=CELEX%3A52020PC0593.
Momtaz, P.P. (2020). Initial coin offerings. *Plos one*, 15, e0233018.
Prospectus (2014). Regulation of the European Parliament and of the Council on the prospectus to be published when securities are offered to the public or admitted to trading on a regulated market. https://eur-lex.europa.eu/legal-content/EN/TXT/?uri=celex%3A32017R1129.
Putniņš, T.J. (2012). Market manipulation: a survey. *Journal of Economic Surveys*, 26, 952–967.
Rock, K. (1986). Why new issues are underpriced. *Journal of Financial Economics*, 15, 187–212.
Vismara, S., Paleari, S., and Ritter, J.R. (2012). Europe's second markets for small companies. *European Financial Management*, 18, 352–388.
Welch, I. (1989). Seasoned offerings, imitation costs, and the underpricing of initial public offerings. *Journal of Finance*, 44, 421–449.

7. A minting mold for the eFranc

Hans Gersbach and Roger Wattenhofer[1]

INTRODUCTION

The current monetary system is the result of an evolution extending over several centuries. How it compares to alternative systems forms a long-standing question. New technologies that could possibly be used in various parts of the monetary system—validating transactions, transferring money, controlling the supply of money—have fueled the academic and public debate on whether and how our monetary system could and should change. The downward trend of cash use in a variety of countries has further fueled the search for alternative types of money (see Figure 7.1).

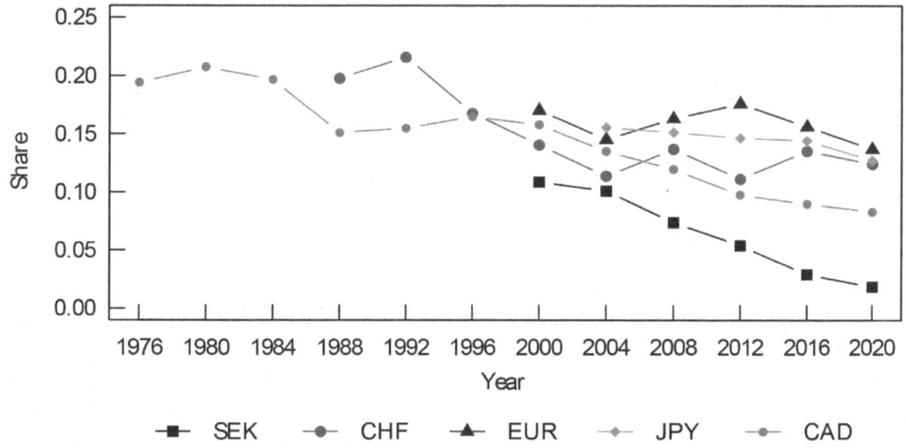

Note: SEK: Swedish Krona, CHF: Swiss Franc, EUR: Euro, CAD: Canadian Dollar, JPY: Japanese Yen.
Source: Based on data from Bank of Canada, Bank of Japan, European Central Bank, Sveriges Riksbank, and Swiss National Bank, as of April 7, 2020.

Figure 7.1 Share of cash in the monetary aggregate M1, average of monthly reported figures

There have been various proposals for changing the current monetary system. At one extreme, there is the so-called "sovereign money proposal" in which money is solely created by the central bank. At the other extreme, the current hierarchical monetary system could be supplemented by a variety of privately issued, competing fiat monies, which do not constitute a claim on the legal tender. However, more modest changes lie between these two extremes. For example, the introduction of a publicly available digital form of the national currency, commonly referred to as Central Bank Digital Currency (CBDC), could be envisioned. Such a CBDC could take several forms (see Schär and Berentsen 2020, and Figure 7.3 in the next section, for example.). In Figure 7.2, we provide an overview of the motivations for issuing a retail CBDC.

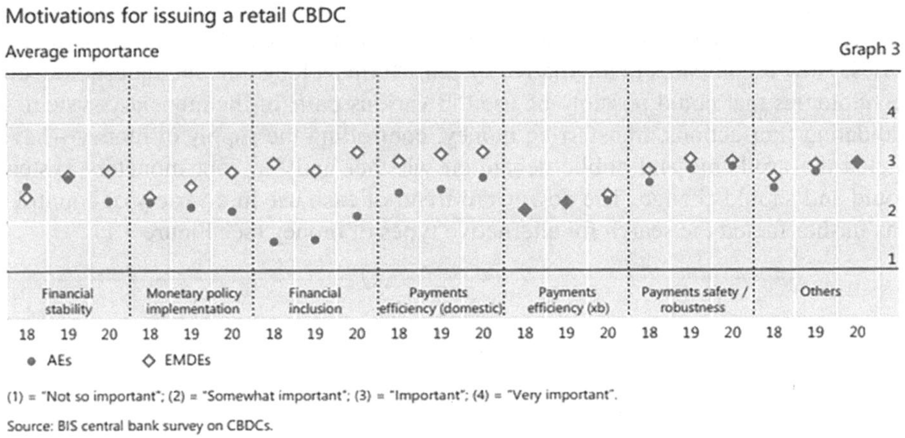

Figure 7.2 *Motives for issuing a retail CBDCs.*

For Switzerland, the two research questions are: Should Switzerland introduce a CBDC? And if so, which technical implementation is the most appropriate?

In this chapter, we argue that an eFranc should be introduced to complement the Swiss monetary system. An eFranc is a non-interest-bearing digital form of the legal tender available to the public. The public can convert banknotes or part of their bank deposits into eFrancs, subject to the banks' ability to obtain the corresponding amount of eFrancs from the central bank. There is free conversion of eFrancs into bank deposits (and into banknotes). For the technical implementation of the eFranc, we suggest a two-layer system combining a permissioned, asynchronous blockchain without consensus which provides a secure environment for validating transactions (base layer), plus a peer-to-peer payment network (top layer).

One may wonder why an eFranc should be introduced in Switzerland, with its traditional strong reliance on cash payments, and reports by the Federal Council on CBDCs that there is no need to introduce an eFranc. This issue is addressed in detail in this chapter, where we stress economic advantages and the fact that the technical implementation that we propose is the minimal possible fault-tolerant implementation. Moreover, it creates a payment system that can continue to function even if the current payment system is successfully attacked. And finally, it opens up a door to more financial innovations.

LITERATURE

The current monetary system has three main actors: the central bank, commercial banks, and the public. These are arranged hierarchically, with the following elements (see e.g. Faure and Gersbach 2021).[2]

The money stock available to the public is composed of deposits at commercial banks (to a large extent) and of banknotes and coins (to a minor extent). Banknotes and coins are physical central bank money (henceforth "cash") and serve as the sole legal tender.

Cash is issued by the central bank to commercial banks, which use it to settle withdrawals of deposits. Deposits (electronic private bank money) represent claims on cash but are issued by commercial banks when they grant loans or purchase assets, or are created when households deposit banknotes with banks.

Reserves (electronic central bank money) are issued by the central bank to commercial banks, which use them to settle claims arising from interbank deposit flows when the public makes payments. Only commercial banks have access to electronic central bank money.[3] Commercial banks have to comply with a set of rules such as liquidity and capital requirements. However, they are not (or only to a minor extent) required to hold central bank money as reserves for their deposits.[4]

Three prominent features of the hierarchical monetary system are of particular importance for our considerations. First, most money is created by commercial banks. Second, the public only has access to cash and bank deposits, but not to electronic central bank money. Third, commercial banks interact with the public and the central bank and are thus the bridge between the central bank and the public.

Before we can talk about alternative monetary systems, we need to outline the objectives that a monetary system should fulfill. The most important objectives can be summarized as follows.

Money should play its traditional roles (unit of account, medium of exchange, store of value), which ultimately requires that its value remains stable—or at least approximately stable—across time. Price stability should always be by far the most important objective in the long run, which requires the presence of an independent central bank.

Disruptions in the monetary system or crises in the wider financial system should be limited to an absolute minimum, and if they do happen, their spillovers to the real economy should be as restricted as possible. The democratic legitimacy of all governance processes and all policies involved should be well founded.

To design a CBDC, one first has to specify the functions it should be able to fulfill, such as accessibility, privacy, real-time and cross-border payments, resilience, and whether it should be a complement or substitute for cash. Second, one has to determine which technical designs best fulfill these functions. A comprehensive discussion of all options is beyond the scope of this chapter (see e.g. Auer and Böhme 2020; Bank of England 2020), yet it is important to provide an overview of the typology of existing CBDCs. We do so in Figure 7.3. We then proceed from two observations that guide our proposal.

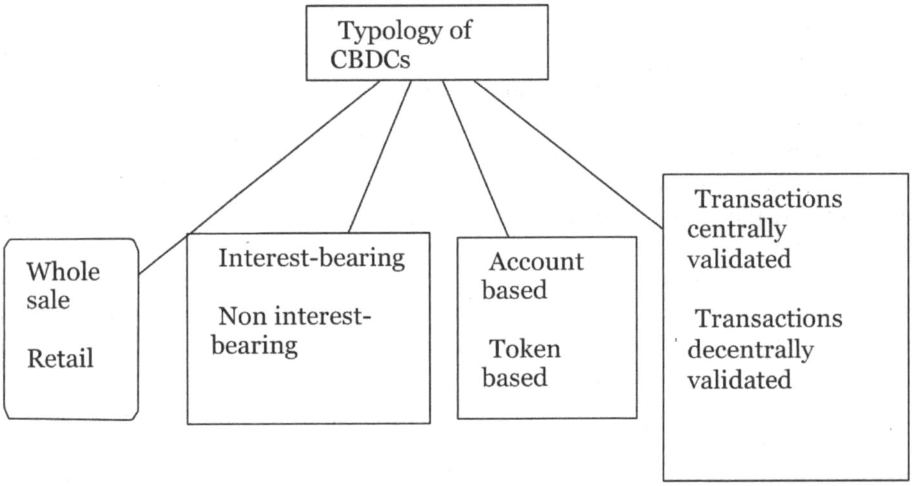

Figure 7.3 Design dimension of CBDCs

First, there are important discussions about the pros and cons of CBDCs. The most important advantages are the disciplining effect on commercial banks (Berentsen and Schär 2018), financial inclusion and financial stability (Ricks et al. 2018; Berentsen and Schär 2018), as well as an improved conduct of monetary policy (Bordo and Levin 2017).

However, Cecchetti and Schoenholtz (2018) argue that a CBDC can also entail financial instability. Among others, Engert and Fung (2017) claim that a CBDC could enhance competitiveness in payments. Similarly, Kahn et al. (2018) present the mitigation of competition problems in the banking sector as a strong argument in favor of the introduction of a CBDC. A panorama of the possible consequences of the issuance of CBDC through central banks is given in Pichler et al. (2019).

The introduction of a CBDC would also pose technical and organizational challenges. The former are addressed by Böhme (2019) and Auer and Böhme (2020), while the latter are discussed by Bindseil (2019). Moreover, Agur et al. (2019) discuss the optimal design of a CBDC, taking into account preferences for anonymity and security, as well as network effects.

Several theory papers assess the effects of a CBDC. In an overlapping generation framework with imperfectly competitive banks, Andolfatto (2018) shows that a CBDC can increase financial inclusion and raise deposit rates through increased competition.

Chiu et al. (2019) also assess this positive competition effect. They calibrate their model for the US economy and show that under suitable interest rate setting, a CBDC may raise bank lending and output in a significant manner. Barrdear and Kumhof (2016) develop a dynamic stochastic general equilibrium model to show how CBDCs lower the real policy rate and thus foster the stimulation of the economy. Similarly, Keister and Sanches (2019) demonstrate that a CBDC is welfare-improving, although in some instances the banks' funding costs increase and lending is reduced, as is welfare.

Böser and Gersbach (2020) show that interest-bearing CBDCs might entail a higher liquidity demand on the side of banks which, in combination with limited liquidity supply by the central bank, may lead to more prudent bank behavior. However, if the CBDC is in widespread use, a limiting liquidity supply by the central bank would endanger the viability of the banking system (see Böser and Gersbach 2020). In turn, relaxing liquidity supply will undo any positive effect of interest-bearing CBDCs on the prudent behavior of banks (see Böser and Gersbach 2020 for this line of reasoning). Hence, a CBDC should not act as a deposit substitute, but as a substitute for cash. Of course, it is not guaranteed that the Swiss public will rapidly adopt the eFranc. Yet since it is stable—always having the same value as bank notes—we expect continuous adoption if the technical requirements are simple. There is no risk if adoption only proceeds slowly. Second, as to the technical design, the basic decision would be between a conventional centrally controlled database and a distributed ledger. While both designs have advantages and disadvantages, we argue in this chapter that a specific decentralized design has a variety of advantages over other potential infrastructure.

eFRANC

We focus on a non-interest-bearing digital form of central bank money for the public. In particular, we focus on the introduction of a token-based form of banknotes with the name "eFranc."[5]

This eFranc is simply a digital form of a banknote; that is, a currency held and traded only on a distributed ledger such as a blockchain, on which transactions are validated decentrally. Everybody should be allowed to hold eFrancs and to make transactions using them.[6] An eFranc should allow secure, anonymous holdings of cash, subject to legal constraints, in particular anti-money laundering and know-your-customer rules.

Ultimately, an eFranc is a close substitute for banknotes and coins but enables combating money laundering at levels that can be as high as bank deposits. Furthermore, an eFranc opens up possibilities for automatizing some of these legal constraints.

Even if the introduction of an eFranc appears to signify only a small change, it entails a new monetary architecture. For instance, it needs appropriate rules and suitable technical requirements. In particular, since the eFranc constitutes an additional form of legal tender, how eFrancs can enter the monetary system has to be specified. Technically, there are two ways that eFrancs can be introduced.

First, mirroring the process by which banknotes enter the economy today, the eFranc could be governed by the following rules, henceforth called the Complement System:

- Creation of the eFranc will occur through the Swiss National Bank (SNB).
- Banks can obtain eFrancs from SNB against eligible collateral.
- The public can transfer part of their bank deposits to eFrancs, subject to the banks' ability to acquire the corresponding amount of eFrancs from the central bank.
- Free conversion of eFrancs into bank deposits (and into banknotes) will be possible.

The Complement System simply adds another (digital) legal tender to the existing monetary system. An alternative approach is the Substitute System. It involves the last three rules in the Complement System, but the first rule now reads:

- Banks can obtain eFranc from the SNB by returning the same amount of banknotes to the SNB.

Hence, in the Substitute System, the eFranc can only be created if the same amount of banknotes goes back to the SNB. In turn, this step requires that banks have to acquire this amount of banknotes beforehand, either from the central bank or if customers return them. While individual acquisition of eFrancs by the public increases the amount of legal tenders in the Complement System and leaves it constant in the Substitute System, the monetary aggregate will not change if the public have a given preference for a mix of eFrancs, cash, and bank deposits. Hence, no matter how eFrancs are introduced, the monetary aggregate consisting of cash, eFrancs, and bank deposits is the same in both systems.

Of course, introducing the requirement that banks have to return physical banknotes to the central bank when they create eFrancs should not add a separate physical process to the system. Since banks regularly acquire banknotes from the central bank, the amount of eFrancs created by a bank could simply be deducted from these regular flows of banknotes to the banks. One could even envision the central bank only verifying the ability of a bank to acquire the required amount of banknotes to be converted to eFrancs, and then decreasing the bank's electronic reserves at the central bank correspondingly. This scenario would be almost equivalent to the Complement System.

We stress that while the SNB controls the creation of eFrancs, the mix between banknotes and eFrancs, and between legal tenders and bank deposits, is impacted by the public and banks. Moreover, the conversion rules in both systems can be more or less restrictive with regard to the conversion of bank deposits into eFrancs, in order to prevent such switches from occurring on a large scale, which would be tantamount to a bank run.[7] At all events, individuals are allowed to switch from eFrancs to bank deposits and, via bank deposits, from eFrancs to banknotes.

Moreover, we envision that banks operate the channels between bank accounts and the blockchain to execute the conversions.[8] In this manner, no further physical and digital infrastructures are needed besides these channels and the blockchain.

Before we address the technical details of the implementation, we now focus on the potential economic advantages and disadvantages of an eFranc.

ADVANTAGES AND DISADVANTAGES

Advantages

An eFranc would have several advantages. First, an eFranc supplements the Swiss monetary system with a digital form of legal tender that is solely controlled by the central bank. The eFranc is a safe nominal asset, since holding eFrancs does not involve a counterparty and so there is no default risk. Since there is a risk that banknotes—the sole legal tender today—may decline in their use, as the COVID-19 pandemic illustrated, the eFranc ensures that the monetary system continues to operate with the widespread use of a legal tender. This concept is important, since a monetary system with the widespread use of a legal tender tends to perform better than one without, for several reasons.

To start with, bank deposits signify legal claims on this tender, and the threat to switch from bank deposits to the safe legal tender disciplines banks. In particular, an eFranc acts as a disciplining device on money creation by banks if the use of banknotes declines. Hence, an eFranc can help to stabilize credit and money creation cycles[9] and thus will help the central bank to pursue its main objective: maintaining a stable value for its currency.

Moreover, the legal status of bank deposits as claims on the legal tender becomes uncertain without the widespread use of the underlying legal tender, and may undermine its status as a medium of exchange. Since the development of an eFranc takes time, avoiding the risk of a monetary system without a legal tender requires the initiation of an electronic legal tender.

There is an important qualification to the stability argument. If an eFranc becomes attractive, and much more attractive than banknotes, instability may arise, since the central bank may need to issue many more eFrancs, and the customers' switch from bank deposits to eFrancs may cause liquidity shortages for commercial banks, and thus generate financial instability.

Second, the Swiss Franc may face increasing competition from private suppliers of digital currencies. This competition may cause a drop in demand for Swiss Francs, with associated seigniorage losses, and potential difficulties for monetary policy, as the transmission channels may be significantly affected. Avoiding this risk can justify the introduction of an eFranc that is as attractive as currencies from private competitors. Yet, it is unclear if and when private suppliers of digital currencies will be an essential threat to national currencies.

Third, the eFranc avoids the costs associated with printing, storing, distributing, and protecting physical banknotes. Of course, operating a distributed ledger is not costless, but with an appropriately distributed ledger design, as discussed in the next section, these costs are considerably lower than for using physical banknotes. Fourth, the use of an eFranc never involves any infection risk, a feature that has suddenly become crucial in the face of the COVID-19 pandemic.[10]

Fifth, an eFranc could ensure anonymity against private persons for all lawful exchanges and can thus recover some properties of physical banknotes. Anonymity is a property that is desired by many citizens as it guarantees freedom to interact with others without the knowledge and potential reaction of third parties. Since an eFranc fulfills anti-money laundering and know-your-customer rules, it does not provide the same level of anonymity as physical banknotes against the government. The state alone is allowed to trace transacting agents back to the distributed ledger, and only in precisely described, exceptional circumstances inscribed in corresponding laws.

Sixth, an eFranc would further limit the possibilities of imposing negative nominal interest rates on market participants. In particular, one consequence of the eFranc is that interest rates on bank deposits will no longer become negative once the monetary system with the eFranc is fully developed. Arguably, this is a desirable property, since it fosters trust in the currency and ultimately helps to stabilize its value. Yet, as much literature has shown,[11] the zero/effective lower bound on nominal interest rates hampers the stabilization of macroeconomic shocks.

Seventh, we envision that transactions with eFrancs can be executed in a technical infrastructure that is independent of the existing payment system involving bank deposits and the associated clearing system. The technical infrastructure on which eFranc transactions take place should be tailor-made, such that it can even become a central part of future payment and clearing systems. In particular, the interface between bank-based payment systems and the new blockchain-based payment system could be designed in such a way that a failure of the first would not spill over to the other, and vice versa, thus enhancing resilience against cyber risks, for instance. An eFranc could also help if parts of the whole current electronic payment system, the Swiss Interbank Clearing System (SIC), incurred disruptions.

Eighth, the blockchain with eFrancs allows for new kinds of advanced financial interaction via so-called "smart contracts," which are mutual agreements embedded in an executable computer code. Thus, the contractual clauses would be executed and enforced automatically, without the need of a third party. While smart contracts and the opportunity of borrowing and operating collateralized lending would create a rich financial system on the blockchain, the technical resilience of the infrastructure must be given first priority.

Alternative Designs

Many advantages of an eFranc can be realized by anybody having a non-interest-bearing CBDC account at the central bank and whose accounts are integrated in the current payment system (see e.g. Berentsen and Schär 2018). Yet, there are also advantages to the proposed blockchain system. First, one wants to make sure that important data is stored in more than one place, because that single place may representan immediate point of failure. This precaution is common in finance. A retail bank also stores the data of a bank account on multiple machines. This data is encrypted as well, so that the information is not easy to tamper with. Those attributes are essentially the two ingredients of our base layer, and we argue that this layer is the minimal possible fault-tolerant implementation. It is also simpler than the alternative design of database and backup databases.

Second, the technical infrastructure for the eFranc is independent of the existing payment system involving bank deposits and the associated clearing system with the central bank. Adding central bank accounts would enlarge the current system, while the infrastructure for the eFranc creates a system that would continue to function as a payment system in which only eFrancs can be used if the current bank or central bank temporarily collapses or is hacked.

Third, once the eFranc infrastructure is in place, financial innovations using the eFranc can—and probably will—develop. In particular, smart contracts, and viable concepts of decentralized borrowing and lending, are expected. These developments are impossible or harder to envision if eFrancs are held at central bank accounts.

Disadvantages and Gradual Implementation

Could an eFranc also have disadvantages? One issue lies in the conduct of monetary policy. While any new form of money has an impact on the transmission channels of monetary policy, banknotes in cryptocurrency form would have the least disruptive effects on monetary policy, as long as bank runs are avoided. This takes us to the second issue: if the interest on bank deposits moves towards zero, or when insolvency concerns of banks are present, the eFranc could lead to financial instabilities. At least initially, this circumstance requires sufficient restrictions on the conversion of bank deposits to eFrancs. Moreover, a well-capitalized banking sector is not only essential for times without an eFranc, but it is even more important when the eFranc has been introduced.

Third, an eFranc needs a functioning blockchain infrastructure; which is not guaranteed at the moment. Since existing proof-of-work blockchains, with their high energy consumption, are not suitable, a new type of blockchain protocol is required, which we will outline later.

These concerns mean that it is advisable to plan three phases, which we illustrate here for the Substitute System:

1. Launch. In this phase, creation, access, and amounts of eFranc holdings on the distributed ledger are limited.
2. Experimentation. Access is granted to the public, while the amounts of eFranc holdings remain limited.
3. Full integration. All three conversion rules apply:
   a. free exchange of physical banknotes into eFranc;
   b. free exchange of eFranc into bank deposits (and banknotes);
   c. exchange of bank deposits into eFranc subject to the banks' ability to acquire the corresponding amount of banknotes from the central bank.

Ultimately, everybody should have the right to make transactions freely on the blockchain by using the eFranc as a means of payment, and to store the eFranc on the blockchain.

While the above process demonstrates the need for a careful, step-by-step introduction in launching the eFranc, two additional considerations are important. First, the full integration phase should not take place when the interest rate on sight deposits is zero or below. Otherwise, we might have conversions of such large amounts of deposits that the stability of the banking system would be threatened. Second, at least for some time, banks should keep logs of all the conversions to eFrancs that customers have ordered.

TECHNICAL IMPLEMENTATION

The Architecture

The advantages of an eFranc discussed in the previous sections can only be harvested if the technical implementation is frictionless and involves few costs. Hence, the technical architecture must satisfy the principles of security, throughput, accessibility, low cost, and programmability (for a differing classification, see Norges Bank 2018). Otherwise, neither the scale and ease, nor the safe use, of eFrancs and thus its advantages can be realized.

The architecture consists of a base layer (bottom) and a payment network (top). Transactions can travel customer-to-customer in the payment network, using a path of middlemen (MM) and channels. Transactions can also directly be sent to the four committee members (CMs) in the base layer. New channels in the transaction network are being established with a funding transaction in the base layer. Committee members can parallelize the verification of transactions, as shown in Figure 7.4 for committee member 4, by sending an incoming transaction to the correct server, based on the input of the transaction.

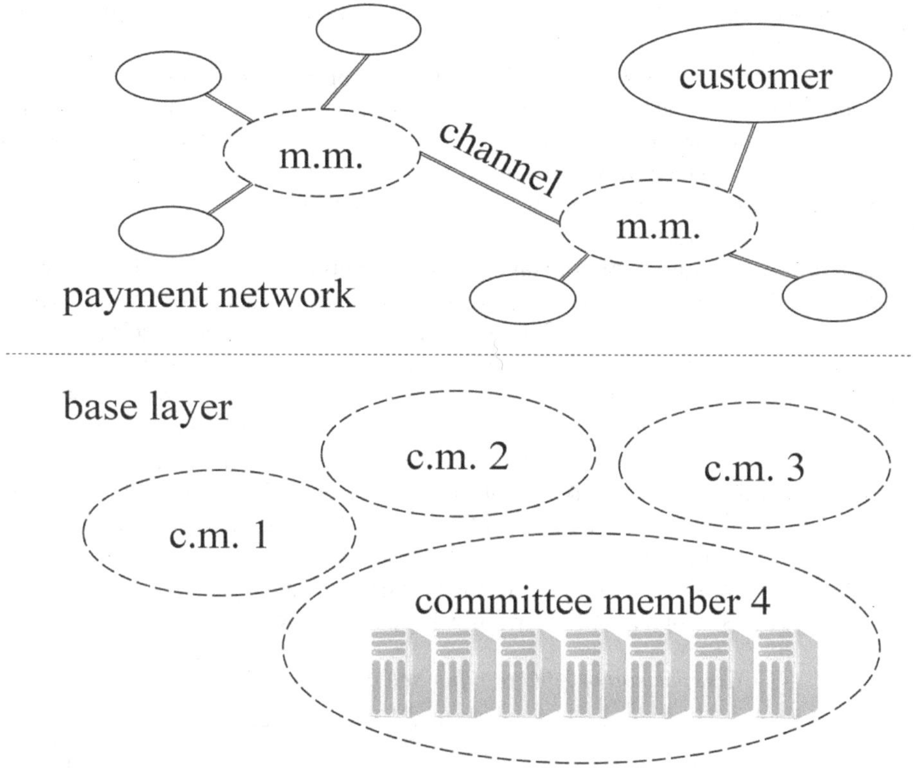

Note: CM: committee members; MM: middlemen.

Figure 7.4 Overview of the technical architecture

A modern architecture will be comprised of two layers, a base layer that validates basic transactions and a payment network that allows for payments between banks or between a bank and its customers. An overview of the whole architecture is depicted in Figure 7.4. We stress that these two layers have no connection to the two-layered architecture in our monetary system, with the central bank and commercial banks forming the top layer and commercial banks, payment partners, and end users forming the base layer.

Base Layer

The base layer provides the security of the system. We propose the use of a permissioned asynchronous blockchain without consensus. The basic idea of this base layer was presented in the Asynchronous Blockchain without Consensus (ABC) protocol by Sliwinski and Wattenhofer (2019). Note that ABC is more highly developed than is necessary for an eFranc design, as it is permissionless. For instance, Meta's Libra/

Diem cryptocurrency advocated for an ABC-like architecture (see Baudet et al. 2020) before the project was halted.

We assume that the cryptographic functionality is provided by asymmetric encryption and hashing. Apart from these cryptographic necessities, the base layer does not employ randomization and is completely deterministic. A deterministic protocol is usually simple, which allows for a swift and precise implementation. Moreover, deterministic protocols are easier to understand for laypersons, which might foster acceptance of the eFranc by the public.

ABC is asynchronous, without making any assumptions about network latency: no matter how slowly messages are transmitted, the protocol is guaranteed to be correct. As such, ABC is fully resilient to all network-related threats, such as delaying messages from some party or denial-of-service attacks. By disabling communication, an adversary could stop the system from creating and approving new transactions, but the adversary cannot invalidate previously approved transactions or approve illegal transactions. In comparison with orthodox blockchains such as Bitcoin, this improves the security of the eFranc. Unlike proof-of-work systems, the security of the eFranc system does not depend on the amount of resources devoted, such as energy, computational power, or memory.

In Table 7.1, we show a summary of the properties of the base layer of the eFranc and the properties of other well-known blockchain approaches.[12]

Table 7.1 *Comparison of ABC to other selected blockchain protocols*

	Bitcoin Ether	PBFT	Ouroboros	Algorand	Honey-Badger	eFranc (ABC)
Permissionless[a]	✓		✓	✓		
Energy-efficient[b]		✓	✓	✓	✓	✓
Finality[c]		✓		✓	✓	✓
Asynchronous[d]					✓	✓
Deterministic[e]		✓				✓
High throughput[f]						✓
Smart contracts[g]	✓	✓	✓	✓	✓	(✓)

Notes: [a] The infrastructure of the protocol is provided by the general public; [b] The total power consumption of the whole system is in the order of 1 kilowatt; [c] As soon as a transaction is approved, the transaction is final and cannot be reverted; [d] There are no timing assumptions; the protocol is correct even if the underlying internet is suffering from severe problems; [e] To keep the protocol simple, randomization is only used in cryptographic primitives; [f] The system can handle a load as high as millions of transactions per second; [g] The system allows for smart contracts that can be called by arbitrary participants.

Source: Adapted from Sliwinski and Wattenhofer (2019).

The participants of the eFranc in the base layer form a committee that should be made up of trusted entities of the Swiss financial system, such as the Swiss National Bank (SNB), the Swiss Financial Market Supervisory Authority (FINMA), the Swiss payment service provider SIX, and possibly some of the core banks in Switzerland such as UBS and Credit Suisse. Since these entities perform quite different functions in the Swiss financial market system, one could also envision the base committee consisting only of larger banks, possibly complemented by large insurance companies.

We envision that the list of validators is part of the legal document (laws and decrees) that make the eFranc and its architecture a public infrastructure. If private entrepreneurs are involved, they can be incentivized by (small) fees to perform the validation services. One might envision that private enterprise could compete to become a publicly certified eFranc transaction validator. The ensuing reputation gain may be high enough to motivate even private enterprises to perform the validation services without any monetary rewards. Each of the validators participates in the committee with a computer authenticated with a known public key. We call the set of participants on the base layer the committee. The eFranc requires that strictly more than two-thirds of the committee members obey the protocol. In other words, if the committee consists of four members, at least three should be "honest."

In the following, we always require this ratio (four members, at least three of them being honest, that is, complying with the protocol). Alternative designs require five honest members out of seven, or seven out of ten. Even if all committee members are trusted, it is still better to include fault-tolerance. This precaution is no different from a bank keeping multiple copies of account data, just in case one of the copies fails.

The main operation consists of a transaction transferring eFrancs from one or more input accounts to one or more output accounts. Transactions can be initiated by anyone, including banks that are not part of the committee.

Every transaction refers to at least one previous transaction, in such a manner that all transactions form a directed acyclic graph (DAG). The initial transaction of the DAG represents the initial stake in the system; that is, no eFranc is assigned to anybody. The eFranc is created with a transaction as well. The input of such a creation transaction is simply signed by the central bank; the outputs are accounts of the commercial banks that have provided cash to the SNB in exchange for the newly created eFranc.

An adversary issuing conflicting transactions is a primary threat to blockchain systems. Traditionally, it has been assumed that blockchains need to feature a technical primitive known as "consensus" to validate exactly one of the transactions issued by a misbehaving party. The eFranc does not need such a costly consensus routine. If an adversary is issuing conflicting transactions, the eFranc only guarantees that at most one transaction is valid.

A transaction, denoted by t, is confirmed by the system if enough (three out of four) committee members (directly or indirectly) acknowledge t. If a transaction receives support (digital signatures) by the committee of three (out of four), no other transaction conflicting with t can be confirmed. In particular, if the owner attempts to execute the transaction t' that is trying to spend (some of) the same input(s) as t, the eFranc system (the honest committee members) will reject t'. If an owner issues two conflicting transactions t and t' at roughly the same time, it is possible that: (case a) either t or t' is confirmed (but not both); or (case b) neither t nor t' are ever confirmed. Case (b) happens if some system committee members see and try to confirm t, while others see and try to confirm t'. The system might remain in this state forever, with the committee being split between t and t', without any clear majority. Crucially, such a situation can only arise if the issuer of t and t' intentionally misbehaves and does not act by accident. In such cases, it is reasonable to punish the issuer with a fine.

Alternatively, one could also enhance the system to be able to deal with conflicting transactions t and t'. One way is to slightly increase the size of the committee in order to establish a consensus on demand. If enough committee members signed a transaction, the transaction is final. However, if two conflicting transactions cannot get enough signatures, a consensus procedure is started to decide which of the two competing transactions is valid. This approach is described in detail in the literature, such as in Sliwinski et al. (2022).

What if an honest participant suggests a transaction t, but only two out of four committee members sign this transaction t? In this case, the issuer of the transaction must simply wait. The issuer can remind the two trailing committee members to sign the transaction t, but no signature can be enforced. Honest committee members will sign all transactions that are correct. They cannot abstain from signing a correct transaction. The only excuse for not signing a correct transaction t is that a committee member has not yet received transaction t, for example because of a damaged internet. As soon as the underlying internet is fixed, transaction t will be signed.

The bottleneck in this system occurs because every committee member needs to verify validity before digitally signing any transaction. We can mitigate this problem in two ways. First, verifying validity and digital signing can take place in parallel. If a committee member is overwhelmed by the number of transactions, it can set up k computers, each being responsible for a different set of transactions. For instance, depending on the last b bits of the input(s) of a transaction, the transaction will be sent directly to the right machine out of $k = 2^b$ machines in total. This machine will independently verify and digitally sign the transaction on behalf of the committee member owning the machine. This way, the base layer can achieve a k times higher throughput than blockchains that rely on consensus, for an arbitrarily large k. The idea is that multiple (parallel) machines build a verifier service. Based on the input of the transaction, the transaction is being verified by the right machine. For instance, assume we have $n = 100$ machines at a verifier (every verifier can have a different number, independently of the others). We take the (hashed) input of the transaction, and compute the modulo n of that number. Then the transaction is being sent to and verified by the machine with the ID equal to the result of that little computation. This machine can then inform the output machines (again modulo n) about their new inputs.

However, an even more efficient remedy would be the introduction of a payment network as a higher layer. This we discuss next.

Payment Network

On this layer, participants do not have to be committee members. Payment channels or payment networks are peer-to-peer agreements between any set of participants.

They permit implementation flexibility, and as such, they will not be discussed in detail in this chapter. More detailed information on payment networks can be found in the literature, including the original papers: Decker and Wattenhofer (2015) and Poon and Dryja (2016).

Payment networks can make use of financial institutions acting as eFranc financial intermediaries or simply as middlemen. A middleman can be a commercial bank, another existing financial institution, or an institution specifically created for operating eFranc transactions.

Small payments can be exchanged back and forth directly between two or more participants or middlemen. Transactions may use sequence numbers, so that the latest state of the channel is always clear. Each transaction will be signed by the issuer of the transaction.

More concretely, let us have two financial middlemen A and B who establish a payment channel. Originally, the two middlemen assign some funds to the channel by transferring some amount of eFrancs to that channel. This eFranc might stem either from their own assets, or could be partially borrowed from the central bank against collateral.

Now the middlemen could send each other transactions. If middleman A wants to make a payment to middleman B, A simply signs a transaction and sends the signed transaction to B. At some point, middlemen A and B might disagree on the total amount of eFrancs they have exchanged so far (that is, on how much money is owed to whom).

In the event of such a dispute, either A or B can call on the underlying base layer. The eFranc base layer will then ask A and B to present their evidence on the current state of the channel. This evidence takes the form of the last signed transactions, reflecting the current state of the payment channel. Based on this evidence presented by A and B, the committee will then close the channel and the funds will be distributed to A and B accordingly. Note that the base layer committee will judge the situation entirely mechanically, without human intervention.

In contrast to the operations on the base layer, this operation is a synchronous one because the committee needs to wait to hear from all involved channel parties (both A and B in our previous example) before making a decision. One might implement some form of timeout if one of the involved channel parties does not answer within a given time frame. Note, however, that such channel disputes should be rare, as one of the involved channel parties must act maliciously for such situations to occur. Since the other channel parties have hard evidence of malicious behavior in the form of signed transactions, such punishable behavior should be even rarer.

Alternatively, one might involve some watchtower for each channel, which will also provide evidence if the base layer committee asks for evidence and one of the participants does not provide it. This variant of a payment network has recently been described by Avarikioti et al. (2019).

Smart contracts can be supported by these payment channels. Indeed, the eFranc will probably have various forms of payment networks, with some channels supporting smart contracts and others not.

Accounts

As a consequence of our two-layered system, various forms of eFranc accounts may exist. Banks (and other financial institutions) will have one or more base layer accounts. These accounts will be used, for instance, to establish new eFranc accounts for consumers.

In addition, banks, as part of the set of eFranc middlemen, will also hold accounts on the payment layer. Some of these accounts will engineer payments among customers, and between customers and service providers. These payment layer accounts may form channels with other eFranc middlemen and, as such, a payment layer account might be directly funded with eFrancs.

Also on the public side, different accounts may exist. For instance, a person may wish to own a base layer account. The advantage is that such an account is relatively anonymous, as only the bank that originally established the account knows the identity of the account holder.[13] The account is independent of the bank that established the account, as the account holder can issue (signed) transactions completely autonomously without interacting with third parties. Such an account is relatively close to cash and shares a major downside risk incurred by cash: if the account holds a large amount of eFrancs, the account holder must protect its digital signature (private key) carefully, since anybody who knows the digital signature can immediately transfer money to another eFranc account. On the other hand, a person may independently store large amounts of eFrancs in a tiny security box.

For eFranc accounts storing large amounts of money, it may be beneficial to create a multi-signature account. In this case, every transaction must be co-signed by both the account owner and their bank (or some other third-party trustee). This type of eFranc account is similar to a bank safe deposit box.

Finally, a person may also have a payment layer account. This account may be used for daily payments of small sums. There might be a payment network between the consumers and a coalition of merchants. A consumer simply sends a signed payment layer transaction to a merchant, for example by holding the consumer's near-field communication (NFC) mode enabled phone against a merchant tag. This type of account is similar to cash and debit cards.

These different account types present various trade-offs with regard to efficiency, security, and privacy.

Offline Payments

One of the fundamental advantages of cash is its availability in disaster situations (for example, earthquakes, revolutions). A situation without internet would pose a challenge to the banking infrastructure, while cash also works offline, without electricity, internet, or computer. Following the example of Sweden, we may eventually become a cashless society. Then, any lengthy interruption to the electricity supply or the internet infrastructure would be problematic. It is of paramount importance for the eFranc to offer some form of emergency offline payments. Such payments are possible with both base layer accounts and payment layer accounts.

We envision the eFranc to be able to withstand at least a situation where neither consumers nor merchants have access to the internet. Both consumers and merchants, however, have a battery-powered device such as a smartphone. These devices can communicate via some short-range means such as NFC or Bluetooth. In an emergency situation, the merchant may decide to accept a transaction from the consumer, although it cannot be validated by the base layer committee or the payment channel mechanism. After accepting the payment, the merchant will present the transaction to these validators at a later stage, when online services are working again.

There are two risks associated with offline payments. First, a fraudulent consumer may have manipulated their phone and present a transaction for which the input is a non-existent (imaginary) account. The merchant can fend off such an attack by only accepting offline payments from accounts already known to the merchant. For instance, the merchant knows the account because the consumer has shopped at the store before; or the consumer may have registered an account in a public list of accounts (known to merchants), so that the consumer can continue to make transactions if only offline payments are possible.

Second, a fraudulent consumer may have little or no money in their account, but nevertheless wants to buy goods and services. Again, for this to happen, the consumer's phone must have been manipulated. Otherwise, the consumer's phone (knowing the account balance) will not sign the transaction. During an offline payment process, such an attack is not detectable by the merchant. However, since the merchant receives a signed transaction from the consumer, the merchant has proof in the form of the signed payment. The fraud will be detected when the internet connection is reestablished, as the transaction cannot be validated by the base layer committee or the payment channel. We assume that such cases of fraud will be rare, as the consumer's name can be identified by law enforcement. Changing the software to commit fraud is a severe breach of the law, and a dishonest consumer will incur prosecution.

In summary, our system may allow offline payments in emergency situations, and even external punishment in case of malicious user behavior. These features are uncommon in blockchain systems as they lack identifiable accounts.

Governance and Challenges

Although transactions on a blockchain rely on decentralized validations of transactions, the maintenance and development of the infrastructure requires additional governance and funding. In particular, improvements to the technology, introducing technical upgrades, and changes of parameters and in communication, have to be taken care of. While some of these tasks can also be decentralized over time, they should be entrusted to a new public entity operating the eFranc infrastructure. It might be conceived in a similar way to SIX, which operates the infrastructure for the Swiss financial system.

Actually, Switzerland is extremely well positioned to develop an eFranc for two reasons. With SIX, it has quite some experience in setting up and operating infrastructures for the financial system. Moreover, Switzerland belongs to the countries in which blockchain technologies are actively developed. As a possible downside, one might be concerned that an eFranc might become more attractive in foreign countries as a storage of value, with side effects on the currency valuation.

Moreover, a number of technical challenges still need to be addressed, as our chapter can only be a first draft of these new processes and structures. In particular, the eFranc might explicitly support offline money.[14] Finally, if the internet is down, no transactions can be verified by the committee. Hence, no new channels and payment systems can be established until the internet resumes its functions. As discussed above, the payment layer can continue to operate for some time if the internet is down.

CONCLUSION

We suggest introducing the eFranc in an experimental phase in the Swiss monetary system. The eFranc would not revolutionize or disrupt the monetary system, but would enable the system to evolve in a controlled manner. Such caution is desirable, as each step towards new technologies has to be adapted and analyzed carefully to maintain the systems in their functions at all times.

NOTES

1. We would like to thank Florian Böser, David Mangini, Tejaswi Nadahalli, Harald Nedwed, the referees and the editors for valuable comments.
2. For an analysis of the current hierarchical monetary system, see Faure and Gersbach (2021). Money creation processes are summarized in McLeay et al. (2014) and Bundesbank (2017).
3. The precise access rules differ across currency areas and may include a varying number of financial intermediaries other than commercial banks.
4. For Switzerland, see https://www.admin.ch/opc/de/classified-compilation/20021117/index.html and https://www.admin.ch/opc/de/classified-compilation/20040259/index.html#a18 for its minimal reserve rules.
5. While cryptological methods play an essential role in digital transactions, with a token-based form of banknotes we mean that its transactions are validated on a distributed ledger.
6. An alternative approach for a digital banknote has been developed by Giori Digital (private discussions with Giori Digital SA on the basis of its Retail CBDC solution).
7. Moreover, in times of large reserve holdings of banks at the central bank, one might introduce incentives or even restrictions for banks to convert these reserves into eFrancs.

8. This does not exclude the emergence of further specialized financial institutions operating these channels.
9. The literature has identified several reasons why commercial banks allocate too much lending capacity to boom states and too little to bad states (see e.g. Gersbach and Rochet 2017).
10. Nevertheless, an eFranc does not imply that physical banknotes should be abolished. The unique features of physical banknotes—for example, complete anonymity, immediate verification of completeness of exchange, and protection against negative interest rates—typically outweigh the disadvantages of facilitated tax evasion and criminal activities. Physical banknotes should remain an option for the public (Wissenschaftlicher Beirat beim Bundesministerium für Wirtschaft und Energie 2017).
11. See Gersbach et al. (2021) for a recent contribution.
12. A further comparison can be made with the solution in which the central bank offers payments accounts to everybody (see Berentsen 2020).
13. One might envisage law enforcement being entitled to learn the identity of the account holder, in the event of the account displaying connections with illegal activities.
14. The current e-krona project of the Sveriges Riksbank intends to develop a "value-based" system that would enable the public to hold electronic central bank money either on a prepaid card or on a mobile phone (https://www.riksbank.se/en-gb/payments-cash/e-krona/, accessed on November 4, 2019). For an analysis of the differences and similarities between a value-based and an account-based system, we refer the reader to Kahn et al. (2018).

REFERENCES

Agur, Itai, Anil Ari, and Giovanni Dell'Ariccia. Designing central bank digital currencies. International Monetary Fund Working Paper, 252, 2019.

Andolfatto, D. Assessing the impact of central bank digital currency on private banks. Federal Reserve Bank of St Louis Working Paper, 026C, 2018.

Auer, R. and R. Böhme. The technology of retail central bank digital currency. *BIS Quarterly Review*, March 2020.

Avarikioti, Georgia, Eleftherios Kokoris Kogias, and Roger Wattenhofer. Brick: Asynchronous State Channels, 2019.

Bank of England. Central bank digital currency: opportunities, challenges and design. Bank of England Discussion Paper, March 2020.

Barrdear, J. and M. Kumhof. The macroeconomics of central bank issued digital currencies. Bank of England Staff Working Paper, 605, 2016.

Baudet, Mathieu, George Danezis, and Alberto Sonnino. Fastpay: high-performance Byzantine fault tolerant settlement, 2020.

Berentsen, A. Plädoyer für den E-Euro—Implikationen für die Gesellschaft. University of Basel Faculty of Business and Economics Working Papers, 2020/17, 2020.

Berentsen, A. and F. Schär. The case for central bank electronic money and the non-case for central bank cryptocurrencies. *Federal Reserve of St Louis Review*, 100(2): 97–106, 2018.

Bindseil, Ulrich. Central bank digital currency: financial system implications and control. *International Journal of Political Economy*, 48(4): 303–335, 2019.

Böhme, Rainer. The technology behind CBDCs: state of the art, design options, and implications. Presentation at the BIS-OeNB Workshop on Digital Currencies, Central Banks and the Blockchain: Policy Implications, Vienna, October 25, https://www.oenb.at/dam/jcr:0b5d72a7-e154-4495-8084-098f470325ff/BOEHME.pdf (accessed February 24, 2020), 2019.

Bordo, M.D. and A.T. Levin. Central bank digital currency and the future of monetary policy. National Bureau of Economic Research Working Paper, 23711, 2017.

Böser, F. and H. Gersbach. Monetary policy with a central bank digital currency: the short and the long term. Mimeo, 2020.

Bundesbank. The role of banks, non-banks and the central bank in the money creation process. Deutsche Bundesbank Monthly Report, 2017.

Cecchetti, S.G. and K. Schoenholtz. Universal central bank digital currency? Blogpost, *Money and Banking*, April 22, 2018.

Chiu, J., S.M. Davoodalhosseini, J. Hua Jiang, and Y. Zhu. Central bank digital currency and banking. Bank of Canada Staff Working Paper, 20, 2019.

Decker, Christian and Roger Wattenhofer. A fast and scalable payment network with Bitcoin duplex micropayment channels. In 17th International Symposium on Stabilization, Safety, and Security of Distributed Systems (SSS), Edmonton, Canada, August 2015.

Engert, W. and B. Fung. Central bank digital currency: motivations and implications. Bank of Canada Staff Working Paper, 16, 2017.

Faure, S. and H. Gersbach. On the money creation approach to banking. *Annals of Finance*, 17: 265–318, 2021.

Gersbach, H., Y. Liu, and M. Tischhauser. Versatile forward guidance: escaping or switching? *Journal of Economic Dynamic and Control*, 127: 104087, 2021.

Gersbach, H. and J.-C. Rochet. Capital regulation and credit flunctuations. *Journal of Monetary Economics*, 90: 113–124, 2017.

Kahn, C.M., F. Rivadeneyra, and T.-N. Wong. Should the central bank issue e-money? Bank of Canada Staff Working Paper, 58, 2018.

Keister, T. and D. Sanches. Should central banks issue digital currency? Bank of Philadelphia Working Paper, 26, 2019.

McLeay, Michael, Amar Radia, and Ryland Thomas. Money creation in the modern economy. *Bank of England Quarterly Bulletin*, 2014.

Norges Bank. Central bank digital currencies. https://www.norges-bank.no/en/news-events/news-publications/Reports/Norges-Bank-Papers/2018/ norges-bank-papers-12018/, 2018

Pichler, P., M. Summer, and B. Weber. Does digitalization require central bank digital currencies for the general public? *Monetary Policy and the Economy*, Q4: 40–56, 2019.

Poon, Joseph and Thaddeus Dryja. The Bitcoin Lightning Network. https://lightning.network/lightning-network-paper.pdf, 2016.

Ricks, M., J. Crawford, and L. Menand. A public option for bank accounts (or central banking for all). UC Hastings Research Paper, 287, 2018.

Schär, F. and A. Berentsen. *Bitcoin, Blockchain and Cryptoassets: A Comprehensive Introduction*, MIT Press, 2020.

Sliwinski, Jakub, Yann Vonlanthen, and Roger Wattenhofer. Consensus on demand. CoRR, abs/2202.03756. https://arxiv.org/abs/2202.03756, 2022.

Sliwinski, Jakub and Roger Wattenhofer. ABC: Asynchronous Blockchain without Consensus. ArXiv ePrint 1909.10926. https://arxiv.org/abs/1909.10926, 2019.

Wissenschaftlicher Beirat beim Bundesministerium für Wirtschaft und Energie. Zur Diskussion um Bargeld und die Null-Zins-Politik der Zentralbank. https://www.bmwi.de/Redaktion/DE/ Publikationen/Ministerium/Veroeffentlichung-Wissenschaftlicher-Beirat/gutachten-wissenschaftlicher-beirat-gutachten-diskussion-um-bargeld.4442 (accessed December 17, 2019), 2017.

8. Lessons from a decade of cryptocurrency hacks, 2011–2021

Ben Charoenwong and Mario Bernardi

OVERVIEW

The cryptocurrency market has grown over 300 000 percent since its inception over a decade ago, attracting a large pool of talented developers and piquing the interests of legendary investors such as Paul Tudor Jones, Ray Dalio, and Stanley Druckenmiller. Unfortunately, the meteoric rise in Bitcoin value has also drawn the attention of bad actors, including hackers, scammers, and fraudsters. We estimate that the damages from the biggest hacks alone, using the Bitcoin price in October 2021, amount to around $88.6 billion. For comparison, analysts estimate the entire Mexican drug trafficking to be worth $13 billion a year (White House 2006).

Cyber hacks are detrimental to the development of crypto businesses. Such hacks can decrease trust in the entire cryptocurrency ecosystem, particularly as a core value proposition of cryptocurrencies is the inability of bad actors to steal the currency. In this chapter, we detail some of the most notable hacks, thefts, and embezzlements over the past decade. For each case, we discuss a brief history, what allowed the hack, and regulatory and cyber security consequences. In general, the hacks can be grouped into three categories:

1. Security breach: this hack happens most often, mainly because the hackers could find a loophole in the security system and exploit the most out of the opportunity, rendering some of the core infrastructure of these exchanges practically without any protection. Breaches are also one of the biggest reasons why exchanges are constantly investing in the newest security measures to better protect their customers' funds.
2. "Human error" hack: this kind of hack typically involves ransom emails or malwares into their system, which allows hackers to obtain the private keys for the exchanges' wallets. Often, this type of hack is the most glaring for most exchanges, as it relates to exchanges' attention to detail. When the actual event happens, some of these exchanges are not even aware of what is taking place, which signals negligence on their part.
3. Agency problem: the last type of hack occurs not because of negligence or inferior security measures, but because of an inside job. Either the founders suddenly disappear alongside the cold wallet containing the customers' funds, or they work with hackers to slowly siphon the funds from the wallet over an extended period. This type of hack is the hardest to avoid because bad actors within the

company are hard to detect. They are well versed in masking their intentions until the opportunity is ripe. Given the history of this kind of hack, it is common for cryptocurrency exchanges to offer some form of insurance against this potential breach.

SAMPLE AND METHODOLOGY

We look at cryptocurrency news sources for cryptocurrency hacks between 2011 and 2021, compiling reporting from CoinDesk, Bloomberg, The Block, SelfKey, Blockworks, and other re-publishers. Where applicable, we also include additional links to the raw documentation that provides the information we collected.

As a reference currency, we include all amounts in Bitcoin (BTC), even if the theft may have involved other currencies. All currency exchange rates are based on the end of the month of the hack, where applicable. The underlying assumption is that the stolen amount is likely not converted into fiat currency immediately, in which case the rising value of the hacked cryptocurrency will raise the US dollar (USD)-implied value of the stolen cryptocurrency. We provide the USD equivalent of the stolen currency as an additional reference. Finally, to the extent that some of the stolen cryptocurrencies were returned or recovered, we do not include the total recovered amount, as some were still being recouped as of this writing in the second half of 2022. Therefore, our findings can be interpreted as an upper bound of the stolen value. The details of each individual event and appropriate references are on the companion site to this textbook.[1]

FINDINGS

Table 8.1 shows the summary of cryptocurrency thefts. Of the three major types of breaches, we find that 20 of the 30 events were security breaches due to authentication systems and private key information not being stored in secure locations. The next most common is human error—accounting for five of the 30 events—whereby an unwitting person falls victim to scams or phishing emails, which then deposit malware. The last category accounting, for two of the thefts, is the agency problem, which refers to an insider to the cryptocurrency exchange who steals the money.

We also find that the hacks clustered after 2017 following the rapid rise of the value of the cryptocurrency market. And despite only accounting for five of the 30 events, the inside jobs carried the highest financial cost, with the most recent Africrypt hack alone accounting for $3.6 billion in losses.

Overall, if the stolen amounts were immediately converted to Bitcoin but then held until today, the stolen cryptocurrencies valued at 1.289 million BTC are equivalent to over $88 billion at its all-time high of $68 789. Instead, if all currencies were immediately converted to USD by the end of the month of the hack, we estimate that the amount stolen would be around $7 billion. Whether the stolen currency amounts

Table 8.1 *Summary of crypto hacks, 2011–2021*

No.	Date	Impetus	Original Amount in Coin Stolen	BTC Equivalent	USD Equivalent	Type
1	June 2011	Mt. Gox Private Key Hack	2 643 BTC	2 643	30 000	Security Breach
2	March 2014	Mt. Gox Transaction Malleability	850 000 BTC	850 000	460 000 000	Security Breach
3	July 2014	Mintpal Hack	8 000 000 Vericoin	3 225	2 000 000	Security Breach
4	January 2015	Bitstamp Malware Attack	19 000 BTC	19 000	5 100 000	Human Error
5	August 2015	BTER Inside Job	7 170 BTC	7 170	1 750 000	Agency Problem
6	May 2016	Gatecoin Hot Wallet Breach	250 BTC and 185 000 ETH	4 463	2 000 000	Security Breach
7	August 2016	Bitfinex-BitGo Theft	119 756 BTC	119 756	66 000 000	Security Breach
8	April 2017	Yapizon Hot Wallet Breach	3 816 BTC	3 816	5 300 000	Security Breach
9	December 2017	NiceHash Payment Compromise	4 736 BTC	4 736	62 000 000	Security Breach
10	January 2018	Coincheck Virus Hack	523 000 000 NEM	47 711	533 000 000	Human Error
11	February 2018	Bitgrail Hack/Exit Scam	17 000 000 NANO	19 044	170 000 000	Security Breach
12	April 2018	CoinSecure Inside Job	438 BTC	438	3 300 000	Agency Problem
13	June 2018	Bithumb and Coinrail Theft	US$71 000 000 of XRP and ETH	10 394	71 000 000	Security Breach
14	September 2018	Zaif Hot Wallet Breach	5 966 BTC, undisclosed BCH, and MonaCoin	9 089	60 000 000	Security Breach
15	December 2018	QuadrigaCX Theft	26 350 BTC or US$130 000 000	26 350	130 000 000	Agency Problem
16	March 2019	Coinbene Inside Job	US$100 000 000 of HPT, NPSX, MXM, and UDOO	25 202	100 000 000	Agency Problem
17	May 2019	Binance Hack	6 270 BTC	6 270	40 000 000	Human Error
18	June 2019	Bitrue Hack	9 300 000 XRP and 2 500 000 ADA	361	3 900 000	Security Breach
19	November 2019	Upbit Security Breach	342 000 ETH	6 771	51 000 000	Security Breach
20	July 2020	Cashaa Malware Hack	336 BTC	336	3 100 000	Human Error

No.	Date	Impetus	Original Amount in Coin Stolen	BTC Equivalent	USD Equivalent	Type
21	September 2020	KuCoin Security Breach	US$281 000 000 of BTC and ETH	26 137	281 000 000	Security Breach
22	December 2020	EXMO Security Breach	US$10 500 000 of BTC, XRP, ZEC, ETC, and ETH	422	10 500 000	Security Breach
23	June 2021	Africrypt Hack	69 000 BTC	69 000	3 600 000 000	Agency Problem
24	August 2021	Poly Network Hack	US$600 000 000 of USDC, BTC, and ETH	12 964	600 000 000	Security Breach
25	August 2021	Liquid Hack	US$91 350 000 of BTC and ETH	1 941	91 350 000	Security Breach
26	October 2021	Cream Finance Hack	US$130 000 000 of ETH and its derivatives	2 102	130 000 000	Security Breach
27	November 2021	Boy x Highspeed Theft	US$139 000 000 of various cryptocurrencies	2 404	139 000 000	Human Error
28	December 2021	Badger DAO Hack	US$120 000 000 of BTC and ETH	2 544	120 000 000	Security Breach
29	December 2021	Bitmart Security Breach	US$196 000 000 of ERC-20 tokens and BSC tokens	4 155	196 000 000	Security Breach
30	December 2021	AscendEX Security Breach	US$77 700 000 of ERC-20, BSC, and Polygon tokens	1 647	77 700 000	Security Breach
			Total Amount Stolen	1 289 886	7 015 030 000	

Note: The table shows the summary of the 30 large cryptocurrency thefts from 2011 to 2021. In many situations, the exact date of the theft is either unknown or not disclosed. Therefore, we include the month in which it occurred. BTC and USD equivalent are converted from the original stolen cryptocurrency at point-in-time prices using the end-of-the-month BTC and USD values. In some cases where no direct pairwise price is available, we consider a three-way conversion through BTC to USD using the mid-price as of the end of the month.

to $7 billion or over $88 billion depends on how quickly the bad actors could convert cryptocurrency into fiat currency. To the extent that many of the bad actors in the cryptocurrency world have some stake in the continual growth of the cryptocurrency market, and to the extent that quickly converting large amounts of stolen currency into fiat currency is not frictionless, we assume that the bad actors would keep the stolen value in Bitcoin to allow easy transport and transaction with other parties in the cryptocurrency market.

Several other patterns also emerge. First, many of the exploits are due to exchanges, due to either direct security breaches or agency problems. Despite the promise of cryptocurrency being decentralized, the main methods of interfacing with the markets are through centralized outlets. In fact, some exchanges do not even provide a wallet to a specific individual. Instead, account holdings are pooled in wallets held directly by the exchange, not the end client. As a consequence of this scenario, successful attackers on the exchange itself can escape with most or all of the value in the exchange wallet directly, affecting numerous end users.

Second, even using a proper wallet (hot or cold) does not fully block against human error arising from susceptible traders falling for phishing expeditions. The fact that cryptocurrency wallet access is a single-authentication point means this problem inherently cannot be addressed without the introduction of some additional level of trust, an intermediary such as a password manager, which can send and interpret multi-factor authentication. One example of such a service is Fireblocks, which takes custody of a user's private key and promises additional layers of security by parsing keys into multiple segments so that no single point of attack can compromise access. Such service providers have started to flourish as the market matures and more institutional capital flows into the market. For human error, the main method to alleviate these issues is simply more education and due diligence. To this end, there are also increasing numbers of training programs and certifications in cryptocurrency and digital assets offered by reputable institutions. However, the incentives to provide these countermeasures against vulnerabilities may be outpaced by the gains from the cryptocurrency market if the price growth is too fast. We discuss the implications of the recent boom in cryptocurrency below.

Third, many crypto exploits themselves have trouble cashing out their theft. The fact that many exploits are on-chain (although they may cross multiple chains) also means that they are somewhat traceable. Therefore, blacklists have formed in response to the exploits, effectively locking out some cryptocurrency funds from the system permanently. In these situations, not only does the value get stolen from an original user, but the entire amount is effectively removed from the monetary system completely due to the blacklists enforced by centralized authorities such as exchanges or large traders. Not all the stolen coins could have been cashed out of the cryptocurrency ecosystem into fiat, but the values reported in Table 8.1 still represent losses to market participants. Even if a wallet is blacklisted for having stolen some cryptocurrency, the wallet may be ostracized from interacting with some of the cryptocurrency community (but not all of the market, since not all participants need to adhere to the blacklist). In addition, bad actors may also use cross-chain on- and off-ramps to launder stolen cryptocurrency and bypass blacklists, to the extent that the decentralized enforcement cannot track cross-chain transactions. Unfortunately, the very nature of decentralized finance with no current regulatory body does not permit authority to ensure that funds can be recovered.

Finally, in addition to the high-profile crypto hacks and exploits, reports of crypto-based cybercrimes, specifically on Bitcoin Abuse—a peer-driven website where victims of cyberattacks disclose the addresses that the alleged criminals use to receive payments—included over 15 000 incidents in 2018, over 75 000 in 2019, over 100 000 in 2020, and over 55 000 in 2021. The website contains the alleged criminal address, total BTC exploited, report date, and the number of affiliated transactions. There are also categories for each type: Blackmail, Darknet Market, Ransomware, Tumbler (using services such as TornadoCash, which mixes users and transactions to reduce on-chain footprint), Sextortion (messages threatening to reveal a history of adult content consumption to email contacts), and Other.

LESSONS FROM CRYPTOHACKS

As the cryptocurrency market continues to rise in value, so will the pay-offs for bad actors. However, as centralized entities such as exchanges handle larger values of transactions and act as custodians for larger amounts, so the reputational cost associated with losing clients' cryptocurrency increases. The past decade of large-scale cryptocurrency thefts has implications for current market participants. These thefts should bring more awareness of how important managing digital assets can be, proving highly beneficial for newcomers to the space. Participants may think that instead of trusting their funds to centralized entities such as exchanges, they may consider using cold wallets. However, that is also not without risks, as losing the cold wallet, or having it stolen physically, still poses potential risks. Which effect will tend to dominate, remains an empirical question.

Nonetheless, the history of hacks in the crypto ecosystem illustrates how nascent the niche is, echoing the equity markets in the early 18th century. While exchanges are keeping up to date with the latest security improvement measures, users need to understand that even the most sophisticated exchanges can be breached. Therefore, emerging insights from behavioral finance and economics from the past several decades of research can provide some insight into the consequences of these hacks and the attention people pay to cryptocurrency markets overall.

Overall, interest in cryptocurrency has dramatically increased over time (Figure 8.1), skyrocketing by over 100 000 percent in search volume interest, and collapsing following the 2018 crash. As its price rose again in 2020, attention on cryptocurrency increased again, with even more adoption by retail traders. The aggregate patterns exhibit a strong consistency with a "fear of missing out" as cryptocurrency prices rose. As discussed above, as prices rise, so too does the pay-off of theft or hacks. Because the costs to secure most cryptocurrencies do not scale with their price, we should not be surprised to see more crypto hacks as the price booms.

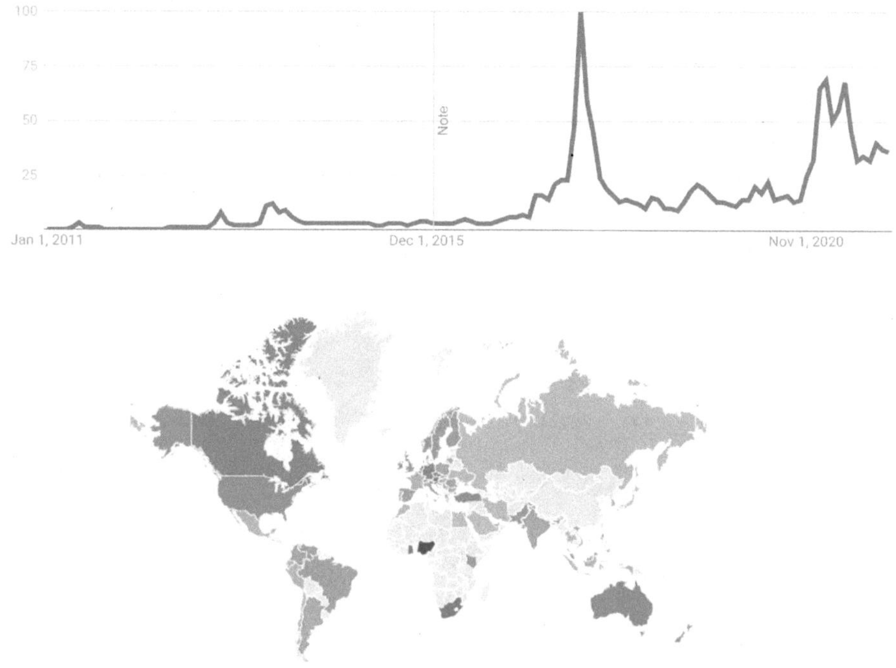

Source: Google search volume of "Bitcoin" over time and across regions.

Figure 8.1 *Attention to Bitcoin from 2011 to 2021*

But digging more specifically into each specific crypto hack also reveals some interesting human psychology insights. While it's true that the exploits cause losses to the existing market participants, the exploit itself is also typically covered in the media. In the same reporting, media outlets typically outline the cryptocurrency's stratospheric gains prior to the crash. So in some sense, even the coverage of the exploit itself, which reveals information on the amount of theft, can induce a fear of missing out—a concept we discuss in more detail below.

For example, consider the Africrypt hack revealed on June 24, 2021, which cost US$3.6 billion in losses at the time of reporting. We see attention towards overall cryptocurrency, defined by Google searches for the terms "cryptocurrency," "bitcoin," "Ethereum," and "crypto," rising overall right at the revelation of the incident (Figure 8.2). So, on the one hand, value was lost from the theft. On the other hand, people became increasingly aware of cryptocurrency more broadly around these events.

The Africrypt hack is not a peculiar case. Even three years before that, in the Coincheck hack revealed on January 31, 2018, for a loss of $523 million, a similar pattern emerges (Figure 8.3), and people started paying more attention to cryptocurrencies overall. An interesting difference is that across these two large-scale events,

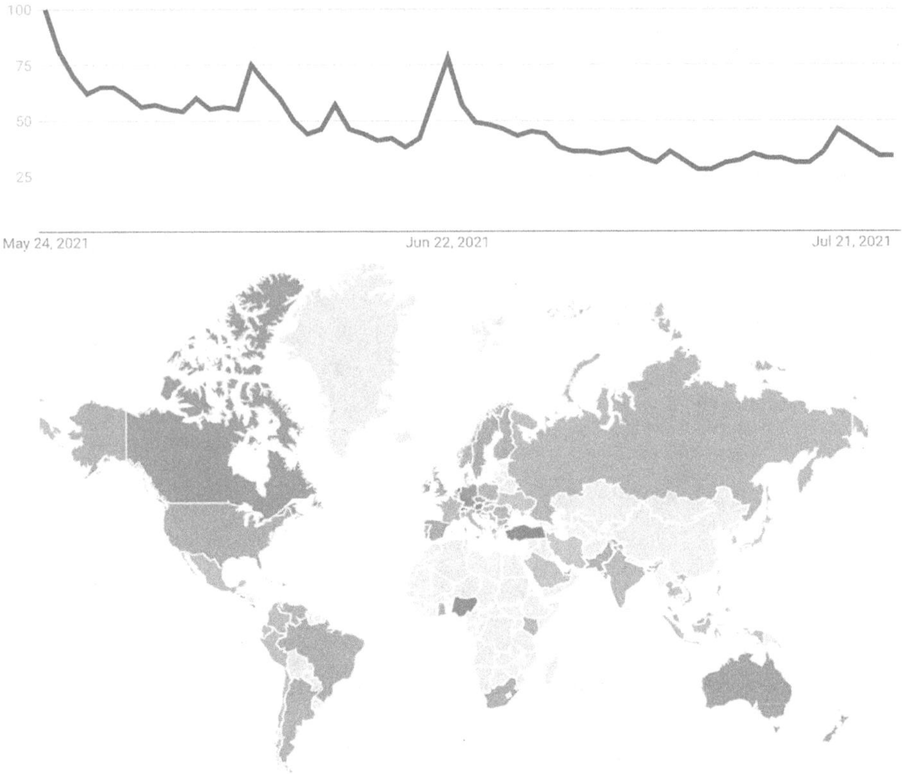

Source: Google Trends.

Figure 8.2 Attention to cryptocurrencies around the Africrypt hack

the countries with the most searches differ. As there are still many non-adopters in the market, the additional awareness of cryptocurrencies overall may actually induce more people to enter the market in the near future following the exploits, in a somewhat "buy-the-dip" mentality.

Motivated by these examples, we discuss additional features of cryptocurrency markets that affect market participant psychology, which may exploit susceptibilities. In addition, we discuss some research that highlights specific features or impossibilities of cryptocurrency markets as lessons for future developers and market participants.

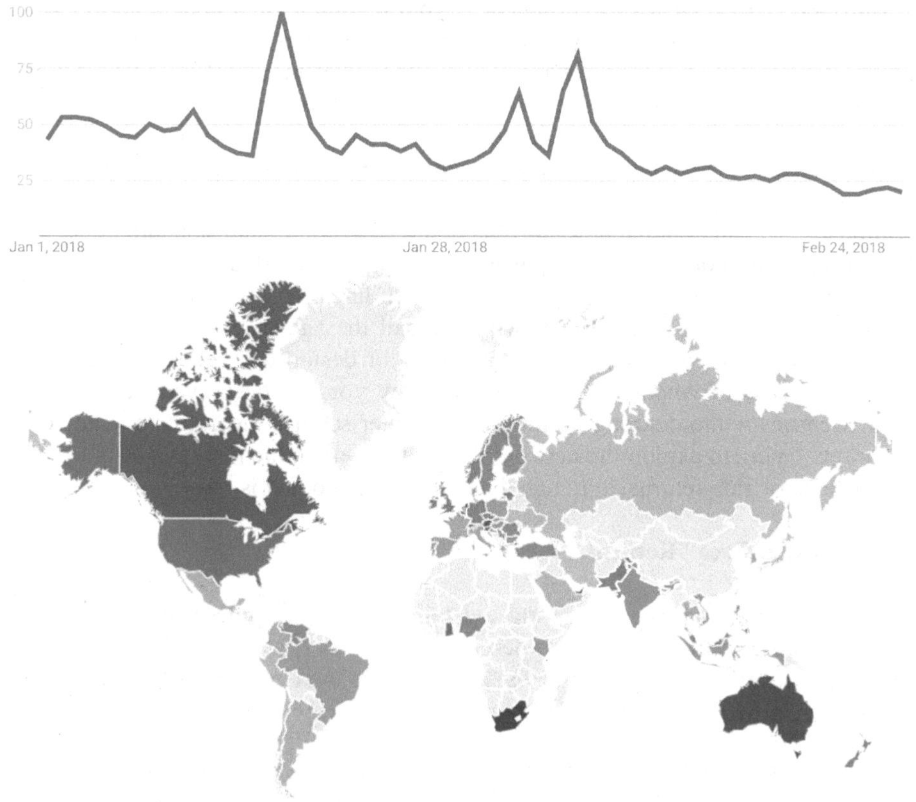

Figure 8.3 *Attention to cryptocurrencies around the Coincheck hack*

A SURE THING AND FEAR OF MISSING OUT

A decentralized finance (DeFi) endeavor attempts to join ideas about computing and economics. Blockchain-powered smart contracts enable new approaches to solving financial problems, and the technology introduces new trade-offs. Specifically, the possibility of a credible and known money supply rule, combined with consensus protocols to maintain a public ledger without reliance on a trusted institution, raises the question of whether the existing monetary and financial system can be replaced with an untrusted, decentralized, self-sustaining system. Further, the rise of blockchains with smart contracting functionality raises the question of whether automated market makers and protocols can replace current financial institutions. This DeFi has even induced existing financial institutions in traditional finance (TradFi) to invest in the ecosystem, perhaps as insurance against the chance that DeFi can disrupt the system. So, there seems to be some promise.

But there are some lessons from the crypto exploits listed above, and research on investments and human psychology. The fear of missing out can induce more uninformed traders to enter the market, fueling what may end up being a Ponzi scheme. A "tell" is the promise of stable and high returns in a very volatile market. Exemplifying this pattern is the fact that many cryptocurrency protocols or vaults display returns as an annual percentage yield (APY)—a term typically used for safe deposits—as compared to risky assets such as the stock market, where S&P 500 returns are typically quoted in terms of annualized averages and standard deviations. Importantly, the notions of both reward and risk are reported. This condition was not so for many cryptocurrency protocols, which later were revealed to be hacks or "rug pulls"—a colloquial term for what we call the agency problem above. Even well-intentioned protocols may crash due to poor design that relies on impossibilities, regardless of whether they were fueled by young, starry-eyed developers in their twemties without strong training in computer science theory, or by bad actors purposely trying to exploit the new uninformed traders in the market. Many of these mark stable or safe returns, although the underlying product is risky.

Crypto "Risk-Free" Returns

Let us go through an example in more detail to illustrate some of these ideas. For example, consider the certificate of deposit—a security typically offered by licensed financial institutions—offered by Hex. According to the United States Securities and Exchange Commission website investor.gov, a certificate of deposit (CD) is:

> A savings account that holds a fixed amount of money for a fixed period of time, such as six months, one year, or five years, and in exchange, the issuing bank pays interest. When you cash in or redeem your CD, you receive the money you originally invested plus any interest. Certificates of deposit are considered to be one of the safest savings options. A CD bought through a federally insured bank is insured up to $250,000. The $250,000 insurance covers all accounts in your name at the same bank, not each CD or account you have at the bank.
>
> As with all investments, there are benefits and risks associated with CDs. The disclosure statement should outline the interest rate on the CD and say if the rate is fixed or variable. It also should state when the bank pays interest on the CD, for example, monthly or semi-annually, and whether the interest payment will be made by check or by an electronic transfer of funds. The maturity date should be clearly stated, as should any penalties for the "early withdrawal" of the money in the CD. The risk with CDs lies in the risk that inflation will grow faster than your money and lower your real returns over time.

In contrast, Hex's advertisement (Figure 8.4) suggests annual interest of 38 percent, possibly even more if the returns can be compounded. The advertisement also touts the benefits from "significant price appreciation," and taps directly into the fear of missing out by claiming that it is "the fastest-appreciating digital asset in history." Importantly, as of October 2022, the term "risk" does not once show up on its main website (not even in the disclosures). The Frequently Asked Questions response to the question, "Is HEX a Ponzi, pyramid scheme, MLM, scam, ICO or security?", is a terse "No." And the response to the question, "Why is there no whitepaper?", is "It's more important to put work into a good website than a good whitepaper. Still there is a technical explanation here which is considered HEX's whitepaper." Again, the term "risk" does not once show up in the technical explanation. So, absent the risk disclosures, why not get rich quickly? The offer sounds amazing, offering a safer and more conservative investment than other cryptocurrencies, meanwhile still offering significant opportunity for growth on top of the guaranteed rate of return.

Source: Hex.com. Accessed May 2022.

Figure 8.4 *Hex Online marketing banner*

For context, Hex was also offering 38 percent returns while competitors such as BlockFi (backed by Coinbase and facing its own legal troubles as of 2022) were offering 3 percent APY, and five-year bank-offered certificates of deposit were yielding 3.15 percent. Not typically discussed is the fact that the Hex return was offered in terms of its own currency; the BlockFi return was offered in terms of Bitcoin. Only the five-year, bank-offered deposit gave returns in United States dollars. But nonetheless, to assuage concerns that it is too good to be true, it relies heavily on the term "certificate of deposit," stating on its website in May 2022 that "this common investment tool is used by hundreds of millions of people worldwide with a market value in the trillions."

Like many other cryptocurrencies, Hex rode the fear of missing out wave for a significant gain with returns of around 30 times the initial investment from January 2021 through September 2021, but collapsing back in 2022 (Figure 8.5). Nonetheless, for insiders who started in 2021 or before at a price point below 1.5 cents, the returns are at least 300 percent. Although new investors coming in around 2021 may have lost significant value, insiders likely still benefited. It turns out that Hex is not unique in the price pattern, and may potentially be misleading in its marketing. Interestingly, Hex.com maintains an active page dedicated to whether it is a scam. On the page, accessed in October 2022, the banner "HEX is not a scam" appears prominently. Whether or not regulators will turn their attention to this certificate of deposit remains to be seen, but the underlying fundamental remains: DeFi can offer opportunities, but there may also be schemes that promise outsized returns with little mention of risk, which may be misinterpreted. In a rising market where uninformed investors are quick to act and slow to read and absorb news, the opportunities for bad actors increase.

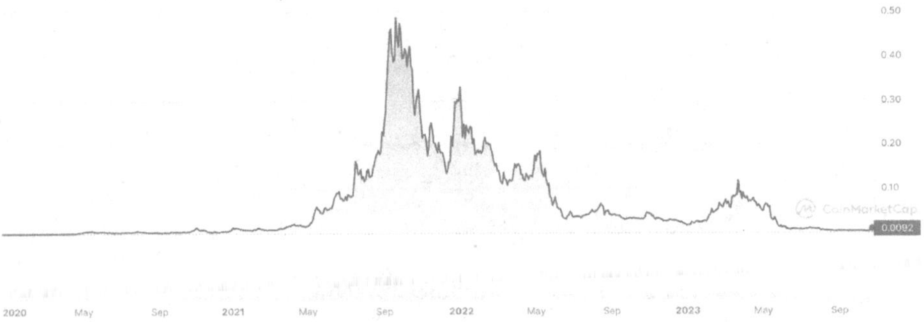

Source: Coinmarketcap. Accessed October 30, 2022.

Figure 8.5 *Hex-to-USD prices*

For DeFi, the feasibility of a positive risk-free rate is important for building a new financial system since it is a building block underlying much of the infrastructure of modern financial engineering. For example, a large portion of derivative finance relies on dynamic replication techniques that will not carry over absent a risk-free asset. As a construction within both economics and computer science, DeFi protocols are subject to both fields' limitations.

Since it aims to use advancements in both computation and cryptography to tackle standard economic problems, DeFi must therefore operate within the intersection of constraints required by both the computer science and economic domains. Research by Charoenwong et al. (2023a) explores a foundational question at the junction of those fields: Can DeFi truly offer a risk-free rate? Relying on well-known theoretical results from computer science dating back to Alan Turing's pre-World War II paper places bounds on what decentralized financial products can be built, and constrains the shape of future developments in DeFi. Among other limitations, the authors show that markets in DeFi are incomplete, and a risk-free rate is inadmissible. Specifically, the paper finds that a general Turing-complete smart contract language is incompatible with a decentralized risk-free positive yield. The result follows from both Turing-completeness and decentralization properties. The former means that a smart contract cannot be proven to halt, while the latter means that allowing an authority to intervene to halt the program is unacceptable as a solution. The research paper's contribution includes showing what classes of products cannot work—what cannot be copied wholesale from TradFi—and viewing recent advances in DeFi through the lens of an economic model based on computational theory. Smart contracts are not alchemy: they cannot generate yield out of nothing. Therefore, all reported DeFi "APYs" inherently contain some risk. It simply is not disclosed in many protocols. Until someone designs a smart contract infrastructure more powerful than a Turing machine, enforcing an environment without risk with only code in a complex decentralized system will not be possible.

Manufacturing Stability from Risky Assets

In the same spirit, many protocols have been created in an attempt to maintain stability in the face of the volatile cryptocurrency market. The market has grown to over US$100 billion. And since 2019, the International Monetary Fund has launched its series titled Fintech Notes, with plenty of writings on stablecoins, and kick-started by the cryptocurrency Libra, launched by what was then still called Facebook, until now with the failure of a handful of stablecoins.

While stablecoins bear some resemblance to pegged fiat currencies of many emerging markets, there are notable differences. For example, it is possible, in principle, to maintain stability via a decentralized smart contract rather than a central bank or other monetary authority with discretionary power. And although the concept of dollarization in international finance and economics traces back hundreds of years, the touted benefits of this stablecoin innovation are their low-cost, global reach (for example, USD Coin by Circle launched in 85 countries in 2019), and transaction speed. They also serve as on-ramp and off-ramp securities between TradFi and DeFi protocols. Many protocols attempt to manufacture a stable token backed by risky assets.

One example of stablecoin is the case of Terra Lab's stablecoin, UST. Before its spectacular collapse in the summer of 2022, UST was a large stablecoin that garnered much attention from investors and skeptics alike. According to reporting by the *Financial Times*, clients could lend their stablecoin for a yield of almost 20 percent annually, touted like a safe deposit, with advertising on Binance in April 2022 (just one month before its collapse) featuring the words "High Yield, Safe & Happy Earn" (Figure 8.6). The advertisement, circulated on the private messaging platform Telegram, was viewed over 100 000 times. It is different from standard securities because the advertisement contained no risk disclosures.

Note: Binance's Telegram message, viewed 117 000 times.
Source: https://www.ft.com/content/d459f435-edff-412c-85a5-0961d50aba69.

Figure 8.6 *Binance Online marketing banner*

Just one month later, mid-May 2022, the value of the Terra Luna token collapsed alongside the value of UST (Figure 8.7). After confidence in UST fell, it entered a death spiral, and no amount of algorithmic trading could maintain its stability. The peg breaking is reminiscent of emerging market economies such as those in the Asian Financial Crisis in 1997, whereby many Southeast and East Asian currencies depreciated with no recovery.

Figure 8.7 *LUNA-to-USD prices*

Inherently, the issue of stablecoins is similar to the provision of a risk-free interest rate in DeFi. In follow-up work, Charoenwong et al. (2023b) study whether it is possible to create a decentralized and capital-efficient stablecoin using smart contracts that algorithmically trade to maintain stability. They show that an imperfectly backed algorithmic stablecoin cannot be provably stable.

Exploits covered above which featured agency problems where stolen funds continue to trade on-chain may also be tracked. Therefore, the role for regulatory enforcement of existing property rights rules seems straightforward. However, the development of new regulatory frameworks surrounding frameworks remains an active area of deliberation.

FINANCIAL REGULATION AND CONSEQUENCES

As the entire crypto market grew in market capitalization, so too did the number of hacks. Simultaneously, more and more attention is also being paid to the need or desire for regulatory guidelines and frameworks for cryptocurrency operators. In Figure 8.8, we show Google attention to the term "crypto regulation" over time.

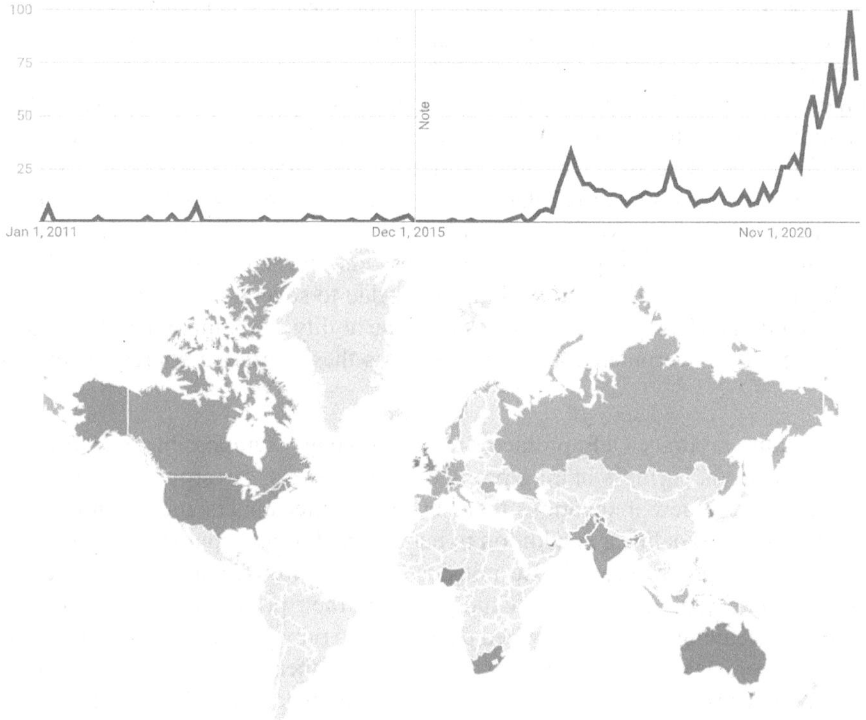

Source: Google Trends. October 2022.

Figure 8.8 *Attention to crypto regulation*

Unsurprisingly, countries with the most capital and with more at stake (both to lose and to gain in the cryptocurrency markets) also had the highest interest. Nonetheless, interest alone also does not mean that government agencies are passing more rules.

Actual regulation itself lags. So, not only does the interest in regulation and regulatory changes typically come after some crisis in the market itself, but the regulatory deliberation and rule-making process itself is also often stymied by a lack of education and familiarity, uncertainty, and partisanship. Regulators around the world walk a fine line. On the one hand, they want to appear embrace new financial innovations, particularly those which can improve financial market access in underserved market segments. On the other hand, most regulators also have a mandate for investor protection, which typically entails increasing the hurdles that individuals need to clear in order to be able to participate in risky markets. In booming markets, regulators are hesitant to pass rules slowing down the market, for fear of backlash from the public for not wanting them to get rich.

Since 2017, regulators around the world have taken different paths. Generally, the regulations can be viewed as positive or negative. “Sandboxes” for new start-ups to operate and experiment represent one example of positive regulation. As an example of negative regulation, we may consider those that specify what business models are banned, or outright ban the use of cryptocurrencies by a particular country’s residents in general.

Figure 8.9 from Coincub summarizes the different types of positive and negative regulations as of October 2022. Although the regulatory landscape is likely to change in the future, what seems clear now is that, by and large, regulators are adopting mostly positive government regulations, permitting the testing and usage of certain financial technology innovations associated with cryptocurrency use.

So what do the large crypto exploits and research in cryptocurrency tell us? From our classifications, large crypto exploits occur due to several main reasons: security breaches, human error, or agency problems. The ability of regulation and regulatory enforcement by government agencies to address these different sources of exploits differs:

1. Regulating arbitrary DeFi protocols to have no bugs is impossible; a well-known problem from Turing’s halting problem. Nonetheless, governments can experiment with the new innovations themselves to better understand common issues and provide guidelines, in addition to hard rules, for new companies to adopt.
2. Regulating human error is also not possible, as to err is human. Little can be done to stop people from accidentally posting their private key online in a code block, or leaving their unencrypted passwords in public view. After all, the whole premise of DeFi was to have a single-factor authentication, where one single point of access suffices for all transactions. Nonetheless, regulators may promote the use of security layers or vaults to protect sensitive information more securely. The key point to note here is that, inherently, by having government agencies that can regulate the market in the first place, we are assuming that society trusts the

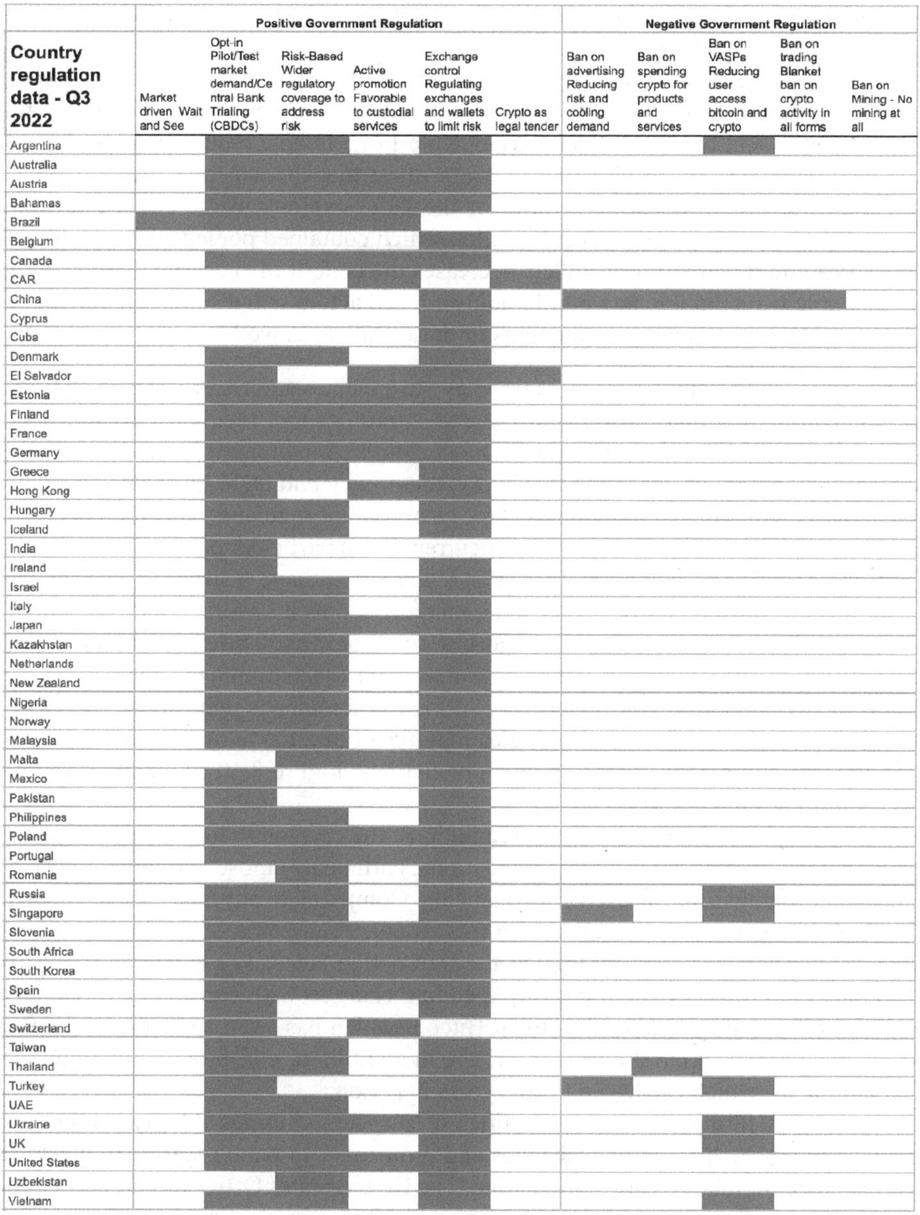

Source: Coincub. https://coincub.com/cryptocurrency-regulation-around-the-world/. Accessed October 17, 2022. Published October 12, 2022.

Figure 8.9 *Country regulations in 2022*

government. If not, then using other kinds of security layers will involve trusting other service providers instead.
3. Therefore, regulation can only mainly address and tackle agency problems. Here, governments can regulate the use of custody, reminiscent of the United States Securities and Exchange Commission Rule 17a-5, which requires broker-dealers who have custody of client accounts to attest that the accounts are segregated from the firms' assets. A handful of the large exploits in the past came from a direct attack on an exchange's wallet, which contained pooled customer funds. Spreading it across more wallets decreases the benefit of successfully exploiting a single wallet in the network. In doing so, bad actors will also be less enticed or attentive to the transaction amounts of these wallets as well.

Because outright banning cryptocurrencies stifles innovation and experimentation, it is not surprising that most countries adopt more positive regulatory frameworks. We also note additional challenges for most countries: regulators compete with one another. By nature of decentralization, cryptocurrency and DeFi protocols generally enjoy participation from individuals across a myriad of regulatory jurisdictions.

One country banning the use of cryptocurrency or a particular protocol may simply shift the adoption to other countries. For regulators to have a strong impact on the ecosystem, it must either be a very large market such as the United States or China, or a coalition of regulators must impose a common set of rules and enforcement mechanisms. Even with the latter, note that even the harmonized regulations on anti-money laundering worldwide vary in their enforcement intensities. Therefore, restricting the use of these technologies may result in a game of Whack-a-Mole as the services and hosting simply move jurisdictions. Figure 8.10 summarizes crypto regulations around the world.

Beyond the consideration of new regulations, the cryptocurrency market also has implications for existing rules and regulations, particularly those pertaining to fraud, anti-money laundering, and terrorist financing. Compared to physical cash payments, blockchain transactions are easier. To this extent, even some of the large exploits may be partially resolved by tracing the transaction steps. For example, the 2016 BitFinex hack was revealed to be by a couple charged with conspiracy to launder US$4.5 billion; the value of the stolen Bitcoin which has risen since the hack. The conspiracy carries up to 20 years in prison, in addition to conspiracy to defraud the United States, which carries up to five years in prison.[2]

Even when finding the exact identities of suspects is impossible, typically centralized nodes such as large exchanges and protocols can band together to blacklist certain nodes or tokens from participating. The United States Office of Foreign Assets Controls recently released a list of blockchain nodes to its Specially Designated Nationals list, commonly known as the "blacklist." Requiring cryptocurrency operators, for example exchanges such as Coinbase, to adhere to these blacklists can cause a segmentation of the cryptocurrency market. Therefore, the stolen funds may not be able to participate with the compliant segment of the market.

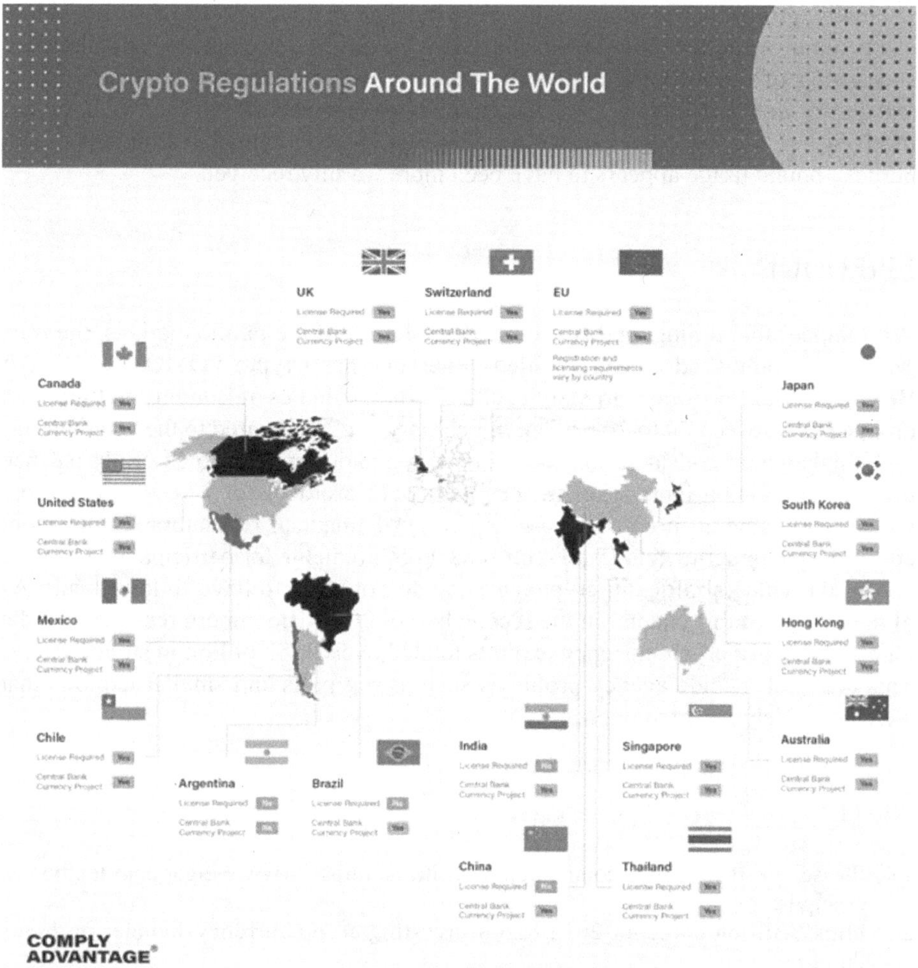

Source: https://complyadvantage.com/insights/cryptocurrency-regulations-around-world/. Accessed October 17, 2022. Originally published July 5, 2018, updated August 25, 2022.

Figure 8.10 Crypto regulations around the world

In this case, law enforcement agencies can weave digital footprints to identify other hackers, sometimes individuals and groups. On the one hand, over the past decade, stealing cryptocurrency and sitting on it would have generated high returns to theft. Moving large amounts of funds is much easier than carrying physical cash. On the other hand, exploits in the blockchain are also more traceable than actual cash theft. But the clear picture is that exploits cause decreases in welfare, as even blacklists that are effective would simply burn and lock up cryptocurrencies from the system.

Finally, governments which adopt more positive regulations tend also to explore using some of the technologies in their own currencies through the establishment and testing of central bank digital currencies (CBDCs). However, their efficiency and utility are still unclear. For example, Nigeria's eNaira appears to have not received a warm welcome. However, Singapore's programmable Singdollar with purpose-bound usage appears to have been more warmly received.

EPILOGUE

With impeccable timing, and reflecting the zeitgeist of the public markets, the *New York Times* published an article titled "Everyone has Crypto FOMO, but Does It Belong in Your Portfolio?" in March 2022. Trading volumes of Bitcoin and Ethereum dropped by between 50 to 70 percent in February 2022 compared to the year before.[3]

A fundamental consideration for financial regulation will be to carefully balance between embracing innovation such as new DeFi protocols or investor protection, which may come at more of a cost to privacy if financial regulators require more anti-money laundering and know-your-client requirements for participants.

Yet, the vulnerabilities in cryptocurrency do not seem to have followed suit. As of the writing of this chapter in the second half of 2022, Bloomberg reported that the number of major cryptocurrency exploits totaled over US$2 billion in stolen tokens. This does not include agency problems such as rug pulls and smaller exploits that were not widely reported upon.

NOTES

1. Please see the book's companion website at https://www.e-elgar.com/textbooks/cronqvist
2. https://edition.cnn.com/2022/02/08/investing/cryptocurrency-laundering/index.html.
3. https://www.nytimes.com/2022/03/24/your-money/Bitcoin-investing-cryptocurrency.html.

REFERENCES

Charoenwong, B., Kirby, R.M., & Reiter, J. "Risk-Free Interest Rates in Decentralized Finance." In 2023 Fifth International Conference on Blockchain Computer and Applications (BCCA) (October 2023a, pp. 466–473). IEEE. Retrieved from https://ieeexplore.ieee.org/document/10338890.

Charoenwong, B., Kirby, R.M., & Reiter, J. "Computer Science Abstractions to Help Reason about Decentralized Stablecoin Design." IEEE Access (2023b). Retrieved from https://ieeexplore.ieee.org/abstract/document/10258164.

White House. "National Drug Control Strategy." Report. February 2006. Retrieved from https://www.justice.gov/archive/olp/pdf/ndcs06.pdf.

9. Financial economics of automated market makers

Alexander Brauneis, Roland Mestel, and Martin Rauch

INTRODUCTION

In traditional financial (TradFi) markets, the trading of assets is organized by employing a central limit order book (LOB). Market participants submit orders to the LOB, stating the volume they wish to trade as well as the maximum (minimum) price at which they are willing to buy (sell). These so-called limit orders are executed on a price-time priority, that is, other market participants who are willing to accept any price will buy (sell) at the lowest (highest) price currently available in the LOB. If two limit orders happen to offer the same price, the one submitted first to the LOB will be executed. Besides new limit orders entering the LOB, existing limit orders may be changed or cancelled at any time. In liquid markets, this usually results in numerous updates of the LOB every second.

In decentralized finance (DeFi)—blockchain-based trading mechanisms—a market designed in the fashion of a TradFi LOB would be infeasible for at least two reasons. First, updates to the LOB would be restricted by the respective blockchain's block time. For instance, with the Ethereum blockchain, updates in an LOB could only happen roughly every 15 seconds. Second, each update to a blockchain-based LOB would be subject to fees paid to miners or validators, which can be substantial. In late 2018, UniSwap was deployed on the Ethereum blockchain. UniSwap is a smart contract-based protocol that overcomes the limitations of LOB trading mechanisms on blockchains by proposing a novel way that facilitates the exchange of assets, referred to as automated market makers (AMMs).[1] In essence, AMMs are pools of two assets where one can be exchanged for the other along predetermined rules. Since UniSwap's inception, a number of similar decentralized exchanges (DEXs) have been deployed to many different blockchains, with a total daily trading volume of more than US$1 billion by the end of 2022. The growing importance of DEXs over the last few years has also attracted the attention of academia. Therefore, DeFi, DEX, and AMM are the subject of a growing body of literature.

Some academic papers explore AMMs from a theoretical perspective. One of the first theoretical analyses was provided by Angeris et al. (2019), who study constant product and constant mean AMMs. Xu et al. (2021) and Mohan (2022) provide an overview of different types of AMM mechanisms. Bartoletti et al. (2021) develop a theoretical model that describes the interactions between AMMs and its users. Others derive optimal levels of liquidity provision and trading fees. Also, the optimal arbitrage problem has been analyzed for AMMs. Evans et al. (2021) analyze how fees should be set in order to maximize liquidity providers' returns. Fritsch and Wattenhofer (2021) prove that in theory a Nash equilibrium for an optimal fee level exists. Aoyagi (2020) studies equilibrium liquidity provision in the light of asymmetric information. Angeris et al. (2019), Angeris and Chitra (2020), as well as Evans (2020), examine the optimal arbitrage model for different AMM mechanisms.

Another topic within the literature on AMMs is impermanent loss (IL). Tiruviluamala et al. (2022) provide a general framework to analyze properties of the IL functions of different AMM protocols. Clark (2020) shows that a liquidity provider's payoff can be replicated with a static combination of futures and options. Khakhar and Chen (2022) propose an algorithm to find a combination of derivatives to hedge liquidity positions. Aigner and Dhaliwal (2021) point out the option-like payoff structure of IL in uniform and concentrated liquidity AMMs. Deng and Zong (2022) extend their research and formally prove that it is possible to statically replicate a liquidity provider's IL with standard European options.

Furthermore, Krishnamachari et al. (2021) propose the idea of dynamic automated market makers (DAMMs), which eliminate the need of arbitrageurs to keep prices in line with reference market prices. Park (2021) theoretically outlines the shortcomings of constant product AMMs, such as that they conceptually incentivize miners to perform front-running, and proposes a different mechanism. The concept of concentrated liquidity, which was implemented by the UniSwap v3 protocol[2] and which allows liquidity providers to set price ranges within which they want to provide liquidity, has also been researched recently. (e.g., Fritsch 2021).

Besides the theoretical literature on AMMs, an increasing number of papers study AMM mechanisms empirically. The focus lies on evaluating the profitability of liquidity provision for different trading pairs, exchange platforms, and AMM mechanisms (Heimbach et al. 2021; Parlour and Lehar 2021), price efficiency and arbitrage opportunities (Barbon and Ranaldo 2021; Wang et al. 2021), interaction of trading activities and liquidity provision between centralized exchanges (CEXs) and DEXs (Barbon and Ranaldo 2021), and potential security concerns (Daian et al. 2019). Because UniSwap is the largest DEX in terms of trading volume, most empirical studies are conducted based on transactions from the UniSwap network.

The remainder of this chapter is structured as follows. It first briefly outlines the main characteristics of AMM, then discusses the mechanics of AMM in detail, before addressing liquidity provision in AMM pools. The final section concludes.

COMPONENTS OF AN AMM MARKET

As outlined in the introduction, implementing an LOB exchange on a blockchain leads to high transaction costs and consumes a lot of storage space. To overcome these inconveniences, most DEXs rely on the concept of automated market making. Contrary to the conventional LOB mechanism, an AMM does not require the matching of a buy and sell order to conduct a trade. Instead, trades are facilitated by a liquidity pool, which technically is a smart contract that holds a specific pair of blockchain based assets, or tokens, in reserve. The rate at which traders can conduct trades against the liquidity pool is determined by the trading function. The latter is a formula that algorithmically provides an exchange rate for which a trader can buy or sell a specific amount of tokens.

Before describing different AMM mechanisms in more detail, it is important to elaborate on the basic components of and the interactions between different groups of participants within an AMM market. In general, an AMM market consists of liquidity providers on the one hand, who send a specific pair of tokens to the liquidity pool, and traders on the other hand, who conduct trades against the liquidity pool.

Liquidity Providers

Liquidity providers (LPs) are market participants who provide liquidity by sending tokens to a liquidity pool. Technically, a liquidity pool in its most simple version is a smart contract that stores two different tokens which will then be used for trading. As a simple analogy, consider a basket which is filled with apples and bananas (provided by LPs). Trade happens by adding one fruit to the basket and taking out a predetermined number of the other fruit. In a similar fashion, cryptoasset pools can be created that allow for the trading of a pair of two tokens. For every single trading pair (for example, ETH/USDT), a distinct liquidity pool has to be created.

To incentivize market participants to provide liquidity to these pools, LPs earn fees for each trade that is conducted against the liquidity pool. LPs can redeem their liquidity at any time, so they are not bound to provide liquidity for a specific time horizon. Since by providing liquidity they enable the execution of trades, the role of a liquidity provider in an AMM can be compared to that of a market maker in a traditional exchange.

Traders

Traders are market participants who want to buy or sell different tokens. In an AMM market, they conduct their trades against liquidity pools. For example, if a trader wants to buy token A in exchange for token B, this trade will be facilitated by the A/B liquidity pool (that is, a liquidity pool that keeps tokens A and B in reserves). In particular, the trader will send a specific number of units of token B to the pool and in exchange will receive a specific number of units of token A and vice versa. The exact number of units of token A she receives for each unit of token B is determined by the trading function used by the liquidity pool. Also, not the entire amount of units of token B sent to the pool will be included in the trade, since a fraction of it will be rewarded to the liquidity providers in the form of trading fees. Traders also play an essential role by conducting arbitrage trades with which they ensure that a token's price in an AMM market always reflects the reference market price, for example, the price in other markets such as centralized crypto exchanges.

Trading Function

The exchange rate at which traders can swap tokens against the liquidity pool is determined by a predefined formula that takes the liquidity pool's token reserves as input. Most DEXs apply a variant of the class of constant function market maker (CFMM) formulas. What all types of CFMMs have in common is that they require the value of a function, which is calculated based on the pool's token reserves, to be constant before and after a trade (hence the notion "constant function").[3] This value, that has to be held constant, is called the invariant, and subsequently referred to as k. The currently most widely applied CFMM is the constant product market maker (CPMM), which is also why we will analyze the constant product function in more detail than other types of CFMMs.

CONSTANT FUNCTION MARKET MAKERS

The trading function algorithmically determines an exchange rate for which traders can conduct trades against the liquidity pool. As already outlined, most DEXs deploy a CFMM formula as their trading function. This section provides an exemplary overview of the most relevant types of CFMMs. While the actual trading functions that are applied by different DEXs may be very complex to model, they essentially build up on standard types of CFMMs. Rather than analyzing the particular design of specific DEXs' trading functions in detail, the aim of this chapter is to foster a better understanding of the general mechanisms of CFMM functions.

Constant Product Market Maker

The constant product market maker (CPMM) is the most prominent CFMM function.[4] The CPMM formula defines the product of the pool's token reserves as the function's invariant k. Let a pool consist of x units of token A and y units of token B, then the product of the token reserves is given by:

$$xy = k \tag{9.1}$$

Trading against a CPMM pool

If a trader wants to buy Δx units of token A in exchange for Δy units of token B, they will effectively remove Δx units of token A from the pool and add Δy units of token B to the pool. The following equation must then hold:

$$(x - \Delta x) \bullet (y + \Delta y) = xy = k \tag{9.2}$$

From equation (9.2), one can derive that, in absence of trading fees, in order to buy Δx units of token A, a trader has to pay:

$$\Delta y = y \bullet \frac{\Delta x}{x - \Delta x} \tag{9.3}$$

units of token B. Equivalently, for Δy units of token B, a trader receives:

$$\Delta x = x \bullet \frac{\Delta y}{y + \Delta y} \tag{9.4}$$

units of token A.

While equations (9.3) and (9.4) compute exchange rates without taking trading fees into account, DEX protocols do actually charge a percentage fee for each trade in practice. The trader pays the fee in units of the token they wish to sell, which reduces the number of tokens that effectively can be swapped for the other token. Let ς be the percentage fee charged for each trade and $\tau = 1 - \varsigma$. Then, if a trader initiates a sale of Δy units of token B, $\varsigma \Delta y$ units of token B will be charged as trading fees and only the remaining $\tau \Delta y$ units of token B can be used for the purchase of token A. Therefore, incorporating trading fees, equation (9.2) modifies to:

$$(x - \Delta x) \bullet (y + \tau \Delta y) = xy = k \tag{9.5}$$

Correspondingly, equations (9.3) and (9.4) will change to:

$$\Delta y = \frac{y \bullet \frac{\Delta x}{x - \Delta x}}{\tau} \tag{9.6}$$

and:

$$\Delta x = x \bullet \frac{\tau \Delta y}{y + \tau \Delta y} \tag{9.7}$$

Equations (9.6) and (9.7) show that whenever trading fees are charged, the number of units of token B a trader has to pay to buy Δx units of token A is higher, or equivalently, the number of units of token A a trader can buy for Δy units of token B is lower, as compared to when there are no trading fees involved.[5] After the trade has been executed, the fee that has been paid by the trader is added to the liquidity pool and thereby rewarded to the liquidity providers, proportional to their pool share.

As equations (9.3) and (9.4) already indicate, the price for which traders can exchange tokens against the liquidity pool is determined by the pool's token reserve ratio (*RR*), which is the ratio between the number of units of each token in the pool. So $RR_{A/B} = \frac{y}{x}$ sets the number of units of token B in proportion to the number of units of token A and thus expresses how many units of token B the pool currently holds for each unit of token A. Analogously, $RR_{B/A} = \frac{x}{y} = \frac{1}{RR_{A/B}}$ denotes the number of units of token A that the liquidity pool currently holds for each unit of token B.

For an infinitesimally small trade size $\Delta y \to 0$ and in absence of trading fees, the ratio at which tokens can be exchanged equals the pool's token reserve ratio.[6] We define this ratio as a token's quoted price. So, token A's quoted price, denoted in units of token B, is given by:

$$P_{A/B} = RR_{A/B} = \frac{y}{x} \tag{9.8}$$

Analogously, token B's quoted price, denoted in units of token A, would be given by $P_{B/A} = RR_{B/A} = \frac{x}{y}$. DEX protocols report a token's quoted price as its current price. So, for example, if the UniSwap ETH/USDT liquidity pool currently holds 100 units of ETH and 10 000 units of USDT, the quoted price $P_{ETH/USDT}$ would be 100 (since $\frac{10000}{100} = 100$).

Assuming that there exists an external market (for example, a centralized exchange such as Binance, Coinbase, Kraken, or others) where tokens A and B are traded as well, based on arbitrage considerations, the pool's token reserve ratio must always reflect the price at which the respective tokens are traded in an external market, which we refer to as the reference market price $P^r_{A/B}$. If this is not the case and, for example, $P_{A/B} < P^r_{A/B}$, arbitrageurs would buy token A for $P_{A/B}$ from the CPMM liquidity pool and sell it for $P^r_{A/B}$ on the reference market. This would cause an increase in the quoted price and a decrease in the reference market price, until ultimately the equilibrium of $P_{A/B} = P^r_{A/B}$ is restored again.[7] Whenever the pool's quoted price and thus its token reserve ratio equals the reference market price, each token's reserve contributes equally to the overall value of the pool's liquidity reserves.

While the quoted price is the price for which an infinitesimally small trade in absence of trading fees could theoretically be conducted, a measure that may be more relevant for a trader is the realized price, which captures the actual ratio at which tokens are exchanged in a transaction:[8]

$$P'_{A/B} = \frac{\Delta y}{\Delta x} \tag{9.9}$$

The realized price tells a trader how many units of token B they have to pay for each unit of token A for a given trade size of Δy. As the following example will illustrate, the realized price will always diverge from the quoted price in a way that $P'_{A/B} > P_{A/B}$. From a trader's point of view, this means that the actual number of units of token B they have to pay to receive one unit of token A will always be larger; or, equivalently, the actual number of units of token A they receive for one unit of token B will always be smaller than the quoted price suggests.

Numerical example

A liquidity pool consists of 50 units of token A and 100 units of token B. For each trade, the pool charges a fee of 1 percent of the trading volume. A trader arrives and wants to sell seven units of token B in exchange for token A.

Liquidity pool composition prior to the trade

Before the trade is conducted, the pool consists of 50 units of token A and 100 units of token *B*. Since the pool's quoted price equals its reserve ratio, we have $P_{A/B} = \frac{100}{50} = 2$. Furthermore, the invariant *k*, which must remain constant before and after the trade, can be calculated according to equation (9.1), that is, $k = 50 \bullet 100 = 5000$.

Trade execution

The trader wants to swap a total of seven units of token *B*, which they send to the liquidity pool. Since the pool charges a trading fee of 1 percent, 0.07 ($= 7 \bullet 0.01$) units of token *B* will be deducted and only the remaining 6.93 ($= 7 \bullet 0.99$) units will enter the trade. In a next step, the liquidity pool will apply the CPMM function to compute the number of units of token A the trader will receive in exchange for 6.93 units of token *B*.[9] Applying equation (9.4) yields:[10]

$$\Delta x = 50 \bullet \frac{6.93}{100 + 6.93} = 3.24$$

Liquidity pool composition after the trade

Consequently, the liquidity pool will exchange 6.93 units of token *B* for 3.24 units of token *A*. Hence, starting from the initial token reserves, the number of units of token A within the pool will decrease to 46.76 ($= 50 - 3.24$), while the number of units of token *B* will increase to 106.93 ($= 100 + 6.93$). Now, it can also be shown that the trade did not change the invariant *k* since $50 \bullet 100 = 46.76 \bullet 106.93 = 5000$. However, the trade did affect the token reserve ratio and thus the quoted price $P_{A/B}$, which changed from 2 to 2.29 $\left(= \frac{106.93}{46.76}\right)$. After the trade has been conducted, the trading fee of 0.07 units of token *B* that has been deducted from the initial amount of units of token *B* that the trader sent to the pool, will be added to the liquidity pool, thereby slightly increasing the pool's token reserves.

Quoted price and realized price

From the trader's point of view, the token swap with the liquidity pool is equivalent to purchasing 3.24 units of token A at a price of 7 units of token *B*. The realized price $P'_{A/B}$ including trading fees is therefore 2.16 $\left(= \frac{7}{3.24}\right)$. The realized price is thus higher than the quoted price $P_{A/B}$ prior to the trade, which was 2. Put differently, while the quoted price suggested a price of two units of token *B* for each unit of token *A*, the trader actually had to pay 2.16 units of token *B* for each unit of token *A*.

Slippage

The divergence between the quoted and the realized price partly stems from the trading fee, since the quoted price discards fees. However, even after deducting the fee, the constant product formula converts 6.93 units of token *B* into 3.24 units of token *A*. This implies a realized price of 2.14 $\left(= \frac{6.93}{3.24}\right)$, which is still markedly above the quoted price of 2. The reason for this deviation, even after adjusting for trading fees, simply lies in the design of the CPMM formula. Consider again equation (9.4), which computes the number of units of token A that a trader receives in exchange for Δy units of token B:

$$\Delta x = x \bullet \frac{\Delta y}{y + \Delta y}$$

However, if tokens could actually be exchanged according to the quoted price, this would yield the following relationship between Δx and Δy:[11]

$$\Delta x = x \bullet \frac{\Delta y}{y} \tag{9.10}$$

By comparing equations (9.4) and (9.10), it is apparent that the CPMM formula will always yield a smaller number of Δx than an exchange according to the quoted price would, since $x \bullet \frac{\Delta y}{y + \Delta y} < x \bullet \frac{\Delta y}{y}$ for arbitrary (positive) values of x, y, and Δy. Geometrically speaking, the CPMM function is convex, hence the marginal number of units of token A that one unit of token B buys is decreasing.

The difference between the quoted and realized price that is caused by the shape of the CPMM formula is referred to as slippage.[12] While there is not one standard measure to express slippage (denoted by S) we define it as the relative difference between the realized and the quoted price:

$$S = \frac{P'_{A/B}}{P_{A/B}} - 1 \tag{9.11}$$

Slippage, as defined in equation (9.11), measures the percentage difference between the realized and the quoted price of token A.[13] Following the numerical example, S amounts to 6.93% $\left(= \frac{2.14}{2} - 1\right)$. In other words, even after adjusting for trading fees, the realized price for each unit of token A, denoted in units of token B, settles at a premium of 6.93 percent on the quoted price. The size of slippage that the trader bears depends on two parameters, namely, the size of the trade (that is, Δy), and the size of the pool (measured in terms of k, the product of the pool's token reserves). To see how each of the two parameters affects slippage, consider Table 9.1, which compares slippage for three different levels of k (pool size) and Δy (trade size) each.[14]

To summarize, the difference between the realized and the quoted price—that is, slippage—will be smaller for larger pool sizes as well as for smaller trade sizes. This is similar to the mechanisms of a traditional exchange, where the divergence between the execution and quoted price of a market order depends on the depth of the order book (which represents the asset's liquidity) and the order volume.

Table 9.1 *Slippage for different pool and trade sizes*

		Trade size		
		$\Delta y = 5$	$\Delta y = 5$	$\Delta y = 10$
Pool size	$k = 15\,000$	0.67%	3.33%	6.67%
	$k = 60\,000$	0.33%	1.67%	3.33%
	$k = 135\,000$	0.22%	1.11%	2.22%

Graphical representation of the CPMM formula

The CPMM function can be plotted in a plane, with the x coordinate indicating the number of units of token A and the y coordinate indicating the number of units of token *B* in the liquidity pool. Starting from the constant product rule $xy = k$, the function $y(x) = \frac{k}{x}$ is a graphical representation of all combinations of token reserves a liquidity pool can hold for a given liquidity level of *k*, as shown in Figure 9.1.

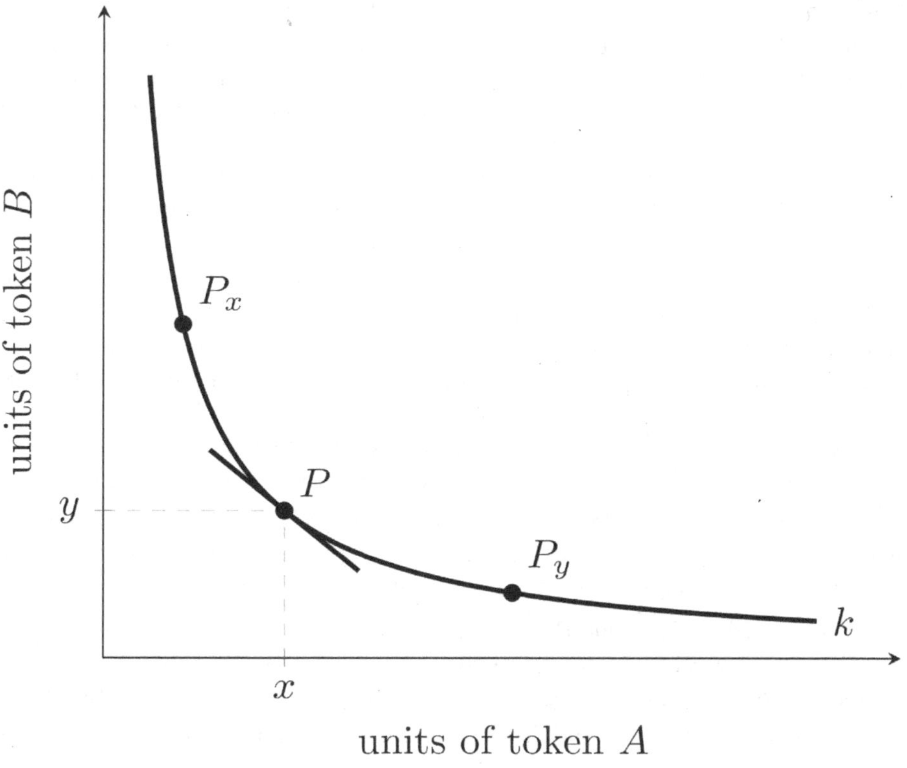

Source: Based on Mohan (2022: 16ff).

Figure 9.1 *Constant product function*

Consider the current state of the liquidity pool depicted in Figure 9.1 to be x units of token A and y units of token B, such that P represents the current token reserve ratio in the coordinate system. If a trader wants to buy token A in exchange for token B, this would decrease the number of units of token A and increase the number of units of token B within the liquidity pool, resulting in a shift of P upwards along the curve to the new pool composition P_x. Conversely, buying token B in exchange for token A would move P downwards along the curve to point P_y, since the trade would increase the number of units of token A and decrease the number of units of token B within the pool.

An arbitrarily small trade size, that is, $\Delta y \rightarrow 0$, would result in a marginal shift of P along the curve. It can be seen that the absolute value of the curve's slope at point P equals $\frac{y}{x}$ and hence is equivalent to the current quoted price $P_{A/B}$.[15] In general, the quoted price in a liquidity pool is equivalent to the absolute value of the slope of the trading function, that is, the derivative of $y(x) = \frac{k}{x}$ which equals $y'(x) = -\frac{k}{x^2}$ and therefore $P_{A/B} = \left|-\frac{k}{x^2}\right| = \left|-\frac{xy}{x^2}\right| = \frac{y}{x}$. The quoted price of token A tends to zero (infinity), if the number of units of token B goes to zero (infinity). However, a trade can never cause a token's reserve to fall to exactly zero, which means that the pool will always hold positive values of either token. This property of CPMM pools is referred to as the no-depletion property.

To see how the pool size affects a trade's realized price, consider Figure 9.2, which shows two trading curves for different levels of k. Since $k_2 > k_1$, one can think of k_1 as being the small and k_2 as being the large liquidity pool.

The initial states of the pools are given by the token reserve combinations of $(x_1|y_1)$ and $(x_2|y_2)$, which translate to points P_1 and P_2 on the curves k_1 and k_2, respectively. As indicated by the thin black lines that tangent points P_1 and P_2, k_1 at point P_1 has the same slope as k_2 at point P_2, which implies that both pools have the same quoted price.[16]

Next, a trader wishes to sell Δy units of token B. If he chooses to conduct the trade against the small pool, the pool's reserve combination would change to $(x_1'|y_1')$, which yields point P_1' on curve k_1. Analogously, if he traded against the large pool, the pool's reserve combination would change to $(x_2'|y_2')$, which yields point P_2' on curve k_2.[17] While the absolute values of the slopes of the tangent lines indicate the quoted price, those of lines $\overrightarrow{P_1P_1'}$ and $\overrightarrow{P_2P_2'}$ represent the realized prices, that is, the number of units of token B the trader has to pay for each unit of token A when selling Δy units of token B to the small and large pool, respectively.[18] Therefore, the difference in the slopes of $\overrightarrow{P_1P_1'}$ and $\overrightarrow{P_2P_2'}$ and their respective tangent lines graphically represents the degree of slippage in each trade. Also, when comparing $\overrightarrow{P_1P_1'}$ and $\overrightarrow{P_2P_2'}$, one can see that the slope of $\overrightarrow{P_1P_1'}$ is steeper than that of $\overrightarrow{P_2P_2'}$, which means that the average price a trader has to pay for each unit of token A is higher when trading against the small pool (that is, k_1). This shows that for a given trade size, slippage is larger when

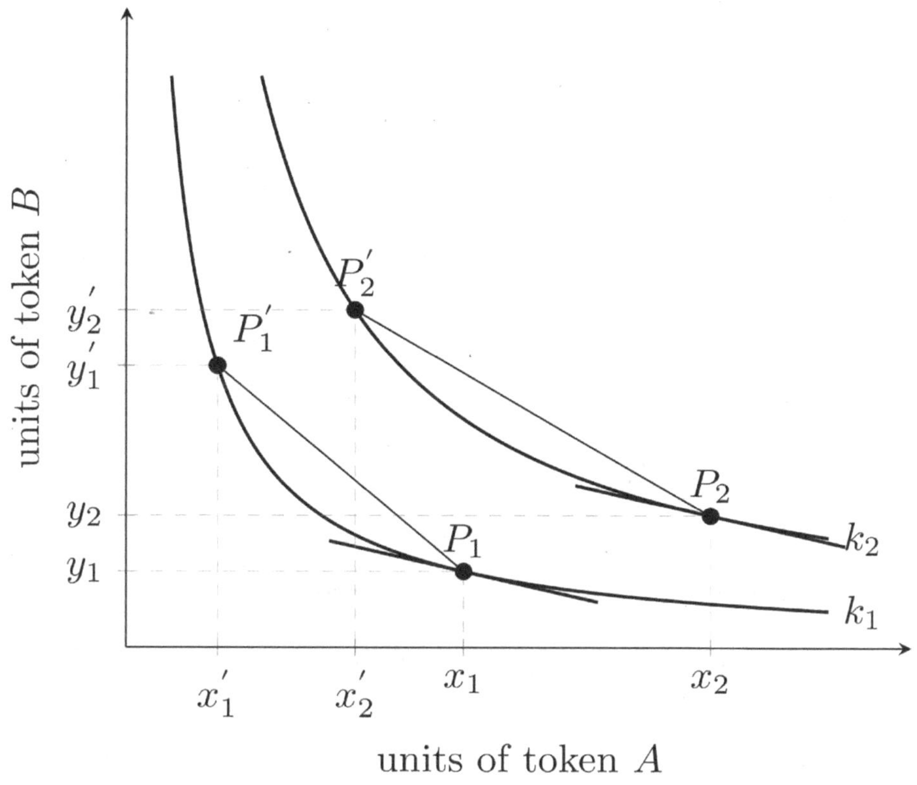

Source: Based on Mohan (2022: 16ff).

Figure 9.2 *Different pool sizes*

the pool size is smaller.[19] While in Figure 9.2 the size of the liquidity pools differs, Figure 9.3 depicts the execution of trades of different sizes against one liquidity pool.

Again, the pool's initial state is given by the token reserve combination of $(x|y)$, which translates to point P on the curve k. Now, a trader wishes to sell a) Δy_s or b) Δy_l units of token B, with $\Delta y_l > \Delta y_s$. While the small trade (that is, Δy_s) causes a shift upwards along the curve to point P_s with token reserves $(x_s|y_s)$, the large trade (that is, Δy_l) changes the token reserves to $(x_l|y_l)$, which corresponds to point P_l on the curve. Analogously to Figure 9.2, the absolute values of the slopes of the tangent line and lines $\overrightarrow{PP_s}$ and $\overrightarrow{PP_l}$ represent the quoted price and the realized prices of the small and large trades, respectively. By comparing lines $\overrightarrow{PP_s}$ and $\overrightarrow{PP_l}$, one can see that line $\overrightarrow{PP_l}$ has a steeper slope, which indicates that the average price a trader has to pay for each unit of token A is higher when conducting the large trade. This is in line with

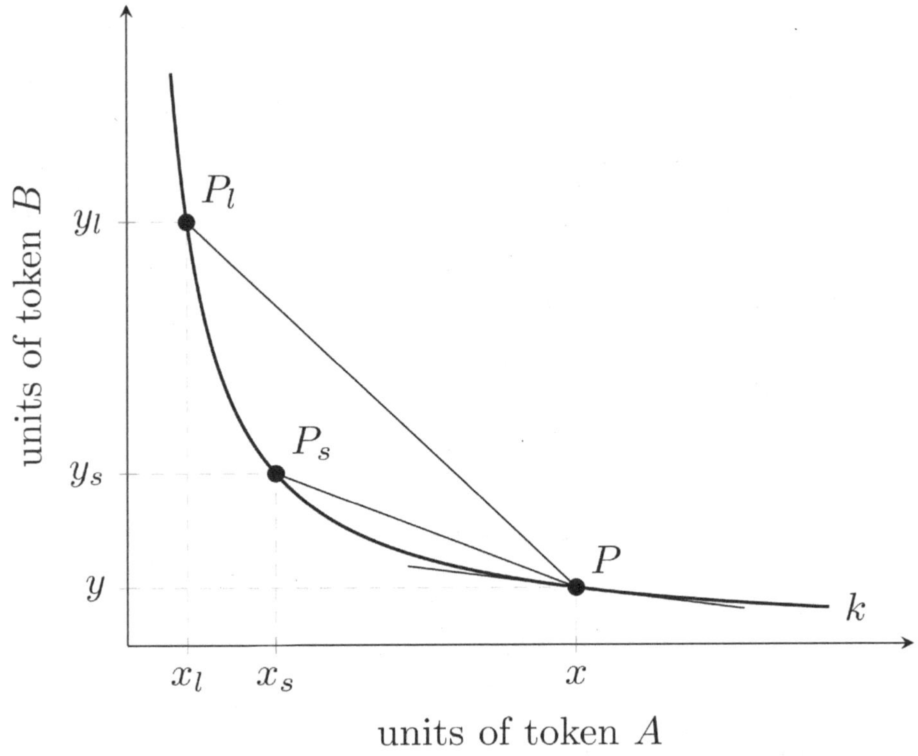

Source: Based on Mohan (2022: 16ff).

Figure 9.3 *Different trade sizes*

the results of Table 9.1, namely, that for a given pool size, the degree of slippage is larger when the trade size increases.

Constant Mean Market Maker

While the CPMM formula is the currently most widely applied AMM mechanism, there exist further variations of CFMM formulas. One of them is the constant mean market maker (CMMM), which can be seen as a generalization of the constant product formula. In the CMMM formula, the invariant k is defined as the weighted geometric mean of the pool's token reserves. Let a pool consist of N distinct tokens with x_n being the number of units and w_n the weight, with $\sum_{n=1}^{N} w_n = 1$, assigned to the reserves of the nth token, then k is given by:[20]

$$\prod_{n=1}^{N} x_n^{w_n} = k \tag{9.12}$$

The token weights determine the share that each token's reserve contributes to the overall pool value. For example, if a pool consists of tokens A, B, and C with token weights $w_a = w_b = w_c = \frac{1}{3}$, this means that the reserves of tokens A, B, and C each contribute one-third to the overall value of the pool's reserves.[21]

CMMM with two tokens

To gain a better understanding of the CMMM formula, consider a CMMM liquidity pool that only consists of two tokens, namely x units of token A and y units of token B, with w_a and w_b being the weights for the reserves of token A and B. In this case, the CMMM formula is given by:

$$x^{w_a} \bullet y^{w_b} = k \tag{9.13}$$

Now if a trader wants to buy Δx units of token A in exchange for Δy units of token B, without taking trading fees into account, the following equation must hold:

$$x^{w_a} \bullet y^{w_b} = (x - \Delta x)^{w_a} \bullet (y + \Delta y)^{w_b} = k \tag{9.14}$$

This means that in order to buy Δx units of token A, a trader has to pay:

$$\Delta y = \left(\frac{k}{(x - \Delta x)^{w_a}}\right)^{\frac{1}{w_b}} - y \tag{9.15}$$

units of token B. Equivalently, in exchange for Δy unis of token B, they will receive:

$$\Delta x = x - \left(\frac{k}{(y + \Delta y)^{w_b}}\right)^{\frac{1}{w_a}} \tag{9.16}$$

units of token A.[22]

While in the CPMM formula the quoted price is simply the ratio between the number of units of each token within the liquidity pool, in the CMMM formula, the token weights need to be considered, so that the quoted price is given by:[23]

$$P_{\frac{A}{B}} = \frac{w_a}{w_b} \bullet \frac{y}{x} \tag{9.17}$$

Analogously to the CPMM formula, the degree of slippage a trader incurs when trading against a CMMM pool equals the relative difference between the realized and the quoted price. Also the relations between the level of slippage and pool and trade size, respectively, are the same as discussed for the CPMM formula.

A special case of the CMMM formula is given when the pool consists of two distinct tokens and both tokens are equally weighted (that is, $w_a = w_b = 0.5$). The CMMM formula is then given by:

$$x^{w_a} \bullet y^{w_b} = \sqrt{xy} = k \tag{9.18}$$

Squaring equation (9.18) yields $x \bullet y = k^2$, which is equivalent to the trading function of the CPMM formula.[24] Therefore, since it is possible to model the CPMM function as a CMMM function with two tokens and equal weights, strictly speaking, the constant product formula can rather be seen as a special type of CMMM functions than a separate type of CFMM function.

CMMM with dynamic token weights

While we have assumed the token weights w_n to remain constant once determined, there also exist DEX protocols that dynamically adjust the token weights according to reference market prices. The intuition thereby is to maintain an equilibrium between the pool's and external prices without relying on the trading activities of arbitrageurs.[25]

To see how adjusting the token weights can keep the pool's price in line with the reference market price, keep in mind that, as illustrated in equation (9.17), a token's quoted price in a constant mean liquidity pool depends on the token reserve ratio and the ratio between the token weights. Now, consider a situation in which token *A's* quote price $P_{A/B}$ is lower than its reference market price $P^r_{A/B}$. If token weights are fixed, the gap between $P_{A/B}$ and $P^r_{A/B}$ would be closed by arbitrageurs buying token A from the pool (thereby increasing $P_{A/B}$, since $P_{A/B} = \frac{w_a}{w_b} \bullet \frac{y}{x}$) and selling it on the reference market, until the equilibrium is restored. However, if the CMMM uses dynamic token weights, $P_{A/B}$ could also be adjusted to $P^r_{A/B}$ by increasing w_a and decreasing w_b until $P_{A/B} = P^r_{A/B}$.[26] By adjusting the token weights, dynamically weighted CMMMs pose an opportunity to keep pool prices in equilibrium with those of external markets, while keeping token reserves constant.

In order to know the current reference market price, dynamically weighted AMMs rely on so-called price oracles. In the context of blockchain technology and smart contracts in general, an oracle is a gateway that transmits external information to the blockchain and thereby allows smart contracts to access this information and process it accordingly. A price oracle therefore reports token prices from external sources to the blockchain, which DEX protocols can subsequently process as a token's reference market price. Dynamically weighted AMMs therefore heavily rely on the accuracy and speed of the oracle.

Constant Sum Market Maker

Another variant of CFMM formulas is the constant sum market maker (CSMM), which defines the invariant k as the sum of the pool's token reserves. Again, consider a pool that consists of x units of token A and y units of token B, then the CSMM function is given by:

$$x + y = k \tag{9.19}$$

While equation (9.19) is the simplest form of a CSMM function, it could also consist of more than two different tokens or multiply each token's reserves with a different factor (for example, $2x + y = k$, or $x + y + z = k$). What all variants of constant sum functions have in common is that the prices at which the pool's tokens are traded do not depend on the token reserve ratio. To see why, consider the equation that must be satisfied when a trader wishes to buy Δx units of token A in exchange for Δy units of token B:

$$(x - \Delta x) + (y + \Delta y) = x + y = k \tag{9.20}$$

By solving equation 20 for Δx and Δy, respectively, it can be shown that in order to buy Δx units of token A, one has to pay:

$$\Delta y = \Delta x \tag{9.21}$$

units of token B and, equivalently, for Δy units of token B, one will receive:

$$\Delta x = \Delta y \tag{9.22}$$

units of token A. This means that a trader can always exchange one unit of token A against one unit of token B, independent of the pool's current token reserve ratio.[27]

Plotting the constant sum function in a coordinate system yields a line with a constant slope, as Figure 9.4 illustrates.[28]

The fact that at any point on the line the slope is constant indicates that, as previously stated, the ratio for which the pool's tokens can be exchanged is independent of the state of the token reserves. So, no matter at which point of the line the current token reserve combination lies, for a given number of Δy units of token B, a trader will always receive the same number of Δx units of token A.[29]

An advantage of the constant sum formula is that trades incur no slippage, since token prices do not change as their reserve combinations move along the line. However, the fact that the pool's token prices stay constant can become very problematic, since this means that they cannot adapt to the reference market price. Precisely, this means that whenever the reference market price deviates from the pool price, arbitrageurs could potentially buy every unit of the undervalued token from the liquidity pool and sell it at the reference market, thereby depleting the pool's entire liquidity and leaving liquidity providers only with reserves of the token whose value has decreased relatively. The fact that one token's reserve can theoretically fall to zero can also be seen when considering the line that represents the constant sum function in Figure 9.4. As already outlined, such a scenario cannot occur when prices are calculated based on a constant product or constant mean function. Therefore, constant sum functions in their pure form are not suitable as trading functions, since they would only work if the tokens' reference prices were perfectly positively correlated. In practice, liquidity pools that trade one stable coin for another (for example, USDT/DAI or USDC/BUSD) could be suitable for employing a CSMM.

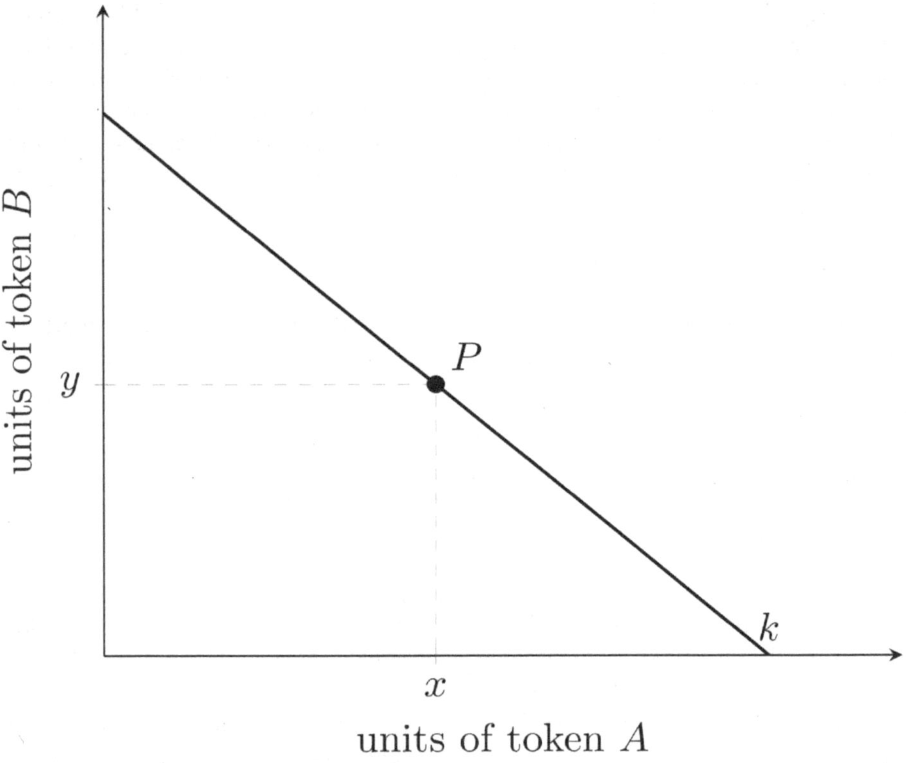

Figure 9.4 Constant sum function

LIQUIDITY PROVISION IN AMM MARKETS

As already briefly discussed, liquidity providers participate in AMM markets by adding a pair of tokens in a specified ratio to a liquidity pool, which will subsequently use the tokens to facilitate trades. In exchange, liquidity providers earn trading fees for each trade that is conducted against the liquidity pool, proportionate to their pool share.

Adding Tokens to a Liquidity Pool

To better understand the process of liquidity provision, consider again a constant product liquidity pool that currently consists of x units of token A and y units of token B. Now, if someone wants to become a liquidity provider, they can add a specific number of units of token A and B to the liquidity pool, thereby increasing the pool's liquidity and reducing slippage for traders. The ratio between token A and B at which the liquidity provider adds them to the pool has to match the current token reserve ratio exactly,[30] since otherwise, changes in the pool's liquidity level would change its quoted price, which in turn would cause a deviation from the reference market price. So, with x^+ being the number of units of token A and y^+ being the number of units of token B the liquidity provider adds to the pool, the following equation must hold:

$$\frac{y^+}{x^+} = \frac{y}{x} \tag{9.23}$$

While adding additional liquidity to the pool must not change the token reserve ratio, it does, however, increase the invariant k. Let $xy = k$ be the invariant before the addition of liquidity, then after the additional liquidity provision, the invariant changes to $x'y' = k'$, with $x' = x + x^+$ and $y' = y + y^+$. Vice versa, removing liquidity decreases k. Once the liquidity provider has chosen a specific number of units of each token (that satisfies $\frac{y^+}{x^+} = \frac{y}{x}$) that they are willing to add to the pool, their pool share (PS) is calculated by setting the number of units of tokens they added in proportion to the overall number of units of tokens within the pool:

$$PS = \frac{x^+ + y^+}{x + y + x^+ + y^+} = \frac{x^+ + y^+}{x' + y'} \tag{9.24}$$

A liquidity provider's pool share determines the fraction of trading fees that are credited to them and is subject to change whenever another liquidity provider adds or removes liquidity. Also, the number of units of each token's reserves that the liquidity provider is entitled to when redeeming liquidity is determined by his pool share. Note that while a liquidity provider's pool share, as defined in equation (9.24), can change as a result of liquidity provision or removal by other liquidity providers, its value (that is, the number of each token's units the liquidity provider is entitled to) remains unaffected by that. To illustrate, consider a pool to consist of one unit of token A and B each, with both tokens being provided by one single liquidity provider, which means that his pool share is 100 percent. Now, if another liquidity provider adds a second unit of each token, the initial liquidity provider's pool share would decrease to 50 percent. However, each token's reserves have doubled, which means that the value of the initial liquidity provider's pool share still equals one unit of token A and B each.

Impermanent Loss

While liquidity providers get compensated for their liquidity provision in the form of trading fees, they are exposed to the risk of changing token prices. To see why changing token prices pose a risk for liquidity providers, we compare the value of a liquidity provider's pool share to the alternative of not providing liquidity and instead simply holding the tokens. Therefore, we introduce the holding portfolio which consists of the respective units of each token that were added to the liquidity pool (that is, x^+ units of token A and y^+ units of token B) and thus represents the alternative of not engaging in liquidity provision.

Then, at the time of liquidity withdrawal there are two portfolios whose values can be compared: that of the holding portfolio, which consists of x^+ units of token A and y^+ units of token B, and that of the liquidity provider's pool share. At the time of liquidity provision, the latter also consisted x^+ units of token A and y^+ units of token B, but this may have changed due to changes in the reference market price. To compare both portfolio values, we choose a numeraire, which, arbitrarily, will be token B. Since the holding portfolio will always consist of x^+ units of token A and y^+ units of token B, its value at the time of liquidity removal, which we refer to as terminal value (TV), is given by:

$$TV_{hold} = x^+ \bullet Pr^t_{A/B} + y^+ \tag{9.25}$$

$Pr^t_{A/B}$ thereby indicates the reference market price of token A, denoted in units of token B, at the time of liquidity removal, which may differ from $Pr_{A/B}$, which we consider to be the reference market price at the time of liquidity provision. The terminal value of the liquidity provider's pool share, at the time of liquidity removal, is given by:

$$TV_{pool} = PS \bullet \left(x^t \bullet Pr^t_{A/B} + y^t\right) \tag{9.26}$$

x^t and y^t denote the number of units of token A and B within the liquidity pool at the time of liquidity removal. The ratio between x^t and y^t will equal $Pr^t_{A/B}$, since, otherwise, arbitrage would be possible. Simultaneously, when assuming that during the time of liquidity provision no further addition or removal of liquidity took place,[31] the product of the token reserves at the time of liquidity removal must still equal k', which yields $x^t = \sqrt{\frac{k'}{Pr^t_{A/B}}}$ and $y^t = \sqrt{Pr^t_{A/B} \bullet k'}$.[32] The following example should illustrate how the value of the holding portfolio and the pool share are calculated.

Numerical example

A liquidity pool consists of 45 units of token A and 90 units of token B. A liquidity provider decides to add 5 units of token A and 10 units of token B to the pool. At the time of liquidity removal, the reference market price $Pr^t_{A/B}$ is given by 2.5.

Liquidity provision and pool share

Before the addition of liquidity, the pool consists of 45 units of token A and 90 units of token B, which translates to $k = 4050$. By adding 5 units of token A and 10 units of token B, the token reserves increase to $x' = 50$ and $y' = 100$, which yields $k' = 5000$. According to equation (9.24), the liquidity provider's pool share is therefore 10 percent. Furthermore, by assuming that the token reserves reflect the reference market price, one can see that $Pr_{A/B}$ at the time of liquidity provision is 2.

Liquidity removal

Now, consider the pool's token composition at the time of liquidity removal. Since $\frac{y^t}{x^t} = Pr^t_{A/B} = 2.5$ and $x^t y^t = k' = 5000$, the pool will consist of $x^t = 44.72$ units of token A and $y^t = 111.80$ units of token B. The liquidity provider can hence redeem 4.472 units of token A and 11.18 units of token B from the pool. In terms of units of token B, this yields 22.36 units, since one unit of token A is worth 2.5 units of token B. However, the terminal value of the holding portfolio, which still consists of 5 units of token A and 10 units of token B, would be 22.5 units of token B. This shows that, without taking trading fees into account, the liquidity provider's terminal wealth would have been 0.14 units of token B higher, had he not added the tokens to the liquidity pool and instead just held them outside the pool.

This divergence between the value of a liquidity provider's pool share and the holding portfolio is referred to as impermanent loss (*IL*) and typically measured in terms of their relative difference.[33] The notion of "impermanence" refers to the fact that the liquidity provider effectively suffers the loss only upon withdrawal. If they instead choose to continue being a liquidity provider, the tokens' price ratio may revert to the initial ratio and impermanent loss would vanish. In the current example, IL would be 0.62% $\left(= \frac{22.36}{22.50} - 1\right)$, which implies that the value of the liquidity provider's pool share is 0.62 percent less than that of the holding portfolio. A general way to calculate impermanent loss is given by:[34]

$$IL = \frac{2\sqrt{c}}{1+c} - 1 \tag{9.27}$$

with $c = \frac{P^{r_t}_{A/B}}{P^{r}_{A/B}}$.[35] A zero impermanent loss, following equation (9.27), can only happen for $c = 1$, implying that the two tokens' price ratio did not change from liquidity provision to liquidity withdrawal. For instance, if the prices of both tokens in the pool double, their relative valuation would still be the same (that is, $P^{r_t}_{A/B} = P^{r}_{A/B}$) and no impermanent loss accrues. However, as soon as the relative valuation of the tokens changes (that is, $P^{r_t}_{A/B} \neq P^{r}_{A/B}$), the liquidity provider will suffer an impermanent loss, irrespective of the direction of the relative price change. What equation (9.27) also illustrates is that impermanent loss is exclusively determined by the degree of the change in the tokens' relative prices (captured by the parameter c) during the time of liquidity provision. The overall pool size and the liquidity provider's pool share, in contrast, do not play a role.[36]

The economic reason for impermanent loss is that whenever one token's price increases relative to the other, arbitrageurs will remove the token that has increased from the pool and replace it with the token that has decreased, until the token reserve ratio falls in line with the reference market price again. This means that the liquidity pool, and hence the liquidity providers that filled the pool with their tokens, will always exchange the appreciating token against the depreciating token. This implies that the number of units of the token that has relatively gained in value that a liquidity provider is entitled to at the time of liquidity removal will be lower, and the number of units of the token that has relatively lost in value will be higher, than the respective amounts of each token they have initially added to the pool. This can be also observed in the previous example, where the number of units of token A (that is, the token whose relative price increased) that the liquidity provider is entitled to decreased from 5 at the time of liquidity provision to 4.472 at the time of liquidity removal, while the number of units of token *B* (that is, the token whose relative price decreased) increased from 10 at the time of liquidity provision to 11.18 at the time of liquidity removal. Figure 9.5 illustrates impermanent loss as a function of the relative change in the token prices. The x axis shows the relative price change between the time of liquidity provision and removal.

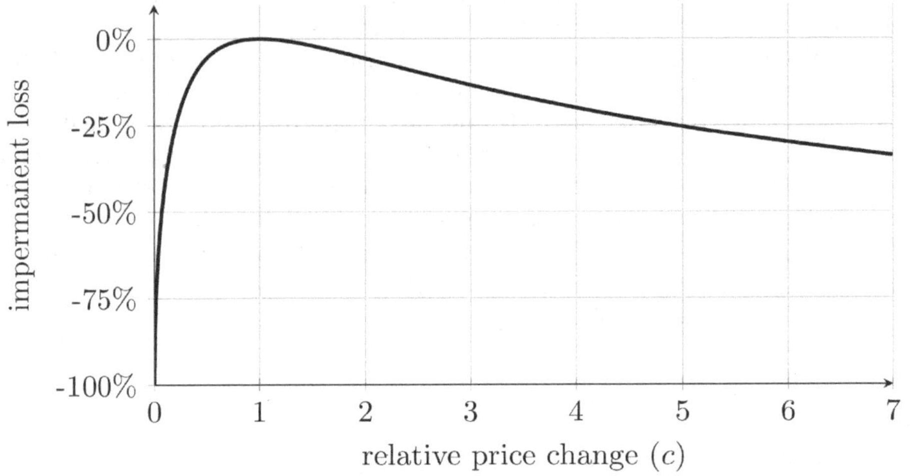

Figure 9.5 *Impermanent loss as a function of the tokens' relative price change*

When simply comparing the values of a liquidity provider's pool share to that of the holding portfolio, it might seem as if liquidity provision would never be profitable. It is important to note, though, that in the impermanent loss framework, trading fees are not taken into account. So, while in most cases liquidity providers will suffer a certain degree of impermanent loss, liquidity provision can still be profitable (compared to holding the tokens outside the pool) whenever the accrued trading fees exceed the impermanent loss.

SUMMARY

With the rise of smart contract based trading mechanisms, decentralized finance has gained traction. In particular, decentralized exchanges (DEXs) such as UniSwap allow for the permissionless, noncustodial exchange of blockchain-based assets, without central authorities and middlemen. Contrary to traditional markets operating limit order books, DEXs employ automated market maker liquidity pools, which is a set of smart contracts (that is, computer code) which aggregately are referred to as the protocol. The protocol stores assets from liquidity providers which can then be used by traders to exchange one asset for another. In its basic version, a liquidity pool holds two tokens in reserves and lets traders swap an arbitrary number of one token for a specific number of the second token in the pool. The exchange rate is determined by the trading function, which is geared to a constant that in turn depends on the pool's reserves. This feature gives rise to the notion of a constant function market maker. While constant product functions are most common, other functions governing the exchange rate of a pool have emerged as well. The exchange rate that a trader effectively obtains depends on the liquidity of the pool, that is, the pool size, as well as the volume they wish to trade. Illiquid pools and large trades entail costs in terms of adverse exchange rates compared to the market's reference price. This effect is referred to as slippage. Providing liquidity, two distinct tokens in a defined ratio, to a pool will come with the benefit of earning fees, and involves the risk of suffering impermanent loss. By the design of automated market makers, the value of a liquidity provider's pool share will be less than that of simply holding the tokens as soon as the price ratio of the two tokens changes after liquidity provision.

NOTES

1. See Adams et al. (2020).
2. See Adams et al. (2021).
3. See, e.g., Angeris and Chitra (2020: 6–7).
4. The CPMM trading function was first popularized by UniSwap; see Zhang et al. (2018).
5. Since $\tau = 1 - \varsigma, \tau < 1$ whenever $\varsigma > 0$.
6. See, e.g., Mohan (2022: 9).
7. An equilibrium where $P_{A/B}$ equals exactly $P^r_{A/B}$ will only be reached in theory, where there exist no trading fees, and infinitesimally small trades are possible. In reality, marginal divergences between the two prices may not be exploited, since trading fees and the price impact incurred by the trade itself may exceed arbitrage profits. Therefore, the token reserve ratio may not always exactly mirror the reference market price.
8. For a given Δy, Δx is calculated according to the CPMM formula presented in equation (9.4).
9. Again, note that while the trader initially sent 7 units of token B to the pool, only 6.93 units can be used to buy token A, since the remaining 0.07 units are charged as trading fees.
10. Alternatively, one could also apply equation (9.7), with $\Delta y = 7$ and $\tau = 0.99$.
11. Exchanging tokens according to the quoted price means that for Δy units of token B, a trader would receive $\Delta x = \frac{\Delta y}{\frac{y}{x}}$ units of token A, since $\frac{y}{x}$ is the quoted price per unit of A, denoted in units of B. Equation (9.10) is a transformation of the expression $\Delta x = \frac{\Delta y}{\frac{y}{x}}$.
12. See Xu et al. (2021: 5).
13. Note that the realized price is calculated after deducting the trading fee.

14. For each trade, $P_{A/B}$ is assumed to be 1.5, so that the values of x and y (prior to the trade) are given by 100, 200, and 300 as well as 150, 300, and 450 for the pools of $k = 15\,000$, $k = 60\,000$, and $k = 135\,000$, respectively.
15. See Mohan (2022: 17).
16. Despite $x_2 > x_1$ and $y_2 > y_1$, both pools have the same reserve ratio $\frac{y_1}{x_1} = \frac{y_2}{x_2}$, which implies that $P_{A/B}$ is equal in both pools.
17. As outlined previously, buying token A in exchange for token B causes an upward shift of the reserve combination along the curve.
18. See Mohan (2022: 19).
19. Also, by comparing the number of units of tokens A and B before and after the trade in each pool, one can see that $x_2 - x_2' > x_1 - x_1'$, while $y_2' - y_2 = y_1' - y_1$. This shows that for adding a given number of units of token B to the pool, the small pool will always return less units of token A than the large pool.
20. In the context of DEXs, the CMMM formula was first introduced by Martinelli and Mushegian (2019: 3).
21. Martinelli and Mushegian (2019: 5–6) provide a formal proof.
22. Analogously to the CPMM formula, trading fees are incorporated by deducting them from Δy in equation (9.14) and correspondingly modifying equations (9.15) and (9.16).
23. This relationship also holds when the pool consists of more than two distinct tokens. So, let A and B be two of N distinct tokens within the pool, then the quoted price of token A, denoted in units of token B, is given by equation (9.17), independent of the size of N. For a formal proof, we refer to Martinelli and Mushegian (2019: 4–5) or Evans (2020: 4).
24. For any given values of x and y, the CMMM formula with equal weights yields exactly the same results as the CPMM formula concerning the pool's quoted and a trade's realized price. Therefore, for a trader, trading against a CPMM liquidity pool is equivalent to trading against a CMMM liquidity pool that applies equal weights to calculate trading quantities of Δx and Δy.
25. See Krishnamachari et al. (2021).
26. See Mohan (2022: 35).
27. If the reserves of tokens A and B are weighted by different factors, such as $a \bullet x + b \bullet y = k$, the exchange rate between the two tokens remains constant as well, but it will differ from one. See Mohan (2022: 31).
28. Analogously to the constant product function that has been plotted, each point on the line represents a token reserve combination whose sum yields a specific value of k.
29. Note that this is not the case for the constant product formula.
30. See Zhang et al. (2018: 3).
31. As previously outlined, liquidity provision or removal by others does change a liquidity provider's pool share, but not its value. So while in fact the pool size (in terms of the product of the pool's token reserves) and, correspondingly, the liquidity provider's pool share may have changed during the time of liquidity provision, the value of the liquidity provider's pool share (without taking trading fees into account) at the time of liquidity removal (that is, TV_{pool}) can be calculated by using the liquidity provider's pool share (that is, PS) and the pool size (that is, k') at the time of liquidity provision.
32. This is obtained by solving $\frac{y^t}{x^t} = P^{r_t}_{A/B}$ and $x^t y^t = k'$ for x^t and y^t.

33. See, e.g., Heimbach et al. (2021: 7).
34. A formal derivation of equation (9.27) is provided by, e.g., Tiruviluamala et al. (2022: 6).
35. Following the numerical example, $c = 1.25$, since $\frac{P^{r_t}_{A/B}}{P^{r}_{A/B}} = \frac{2.5}{2}$. So, *IL*, according to equation (9.27), would be $0.62\,\%$ $\left(= \frac{2 \cdot \sqrt{1.25}}{1 + 1.25} - 1 \right)$, which is exactly the result that was obtained by explicitly calculating the values of the pool share and the holding portfolio.
36. Obviously, in terms of absolute values, impermanent loss increases with the amount of tokens the liquidity provider added to the pool. However, measured as a relative difference, it does not. If, in the current example, the liquidity provider would have added 10 units of token A and 20 units of token *B* instead of 5 and 10, respectively, the difference between the values of the holding portfolio and the pool share would be 0.28 units of token *B* (which is more than the 0.14 units in the initial example), but the relative difference would still be 0.62 percent.

REFERENCES

Adams, H., Zinsmeister, N., and Robinson, D. (2020): *Uniswap v2 Core*. Retrieved from https://uniswap.org/whitepaper.pdf.

Adams, H., Zinsmeister, N., Robinson, D., Keefer, R., and Salem, M. (2021): *Uniswap v3 Core*. Retrieved from https://uniswap.org/whitepaper-v3.pdf.

Aigner, A. and Dhaliwal, G. (2021): *Uniswap: Impermanent loss and risk profile of a liquidity provider*. Available at arXiv: https://doi.org/10.48550/arXiv.2106.14404.

Angeris, G. and Chitra, T. (2020): *Improved price oracles: Constant Function Market Makers*. Available at arXiv: https://doi.org/10.48550/arXiv.2003.10001.

Angeris, G., Kao, H.-T., Chiang, R., Noyes, C., Chitra, T., and Youngblom, R. (2019): *An analysis of uniswap markets*. Available at arXiv: https://doi.org/10.48550/arXiv.1911.03380.

Aoyagi, J. (2020): *Liquidity provision by automated market makers*. Available at SSRN: http://dx.doi.org/10.2139/ssrn.3674178.

Barbon, A. and Ranaldo, A. (2021): *On the quality of cryptocurrency markets: Centralized versus decentralized exchanges*. Available at SSRN: http://dx.doi.org/10.2139/ssrn.3984897.

Bartoletti, M., Chiang, J. H.-y., and Lluch-Lafuente, A. (2021): *A theory of automated market makers in DeFi*. Available at arXiv: https://doi.org/10.48550/arXiv.2102.11350.

Clark, J. (2020): *The replicating portfolio of a constant product market*. Available at SSRN: http://dx.doi.org/10.2139/ssrn.3550601.

Daian, P., Goldfeder, S., Kell, T., Li, Y., Zhao, X., Bentov, I., and Juels, A. (2019): *Flash boys 2.0: Frontrunning, transaction reordering, and consensus instability in decentralized exchanges*. Available at arXiv: https://doi.org/10.48550/arXiv.1904.05234.

Deng, J. and Zong, H. (2022): *Static replication of impermanent loss for concentrated liquidity provision in decentralised markets*. Available at arXiv: https://doi.org/10.48550/arXiv.2205.12043.

Evans, A. (2020): *Liquidity provider returns in geometric mean markets*. Available at arXiv: https://doi.org/10.48550/arXiv.2006.08806.

Evans, A., Angeris, G., and Chitra, T. (2021): *Optimal fees for geometric mean market makers*. Available at arXiv: https://doi.org/10.48550/arXiv.2104.00446.

Fritsch, R. (2021): *Concentrated liquidity in automated market makers*. In D. Song, R. Wattenhofer, A. Gervais, and P. Jovanovic (eds), *Proceedings of the 2021 ACM CCS Workshop on Decentralized Finance and Security* (pp. 15–20). New York: ACM.

Fritsch, R. and Wattenhofer, R. (2021): *A note on optimal fees for constant function market makers*. In D. Song, R. Wattenhofer, A. Gervais, and P. Jovanovic (eds), *Proceedings of the 2021 ACM CCS Workshop on Decentralized Finance and Security* (pp. 9–14). New York: ACM.

Heimbach, L., Wang, Y., and Wattenhofer, R. (2021). *Behavior of liquidity providers in decentralized exchanges*. Available at arXiv: https://doi.org/10.48550/arXiv.2105.13822.

Khakhar, A. and Chen, X. (2022). *Delta hedging liquidity positions on automated market makers*. Available at arXiv: https://doi.org/10.48550/arXiv.2208.03318.

Krishnamachari, B., Feng, Q., and Grippo, E. (2021). *Dynamic curves for decentralized autonomous cryptocurrency exchanges*. Available at arXiv: https://doi.org/10.48550/arXiv.2101.02778.

Martinelli, F. and Mushegian, M. (2019): *A non-custodial portfolio manager, liquidity provider, and price sensor*. Retrieved from: https://balancer.fi/whitepaper.pdf.

Mohan, V. (2022): Automated market makers and decentralized exchanges: a defi primer. *Financial Innovation*, 8(1), 1–48. Available at Springer Open: https://doi.org/10.1186/s40854-021-00314-5.

Park, A. (2021): *The conceptual flaws of constant product automated market making*. Available at SSRN: http://dx.doi.org/10.2139/ssrn.3805750.

Parlour, C.A. and Lehar, A. (2021): *Decentralized exchanges*. Available at SSRN: http://dx.doi.org/10.2139/ssrn.3905316.

Tiruviluamala, N., Port, A., and Lewis, E. (2022): *A general framework for impermanent loss in automated market makers*. Available at arXiv: https://doi.org/10.48550/arXiv.2203.11352.

Wang, Y., Chen, Y., Wu, H., Zhou, L., Deng, S., and Wattenhofer, R. (2021): *Cyclic arbitrage in decentralized exchanges*. Available at arXiv: https://doi.org/10.48550/arXiv.2105.02784.

Xu, J., Paruch, K., Cousaert, S., and Feng, Y. (2021): *Sok: Decentralized exchanges (DEX) with automated market maker (AMM) protocols*. Available at arXiv: https://doi.org/10.48550/arXiv.2103.12732.

Zhang, J., Chen, X., and Park, D. (2018): *Formal specification of constant product* ($x \bullet y = k$) *Market Maker model and implementation*. Retrieved from: https://github.com/runtimeverification/verified-smart-contracts/blob/uniswap/uniswap/x-y-k.pdf.

10. Systematization of knowledge: constant function market makers

Michele Fabi, Myriam Kassoul, and Julien Prat

INTRODUCTION

The advent of blockchain technologies has given rise to a fast-growing stream of financial innovations gathered under the term "decentralized finance" (DeFi). They rely on blockchains and smart contracts to provide decentralized implementations of financial services. The main promise of DeFi is to replace human interventions, and all the moral hazard that they entail, with algorithmic protocols. At its most ambitious, DeFi attempts to do away with the trust in financial intermediaries upon which the legacy system is built.

One the most important building blocks of DeFi are automated market makers (AMMs), algorithms that pool resources to run decentralized exchanges. Although the first AMMs were invented in the 1980s, long before the popularization of blockchains, they are currently receiving much attention as their modern upgrades are particularly suited to running decentralized exchanges. Due to their growing adoption, AMMs are also becoming the focus of renewed academic scrutiny.

This chapter provides an overview of the emerging literature on AMMs. It looks at the history of automated market making to provide some perspective, and then reviews recent innovations. AMMs were first introduced in prediction markets to substitute human intermediaries with algorithmic rules. Their aim was to elicit information about the beliefs of participants, rewarding them for making correct predictions. We explain how researchers were able to derive clear connections between the AMM prices, the cost function of the market maker, and risk-neutral security pricing.

AMMs for prediction markets were theoretically motivated, their practical implementation being grounded in explicit principles. By contrast, AMMs for DeFi were introduced by practitioners who adopted heuristic solutions to solve the challenges of decentralized market making. The new type of AMMs that have nowadays almost completely superseded limit order books (LOBs) in decentralized environments are constant function market makers (CFMMs). Instead of relying on complex matching mechanisms, CFMMs determine asset prices using a deterministic trading function of their inventory. Liquidity providers adjust the level of this trading function by supplying or withdrawing liquidity. Traders swap their assets with the CFMM in a way that keeps the trading function constant.

We present the burgeoning literature that studies the theoretical properties of CFMMs as well as several empirical papers testing its predictions. Our review illustrates that, in spite of their simplistic approach, CFMMs possess several desirable features. First, they satisfy the oracle property as their equilibrium in the absence of arbitrage opportunities tracks market prices. Also, under a set of reasonable design restrictions, CFMMs can be fine-tuned so as to replicate the payoffs that liquidity providers would obtain from investing in traditional financial instruments. The joint surplus of traders and liquidity providers can be optimized by adjusting the curvature of the trading function: curved functions are more suited to pools of volatile assets, whereas flatter functions are more suited to stable, mean-reverting assets such as stablecoins. We explain how these findings follow from standard microeconomic principles since the problem of arbitrageurs is isomorphic to the derivation of the compensated demand function in consumer theory (Fabi and Prat 2022).

After having discussed the optimal design of CFMMs, we survey the literature that studies the competition between centralized and decentralized exchanges. Decentralized protocols have grown exponentially over the last years, becoming serious competitors to centralized exchanges that operate mostly through limit order books. A recent line of research investigates how traders and liquidity providers allocate their assets across these two types of exchanges. It builds on the market microstructure literature and identifies several motives and counter-motives for liquidity provision and trade. Trade is motivated either by exogenous motives, resulting in noise trading, or by arbitrage. Liquidity provision is motivated by returns from fees and capital gain on reserves, but discouraged by adverse selection costs, intrinsic to all types of AMMs. Adverse selection arises because providers lock their funds in the AMM, which prevent them from swiftly reacting to price shocks. Adverse selection costs depend on the relative amount of informed to noise trading. In centralized exchanges (CEXs), adverse selection is measured by the signal-to-noise ratio. In decentralized exchanges (DEXs), adverse selection is measured by the impermanent loss, a function of the curvature of the trading function. The literature highlights that competition among trading platforms leads to a stable equilibrium distribution of liquidity and explains empirical distribution of liquidity in popular DEXs such as Uniswap.

The last branch of literature addresses issues related to privacy and, more specifically, to miner extractible value (MEV), a fundamental challenge for all trades processed on a public blockchain. MEV is the profit that malicious bots can make by defrauding users using insider information. Doing so on a blockchain is particularly easy since transactions are stored in a public memory pool. We present the literature documenting the significance of MEV for popular DEXs and the solutions that have been proposed to alleviate this problem. The last section concludes by discussing promising directions for further research.

AMMs FOR PREDICTION MARKETS

AMMs predate the advent of decentralized finance. They were first introduced to streamline prediction markets, that is, securities markets whose primary objective is to aggregate information about probabilities of future events, such as election results or weather forecasts.[1] Algorithmic solutions are deemed promising because they have the potential to alleviate the thin market problem that often beleaguers prediction markets.

The traditional way to foster market liquidity is to rely on the intermediation of professional market makers who act as counterparties to buy and sell orders. AMMs raise the possibility of replacing human market makers with automated algorithms. In order to provide a workable solution, the algorithm has to solve the two following challenges. First, information must be elicited. Traders who interact with the AMM should find it optimal to reveal their beliefs about the probability distribution of future events. Second, the algorithm has to aggregate opinions by producing an estimate which summarizes the information revealed by all the previous trades.

Information Elicitation

The information elicitation problem was analyzed long before the creation of prediction markets. Consider an agent who entertains the belief $\boldsymbol{p}$ about the distribution of the random variable $\boldsymbol{X}$. The elicitation mechanism asks the agent to report a distribution $\boldsymbol{r}$ based on the knowledge that she will receive the reward $c_i = s(\boldsymbol{r}, \boldsymbol{X}_i)$ if $\boldsymbol{X}_i$ turns out to be the true state of $\boldsymbol{X}$. The design problem consists in finding a *scoring rule* $s(\boldsymbol{r}, \boldsymbol{X}_i)$ such that:

$$p = \underset{r}{\operatorname{argmax}} \ \mathbb{E}_{\mathbf{p}}\left[s(\boldsymbol{r}, \boldsymbol{X}_i)\right], \qquad (10.1)$$

where E_p is the expectation operator associated to the agent's belief $\boldsymbol{p}$. A rule $s(\boldsymbol{r}, \boldsymbol{X}_i)$ that satisfies eqation (10.1) is called a proper scoring rule, since the best response of the agent is to truthfully report their belief $\boldsymbol{p}$.

A naive approach would consist in replacing the score with the reported probability, so that $s(\boldsymbol{r}, \boldsymbol{X}_i) = \boldsymbol{r}_i$. However, this rule does not induce truthful reporting. It is not a proper scoring rule because its linearity induces the forecaster to place all probability weights on the events that she deems the most likely to occur.

Truthful reporting therefore excludes linear rules. But does it identify a unique solution? Unfortunately, no. The quadratic scoring rule proposed by Brier (1950) was quickly followed by Good's (1952) introduction of the logarithmic scoring rule. These two seminal contributions spurred a research agenda whose objective was to provide additional criteria for the selection of scoring rules. For instance, Winkler (1969) showed that Good's logarithmic rule is the only rewarding scheme which allows the designer to use standard likelihood methods for the evaluation of the forecaster's performance. As we will show below, the need to come up with additional criteria to narrow down the design space remains one of the main motivations for ongoing research on AMMs.

Information Aggregation

Since proper scoring rules elicit beliefs, why shouldn't we harvest the wisdom of crowds by combining beliefs elicited from multiple forecasters? The answer from the literature on opinions pooling is full of caveats (see, e.g., Genest and Zidek 1986), showing that more often than not, the pooled distribution is indistinguishable from one of the individual distributions.

The difficulty in pooling opinions explains why it remains common for forecasts to rely on the advice of a single expert. Prediction markets, on the other hand, do not shy away from the information aggregation challenge. Instead of trying to compute one summary statistics out of disparate beliefs, they leverage the economic incentives of forecasters. Betting markets indicate that individuals are willing to place wagers on future events and that they use each other's bets to update their priors, resulting in reliable probability estimates (Hausch et al. 1994).

A market structure similar to that of betting markets can be algorithmically emulated. As originally proposed by Hanson (2003, 2007), the first step consists in using scoring rules sequentially so as to construct a market scoring rule. The state of the market scoring rule is equal to the report $\boldsymbol{r}$ of the last person that has interacted with the rule. The state is public information and anyone can update it by submitting a new report. Once the actual value $\boldsymbol{X}_i$ is revealed, the payout Π to the agent that made the nth update is equal to $\Pi\left(\boldsymbol{r}^n,\boldsymbol{X}_i \middle| \boldsymbol{r}^{n-1}\right) = s(\boldsymbol{r}^n,\boldsymbol{X}_i) - s\left(\boldsymbol{r}^{n-1},\boldsymbol{X}_i\right)$. Given that agents cannot modify the previous report $\boldsymbol{r}^{n-1}$, maximizing one's expected payoff amounts to maximizing the expected value of $s(\boldsymbol{r}^n,\boldsymbol{X}_i)$, which is equivalent to solving equation (10.1). Hence, when the scoring rule s is proper, agents whose beliefs differ from the last report are incentivized to update it by submitting their own truthful report.

Although market scoring rules achieve our goal of sequentially eliciting truthful forecasts, their implementation is not very user-friendly. Reports are not standard bets as agents have to submit probability distributions.[2] A more natural implementation would allow traders to buy and sell securities whose payoffs are attached to the realization of specific outcomes. This is where the introduction of cost functions becomes useful. More specifically:

1. Let N denote the number of mutually exclusive and exhaustive outcomes of the random variable $\boldsymbol{X}$ to be predicted. The AMM offers to trade N distinct securities, each paying \$1 per share if its corresponding outcome is realized.
2. The AMM cost function $C(\boldsymbol{q})$ returns the total amount of money spent by traders as a function of the vector $\boldsymbol{q}$ that keeps track of the overall number of shares held for each of the N securities. The AMM quotes a marginal price $p_i(\boldsymbol{q})$ for security i that is equal to $\partial C(\boldsymbol{q})/\partial \boldsymbol{q}_i$.
3. Anyone can at any time buy or sell shares. The AMM charges $C(\boldsymbol{q}') - C(\boldsymbol{q})$ for a trade that changes the number of outstanding shares from $\boldsymbol{q}$ to $\boldsymbol{q}'$.
4. Once the outcome is realized, the traders that bought the winning security receive \$1 per share from the AMM, while those that did not receive nothing.

The connection between cost functions and market scoring rules is not obvious. Yet, Chen and Pennock (2012) show that the cost function can always be chosen so as to replicate the incentives of participants interacting with a market scoring rule. The equivalence holds under the additional constraint that the vector of marginal prices belongs to its probability simplex, that is, $\sum_{i=1}^{N} p_i(\boldsymbol{q}) = 1$ for all $\boldsymbol{q} \in \mathbb{R}_{+}^{N}$. This restriction ensures that the price of a security indicates the probability of its predicted outcome.

The most popular cost function is the one associated to the logarithmic market scoring rule $s(\boldsymbol{r}, \boldsymbol{X}_i) = b \cdot \log(\boldsymbol{r}_i)$. It reads:

$$C(\boldsymbol{q}) = b \cdot \log\left(\sum_{i=1}^{N} \exp\left(\frac{q_i}{b}\right)\right)$$

The coefficient b>0 is called the liquidity parameter because it controls the elasticity of the price response of the AMM: The larger b is, the less reactive prices are, and so, the more liquid the AMM is. Then, given that the owner of the AMM chooses the value of b, shouldn't they set it as high as possible? The reason why one should refrain from doing so is that the liquidity parameter also controls the amount of money that the AMM can lose. A fundamental property of market scoring rules is that, although running an AMM might be costly, the losses can usually be bounded *ex ante*. For the logarithmic market scoring rule, the worst-case loss, $b \cdot \log(N)$, is linearly increasing in b.[3] Hence the owner of the AMM faces a fundamental trade-off between risk exposure and market liquidity.

Another result in Chen and Pennock (2012) that yields intriguing connections between prediction markets and DeFi is their construction of utility-based market makers. Consider a market maker with utility function U for money and subjective prior about the distribution of the random variable X. A constant utility cost function charges users the exact amount that keeps the market maker indifferent between accepting and declining the trade. Accordingly, "the market maker starts the market with some initial expected utility and then keeps this expected utility level during the whole process of trading" (Chen and Pennock 2012: 51). It turns out that a broad class of market scoring rules[4] satisfies this constant utility requirement when the market maker displays hyperbolic absolute risk aversion. This equivalence result provides a microfoundation for the parametric specification of the AMM, making it possible to directly import the market maker's priors into prices. We will see below that obtaining similar results for CFMMs is one of the main open questions of DeFi.

CFMMs AND DECENTRALIZED FINANCE

The previous section illustrates how research on AMMs for prediction markets progressed in a systematic way. Starting from a well-defined problem, researchers used scoring rules as building blocks to clarify and streamline the design of AMMs. The emergence of AMMs in decentralized finance followed a completely different process. To fully grasp the motivation behind the introduction of CFMMs, it is instructive to go back to their genesis in a proposal first floated by Buterin (2016). The rationale for introducing CFMMs was not to tackle a clear conceptual problem, but rather to expediently solve some practical challenges posed by market marking on blockchains that limit order books were not able to address.

Motivation for CFMMs

Blockchains have many promises but, as of today, most applications are centered on DeFi. Their fundamental benefit is to algorithmically handle the settlement and enforcement of contracts, thereby avoiding the risks and costs associated to financial intermediation. Decentralized exchanges such as Uniswap, Sushiswap, and Curve constitute the core of DeFi. They leverage blockchain infrastructures to allow their users to swap digital assets "atomically" (that is, without counterparty risk).

The main technical hurdle posed by decentralized market making is due to the fact that code execution on blockchains is slow and costly. Traditional AMMs and LOBs are not suited to these limitations because they require many iterations to perform simple asset transfers (Angeris et al. 2022).[5] The inefficient usage of resources entailed by traditional market structures is not only costly to the traders directly involved in a transaction, but also generates a negative externality on all blockchain users.

CFMMs use a simple, minimalist approach to improve resource efficiency: They only need to keep track of a liquidity pool and its reserve vector $\boldsymbol{R} \in \mathbb{R}_+^N$ for the N tradable assets. The fact that CFMMs' internal states are small relative to LOBs makes them extremely light, as can be seen from their publicly accessible codes.[6] We now explain how the smart contracts of CFMMs price swaps by using a deterministic function of the reserves.

Functioning of CFMMs

The market actors that interact with a CFMM classify broadly according to two roles. On the one hand, liquidity providers (LPs) determine the size of the liquidity pool. They can inject additional reserves but do not affect the relative share of the assets listed in the pool. In exchange, they obtain shares of the liquidity pool in the form of LP tokens. These LP tokens, besides giving liquidity providers the right to withdraw the pool's reserves in proportion to their shares, also allow them to collect trading fees.

On the other side of the market, traders or users interact with the CFMM by supplying some assets and withdrawing others. The amount of output $\boldsymbol{O} \in \mathbb{R}_+^N$ a trader is entitled to receive is determined by their input, $\boldsymbol{I} \in \mathbb{R}_+^N$, and the CFMM's reserves $\boldsymbol{R}$ so as to keep the trading function constant at its pre-trade value. That is:

$$f(\boldsymbol{R} - \boldsymbol{O} + \boldsymbol{I}) = f(\boldsymbol{R}).$$

The trading function f is usually positive, smooth, strictly increasing, and strictly quasi-concave. These are very convenient properties as we will see in the next paragraphs.

The level curve of f attained at current reserves is often called the bonding curve. In relation to the trading function, the division of interactions between the CFMM and market actors can be described as follows: liquidity providers shift the CFMM to a different bonding curve, while traders move reserves along a fixed bonding curve (see Figure 10.1).

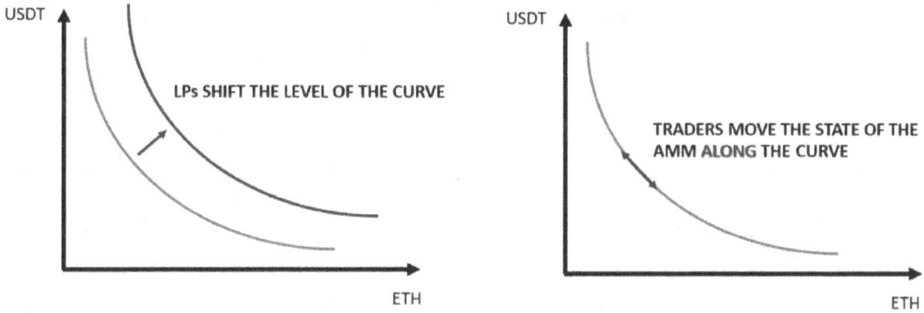

Figure 10.1 *Bonding curve movements*

In practice, some CFMMs implement additional operations besides liquidity provision and swap as described above, making the classification of market actors blurrier.[7] It is nevertheless useful to keep in mind the provider–trader dichotomy as a benchmark.

CFMMs usually charge traders with a proportional fee, $1 - \gamma \in [0,1)$, on their trades. In this case, the output $\boldsymbol{O}$ the traders receive for an input of I assets will be determined by counting only $\gamma \boldsymbol{I}$ of the input in the trading function equality, so that $f(\boldsymbol{R} - \boldsymbol{O} + \gamma \boldsymbol{I}) = f(\boldsymbol{R})$. The other $(1 - \gamma)$I will directly feed the liquidity pool's reserves, which after the swap will amount to $\boldsymbol{R}' = \boldsymbol{R} - \boldsymbol{O} + \boldsymbol{I} > \boldsymbol{R} - \boldsymbol{O} + \gamma \boldsymbol{I}$ for $\gamma > 0$. Notice that for f strictly increasing:

$$f(\boldsymbol{R}') > f(\boldsymbol{R} - \boldsymbol{O} + \gamma \boldsymbol{I}) = f(\boldsymbol{R}).$$

Transaction fees therefore shift the bonding curve upwards owing to the increased liquidity in the pool.

Table 10.1 summarizes the characteristics of several CFMMs from various blockchains.

Example: Uniswap

The most popular type of CFMM is the constant product market maker (CPMM) introduced by Uniswap, a DEX organized as a collection of liquidity pools for asset

Table 10.1 *Top ten CFMMs by total value locked (TVL)*

CFMM	Launch	Trading function	#pools	TVL	Blockchain(s)
Curve	Jan. 2020	Stableswap[i]	257	\$5.88b	Ethereum, Polygon,Arbitrum, Optimism, …
Uniswap	Nov. 2018	CPMM[ii]	1239	\$4.3b	Ethereum, Polygon, Arbitrum, Optimism, Celo
Pancakeswap	Sept. 2020	CPMM	108	\$2.92	BSC
Balancer	March. 2020	G3MM[iii]	186	\$1.83b	Ethereum, Polygon, Arbitrum
Sunswap	Jan. 2022	CPMM and Stableswap (for stablecoin pools)	237	\$962.59m	TRON
Sushiswap	Sept. 2020	CPMM	688	\$831.22m	Ethereum, Arbitrum, Polygon, Harmony, Gnosis, …
VVS Finance	Nov. 2021	CPMM	18	\$451.47m	Cronos
DeFichain DEX	May 2020	CPMM	57	\$314.3m	DefiChain
BiSwap	May 2021	CPMM	87	\$273.11m	BSC
Osmosis	June 2021	Customizable[iv]	261	\$220.68m	Osmosis

Notes: [i] Stableswap: $f(\boldsymbol{R}) = \alpha \sum_{i=1}^{N} \boldsymbol{R}_i - \beta \left(\prod_{i=1}^{N} \boldsymbol{R}_i \right)^{-1}$, for $\alpha > 0$, $\beta \geq 0$.
[ii] CPMM: $f(\boldsymbol{R}) = \boldsymbol{R}_1 \cdot \boldsymbol{R}_2$.
[iii] G3MM: $f(\boldsymbol{R}) = \prod_{i=1}^{N} \boldsymbol{R}_i^{w_i}$, for $\sum_{i=1}^{N} w_i = 1$.
[iv] Customizable: can be customized in each liquidity pool.

pairs. CPMMs use the trading function $f(\boldsymbol{R}) = \boldsymbol{R}_1 \cdot \boldsymbol{R}_2$. The quantity I_1 of asset 1 required by the CFMM to output O_2 units of asset 2 is therefore given by:

$$I_1 = O_2 \frac{\boldsymbol{R}_1}{\boldsymbol{R}_2 - O_2}. \tag{10.2}$$

The CFMM determines the terms of swap among assets though the quantity function $q: \mathbb{R} \times \mathbb{R}_+^N \rightarrow \mathbb{R}$ (Angeris and Chitra 2020). $q(\Delta_2; \boldsymbol{R})$ is the purchase cost of Δ_2 units of asset 2; that is, in equation (10.2), $I_1 = q(O_2; \boldsymbol{R})$. Conversely, $\left| q(-\Delta_2; \boldsymbol{R}) \right|$ is the sale revenue for the converse operation.[8]

Notice that in equation (10.2), $I_1 = q(O_2; \boldsymbol{R})$ is increasing in $\boldsymbol{R}_1$ and O_2, but decreasing in $\boldsymbol{R}_2$. This is on purpose, since the CFMM has to incentivize users to keep the pool balanced, making it expensive to drain reserves and cheap to refurnish them when they are scarce. Moreover, the quantity function is convex in O_2 and makes total reserve depletion impossible as:

$$\frac{d}{dO_2}q(O_2;\boldsymbol{R}) > 0, \frac{d^2}{dO_2^2}q(O_2;\boldsymbol{R}) > 0 \quad (10.3)$$

and:

$$\lim_{O_2 \to \boldsymbol{R}_2} q(O_2;\boldsymbol{R}) = \infty .$$

The properties in equation (10.3) can be summarized as convex pricing. The marginal price, or simply *price* dI_1/dO_2 (of asset 2) is given by:

$$p(\boldsymbol{R}) \equiv p = \lim_{O_2 \to 0} \frac{q(O_2;\boldsymbol{R})}{O_2} = \frac{\boldsymbol{R}_1}{\boldsymbol{R}_2}.$$

More generally, the vector of prices quoted by a CFMM is proportional to the gradient of the trading function, that is, $\boldsymbol{p} = \lambda \nabla f(\boldsymbol{R})$, where $\lambda > 0$ is a scaling constant. This means that marginal prices are proportional to the slope of the supporting hyperplane of the trading set $\{(\mathbf{I}, \boldsymbol{O}) : f(\mathbf{R} + \mathbf{I} - \mathbf{O}) \geq f(\mathbf{R})\}$; that is, the set of trades that keep the market maker weakly above its bonding curve (see Figure 10.2 that shows the trading set shaded in gray and its supporting hyperplane tangent at the market reserves). Taking asset k as numeraire, so that $p_k = 1$, and setting $\lambda = 1/\nabla_k f(\boldsymbol{R})$, we get $p_i = \nabla_i f(\boldsymbol{R})/\nabla_k f(\boldsymbol{R})$ for all $i = 1, \ldots N$ (Angeris and Chitra 2020; Fabi and Prat 2022).

Properties of CFMMs

The organizing principles of CFMMs still elude researchers. This situation is largely explained by the fact that CFMMs were not introduced to solve a clear problem but instead to expediently address some practical challenges. Despite research being still in its infancy, some promising contributions have been made over the last few years.

The pioneers of research on CFMMs are Angeris et al. (2021a, 2021b, 2021c, 2021d, 2021e, 2022; and Angeris and Chitra 2020). They point out that much can be gathered about the behavior of CFMMs by studying the shape of their trading sets.

Price oracle

The first topic these authors analyze is the decentralized oracle problem. A CFMM solves the decentralized oracle problem if its price closely tracks the fundamental price, usually assimilated to the price on a centralized exchange such as Binance. Decentralized oracles are of great value for the ecosystems hosted by a blockchain. Thanks to them, other DeFi applications can read prices directly on-chain, thereby avoiding a potential single point of failure originating from the interaction with exter-

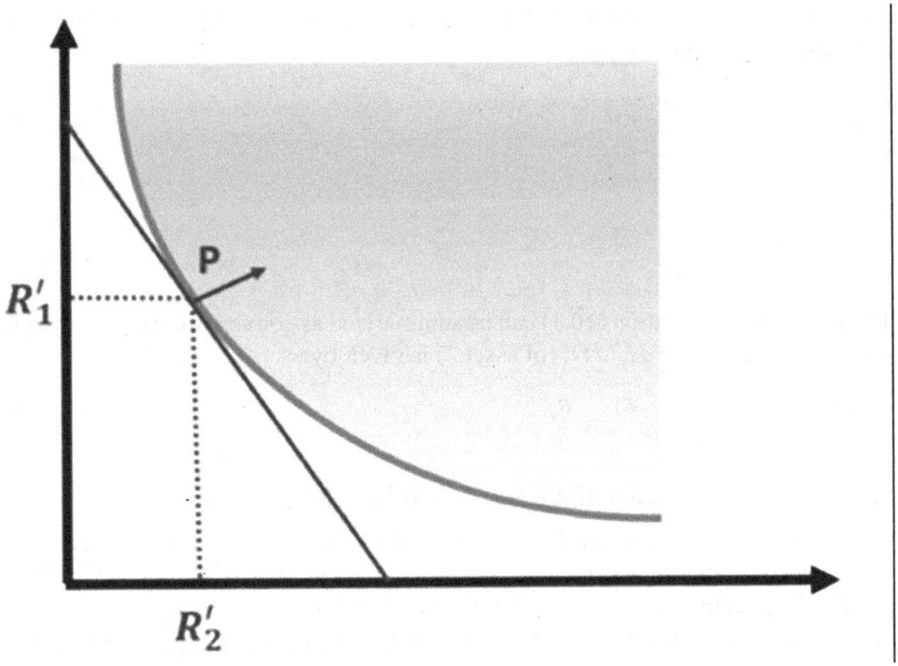

Figure 10.2 CFMM pricing

nal applications. This is why major DEXs implement a price oracle API that retrieves their historical price averages.[9]

Angeris et al. (2020) show that if the trading set is convex—that is, if the trading function is strictly quasi-concave—the CFMM does have a unique no-arbitrage equilibrium in which the CFMM tracks the reference price.

To illustrate how the no-arbitrage condition ensures that the CEX and the DEX quote the same price, consider Uniswap's CFMM with reserves $\boldsymbol{R}_1, \boldsymbol{R}_2$. Suppose that asset 1 is the numeraire and the CEX quotes a market price of p for asset 2. Suppose also that both DEX and CEX charge no fees. Now, whenever $p \neq \boldsymbol{R}_1/\boldsymbol{R}_2$, an arbitrageur can profit from trading across the DEX and the CEX. For $p > \boldsymbol{R}_1/\boldsymbol{R}_2$, asset 2 is underpriced in the DEX. The arbitrageur can then swap asset 1 for asset 2 on the DEX and sell it to the CEX, cashing in the price difference. If $p < \boldsymbol{R}_1/\boldsymbol{R}_2$, then asset 1 is underpriced in the DEX, leading to a symmetric arbitrage opportunity. A strictly convex trading set guarantees that there exists a unique post-arbitrage reserve level with the implied price matching that of the CEX. Note that the oracle property is robust to the addition of transaction fees γ in the DEX. More precisely, fees cause the DEX price p^{DEX} to track the CEX price p^{CEX} within tight bounds, $p^{DEX} \in \left[\gamma p^{CEX}, \gamma^{-1} p^{CEX}\right]$.

Angeris et al. (2021e) simulate the price oracle property for Uniswap using agent-based techniques. Other authors provide empirical evidence with real-world data. Lo and Medda (2020) use an ARDL-ECM (autoregressive dynamic lag error correction model) to estimate the cointegrating relationship between Uniswap's ETH-USDT exchange rate and the exchange rates for the same pair offered by several centralized exchanges. Lehar and Parlour (2021) find that price differences between Binance and Uniswap are usually below 1 percent when liquidity is abundant.

The empirical literature also investigates the discovery of fundamental prices directly on DEXs. A market discovers the fundamental price of an asset when its quoted price is efficient (that is, it reflects the value of the asset). When a DEX quotes fundamental prices, not only those prices and the ones posted by coexisting CEXes are close under no arbitrage, but the DEX itself becomes the reference market. In other words, the CEXs adjust their prices towards the ones quoted by the DEX, not the other way around. Han et al. (2021) argue that Binance traders do indeed consider Uniswap prices as efficient. Specifically, they show that when liquidity provision on Uniswap increases, Binance traders tend to gravitate more towards Uniswap's price, whereas Uniswap traders become less sensitive to Binance's price.

Fabi and Prat (2022) highlight a striking equivalence among the CFMM's no-arbitrage equilibrium and the expenditure minimization problem (EMP) in micro-economic theory. For a bonding curve set at $f(\boldsymbol{R}) = K$, they show that equilibrium reserves equal the Hicksian demand $\boldsymbol{h}(\boldsymbol{p};K)$ of a consumer given indirect utility K and commodity prices $\boldsymbol{p}$. The LP value function (that is, the value of the pool) equals the expenditure function $V(\boldsymbol{p};K)$ under the same interpretation as before. From now on, we omit to state the level of the trading function (that is, the indirect utility in the EMP) when unnecessary, and just write $\boldsymbol{h}(\boldsymbol{p})$ and $V(\boldsymbol{p})$.and commodity prices $\boldsymbol{p}$. The LP value function (that is, the value of the pool) equals the expenditure function $V(\boldsymbol{p};K)$ under the same interpretation as before. From now on, we omit to state the level of the trading function (that is, the indirect utility in the EMP) when unnecessary, and just write $\boldsymbol{h}(\boldsymbol{p})$ and $V(\boldsymbol{p})$.

CFMMs equivalence

Angeris et al. (2020) study the classification of CFMMs. They find that two CFMMs are equivalent if their trading functions generate the same trading sets. This is intuitive since trading functions and their bonding curves are designed to represent trading sets, in the same way that utility functions represent preferences or transformation functions represent production processes in microeconomic theory (Mas-Colell et al. 1995: chapters 3 and 5). More formally, two CFMMs with trading functions f and g are equivalent if $f = v \circ g$ where v is a monotonically increasing function.

Accordingly, under some specific parametrization, Uniswap and its multi-asset generalization Balancer are actually indistinguishable. Balancer uses the trading function:

$$f(\boldsymbol{R}) = \prod_{i=1}^{N} \boldsymbol{R}_i^{w_i} \tag{10.4}$$

with weights $w_i \in (0,1): \sum w_i = 1$. For $n = 2$ and $w_1 = w_2 = \frac{1}{2}$, the Uniswap trading function $g(\boldsymbol{R})$ can be written as:

$$g(\boldsymbol{R}) = \left[R_1^{\frac{1}{2}} R_2^{\frac{1}{2}}\right]^2 = [f(\boldsymbol{R})]^2,$$

thus proving the equivalence with Balancer for this parametrization, while, for $w_i \neq \frac{1}{2}$, the equivalence breaks down.

Optimal curvature

As previously stated, CFMM pricing should discourage traders to create excessive movements in the pools' reserves. This is especially important to limit the cost of adverse selection for liquidity provision, originating whenever an arbitrageur takes advantage of a discrepancy between the CFMM's prices and the prices quoted in the reference market. In DeFi jargon, the cost of adverse selection is called impermanent loss (IL).

A way to mitigate excessive arbitrage, and thus impermanent losses, is by having trading functions that induce convex pricing, as in the case of Uniswap (equation 10.3). This requires positive slippage, defined as the derivative of the price with respect to output; that is, for a two-assets pool:

$$\frac{d}{dO_2} p\left(R_1 + q(O_2; \boldsymbol{R}),\ R_2 - O_2\right) > 0.$$

Angeris et al. (2022) and Fabi and Prat (2022) show that slippage is positive if the trading sets are convex, a property that is satisfied if and only if the trading function is strictly quasi-concave or if it exhibits positive Gaussian curvature.

Some curvature in the trading function is thus desirable to create slippage and limit the harms of arbitrage, but excessive curvature can discourage traders. What, then, is the optimal curvature of a trading function? The answer that Angeris et al. (2022) provide is that low-curvature CFMMs are more suited to low-volatility, mean-reverting assets, such as stablecoins, whereas high-curvature CFMMs are most suited to volatile assets. Trading of the first asset type is not information-driven, hence reserves are likely to move according to small random shocks that pose little risk of depletion. In this context, it is natural to let swaps take place at low slippage. On the other hand, trading of volatile assets is more susceptible to arbitrage, which can cause large reserves movements and harm liquidity providers. In this case, setting a higher slippage via curvature shields LPs. Optimal CFMM curvature resembles classical results in the order book literature (Glosten and Milgrom 1985). In that context, to reduce adverse selection, market makers eliminate excessive orders. Analogously, in CFMMs, the smart contract discourages excessive trading by implementing a steeply curved trading function.

Given that the slippage of any convex price function can be bounded from below using a linear function of the traded tokens, Angeris et al. (2022) uses this lower bound to compute the maximum trade size that makes liquidity provision profitable.

The main takeaway from analyzing CFMM curvature and LP returns is that an optimal CFMM should adjust curvature dynamically based on the volatility of their traded assets (Krishnamachari et al. 2021). To the best of our knowledge, Krishnamachari et al.'s design has not yet been implemented. However, alternative dynamic curves are already used by some recent AMMs.[10]

Replication

The other fundamental aspect covered in the series of papers by Angeris and coauthors is payoff replication via CFMMs (Angeris et al. 2021b). The problem of payoff replication deals with the inversion of the liquidity providers' value function. We have already explained how to compute LPs' value under no-arbitrage for a given trading function. Now we address the converse question: Starting from a desired payoff profile for liquidity providers, can we find a trading function which replicates that specific payoff? The authors manage to do so for a comprehensive class of LP payoff functions. This problem has the same flavor as the one addressed by Chen and Pennock (2012) for prediction markets, since they showed how to derive the AMM associated to a particular cost function.

To solve the replication challenge, Angeris et al. (2021b) exploit duality theory. They prove that the dual problem associated to the maximization of arbitrageurs' gains corresponds to the minimization of LPs' value. In analogy with demand theory, the process of finding the trading set that achieves a given LP payoff is analogous to recovering consumer preferences from a given expenditure function (Fabi and Prat 2022).

Angeris et al. (2021b) establish a bijection between the family of LP value functions that are concave, positive, increasing, homogeneous of degree 1 in the market price and CFMM with convex trading sets. Each property of the class of payoff functions that can be replicated has economic interpretations. Concavity of the value function is analogous to requiring that LPs face impermanent losses; positivity implies that the LP cannot run a deficit; increasing functions ensure that the value of the portfolio grows as the assets appreciate. Homogeneity of degree 1 is simply a scaling property: if all prices are scaled proportionally, so is the value of the LPs' portfolio.

Privacy

So far, we have seen that convexity of the trading set is a desirable property. However, it also has the drawback of causing a loss of privacy for users, as explained by Angeris et al. (2021d). Since the history of pool reserves is public, the quantity function derived from a convex trading set can be inverted so as to recover the exact sequence of trades that led a liquidity pool to its current state. Transactions batching is not a viable solution as it considerably worsens users' terms of trade owing to the price impact. Randomizing also worsen the price impact because of convex pricing. Moreover, the central limit theorem implies that one can efficiently extract the random noise component from prices.

DECENTRALIZED PLATFORM ECONOMICS

We have covered the main properties and optimal design of CFMMs. We now turn our attention to the market structure that they generate. The economics literature on platforms uses the term "two-sided market" to refer to markets that have two distinct sides exerting direct positive externalities on each other (Rochet and Tirole 2003). This is exactly the case for DEXs that operate through a CFMM. As mentioned in the previous sections, the two market sides are liquidity providers and traders. Liquidity providers benefit from higher trade volumes by earning more fees. Traders benefit from higher liquidity by getting lower slippage from the CFMM.

A small but fast-growing literature studies the platform economics of decentralized exchanges. The earliest contributions on this topic are by Aoyagi and Ito (2021), Capponi and Jia (2021), and Lehar and Parlour (2021). These papers propose variations of the same benchmark model to study the rents of traders and liquidity providers who participate to a constant-product DEX or a CEX, together with the resulting allocation of liquidity among the competing exchanges.

Comparison of CFMM and LOB Exchanges

Although this strand of literature outlines many similarities with classical market microstructure models, it also highlights important differences. For example, in LOBs, LPs choose both the quantity they want to supply as well as the minimum sale price of their assets. By contrast, when interacting with a CFMM, LPs choose only their supply, while the price of the liquidity is given by a function of the CFMM's reserves. Once liquidity is supplied, it cannot be conditioned on the price. Due to this feature, the rents from liquidity provision in CFMMs are mutualized, whereas in LOBs liquidity provision is competitive. This feature creates an important difference in the composition of LPs' rents for the two market mechanisms. In LOBs, if LPs compete on prices, their revenues come mainly from setting price slippage strategically. On the other hand, in CFMMs, slippage revenues are captured by arbitrageurs, so LPs revenues come from transaction fees (Lehar and Parlour 2021).

Interestingly, Uniswap's latest upgrade (Uniswap V3) closes part of the gap between CFMMs and LOBs by introducing concentrated liquidity. This functionality allows LPs to supply reserves only within specific price ranges of the traded pair. The advantage of this additional feature for a liquidity provider is that, when the exchange rate matches the range at which they supply liquidity, they can achieve the same fee income as in a standard constant-product pool supplying lower liquidity. The drawback of liquidity concentration is that exchange rates which fall outside of the specified price range can cause substantial losses for LPs. Liao and Robinson (2022) show that, despite its recent launch in 2021, Uniswap V3 was able to collect more liquidity than some of the most popular CEXes (Binance, Coinbase, Kraken, Gemini).

Incentives for Liquidity Providers

The economic literature on two-sided markets underlines that platforms must attract the market side whose demand is more elastic to rents (Rochet and Tirole 2003). In the case of DEXes, the elastic side of the market are liquidity providers. In line with theory, existing DEXes strive to attract liquidity providers, competing against each other and against CEXs.

Yield farming

The process through which LPs harvest the rewards from competing DEXs is known as yield farming. Its revenues are mostly made of two components. First, LP tokens, which allow LPs to accrue transaction fees and claim a fraction of the DEX that they furnish. Second, governance tokens, that carry voting rights on DEXs' strategic decisions (for example, the level of trading fees associated to a given liquidity pool).

The open, unregulated nature of DeFi makes liquidity competition particularly harsh for DEXs. Such competition gives rise to frequent mushrooming of yield farming opportunities. Their landscape is so vast and transient that LPs rely on aggregators, such as Yearn or 1inch, to optimize their liquidity positions across multiple DEXs. To the best of our knowledge, yield farming has received limited academic attention. We therefore present only two major cases of yield farming opportunities that could inspire future research.

Example: Vampire attacks

Some yield farming opportunities originate from DEXs' attempts to enter a market. Network effects should make it difficult for new DEXs to attract liquidity towards them rather than towards well-established protocols. Yet, the open nature of smart contracts combined with traders seeking yield-farming opportunities open the way for newcomers to use cloning strategies. The most common of them is called vampire attack. It entails a DEX siphoning liquidity from another protocol by offering its liquidity providers attractive deals. The first example is the SushiSwap attack, which allowed SushiSwap (a Uniswap fork) to appropriate over $1B of liquidity from Uniswap in less than a week. SushiSwap offered SUSHI tokens to Uniswap LPs as extra rewards in exchange for migrating their Uniswap LP tokens on SushiSwap through the Masterchef smart contract.[11] In response, Uniswap launched in September 2020 its governance token, the UNI token, along with an airdrop of 400 UNI to users who had previously used Uniswap V1 or V2. Vampire attacks have been common in DeFi space and, unfortunately for the victim protocol, give to LPs attractive profit opportunities, at times combined with the entertainment of gamification.[12]

Example: Curve wars

Other yield farming opportunities originate from DEXs' efforts to establish a dominant market position, as in the "Curve wars" that started around May 2020 and which is still ongoing. The Curve wars are competitions among DeFi protocols for the control of Curve's liquidity. Curve being the biggest DEX by total value locked

($5.83 billion at the time of writing in November 2022), DeFi protocols have a strong interest in having their tokens traded on Curve at competitive rates. This enables them to attract yield farmers and thus to establish prominence over their competitors.

A protocol can achieve this goal by holding a big share of Curve's liquidity tokens, the CRV. These can be locked into Curve and converted into Curve's svCRV governance tokens. Besides providing passive yields, svCRV allow their owners self-vote for pool gauging; that is, directing new emissions of CRV tokens to themselves. Generous CRV emissions attract yield farmers and explain the importance of controlling the outstanding token basis of CRVs.

In a similar fashion to Vampire attacks, Convex Finance (Convex for brevity) managed to control the majority of CRV tokens through a cloning mechanism. It devised a protocol that allowed CRV owners to sell their voting rights on Curve for more liquid assets with boosted financial yield, the CvxCRV tokens minted by Convex. Then Convex allowed its LPs to vote on Curve's governance by locking its native tokens, the CVX. In this way, Convex effectively took control over Curve.

Despite Convex being in control of most CVXs in circulation, Curve's governance is to some extent still contestable. Vote buying (or "bribing") protocols such as Bribe.cvx or Votium allow owners of CRV or CVX tokens to delegate their votes in exchange for side payments. Some protocols such as Llama Airforce Union even optimize vote buying for CVX holders.

Adverse selection costs

The downside of liquidity provision in DEXs is adverse selection costs. These arise whenever reference prices change because LPs have their funds locked in liquidity pools, and so cannot react before arbitrageurs take advantage of the price discrepancy.

The usual metric of adverse selection in CFMMs is the impermanent loss (IL), as already mentioned. Fabi and Prat (2022) use a static model to compute the IL as the arbitrage profit from a price shock. They show that the impermanent loss caused by a price move from $\boldsymbol{p}^0$ to $\boldsymbol{p}^1$ is given by:

$$IL(\boldsymbol{p}^0,\boldsymbol{p}^1) = \boldsymbol{p}^1 \cdot \left[\boldsymbol{h}(\boldsymbol{p}^0) - \boldsymbol{h}(\boldsymbol{p}^1)\right] \tag{10.5}$$

$$= \boldsymbol{p}^1 \cdot \nabla_p V(\boldsymbol{p}^0) - V(\boldsymbol{p}^1) \geq 0. \tag{10.6}$$

The second equality in eqation (10.6) follows from $\boldsymbol{h}(\boldsymbol{p}) = \nabla_p V(\boldsymbol{p})$ (Shephard's lemma), and the final inequality from the concavity of V in $\boldsymbol{p}$. Fabi and Prat (2022) demonstrate through equation (10.6) that IL is increasing and convex in $\boldsymbol{p}^1$.

Milionis et al. (2022) develop a continuous-time model of liquidity provision and propose a new measure of adverse selection costs called loss-versus-rebalancing (LVR), which is simply the sum of IL in equation (10.5) over all price changes in a given time period. They call their measure loss-versus-rebalancing rather than impermanent loss to underline that they do not keep reserves fixed at their initial value throughout the history of arbitrages. In a static model, LVR and IL coincide.

However, in a dynamic model, IL does not take into account the impact of reserves rebalancing after each arbitrage. Formally, assuming that prices evolve according to a sequence $\boldsymbol{p}^0, \boldsymbol{p}^1, \ldots, \boldsymbol{p}^{n+1}$ and that arbitrageurs trade with the CFMM in periods 1 to n:

$$LVR = \sum_{k=1}^{n} IL(\boldsymbol{p}^{k-1}, \boldsymbol{p}^k)$$

$$= \sum_{k=0}^{n} \boldsymbol{h}(\boldsymbol{p}^k)\left[\boldsymbol{p}^k - \boldsymbol{p}^{k-1}\right] - \left[\boldsymbol{V}(\boldsymbol{p}^{n+1}) - \boldsymbol{V}(\boldsymbol{p}^0)\right]. \tag{10.7}$$

Milionis et al. (2022) solve the continuous-time limit of equation (10.7) assuming a geometric Brownian motion for $\boldsymbol{p}$. For a timespan of length T, they demonstrate that:

$$LVR \longrightarrow \int_0^T l(\boldsymbol{p}_t)dt,$$

and they solve in closed-form the instantaneous LVR rate $\boldsymbol{l}(\boldsymbol{p}_t)$, expressing it as a function of price volatility and curvature of the LP expenditure function. For a single risky asset with price volatility σ, the instantaneous LVR reads:

$$l(p) = -\frac{\sigma^2 p^2}{2}\frac{d^2}{dp^2}V(p). \tag{10.8}$$

Milionis et al. (2022) estimate LVR applying equation (10.8) to Uniswap and Balancer (see equation 10.4). They find that daily TVL is about 3bp and that LPs' annual yield is about 8 percent.

Incentives for Traders

The recent models of competing exchanges distinguish traders as either noise or informed traders (that is, arbitrageurs). Noise traders have exogenous reasons to trade; they either swap in or out a fixed quantity of assets with equal probability. Informed traders trade with the CFMM to profit from price discrepancies among exchanges.

The interactions between liquidity providers and traders determine the inventory of liquidity pools as well as the distribution of liquidity among competing DEXs and CEXs. The literature keeps CEX and DEX platforms passive but endogenizes the allocation of trades and liquidity across such platforms. It shows that the impact of trader participation on the liquidity of DEXs is in line with established results in the market microstructure literature (Kyle 1985; Glosten and Milgrom 1985; Easley and O'Hara 1987). Informed trading discourages liquidity provision as it causes impermanent losses. Noise trading attracts LPs as it allows them to profit from fees while avoiding large movements in reserves. In the case of DEXs, informed trading also causes temporary capital gains thanks to convex CFMM pricing: if noise trades net out in expectation, then expected pool reserves increases due to the (strict) convexity of the bonding curve. Formally, for a distribution over trades Δ with $\mathbb{E}[\Delta] = 0$, Jensen's inequality implies that:

$$E[q(\Delta\,;\boldsymbol{R})] \geq q(\mathbb{E}[\Delta]\,;\boldsymbol{R}) = 0. \tag{10.9}$$

The intuition behind equation (10.9) is that for convex bonding curves, buying assets from a CFMM is more expensive than selling them.

The problem with such capital gains is that they are completely cancelled out after a single arbitrage. Hence the only lasting factors for liquidity providers originate from transaction fees and asset volatility. In models such as Capponi and Jia (2021) and Lehar and Parlour (2021) where traders' platform choice is exogenous, both fees and volatility have very clear direct effects on equilibrium liquidity: positive for fees, negative for volatility. However, other contributions point out that equilibrium effects which also take into account traders' reactions can be subtler.

Hasbrouck et al. (2022) argue that only moderate fee rates stimulate liquidity provision. Excessive rates instead fire back on LPs due to the disincentive that they entail for traders. Surprisingly enough, Hasbrouck et al. (2022) show that charging low trading fees rather than none can attract traders. Since collected fees are poured back in the liquidity pool, they reduce slippage, in turn making the CFMM more attractive to traders if the lower slippage compensates the higher fees.

Aoyagi and Ito (2021) model a CEX–DEX duopoly. They highlight that higher DEX liquidity generates positive spillovers on the CEX. In their model, an exogenous increase in DEX liquidity causes both types of traders to migrate from the CEX to the DEX, but not to the same extent. Informed traders are more likely to migrate than noise traders due to their higher sensitivity to slippage. The signal-to-noise ratio of the CEX therefore decreases, leading to lower bid–ask spreads in its LOB.

The theoretical results discussed above are supported by empirical evidence. Lehar and Parlour (2021) conduct a regression analysis on Uniswap daily data for 1376 pools. They show that, as predicted by their model, liquidity is negatively affected by volatility and positively affected by noise trading. Lehar and Parlour (2021) argue that the stability of reserves is guaranteed by Ethereum's gas fees, which prevent LPs from draining pools in response to extreme market events (contrarily to what is usually observed in LOBs). They support their stability hypothesis by observing that the 41 percent ETH price decline which occurred on May 19, 2021 caused a withdrawal of only 17 percent of Uniswap's liquidity.

Capponi and Jia (2021) analyze a dataset ranging from April to December 2021, collected from major CEXs and 12 liquidity pools, half from Uniswap, half from SushiSwap. They also find empirical support for a negative relationship between volatility and liquidity, and a positive relationship between liquidity and noise trading. They test and confirm that gas fees and asset volatility are positively correlated.

Finally, Heimbach et al. (2021) also analyze Uniswap data from its deployment in May 2020 to January 2021 in order to describe liquidity distribution across pools. They find that pool participation follows a power law: most LPs participate to a single pool, and 96.5 percent of them participate to at most five pools at once. They argue that LPs' cautiousness is the most plausible explanation for liquidity concentration. LPs tend to participate only to pools whose risks they can assess with confidence. Such an evaluation is easier for the few popular pools to which most LPs participate, rather than for the many small pools in the tail of the liquidity distribution.

MINER EXTRACTIBLE VALUE

We have seen that CFMM is a simple and versatile technology. Nonetheless, its minimalistic design is not without drawbacks. The most notorious one is miner extractible value (MEV).

Technically, MEV are profits that blockchain miners or speculators can earn through the reordering of transactions within blocks. Transaction reordering is harmless to blockchains featuring simple transactions such as Bitcoin, but not for CFMMs and DeFi applications. For instance, when two buy orders are sent to a CFMM, one after another, the pricing formula results in a better deal for the first order.[13]

The name "miner extractible value" comes from the fact that miners are in control of transaction ordering within blocks and can freely select according to strategic or even malicious motives. Most of the time, however, aggressive block reordering is not performed by miners but rather by arbitrage bots that continuously scan the memory pool ("mempool") to spot profit opportunities, and engage in gas auctions to claim them (see, for example, Figure 10.3). This behavior indirectly benefits miners who ultimately get the rents from bots' auctions (Capponi and Jia 2021). MEV priority auctions are problematic for the whole ecosystem as all participants bear the congestion externality they generate. Ethereum's mempool is teaming with bots that profit from MEV opportunities at the expenses of users. This is why practitioners refer to it as a "dark forest," a term originally coined in the science fiction novel *Remembrance of the Earth's Past* (Liu 2008) and popularized in the context of blockchains by a blog article (Robinson and Konstantopoulos 2020).[14]

Front-Running

Daian et al. (2019) is the first academic contribution that documents the significance of MEV. It studies its consequences and simulates bots' priority gas auctions. Analyzing bot activity on Ethereum, Daian et al. (2019) find that miners often earn more from MEV than from block rewards. They further show that, to fully exploit MEV rents, miners should rewind and fork the blockchain, committing a so-called time bandit attack. There is no account of a time bandit attack having happened on a popular blockchain, but its profitability represents a concrete consensus layer threat. Ironically enough, the evidence collected in Daian et al. (2019) was partly a side-effect of the same authors publishing a preliminary report on arbitrages in DEXs (Bentov et al. 2017). Its publication attracted the attention of developers who designed bots that could exploit the arbitrage opportunities identified in the report.

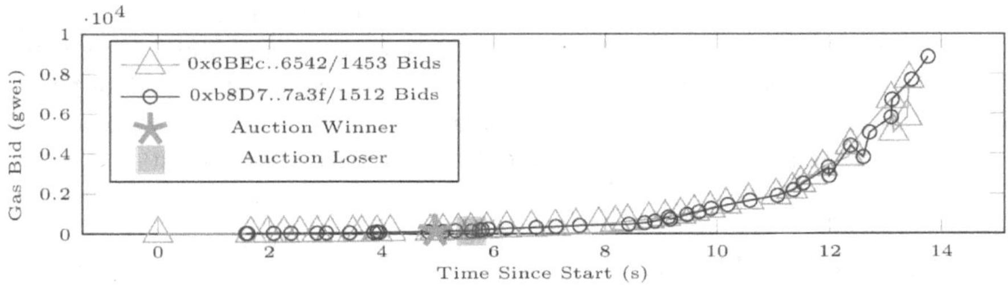

Seconds Elapsed	Quantity @ Price Bid	Ethereum Transaction Origin (Public Key Hash)	Nonce	Transaction Hash
0.000	192085 @ 25.10	0x6BEcAb24Ed88Ec13D0A18f20e7dC5E4d5b146542	1453	0xd32653ca9694a6d1299335f3c04f74cc159bee48c1d32d3a421db08c638ffc78
1.593	231520 @ 25.00	0xb8D76f4BC2518F8eb508bf0Ccca76f8F9DD57a3f	1512	0xb901e6dc2c229fd9105448fcc23caebdedb476c21b6c6c7ddf8d2df4e838d2c7
1.624	231520 @ 28.75	0xb8D76f4BC2518F8eb508bf0Ccca76f8F9DD57a3f	1512	0x9f592504eb71a7452b7a395a7f5ecd34eaa5d090da1162e74221562af54c8f67
1.679	227534 @ 28.81	0x6BEcAb24Ed88Ec13D0A18f20e7dC5E4d5b146542	1453	0x83e2a6774654a9540c3fad8837afcc88b4c932ab2374819254f887305c3a4b22
...	...	...	...	...
4.949	227534 @ 134.02	0x6BEcAb24Ed88Ec13D0A18f20e7dC5E4d5b146542	1453	0xc889bd13594f75e4dd824f04f0c2ad03896cb7ec6518df02455e9560367bb9c4
5.599	231520 @ 133.76	0xb8D76f4BC2518F8eb508bf0Ccca76f8F9DD57a3f	1512	0xaa86d782328c0c9c422e3f2a3170ff41ae21a27ad395c48db76b0080898f85db
...	...	...	...	...
13.383	227534 @ 5834.77	0x6BEcAb24Ed88Ec13D0A18f20e7dC5E4d5b146542	1453	0xb0dc97140394c5f65332ebc459d5e66f89099dbb4d335c866b32280270102858
13.416	227534 @ 7716.48	0x6BEcAb24Ed88Ec13D0A18f20e7dC5E4d5b146542	1453	0x1825be6951577e72a1dafc8de564ce1ccfe5d284173e11e77b2e7f6b1b44571c
13.462	231520 @ 7701.08	0xb8D76f4BC2518F8eb508bf0Ccca76f8F9DD57a3f	1512	0xa9823358c99149f0e6343c604c35988468d01d02868437d8251b3cee282dc92b
m13.759	231520 @ 8856.24	0xb8D76f4BC2518F8eb508bf0Ccca76f8F9DD57a3f	1512	0x366c30a534b5f3d8a6d251f97d401997624d1fe8d3af07ede4d19105dc970942

Note: The graph shows the gas bids of two observed bots over time, while the table details the bots' initial and final bids and the two mined bids (enclosed within continuation dots).
Source: Daian et al. (2019).

Figure 10.3 One example of price gas auction (PGA) that was observed over the Ethereum peer-to-peer network

Qin et al. (2021) quantify the MEV on Ethereum from December 2018 to August 2021. They find it to be over four times the value of block rewards and transaction fees combined. The highest MEV opportunity was worth US$4.1 million, more than 600 times the sum of block reward and transaction fees for an average block. They argue that this MEV opportunity was sufficient to incentivize a miner with only 0.1 percent of the network mining capacity to commit a time bandit attack.

Sandwich Attacks

The most common form of MEV on DEXs are sandwich attacks. A sandwich attack can be performed on both buy and sell orders. It involves the combined front-running and back-running of a target transaction. When a bot (or miner) is notified of some pending buy order on a CFMM, it can forge a buy and a sell order of equal amounts and squeeze the user's transaction within these two. In doing so, the attacker earns a profit as convex bonding curves make it profitable for the bot to buy assets and sell them back when their reserves are higher. These sorts of manipulations also take place in traditional finance, especially through algorithmic trading (Michel 2022). However, CFMMs makes the attackers' life easier, as all pending transactions are public.

The seriousness of MEV is also highlighted by Park (2021), who compares constant product pricing with traditional LOBs. Although he finds that CFMMs satisfy the desirable feature of not inducing users to break their orders into smaller ones, nor split them across multiple DEXs, Park also proves that CFMMs with constant-product pricing are always vulnerable to sandwich attacks.

To see why, consider the CFMM moving as in Figure 10.4 and suppose that the initial reserves of the two assets are $\boldsymbol{R}$. The attacker observes the mempool and notices that a trader wants to buy O_2 units of asset 2. The attacker first front-runs the trader with the same operation and then back-runs the trader by inverting it. To front-run the trader, the attacker pays $I_1 = q(O_2;\boldsymbol{R})$ of asset 1, moving reserves to $\boldsymbol{R}^I = \boldsymbol{R} + \boldsymbol{\Delta}$, with $\boldsymbol{\Delta} = (q(O_2;\boldsymbol{R}), -O_2)$ (movement I). Then, the original trade is executed, but now, the trader pays $q(O_2;\boldsymbol{R} + \boldsymbol{\Delta})$ instead of $q(O_2;\boldsymbol{R})$ to receive output O_2, moving the CFMM reserves to $\boldsymbol{R}^{II} = \boldsymbol{R} + (q(O_2;\boldsymbol{R}) + q(O_2;\boldsymbol{R} + \boldsymbol{\Delta})\ , -2O_2)$ (movement II). Finally, by back-running the trade, the attacker returns the reserves to $\boldsymbol{R}^I$, thereby paying back O_2 of asset 2 and receiving $q(O_2;\boldsymbol{R} + \boldsymbol{\Delta})$ of asset 1 (movement III). At the end of the sandwich attack, the attacker has 0 units of asset 2 but ends up with a positive balance,

$$q(O_2;\boldsymbol{R} + \boldsymbol{\Delta}) - q(O_2;\boldsymbol{R}) > 0,$$

of asset 1, which corresponds to the extra input price the user pays owing to the sandwich attack. Given that the inequality follows from the convexity of the quantity function, sandwich attacks are always profitable for any CFMM with convex trading sets (Fabi and Prat 2022).

The practical consequence of sandwich attacks for users is that they cause involuntary price slippage. In other words, the price at which an order is meant to be executed might not correspond to the actual execution price. To defend against sandwich attacks, DeFi platforms allow users to set a maximum slippage tolerance. Tuning the tolerance threshold is not trivial, as it makes users vulnerable to arbitrage if set too low, but stops most of their trades if set too high. Heimbach and Wattenhofer (2022) compute the optimal slippage tolerance as a function of the size of the trade and the characteristic of the pool. Their simulations indicate that customized tolerance rules outperform the constant slippage tolerance implemented by popular DEXes.

Solutions to MEV

Flashbots is the leading proposal to alleviate MEV. Its key idea is to remove block building capabilities from miners and to transfer them to dedicated agents. In Flashbots, block builders are called searchers. They scan the mempool in search for transactions carrying profitable MEV opportunities, bundle them together, and auction these bundles to miners through a private relay channel.[15] This design reduces the dangers of MEV in two important ways. First, as miners can no longer decide the internal block ordering, they have no incentive to commit a time bandit attack. Second, the private communication channel between builders and miners eliminates the congestion costs generated by priority auctions.

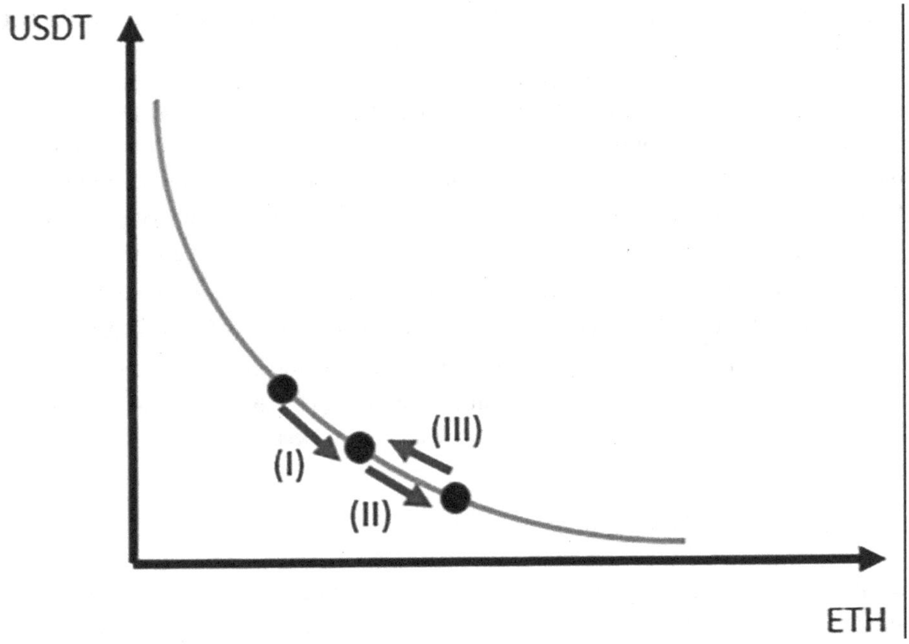

Figure 10.4 *Sandwich attack*

The separation between builders and miners is part of the design proposal for the new Ethereum V2 running on proof-of-stake. It entails important consensus layer modifications which Ethereum's developers have not yet finalized. However, they are already proposing a temporary solution through the Builder API. Ethereum's consensus layer clients can install it to request data directly from the network of block builders, which operates through execution layer clients.

CONCLUSION

We have presented the state of research on AMMs in decentralized finance. Born as tools to facilitate information elicitation in prediction markets, AMMs have morphed into the CFMMs now used in decentralized exchanges. These modern variants are suited to blockchains thanks to their lightweight design. We have explained how decentralized exchanges operated by AMMs give rise to two-sided markets whose success crucially depends on their ability to attract liquidity. Finally, we have discussed the problems raised by miner extractible value, highlighting possible solutions and open challenges.

Although a rigorous theory of decentralized market making does not yet exist, much progress has been accomplished over the last few years. A vocabulary has been elaborated to rigorously describe the design space. Equilibrium models have been built to study existing applications and to provide suggestions for their improvement. With these foundations laid down, the stage is set for a new wave of research on the general optimality principles of CFMMs. In this enterprise, standard microeconomic theory is likely to prove particularly useful since it accurately describes the inner workings of CFMMs (Fabi and Prat 2022). Besides providing theoretical insights on market design, we also expect future contributions to foster our understanding of the interaction between different types of exchanges. The cut-throat competition to attract liquidity is one of the most striking feature of DeFi. Its study will require more advanced models and better empirical evidence on equilibrium liquidity provision.

Building a solid theory of CFMMs is a challenging endeavor as the technology evolves at an ever-increasing pace. Keeping up with this continuous stream of innovations may seem unfeasible, and yet, recent contributions have considerably closed the gap separating theory from practice, making it realistic to envision a new stage of DeFi where protocol design would draw on scientific insights rather than on serendipity and educated guesses.

NOTES

1. Prediction markets are also called information markets. Successful examples include Iowa electronic markets and the Hollywood stock exchange.
2. Another implementation challenge arises from the fact that payoffs are negative in some states of the world. The market scoring rule therefore has to be complemented with an escrow mechanism requesting from each forecaster that they deposit an amount equal to their losses in the worst-case scenario, that is, $\min_{\boldsymbol{X}_i} \Pi\left(\boldsymbol{r}^n, \boldsymbol{X}_i \middle| \boldsymbol{r}^{n-1}\right)$.
3. Note that the worst-case loss is independent of the number of forecasts because the AMM only has to pay the last trader. This result immediately follows from the definition of the AMM's overall payout: $\sum_{n=1}^{T} s\left(\boldsymbol{r}^n, \boldsymbol{X}_i\right) - s\left(\boldsymbol{r}^{n-1}, \boldsymbol{X}_i\right) = s\left(\boldsymbol{r}^T, \boldsymbol{X}_i\right) - s\left(\boldsymbol{r}^0, \boldsymbol{X}_i\right)$, where T is the index of the last trader.
4. More precisely, weighted pseudospherical scoring rules, as defined by Jose et al. (2008), which include logarithmic scoring rules as one of their limit cases.
5. A CFMM takes constant memory to operate and constant time to process each trade. On the contrary, the memory and time taken by an LOB to process a set of trades scale linearly and quadratically in the number of trades to be processed.
6. The codes for Uniswap's smart contract can be found at https://github.com/Uniswap.
7. For example, some CFMMs (for example, Bancor) implement a "unilateral liquidity provision" functionality for supplying reserves only of part of the supported assets. We can treat unilateral liquidity according to our binary classification as a composed operation, made of balanced liquidity provision and subsequent swap. Also, as explained below, a swap that charges transaction fees can be thought of as a composed operation.
8. The quantity function for a swap among generic assets *ij* has additional indexes $q_{ij}(\Delta_j)$.
9. For Uniswap the price oracle API can be retrieved at: https://docs.uniswap.org/protocol/concepts/V3-overview/oracle.

10. For example, Dodo uses a dynamic bonding curve (https://docs.dodoex.io/english/).
11. The MasterChef contract can be found here: https://docs.sushi.com/docs/Developers/Sushiswap/MasterChef.
12. Enzo finance recently carried out a vampire attack against six Ethereum exchanges masked as a videogame (https://decrypt.co/87778/enso-finance-vampire-attack-six-ethereum-defi-competitors).
13. Exposure to MEV is another reason why LOBs are unsuited to blockchains.
14. "Dark forest" is the name of a fictional hypothesis on the state of the universe on which the novel fantasizes. According to the dark forest hypothesis, the universe is an adversarial environment populated by advanced civilizations. They hide from each other, as an encounter would trigger devastating wars. By analogy, Ethereum's mempool is said to be a dark forest because it is populated by arbitrage bots that engage in costly bid auctions if they detect each other.
15. Private relay channels serve the same function as dark pools in the context of centralized LOBs.

REFERENCES

Angeris, G., Agrawal, A., Evans, A., Chitra, T., and Boyd, S. (2021a). Constant function market makers: multi-asset trades via convex optimization. *arXiv preprint arXiv:2107.12484*.

Angeris, G., and Chitra, T. (2020). Improved price oracles: constant function market makers. In *Proceedings of the 2nd ACM Conference on Advances in Financial Technologies* (pp. 80–91).

Angeris, G., Chitra, T., and Evans, A. (2021b). Replicating monotonic payoffs without oracles. *arXiv preprint arXiv:2111.13740*.

Angeris, G., Chitra, T., and Evans, A. (2021c). How liveness separates CFMMs and order books. https://angeris.github.io/papers/cfmm-ob.pdf.

Angeris, G., Chitra, T., and Evans, A. (2021d). Differential privacy in constant function market makers. In *International Conference on Financial Cryptography and Data Security* (pp. 149–178). Springer, Cham.

Angeris, G., Chitra, T., and Evans, A. (2022). When does the tail wag the dog? Curvature and market making. https://cryptoeconomicsystems.pubpub.org/pub/angeris-curvature-market-making/release/2?readingCollection=082fed82.

Angeris, G., Kao, H.T., Chiang, R., Noyes, C., and Chitra, T. (2021e). An analysis of Uniswap markets. https://cryptoeconomicsystems.pubpub.org/pub/angeris-uniswap-analysis/release/15.

Aoyagi, J., and Ito, Y. (2021). Coexisting exchange platforms: limit order books and automated market makers. SSRN working papers. https://papers.ssrn.com/sol3/Papers.cfm?abstract_id=3808755.

Bentov, I., Breidenbach, L., Daian, P., Juels, A., Li, Y., and Zhao, X. (2017). The cost of decentralization in 0x and Etherdelta. https://hackingdistributed.com/2017/08/13/cost-of-decent/.

Brier, G.W. (1950). Verification of forecasts expressed in terms of probability. *Monthly Weather Review*, 78(1), 1–3.

Buterin, V. (2016). Let's run on-chain decentralized exchanges the way we run prediction markets. Reddit. http://reddit.com/r/thereum/comments/55m04x/lets_run_onchain_decentralized_exchanges_the_way.

Capponi, A., and Jia, R. (2021). The adoption of blockchain-based decentralized exchanges. *arXiv preprint arXiv: 2103.08842v1*.

Chen, Y., and Pennock, D.M. (2012). A utility framework for bounded-loss market makers. *arXiv preprint arXiv:1206.5252*
Daian, P., Goldfeder, S., Kell, T., Li, Y., Zhao, X., Bentov, I., ... and Juels, A. (2019). Flash Boys 2.0: frontrunning, transaction reordering, and consensus instability in decentralized exchanges. *arXiv preprint arXiv:1904.05234*.
Easley, D., and O'Hara, M. (1987). Price, trade size, and information in securities markets. *Journal of Financial Economics*, 19(1), 69–90.
Fabi, M., and Prat, J. (2022). The economics of constant function market makers. Mimeo.
Genest, C., and Zidek, J. (1986). Combining probability distributions: a critique and annotated bibliography. *Statistical Science*, 1(1), 114–135.
Glosten, L.R., and Milgrom, P.R. (1985). Bid, ask and transaction prices in a specialist market with heterogeneously informed traders. *Journal of Financial Economics*, 14(1), 71–100.
Good, I.J. (1952). Rational decisions. *Journal of the Royal Statistical Society*, Series B, 14(1), 107–114.
Han, J., Huang, S., and Zhong, Z. (2021). Trust in DeFi: an empirical study of the decentralized exchange. *Available at SSRN 3896461*.
Hanson, R. (2003). Combinatorial information market design. *Information Systems Frontiers*, 5(1), 107–119.
Hanson, R. (2007). Logarithmic market scoring rules for modular combinatorial information aggregation. *Journal of Prediction Markets*, 1(1), 3–15.
Hasbrouck, J., Rivera, T.J., and Saleh, F. (2022). The need for fees at a DEX: how increases in fees can increase DEX trading volume. *Available at SSRN 4192925*.
Hausch, D.B., Lo, V.S., and Ziemba, W.T. (1994). *Efficiency of Racetrack Betting Markets*. Academic Press, San Diego, CA.
Heimbach, L., Wang, Y., and Wattenhofer, R. (2021). Behavior of liquidity providers in decentralized exchanges. *arXiv preprint arXiv:2105.13822*.
Heimbach, L., and Wattenhofer, R. (2022, May). Eliminating sandwich attacks with the help of game theory. In *Proceedings of the 2022 ACM on Asia Conference on Computer and Communications Security* (pp. 153–167).
Jose, V.R.R., Nau, R.F., and Winkler, R.L. (2008). Scoring rules, generalized entropy, and utility maximization. *Operations Research*, 56(5), 1146–1157.
Krishnamachari, B., Feng, Q., and Grippo, E. (2021). Dynamic curves for decentralized autonomous cryptocurrency exchanges. *arXiv preprint arXiv:2101.02778*.
Kyle, A.S. (1985). Continuous auctions and insider trading. *Econometrica: Journal of the Econometric Society*, 53(6), 1315–1335.
Lehar, A., and Parlour, C.A. (2021). Decentralized exchanges. Working paper.
Liao, G., and Robinson, D. (2022). The dominance of Uniswap v3 liquidity. https://uniswap.org/blog/uniswap-v3-dominance.
Liu, C. (2008). *The Dark Forest*. Tor Books, New York.
Lo, Y.C., and Medda, F. (2020). Uniswap and the emergence of the decentralized exchange. *Journal of Financial Market Infrastructures*, 10(2), 1–25.
Mas-Colell, A., Whinston, M.D., and Green, J.R. (1995). *Microeconomic Theory* (Vol. 1). Oxford University Press, Oxford.
Michel, C. (2022). Pricing lp tokens—warp finance hack. https://cmichel.io/pricing-lp-tokens. Accessed: July 30, 2022.
Milionis, J., Moallemi, C.C., Roughgarden, T., and Zhang, A.L. (2022). Automated market making and loss-versus-rebalancing. *arXiv preprint arXiv:2208.06046*.
Park, A. (2021). The conceptual flaws of constant product automated market making. *Available at SSRN 3805750*.
Qin, K., Zhou, L., and Gervais, A. (2021). Quantifying blockchain extractable value: how dark is the forest? *arXiv preprint arXiv:2101.05511*.

Robinson, D., and Konstantopoulos, J. (2020). Ethereum is a Dark Forest. Paradigm blogpost. https://www.paradigm.xyz/2020/08/ethereum-is-a-dark-forest.
Rochet, J.C., and Tirole, J. (2003). Platform competition in two-sided markets. *Journal of the European Economic Association*, 1(4), 990–1029.
Winkler, R.L. (1969). Scoring rules and the evaluation of probability assessors. *Journal of the American Statistical Association*, 64(327), 1073–1078.

11. Systematization of knowledge: mechanism design and the Ethereum blockchain transaction fee market

Fernando Molina and Pablo Roccatagliata

INTRODUCTION

Ethereum uses a block size limit and a fee market to regulate and incentivize the inclusion of some transactions over others and prevent users from spamming the network. This mechanism determines, for every transaction to be added to a block, the price paid by its creator, using a first-price auction: the user makes a bid that will be earned by the miner of the block that decides to include the transaction. The users are therefore bidding for limited (scarce) space on each block.

Three major problems exist with this first-price auction mechanism.[1] First, there is a mismatch between volatility of transaction fee levels and social costs of transactions. Ethereum minimum gas fees could range from 2 gwei (10^9 gwei = 1 ETH) to 20–50 gwei. This makes a correct base fee extremely difficult to estimate and this volatility leaves the network in an unusable state. Figure 11.1 shows Ethereum average as prices.

The second problem lies in the inefficiencies of first price auctions. Miners pack blocks up to the maximum block size and pick transactions to obtain the maximum profit, so their incentive is to pick the transactions with the highest bid. This mechanism is well known for being highly inefficient[2] and also has a very complex fee estimation that could lead to frequent fee overpayment.

The instability of blockchains with no block reward represents a third major problem. Blockchains where there is no issuance in the long term could lead to network instability. Problems such as undercutting attacks—51 percent attack with less than 51 percent of the hash power or selfish mining—could occur in this setting (Carlesten et al. 2020).

A fourth problem, known as needless delays for users, is presented later in the Ethereum Improvement Proposal (EIP) document: transactions often have to wait for several blocks before being included. No one benefits from the fact that blocks have the same size and can not meet block-by-block differences by demand. This fourth problem impacts the approach of how all these setbacks will be resolved. All of these issues related with the first-price auction mechanism are not only a fee problem but also a block size problem.

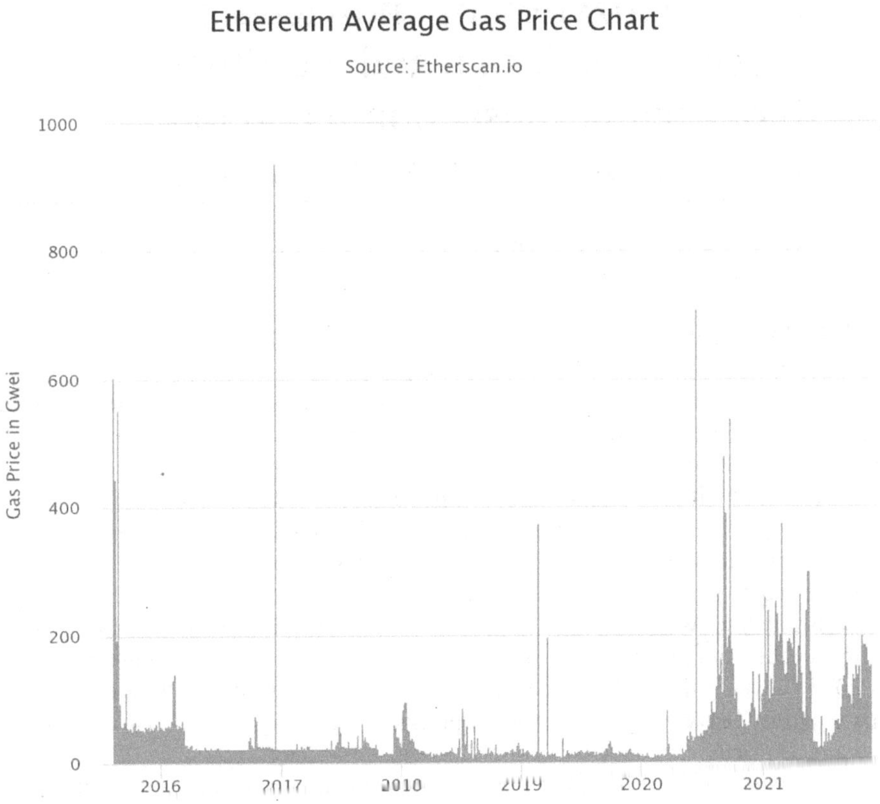

Source: Etherscan.

Figure 11.1 *Gas price in gwei*

EIP-1559

Background

Buterin et al. (2019) introduced EIP-1559, called "Fee market change for ETH 1.0 chain" that outlines several changes in the status quo of transaction fee markets. Roughgarden (2020), in his economic analysis of EIP-1559, summarizes this proposal in eight key ideas:

1. Each block now has a new concept associated called a base fee, that is defined as a reserve price per unit of gas, which transactions are required to pay to be included in a block.[3]
2. The base fee is a function of the preceding blocks only and does not depend on the transactions included in the current block. It is a deterministic value.

3. All the base fee revenues are burned and not earned by the miners as before.
4. New blocks have a maximum block size of 25 million gas. The old maximum, 12.5 million gas, now serves as the target block size.
5. This new mechanism will adjust the base fee upward or downward whenever the size of the last block is bigger or smaller than the target block size. The base fee (r_{cur}) for the current block will use the following formula: $r_{cur} := r_{pred} \cdot \left(1 + \frac{1}{8} \cdot \frac{s_{pred} - s_{target}}{s}\right)$
6. A transaction now includes a tip or a priority fee and a fee cap. A transaction will be included in a block only if its fee cap is at least the block's base fee.
7. The payment is defined by: $g \, . \, min\{r + \delta, c\}$ with δ as the tip, r as the base fee, c the fee cap and g as the gas limit.
8. The miner will get as payment: $g \, . \, min\{\delta, c - r\}$ and the revenue from the base fee (g.r) is burned.

Interestingly, EIP-1559 implements backwards compatibility and can process legacy Ethereum transactions and still include them in blocks, but they will not benefit directly from the new pricing system, since converting legacy transactions results in entirely consuming the former gas price by either the base fee or the tip. The new type of transactions are called dynamic fee transactions.

Benefits

Now that we have defined how EIP-1559 works, let us see which are the benefits associated with this new mechanism. First, it mitigates the economic inefficiencies from the social cost of mismatch due to fee volatility. This new mechanism works like a fixed fee in the short run and a cap in the long run. Second, it eliminates first-price-auction inefficiencies, making fee estimation much simpler. This auction is replaced by a fixed price sale. Third, it mitigates the instability issues with fee-only blockchains offering something similar to a permanent block reward. Finally, miners could include very-low-fees or very-high-fees transactions where the fee would go to themselves, but with EIP-1559 the base fee can only be manipulated at a very high cost. Gas prices are measurable.

EIP-1559 was implemented in the 12965000[4] block when it was introduced at the London Fork on August 5, 2021. With one year of information, written in October 2022, this chapter dives into how this improvement worked, and how we can estimate the only part that remains non-deterministic: the priority fee or tip.

PREVIOUS LITERATURE

The goal of this chapter is to train a forecasting model for the tips component of Ethereum fees. There is still a dearth of research on mining techniques and blockchain transaction fees.

Pierro and Rocha (2019) investigated the factors that affect transaction fees and assessed their predictive power using Granger causality. Recurrent neural networks were used by Werner et al. (2020) to forecast the lowest gas price. In order to measure the correlation between gas price and pending time, De Azevedo Sousa et al. (2020) estimated Pearson and Spearman coefficients, reporting non-significant values. Carl and Ewerhart (2020) note that miners' priorities have not been taken into account, and the gas price itself may be a lagged endogenous variable (as longer expected pending time may lead to higher gas prices, which a simple correlation cannot account for). The authors attempt the identification of a statistical model for the economically relevant threshold gas price, which had not been attempted before.

Liu et al. (2022) use a regression discontinuity design to identify the causal impact of EIP-1559 on the dynamics of Ethereum. Their results show that EIP-1559 enhances user experience by minimizing intrablock gas pricing variations and cutting down on user wait times. On the other hand, the impact of EIP-1559 on gas fee levels and the security of the network is negligible.

This chapter expands on the work by Carl and Ewerhart (2020), in different directions. First, we analyze the period after the implementation of EIP-1559. Second, we include additional exogenous variables such as fees on competing blockchains and the fear index, allowing for reach models to be trained.

EXPLORATORY ANALYSIS

For the exploratory analysis, we used Dune Analytics, a well known crypto analytics tool used to create different queries with different complexity, and create a group of datasets analyzed using notebooks in Python. Dune creates these intermediary tables that have all the information we need related with blocks and transactions of the Ethereum blockchain. For the datasets created with Dune, we used a library called DuneAnalytics[5] and then created our own analysis in the notebooks.

Blocks and Transactions

EIP-1559 was implemented in the 12965000 block. To process a whole year of this mechanism working, we use all the blocks from the beginning to the 15282336 block. The dataset therefore includes 2 317 336 blocks with 431 799 391 transactions.

There is an interesting discovery in this group of blocks: we found 54414 empty blocks, in other words, blocks without any transactions. This scenario is not new with EIP-1559 because before its implementation, miners could mine an empty block. When a miner is compiling a new block (that can take one second), their hash power is idle so they set it to mine an empty block and sometimes this empty block is broadcasted to the network because it compiles before the target block.

Before EIP-1559, when a block is completely full, the next block will have a higher base fee. Of course if you have, for example, four full blocks in a row, the base fee can rise very quickly and most probably the mempool will have transactions that have a base fee below the fee needed. Miners will process an empty block in this scenario. This empty block will induce a reduction of the base fee in the next block.

Legacy Transactions versus Dynamic Fee Transactions

As we have explained, EIP-1559 implements backwards compatibility and supports both legacy and dynamic fee transactions. Despites all the benefits of dynamic fee transactions, legacy fee transactions are still observed. The legacy transactions had higher values at the beginning, and in some cases we have blocks with more legacy transactions rather than dynamic fee transactions.

Over time, the count for dynamic fee transactions is increasing. However, some anomalous cases persist, such as block number 15274011[6] processed on August 4, 2022, that presented 1409 legacy transactions versus five dynamic fee transactions.

The mean of the legacy transactions per block is 58.59 while the mean for dynamic fee transactions is 132 per block. The latter also, and the last ones, have a higher third quartile (197 versus 74). It is striking that both types of transactions have a high number of outliers, having maximum values of 1425 and 1427, respectively.

Block Utilization Rate

As we discussed previously, the new block size is 25 million gas and the old block size, which was 12.5 million gas, is the new target block size. We define the utilization rate as the sum of the gas used by each transaction inside a block divided by the gas limit of the block that, as it was already detailed in the new EIP-1559 formula, can vary depending on the network congestion. Figure 11.2 shows the utilization rate at different hours of the day. The data includes a full year and 2.3 million blocks.

It seems that the dispersion of the utilization rate is lower in the first hours of dawn, but is the most congested and with the largest dispersion in the morning until midday. The median for all the hours remains near to 0.48 with the exception of the 17 and 19 hours that are lower.

ETH Burned

As another interesting feature of EIP-1559, all the base fee is now burned and no longer earned by the miners. After a year, we can calculate a mean of 1.10992 ETH burned per block, with a maximum of 220.93 ETH burned in a single block and a third quartile that is 1.45 ETH (Figure 11.3).

An important amount of ETH was burned in the first blocks of the EIP-1559 implementation but, besides some outlier blocks, the farther we move from the EIP-1559 implementation date, we find a decrease in the ETH burned.

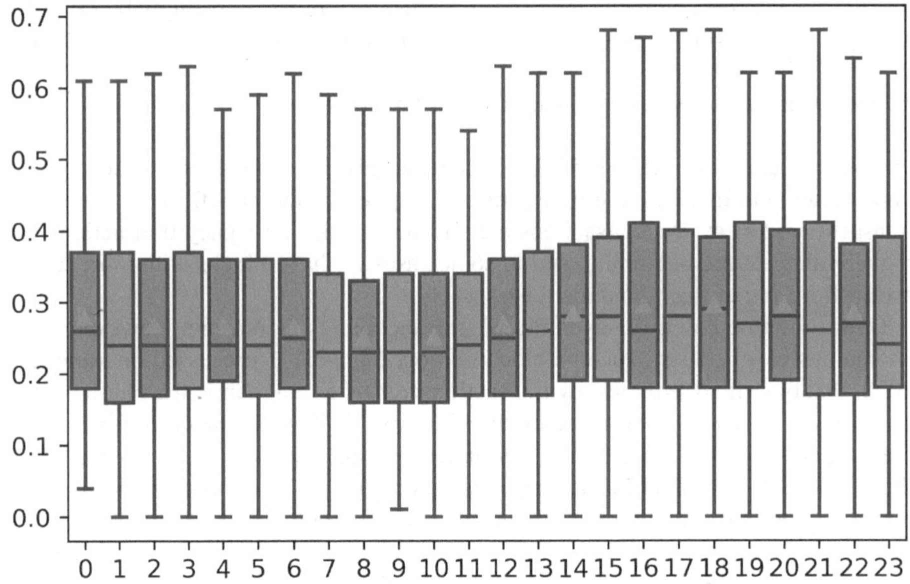

Figure 11.2 Analysis of the block utilization rate over different hours

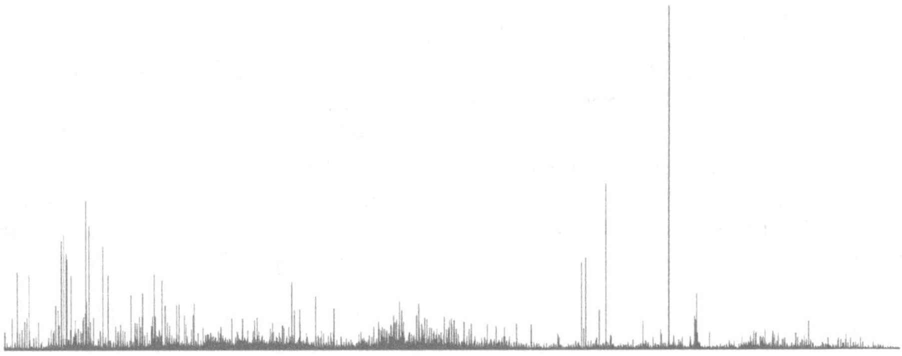

Figure 11.3 Distribution over time of the amount of ETH burned

Base Fee and Tip

Under EIP-1559 the transaction fee is now composed of two parts: the base fee and the tip or priority fee, as explained above. These fees are measured in gwei (also called Shannon), that is, 1*10^9 wei, where wei[7] is the smallest unit of measure in the Ethereum ecosystem, representing 1×10^{-18} ETH. The base fee now follows a deterministic function but the tip is fully dependent on demand conditions.

In Figure 11.4, we can see the evolution over time of the base fee. Other than one great spike, on block 14688911, the base fee evolves in a stable manner. In fact, when the network starts to get congested, you can see how the base fee rises and then decreases, in a process that can last a few blocks. The network was more congested in the first blocks before EIP-1559 implementation, and it is more relaxed in the last couple of months of available data.

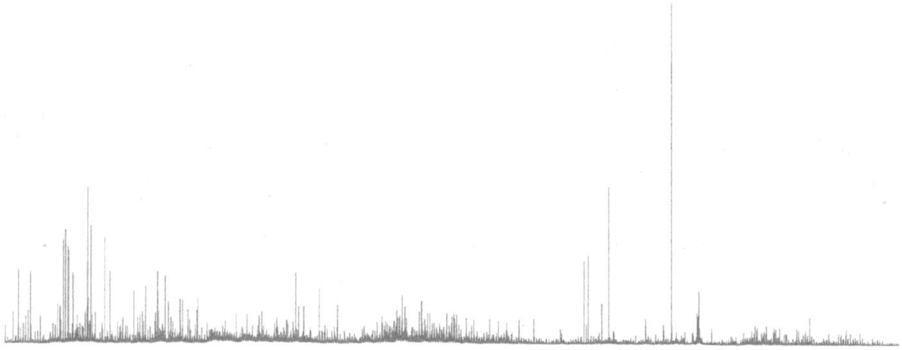

Figure 11.4 *Distribution over time of the base fee*

For tips, Figure 11.5 displays the average of all the tips for each transaction included in a block. The rejected transactions are those with tips below the tip of the least generous tip offered and included.

Figure 11.5 *Distribution over time of the tip*

A user has to "guess" their optimal tip to bid for space in a block. A low tip might cause the transaction to be excluded from the next block. A high tip provides a higher chance of the transaction being included, but the cost may be higher than the private valuation of the transaction for the user. In the following sections, we will attempt to forecast the minimum tip that a user should offer to get our transaction included in the next hour.

DATA

Blocks and Transactions Data

Our first dataset consists of all the blocks and transactions (and their metadata) from August 5, 2021 12:33 PM UTC to August 5, 2022 12:33 PM UTC. These are the blocks numbered 12965000 to 15282336. Approximately every 15 seconds, a new block is created. It would be very optimistic to have our analysis block by block, so we decided to predict the minimum tip so our transaction will be picked and processed with high probability in the next hour. All the data that we gather from blocks and transactions is grouped by hour for this purpose; this leaves us with 8671 hour-rows observations. Table 11.1 shows features for transactions and blocks of Ethereum.

Table 11.1 Features for transactions and blocks of Ethereum

block_time	Date and hour. Example: 2021-08-05 12:00
base_fee	The sum of all the base fees that were paid on a specific date and hour. The base fee of each block is calculated as the sum of base fee per gas of the block x the gas used of each transaction. Its unit of measure is ETH.
gas_used	The sum of all the blocks' gas used limit in a specific hour.
gas_limit	The sum of all the blocks' gas limit in a specific hour.
blocks	Amount of blocks in one hour.
legacy_tx	Amount of legacy transactions in one hour.
tx	Amount of transactions in one hour.
sum_priority_fee_eth	The sum of all the priority fees paid in an hour to miners. Its formula is defined by the sum of all the tips paid in each transaction in an hour x gas used. Its unit of measure is ETH.

Additionally, we include three more columns which contain the *median_tip*, *q1_tip*, and *q3_tip*. If we take a random sample of 1000 blocks in our dataset, we see that 54 percent of them do not order its transaction using a logical or economical criterial where the first transaction in the block will be the one that pays the most (Figure 11.6). That is what we call "unconventional order." In the remaining 46 percent of the blocks, the transactions are included based on tip bids. For our study, this will not be a trivial problem because we have more blocks that are created and organized using order criteria than tip level.

Our target variable is the minimum tip that we have to pay to miners so our transaction will get picked in the next hour blocks with a high probability. This threshold level is defined as the minimum tip paid for each block. The median of this minimum

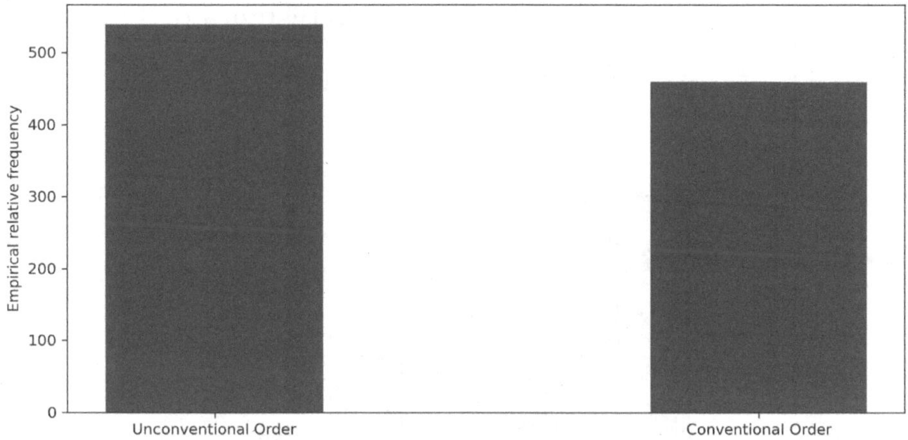

Figure 11.6 Order distribution of 1000 sample blocks

tips guarantees a 90 percent probability of inclusion in the blocks produced during the next hour (Carl and Ewerhart 2020).

However, as we have more blocks that are organized in an unconventional way, we have 2699 out of 8671 rows with zero tip offered. This is a problem because all our predictive models will underestimate our real target, assuming that these zero tips will eventually take a minor share of the minimum tip for included transactions as EIP-1559 adoption continues over time. Therefore we recompute the hourly median of the minimum tip for inclusion by excluding the bids below 1 gwei in the calculation of the median (Figure 11.7). This is the level suggested by Metamask, one of the most popular software wallets with 30 million monthly users across, as a default "guess" for tips when users select slow transactions.

ETH Price Data

ETH is the native token in the Ethereum blockchain. When you make a swap in a decentralized exchange, interact with a contract, or simply send ETH to another wallet, you will have to pay a fee in ETH to use the network. This fee is an incentive for a block validator to process and verify the transaction you are sending.[8] Because of this, ETH price is expected to be correlated with the movements of the priority fee or tip.

The data for ETH price is from Binance, an exchange with 2 billion average volume per day and 1.4 million transactions per second.[9] ETH price is queried for the same timestamp values of the blocks mentioned in the previous section, with a granularity by minute. Binance API has some gaps when we query the values, a problem we address when merging our datasets, taking the last known value. The table includes open, high, low, close, and volume traded (OHLCV) for every hour of the defined timeframe but we only use the close value in our analysis.

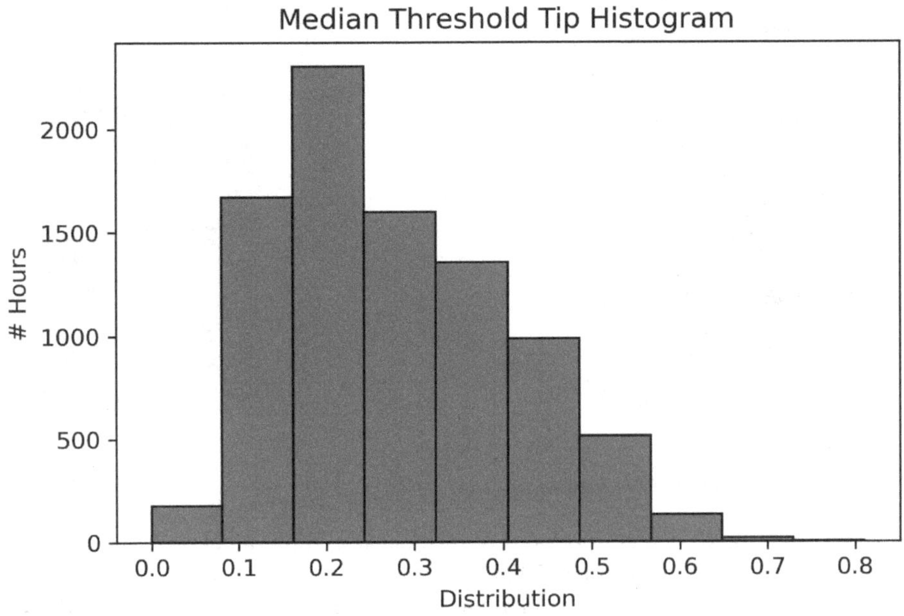

Figure 11.7 *Median threshold tip distribution*

Substitute Chains Data

Ethereum is not the only blockchain that can process transactions using smart contracts with security provided by economic incentives. There are several layer 1 blockchains, but for our study we selected two that are forks (or also called side chains) of Ethereum: Polygon and Binance Smart Chain (BSC). A decrease (increase) in the transaction cost in this alternative blockchain should induce an increase (decrease) in transactions in the Ethereum network. This substitution effect may be hampered by security concerns for highly valuable transactions.

BSC has a first price auction mechanism. We collect data on: *gas_used*, *gas_limit*, *tx*, *blocks*, and the hourly median fee of the blocks in that hour as *hourly_median_fee_tx* from blocks 9769111 to 20203942. Interestingly, during the sampling period, BSC uses a different mechanism called proof-of-stake (POS). In September 2022[10] Ethereum transitioned to POS. This change explains why we have a larger number of blocks in BSC over this period.

Polygon implemented EIP-1559 on January 10, 2022[11] and we have the same information as we got in our Ethereum dataset over the period included in the analysis. For the previous blocks, we only take the same information that we took from BSC, but not the *hourly_median_fee_tx*. For the periods where we do not have tip information, we impute these rows with 0. Also, we have found a gap of four hours where there is no information about Polygon because there was a halt in the network.[12] For this case, we also impute these rows with 0.

NFT Data

Non-fungible tokens (NFTs) are a very popular use case for blockchain. NFT is a standard that is used to uniquely identify codes and metadata that distinguish them from each other. NFTs experienced a boom in 2021.[13]

The main problem with this use case of cryptography is related to the so-called "mint event" that is the launch of a project. Higher fee prices are paid in order to get one of the first pieces of NFT art as users can later sell these items in the secondary market for a higher price. In these minting events, the network may get highly congested and fees can skyrocket. For our study, we decided to include in the dataset the number of sales, the floor price (that is, the lowest price of an NFT collection), and the volume traded daily of the 20 NFT collections with the higher market cap according to the NFT Price Floor site. These collections are: Cryptopunks, Bored Ape Yacht Club, Mutant Ape Yacht Club, Autoglyphs, Chromie Squiggle, Fidenza, Azuki, Moonbirds, Doodles, Ringers, Meebits, Pudgy Penguins, Cool Cats, World of Women, goblintown.wtf, CryptoDickbutts, Mfers, DeadFellaz, Beeple: Everydays—The 2020 Collection, and Clonex.

TVL Data

An interesting metric to measure the success and the progress of a decentralized finance (DeFi) protocol is the total value locked (TVL). Each project will define TVL differently, but we can define it generally as the total value of all assets locked into a protocol, a project, or a specific blockchain. This metric is relevant for our study because a bigger TVL is an indicator of effective usage and adoption; changes in TVL add additional information to forecast changes in fees. Therefore, we included the TVL of the three blockchains that are already in our dataset: Ethereum, Polygon, and BSC. This daily data is gathered using the application programming interface (API) of Defillama, a well-known data site for decentralized protocols.

Fear and Greed Index

When investors switch to risk-off mode the appetite for transactions in DeFi protocols on minting of new NFTs might decline. Consequently, we used the Fear and Greed Index to gauge market sentiment. The Multifactorial Crypto Market Sentiment Analysis Index is calculated on a daily basis by the website Alternative.me[14] by analyzing emotions and sentiments from different sources such as social media, news, surveys, volatility, and volume, and computing all of this into a simple number. Smaller numbers mean that the market is not confident and will be associated with lower prices. High numbers of the index indicate the opposite. This index goes from 0 to 100, where 0 is extreme fear and 100 is extreme greed.

Complete Dataset

We merge all the datasets using the timestamps on all the datasets. We then have a dataset with a row for each hour, with all the information related to block, transactions, fees, ETH price, other networks information, Fear and Greed Index, TVL, and NFT data.

MODELING

After processing the data, we can train several machine learning models to forecast the hourly median of the minimum accepted tip for a transaction to be included in a block. As mentioned, this median guarantees inclusion over the next hour with probability over 90 percent. The benchmark will be an autoregressive integrated moving average (ARIMA) model following the analysis made by Carl and Ewerhart (2020). ARIMA models are a usual benchmark in time series forecasting, given their simplicity and interpretability. Additionally, we train more complex machine learning models such as Lasso, Random Forest, and the XGboost model that try to improve the predictive performance of the baseline.

Feature Engineering

Some further changes are needed before we start training our machine learning models. First, we need to rename the column names and assign the correct data type to the timestamp column. Next, we need to reshape the dataset. When training machine learning models to predict future tips, we have to process historical information and learn from it. In the original shape of the dataset, we have all the information about blocks, transactions, and other data about a specific date and hour in one row. Table 11.2 shows example rows of the dataset.

Table 11.2 Example rows of the dataset

block_time	*base_fee*	*tx*	*legacy_tx*	...	*blocks*
2021-08-05 14:00	82.87	46939	45948	...	277
2021-08-05 15:00	64.96	48827	47237	...	254
2021-08-05 16:00	80.7	48625	47726	...	254
2021-08-05 17:00	845.72	39934	38290	...	293

The objective of this study is to predict the minimum tip (priority fee) so that our transaction would be processed in the next hour with a high probability. Therefore, we create new features with all the information of the blocks, transactions, and other relevant info for the N previous blocks, and we drop all the information of that row related to that block except the minimum priority fee that would be our target feature. The feature names are renamed with "_N", where the N refers to the

Table 11.3 *Example with N = 1 transformation*

block_time	*base_fee_1*	*tx_1*	*legacy_tx_1*	...	*blocks_1*
2021-08-05 14:00	64.96	48827	47237	...	254
2021-08-05 15:00	80.7	48625	47726	...	254
2021-08-05 16:00	845.72	39934	38290	...	293
2021-08-05 17:00	89.87	47702	46577	...	262

information about the N rows before that hour. Table 11.3 gives an example with N = 1 transformation.

Before training any models with the variables in levels, we checked that the series are mean stationary using the Dickey Fuller test. This step is necessary to avoid spurious regressions when working with time series data. In particular, the test results for each series allow us to reject the unit root hypothesis in favor of the hypothesis that each series is stationary at the 5 percent significance level.

Finally, as all the features have different scales and units of measure, we standardize all the features removing the mean and scaling to unit variance. This step is necessary as for some of the statistical learning algorithms to be used, different scales cause predictive underperformance. For the target variable we also apply a derivation of a BoxCox transformation called BoxCox1p in order to stabilize the variance of the target variable.

Data Leakage

We explained above that each row of our dataset contains information of the previous rows. For our models, we create different datasets containing information about the last hour, three past hours, five past hours, ten past hours, and 24 past hours.

The risk is that we could be training our model with data that should not be available in advance when forecasting the minimum tip (look-ahead bias). In time series analysis this information propagates through time correlation of the features. For example, if we take N equal to 3 and we leave the hour 2021-08-07 15:00 in our validation dataset, we cannot have in our training dataset information about the rows that contains hours 2021-08-07 14:00, 2021-08-07 13:00, and 2021-08-05 12:00, because we will be providing our model with information that it should not have at training time.

In order to address this issue, we use the embargo technique, which can be utilized when there is no specific time period that must be prohibited from the neighboring training and test folds to prevent leaking due to the nature of the classification output generating process. It involves deleting a portion of the samples from the train fold that immediately follow the start of the test fold. It should be noted that samples towards the end of the test fold that are close to another training fold do not need to be removed, because they will not help to train the model for the first set of labels. The share of embargoed observations is often small (1 percent or less), and it offers enough data trimming to complete the training phase without noticeable leakage. For the same example, as we retain the hour 2021-08-07 15:00 for validation, we erase for our training model the rows with the hours 2021-08-07 14:00, 2021-08-07 13:00, and 2021-08-05 12:00, and we repeat this process for each row in the validation dataset.

Validation Techniques

For this study, we use K-Fold Cross Validation with three folds for each model that we train. We simulate a division between "known data" and "unknown data" and then we use the first group to train our model with specific hyperparameters, and then test it against the second group, repeating this three times. We have to be very careful in this process for two main reasons.

Our dataset has time series information; in other words, each sample is tagged with a specific date and time. Each row has a specific timestamp and is followed by another row an hour later. This is not a trivial situation for training our models with cross-validation, because the randomization in the standard cross-validation algorithm does not preserve the time ordering,[15] and we end up making predictions of the min tip using information about future blocks that are still not created. Also, time series data is often strongly correlated along the time axis and randomization can create situations where we have in our training set strongly correlated values with our validation set. This means that the two concepts of "known" and "unknown" data become overlapped, making our metrics of performance too optimistic. Because each row has information about previous hours, for each row we cannot have N previous hours in the training dataset.

For the first problem, we used the walk forward method explained by López de Prado (2018). This technique solves the problem by restricting the full sample set differently for each split. First, we split our dataset into *k* equal splits of contiguous hours/rows and we only use *p* contiguous rows to train our model. If we mix both solutions, we can get, for example:

- Train dataset: split 1 to p, validation dataset: split $p+1$.
- Train dataset: split 2 to $p+1$, validation dataset: split $p+2$.

For the second problem, we embargoed the information erasing the N (being N = 1, 3, 5, 10, or 24) previous hours/rows from the training set for each hour/row on the validation set. We create a "gap" between the validation set and training set.

Our target metric for this exercise is the mean absolute error (MAE), as we are forecasting an hourly median. The median is known to be the minimum argument for the MAE function. The MAE measures the average of the absolute errors:

$$MAE = \frac{1}{n}\sum_{j=1}^{n} |e_j|$$

As the size of the MAE might be difficult to interpret, a common transformation is to divide by the average level of the target to obtain the mean absolute percentage error (MAPE), which represents the average of the percentage errors.

ARIMA

In our next step, we train different models using different parameters of the p (number of autoregressive terms), d (number of non-seasonal differences needed for stationarity), and q (number of lagged forecast errors in the prediction equation) parameters of the ARIMA functions. Our best model, the one that got a lower Akaike information criterion (AIC) score, was an ARIMA(4,1,1) with a score of -23578.932.

Finally, we perform cross-validation taking 100 randomly selected dates and hours from our dataset, with the strategies to prevent leakage presented in the previous section, to train the models and then validate the performance predicting the next 24 hours. We are going to train three different models: our most performant ARIMA(4,1,1), a naive model (second model) ARIMA(0,0,0), and a simple model (third model) ARIMA(0,1,0). In coincidence with the AIC results obtained previously, the best model was the ARIMA(4,1,1). The results are shown in Figure 11 8. Finally, we use our best ARIMA model to predict the median and other quartiles of the threshold tip (Figure 11.9).

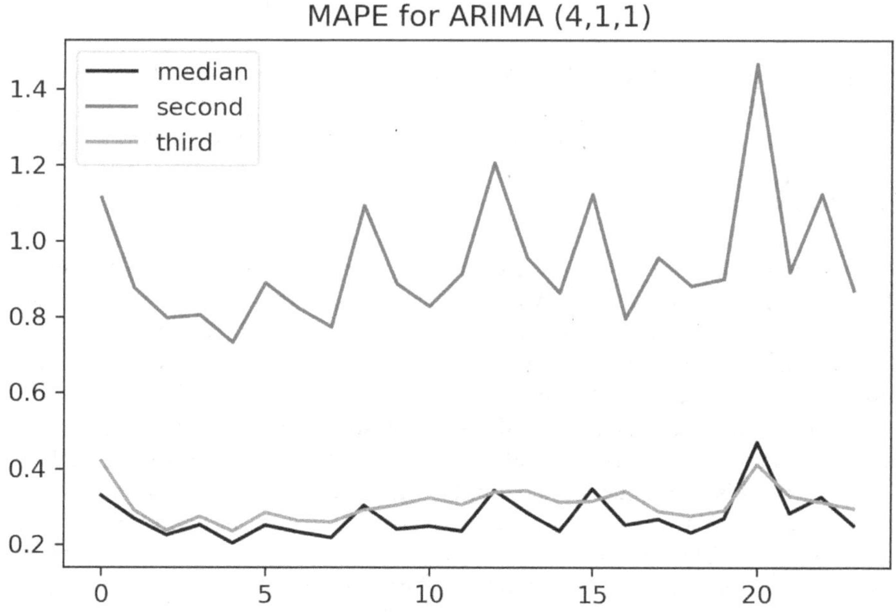

Figure 11.8 Our ARIMA models performance predicting the threshold median tip

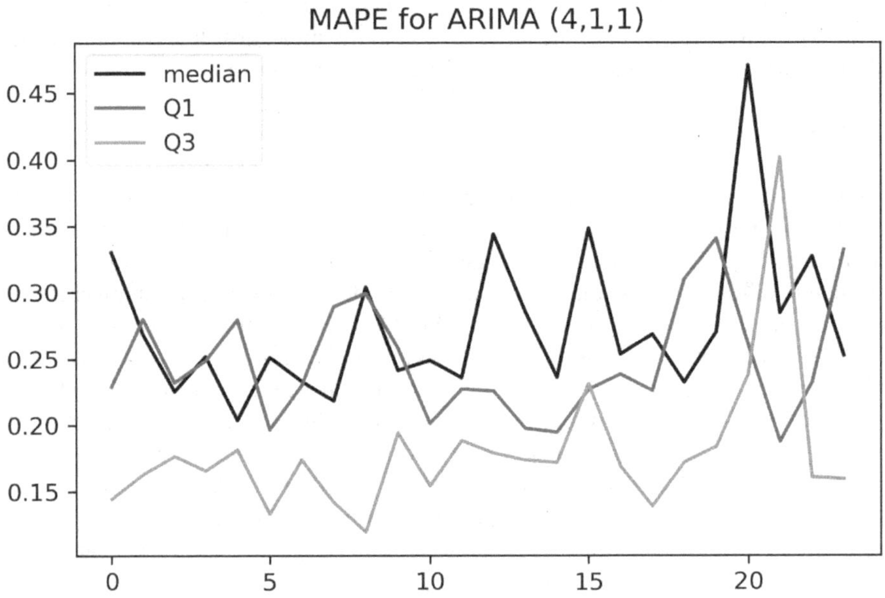

Figure 11.9 *Our ARIMA models performance predicting the threshold median tip*

It is interesting to see that our best ARIMA model can predict with less percentage error the Q1 and Q3 thresholds in comparison to the median threshold. This is a good indicator that more complex algorithms might improve predictive performance.

Lasso Regression

Our second model is a Lasso regression, but this time we use our whole dataset with 91 features. As explained above, we apply embargoes for each of the rows creating five different datasets and using a list of N with N = 1, 3, 5, 10, and 24. Different Ns create different datasets with more or less features. None of these datasets have information about the current date and hour.

It is important to clarify that for the five datasets, standardization is performed, and we use time series walk-forward cross-validation with three folds, as explained above. Using this technique we attempt to see which is the best dataset that minimizes MAE, while we try to get the best hyperparameters of our Lasso regression. In this case, we try different alphas using a list of 0, 0.03, 0.05, 0.1, 0.3, 0.5, 0.5, 0.8, and 1. Finally, we obtain that our best model for the Lasso regression is the dataset with N = 24 and alpha = 0.03. This model gives us an MAE of 0.054 in training. When we compute the different importance that the model gives to the different features, we get the chart in Figure 11.10.

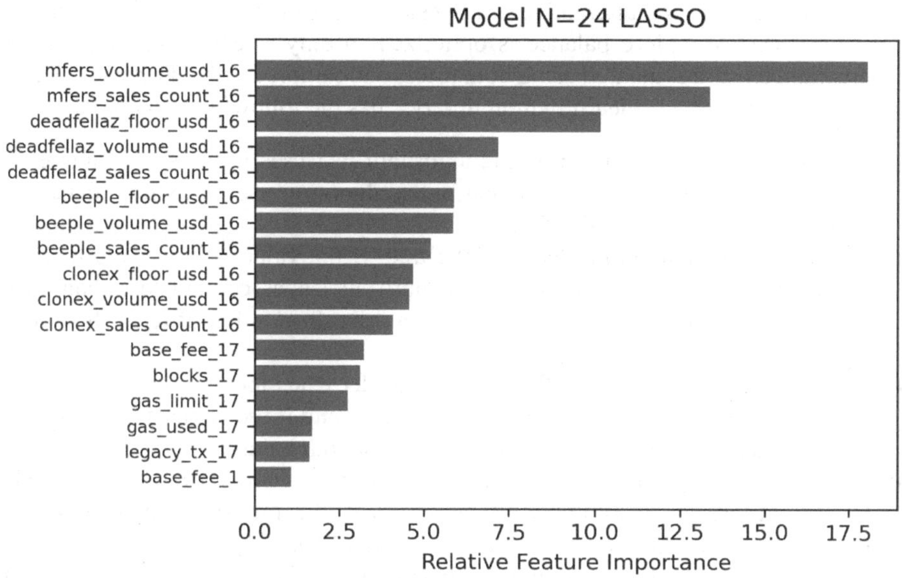

Figure 11.10 *Feature importance for Lasso regression N = 24*

This feature importance is calculated taking into account the different estimated coefficients for each feature of the model. It was expected that NFT data will have an important factor in these predictions. Almost half of these features are related with different and important NFT projects, and they are all related with metrics and information that occurred 16 or 17 hours before the timestamp we are estimating. Taking into account how quickly the gas and tips can increase and decrease over time, this seems a little distant in time, and can be probably an indicator of overfitting in training.

Random Forest

For training our Random Forest model, we again use the K-Fold CV method defined as we did the Lasso regression, but with a few new issues to take into consideration.

Before we start training our Random Forest model, we need to first define how we are going to find the best hyperparameters for our problem. One way to do this is doing a grid search and exhaustively training Random Forests for all the possible combinations of hyperparameters. We have 4320 possible combinations and, taking into account that we are going to select three folds for each model we train, we are going to have 12960 decision trees to train, which is a computational and time-consuming task. The grid search heuristic also carries higher overfitting risks. Another alternative is random search, which basically takes random combinations of hyperparameter values over the defined grid, and repeats the process a certain amount of times. This method can achieve the best hyperparameters combination if we iterate sufficiently. A preferred alternative is Bayesian optimization. Under this heuristic, the exploit versus explore balance is optimized so only selected combinations of hyperparameters are evaluated using both priors and sample results. For example, the Random Forest class in sklearn Python library[16] has the following hyperparameters:

- *bootstrap*: if the value is True, the algorithm just uses a bootstrap sample for building trees. But if the value is False, the algorithm uses the whole dataset to train the trees. We test both values.
- *max_depth*: the maximum depth of the tree. If the value is None, the tree can expand until all the nodes are pure or until all leaves contain less than *min_samples_split* samples. In our case, we test a list from a list of ten values from 10 to 30.
- *max_features*: the number of features to consider when looking for the best split. If the value is "auto" it considers the N features, and if the value is "sqrt" it considers the square root of the N features. We test both values.
- *min_samples_leaf*: the minimum number of samples required to be at a leaf node. Split points are considered only if there is at least this minimum value in each of the new branches. Our testing values are 2, 5, and 10.
- *min_samples_split*: the minimum number of samples required to split an internal node. The possible values are 1, 2, and 4.
- *n_estimators*: the trees trained in a particular forest. We test a list of 100 to 1000, with ten possible values.

After training 150 models using cross-validation over the five different datasets, we obtained that the best model is the one that uses the dataset with N = 5, and the hyperparameters shown in Table 11.4.

Table 11.4 Best hyperparameters for Random Forest N = 5

bootstrap	*max_depth*	*max_features*	*min_samples_leaf*	*min_samples_split*	*n_estimators*
True	27	sqrt	4	10	200

We obtained an MAE of 0.052 in training, lower than our best Lasso regression. To study how this Random Forest model makes its predictions, we need to calculate the normalized total reduction in the gini coefficients granted by each feature over the multiple splits, known as the Gini importance.

This time, we see that the most important features are all related with NFT projects and at this point of the study, this is no surprising news. But it is interesting to see how much importance the model gave to the Beepple NFT project, especially to the sales count that occurred two days after our prediction. Again, this could be a sign of overfitting. Figure 11.11 illustrates the feature importance for Random Forest N = 5.

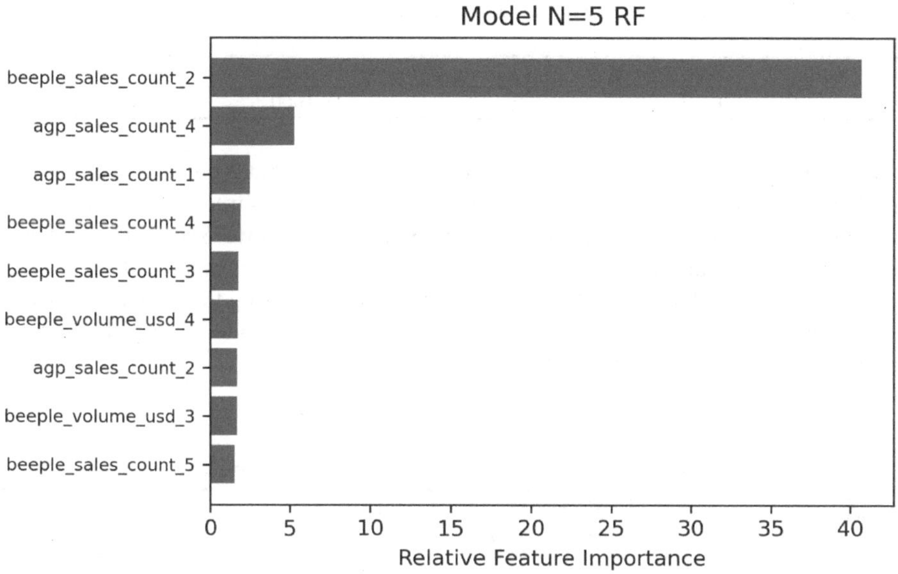

Figure 11.11 *Feature importance for Random Forest N = 5*

XGBoost

Finally, we try boosting a sequential learning algorithm with stellar performance for problems with tabular data. This algorithm tries to learn, predict, and then learn from its mistakes in the next iteration and update the model to focus on the observations where the ensemble of previous models continues to fail. XGBoost in particular uses gradient boosting approaches, trying to find a more direct path to the minimum error, simplifying calculations and improving speed converging more quickly.

Again, we use the five datasets to train different models, to fetch the best hyperparameters using Bayesian optimization over time series walk-forward cross-validation. Some of the hyperparameters include:

- *n_estimators*: number of gradient boosted trees. We test a list of 200 to 2000 with ten possible values.
- *colsample_bytree*: subsample ratio of columns when constructing each tree. In our case there is a list of values with 0.4, 0.5, 0.6, and 0.7.
- *learning_rate*: boosting learning rate, also called "eta." This is a list from 0.1 to 1, with five values.
- *max_depth*: maximum tree depth for base learners. We use a list of ten values from 10 to 20.

After training 150 models, we obtained that the best model is the one that uses the dataset with N = 5 and the hyperparameters as shown in Table 11.5.

Table 11.5 Best hyperparameters for XGBoost N = 5

max_depth	*learning_rate*	*colsample_bytree*	*n_estimators*
15	0.325	0.6	1600

If we compare these values with Random Forest, we see that XGBoost needed more gradient boosted trees to converge to the best MAE, but this tree has less max depth in comparison. We obtained a MAE of 0.063 in training, a lower score in comparison to Random Forest and our Lasso regression. XGBoost also gives a lot of importance to all the metrics related with NFT projects and it is interesting to see that the Beeple project appears again as a very important predictor in our model. Figure 11.12 illustrates feature importance for XGBoost N = 5.

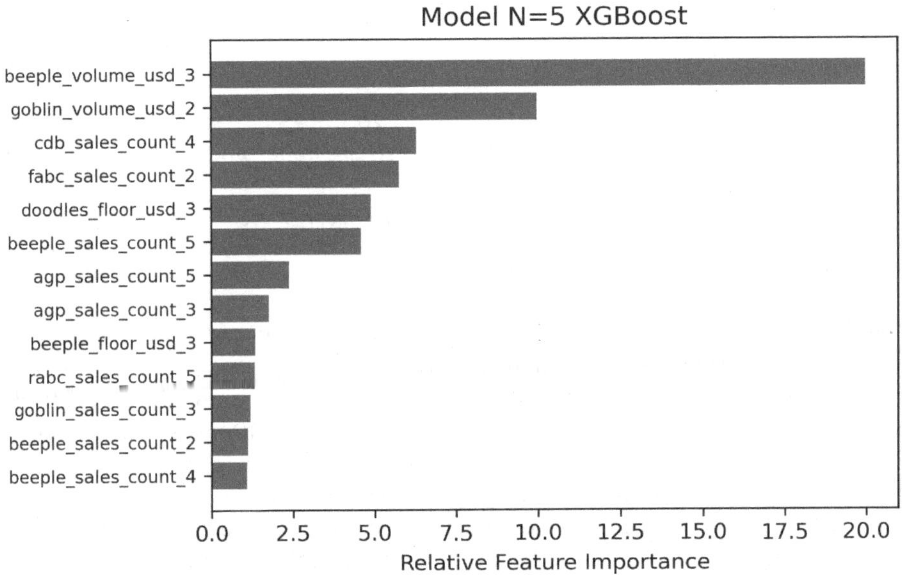

Figure 11.12 Feature importance for XGBoost N = 5

Final Results and Validation Data

For the final exercise, we test all the models with "real data." A new dataset is created specifically for this part of the study to validate how our models would have worked at a particular moment. Our last block in the training dataset was 15282336 and it has the timestamp of Aug-05-2022 12:33:47 PM. For this new dataset, we use information about blocks 10000 after our dataset finished: from block 15292336 (Aug-07-2022 01:50:40 AM) to block 15451335 (Sep-01-2022 06:35:47 AM). As we did for the training dataset, we gather information about TVL from Ethereum,

BSC, and Polygon, NFT data from all the projects, and ETH price for this period of time. For the information related with BSC, we use data from the blocks 9769111 to 20203942, and for Polygon from the blocks 17647148 to 31587150. For this validation dataset, we now have 606 rows/hours. With this new dataset, we predict the threshold minimum tip and we compute the MAE for each model (Table 11.6).

Table 11.6 *MAE for the validation dataset using our models*

Model/Metric	*Lasso*	*Random Forest*	*XGBoost*
N	24	5	5
MAE	0.0377	0.0295	0.0347

XGBoost had a better performance in validation than in training, but Random Forest is still the best-performing model. When we take a closer look at our prediction errors (Figure 11.13), we find an interesting problem. Both Random Forest and XGBoost tend to underestimate the values of the threshold and have lower MAEs. This is not trivial, because if a user takes this forecast as their guess, then the probability of inclusion over the next hour will be smaller than required. On the other hand, Lasso regression has the worst performance, tends to overestimate the target, and only 26

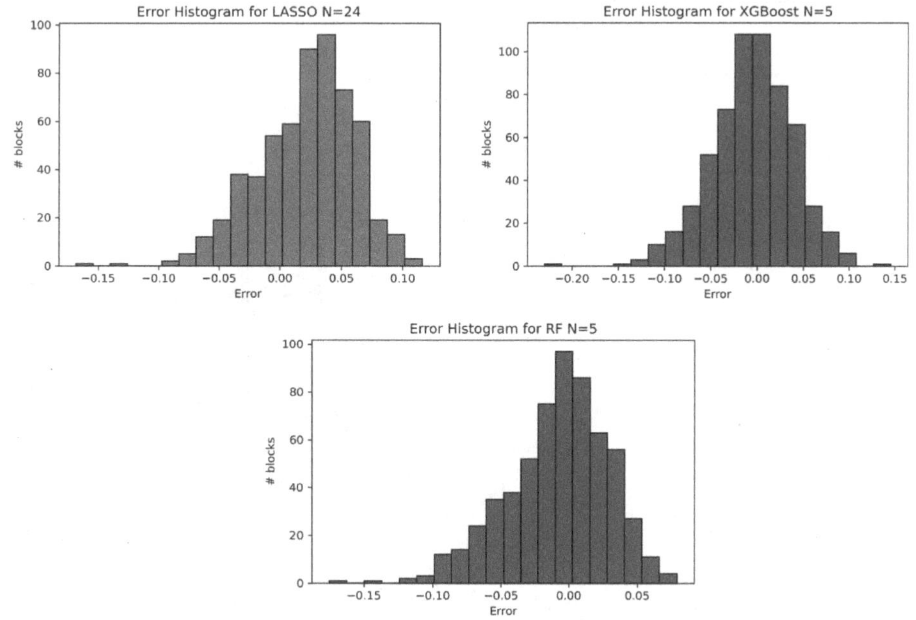

Figure 11.13 *Error histograms for Lasso, Random Forest, and XGBoost in validation*

percent of its predictions have negative errors. We can say that both decision tree models are optimistic models that tend to make predictions lower than the real value, and our Lasso regression is pessimistic because it tends to make higher predictions.

An interesting solution is to average the results from all the models (Figure 11.14). This is known as the ensemble average, defined as the average of the outputs of different models in order to optimize the problem between bias and variance. Although stacking techniques provide an optimal way to combine the models' forecasts, a simple average usually outperforms out of sample in time series analysis (Elliot and Timerman 2016), given varying parameters over time among other causes. From the Random Forest model perspective, we would be paying a little bit more because our error will be average with the two other models, but we will be improving our success transactions. The opposite situation occurs if we make the study from Lasso's perspective. After applying the average to the results of the three models, we obtained that our MAE is now 0.0306. This is a little higher than the Random Forest figure, but now we have 42 percent of our transactions being picked up in the next hour paying a minimum tip.

CONCLUSIONS AND FURTHER RESEARCH

During the course of this project, we have studied how the implementation of the EIP-1559 transformed the Ethereum ecosystem and its impact in the fee mecha-

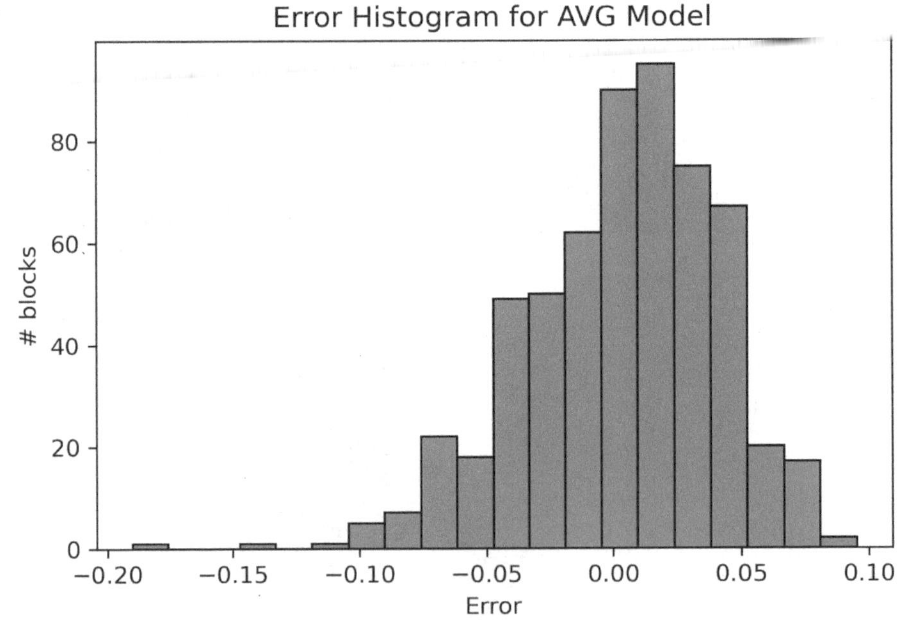

Figure 11.14 Error histogram for the average model

nism. This adjustment was a necessary change that improved highly volatile fees and network congestion. The Ethereum blockchain has benefited from this change, including side effects such as reducing the ETH token emission.

This chapter expands on the work by Carl and Ewerhart (2020), in different directions. First, we analyze the period after the implementation of EIP-1559. Second, we include additional exogenous variables such as fees on competing blockchains and the fear index, allowing for each model to be trained. Third, we performed feature importance exercises, revealing the importance of the NFT ecosystem; transaction fees in other competing networks, such as Binance Smart Chain or Polygon, did not show an important influence on the forecasts. A similar result was obtained for market sentiment and ETH price. The observed MAPE for the selected models is below 5 percent; therefore IEP-1559 seems to have succeeded in simplifying the "guess" process for the right fee (tip) for users to bid in order to get their transaction included in the next block.

The data for this chapter depicts the period before the merge[17] and proof-of-stake changes occurred. An interesting continuation of this analysis will be using data after these changes took place. Also, additional exogenous variables could be included. Harvey et al. (2022) point out that although in normal times there is little correlation between cryptoassets and conventionally risky assets, this correlation increases in the left tail of these traditional risky assets, therefore additional variables such as the VIX index could be included.

NOTES

1. These problems were presented by Vitalik Buterin, one of the co-founders of the Ethereum Foundation, in 2018. Source: https://github.com/zcash/zcash/issues/3473.
2. Buterin made a post explaining the problems on first price auctions that was the precursor of EIP-1559. https://ethresear.ch/t/first-and-second-price-auctions-and-improved-transaction-fee-markets/2410.
3. A miner could also include a transaction that did not pay the full base fee, but it must compensate for the difference from its block reward.
4. Block 12965000. https://etherscan.io/block/12965000.
5. Unofficial Python Library for Dune Analytics. https://github.com/itzmestar/duneanalytics.
6. Block 15274011. https://etherscan.io/block/15274011.
7. Ethereum glossary. https://ethereum.org/en/glossary/#wei.
8. What's unique about ETH? https://ethereum.org/en/eth/.
9. About Binance. https://www.binance.com/en/about.
10. https://ethereum.org/en/developers/docs/consensus-mechanisms/pos/.
11. https://polygon.technology/blog/polygon-is-bringing-eip-1559-upgrades-to-its-network-with-a-testnet-release.
12. This problem was related to the Heimdall implementation in Polygon that forced the core team to implement a hotfix, stopping the network for a few hours. https://forum.polygon.technology/t/pos-chain-downtime-and-heimdall-issue/2324.

13. Year 2021 is also known as the "NFT summer" for crypto. A market report published by Verified Market Research (VMR) valued the global NFT market at $11.3 billion for the year. https://www.verifiedmarketresearch.com/product/non-fungible-tokens-market/.
14. https://alternative.me/crypto/fear-and-greed-index/.
15. There are some caveats when using autoregressive models in particular. A good reference is Hyndman, https://www.sciencedirect.com/science/article/abs/pii/S0167947317302384?via%3Dihub.
16. https://scikit-learn.org/stable/modules/generated/sklearn.ensemble.RandomForestRegressor.html.
17. The Merge is the upgrade from the original proof-of-work mechanism to proof-of-stake of the Ethereum blockchain that occurred on September 15, 2022 and reduced Ethereum's energy consumption by ~99.95%. https://ethereum.org/en/upgrades/merge/.

REFERENCES

Buterin, V. Blockchain resource pricing. 2019. https://ethresear.ch/uploads/default/.

Carl, David, and Christian Ewerhart. Ethereum Gas Price Statistics (December 22, 2020). University of Zurich, Department of Economics, Working Paper No. 373, 2020. Available at SSRN: https://ssrn.com/abstract=3754217.

Carlesten, Kalodner, and Narayanan Weinberg. *On the Instability of Bitcoin Without the Block Reward.* 2020. https://www.cs.princeton.edu/~arvindn/publications/mining_CCS.pdf.

De Azevedo Sousa, J.E., V. Oliveira, J. Valadares, G. Dias Gonçalves, S. Moraes Villela, H.S. Bernardino, and A.B. Vieira. An analysis of the fees and pending time correlation in Ethereum. *International Journal of Network Management.* July 2020, https://opendl.ifip-tc6.org/db/conf/lanoms/lanoms2019/196411_1.pdf.

Elliot, G., and A. Timerman. *Economic Forecasting.* Princeton University Press, 2016.

Harvey, Campbell R., Tarek Abou Zeid, Teun Draaisma, Martin Luk, Henry Neville, Andre Rzym, and Otto van Hemert. *An Investor's Guide to Crypto.* September 1, 2022. SSRN: https://ssrn.com/abstract=4124576 or http://dx.doi.org/10.2139/ssrn.4124576.

Liu, Y., Y. Lu, K. Nayak, F. Zhang, L. Zhang and Y. Zhao. Empirical Analysis of EIP-1559: Transaction Fees, Waiting Time, and Consensus Security. 2022. *arXiv preprint.* arXiv:2201.05574.

López de Prado, Marcos. *Advances in Financial Machine Learning.* Wiley, 2018.

Pierro, G.A., and H. Rocha. The influence factors on ethereum transaction fees. In 2019 IEEE/ACM 2nd International Workshop on Emerging Trends in Software Engineering for Blockchain (WETSEB). IEEE, Montreal, QC, Canada, 24–31. https://doi.org/10.1109/WETSEB.2019.00010.

Roughgarden, T. Transaction Fee Mechanism Design for the Ethereum Blockchain: An Economic Analysis of EIP-1559. 2020. *arXiv preprint.* arXiv:2012.00854.

Werner, S.M., P.J. Pritz, and D. Perez. Step on the Gas? A Better Approach for Recommending the Ethereum Gas Price. In: P. Pardalos, I. Kotsireas, Y. Guo, and W. Knottenbelt (eds) *Mathematical Research for Blockchain Economy.* Springer Proceedings in Business and Economics. Springer, Cham. 2020. https://doi.org/10.1007/978-3-030-53356-4_10.

12. Systematization of knowledge: the advent of a new incentive, maximal extractable value

Burak Öz and Felix Hoops

INTRODUCTION

Information has always had value in finance. Knowing about an upcoming product launch might allow someone to buy into a company early. A politician, knowing about an upcoming regulatory change or an adjustment to financial policy before it is publicly announced, could benefit from buying or selling a corresponding company's stock. A brokerage employee might be aware of a trade in advance and use that to improve their own trading strategy. In all of these scenarios, an actor has information about an impending value shift in the market. And, critically, that information is not publicly available and thus constitutes insider information. Acting on such information, be it directly or indirectly, is insider trading. After much debate in the early 20th century, also on the fundamental question of whether insider trading is to be viewed negatively at all, the practice is now widely outlawed in traditional markets and regarded as a form of market manipulation.

Among the initially described forms of insider trading, some are based on circumstantial, that is, external information, while others are based on market information. Those latter forms are of interest in the context of decentralized finance, as blockchains change the workings of the market, not the externalities. Frontrunning and backrunning are two simple instances of insider trading based on pure market information. The former means executing a trade before a targeted market order, and the latter afterwards. In both cases, the aim is to profit from the resulting shift in value of the underlying asset. To maximize profit, that market order ideally moves a large quantity of value. Consider knowing about an upcoming large-scale purchase of a stock: knowing that it will drive up market value, one can buy the same stock before that purchase executes, netting an instant unrealized return on that position. This scenario is considered frontrunning. Selling any held position in the stock directly after the targeted market order executes, to realize as much of the value shift as possible, is considered backrunning.

Financial author Michael Lewis (2014) helped to publicize the problem through his book *Flash Boys: A Wall Street Revolt* about high-frequency trading. The title comes from the term "flash order"[1] describing the practice of showing a market order to a closed circle of actors shortly before listing it publicly. While this is legal in the

United States, critics such as Lewis view this as a form of frontrunning and, thus, market manipulation.

In contrast to traditional finance, public blockchains and their pending transactions are freely accessible by anyone. Thus, market information has been democratized, requiring a fresh look at insider trading strategies from traditional finance. After all, can it be considered malicious insider trading, if there are no insiders? This re-evaluation began back in 2019 when researchers published their findings on automated and problematic trading strategies on Ethereum (Daian et al. 2019). They paid tribute to Lewis's book by titling their paper "Flash Boys 2.0," suggesting that, like traditional finance, decentralized finance might not be as free and democratized as it is made out to be. Among other things, they discovered that Ethereum miners had an even more important role in the system than initially intended. As block proposers, miners are in the unique position to have the final say about what transactions are executed as part of the block and in what order. Consequently, they have all the power to legally frontrun, backrun, or even replace any transaction. For a simple value transfer, such as a payment for a good or a service, that does not constitute a problem. However, with the adoption of smart contract-enabled blockchains, led by Ethereum, and the subsequent rise of decentralized exchanges (DEXs), the block proposer's power position became problematic. They were now in an unfair position to extract value from the blockchain in a way that was never intended. This value is bundled under the term "miner extractable value" (MEV). Arguably, MEV is the most important contribution of the "Flash Boys 2.0" paper. It introduces an incentive shift at the consensus level, which has wide-reaching consequences for the whole blockchain ecosystem.

Trivial MEV strategies include replacing transactions that leverage an arbitrage opportunity with a functionally identical transaction that secures the value of that opportunity for the block proposer. That scenario is possible because these strategies, such as arbitrage trading, have no dependency on who they are executed by. Anyone seeing such a transaction is able to replicate it for themselves. This move would effectively steal this value from the original transaction creator.

To better understand this concept, let us consider a more sophisticated attack. Traders in decentralized finance usually express their price tolerance on a market order via a slippage tolerance, which is set as a percentage of the expected price. If the market order cannot be executed within the designated slippage, it is dropped. Thus, setting slippage too low can lead to missing out on trades that would have still been lucrative, but just outside the slippage tolerance. On the other hand, setting it too high opens up lucrative frontrunning and backrunning opportunities. Someone could frontrun the transaction in a carefully calculated way that ensures pushing the price of the asset in question to the maximum within the slippage tolerance, and then immediately backrun it to secure a profit seemingly out of thin air. This is called a sandwich attack, because it sandwiches the targeted transaction between the attacker's transactions. And critically, it is labeled as an attack because it actively harms the creator of that targeted transaction. As we discuss in more detail in the section on MEV forms, MEV is not necessarily always extracted at the expense of another market actor.

At the time of publishing "Flashboys 2.0," all the described phenomena or strategies were largely theoretical, with little realization in practice. But it would not take long for their theories to be proven right: during what is now known as "DeFi summer 2020," bots working with strategies described in the paper, starting with simple arbitrage trades, were first confirmed in the real world. Confirmed as at least partially realistic in its raised concerns, "Flashboys 2.0" has since served as a starting point for many researchers to try and understand these phenomena better. One of the first findings was that miners seemingly avoided manipulating block contents for their own gain. That is most likely due to them realizing that it is vital that users know, or at least trust, that the miner will not use their transaction data against them. If, on any blockchain, users do not feel comfortable to send their transactions to a miner, that chain is doomed to be abandoned.

However, that did not deter others from analyzing the pending transactions in the Ethereum transaction pool, using bots to find unrealized value that they can claim for themselves. Why do long-winded, strategy-based analysis of the Ethereum block data if you can just wait for someone to find unrealized value and copy their transaction? Ultimately, that led to constant bidding wars, where large numbers of bots tried to get their transaction committed to the chain by offering higher transaction fees to the miners. These fees could get as high as comprising 90 percent of the value realized within a given transaction. In the end, miners still profited off these value opportunities without directly manipulating transaction order or inclusion.

Later on, it was discovered that blockchains not using proof-of-work (PoW), and consequently not having miners, also exhibited similar value opportunities. That led to the renaming of MEV: from miner extractable value to maximal extractable value. At the same time, the term's definition shifted. While there is no one true definition that we could cite here, the Ethereum community's understanding considers all value that can be realized during block creation by manipulating transaction order or inclusion apart from intended rewards, being the block reward and gas fees.

Understanding MEV is not only relevant to realizing value for oneself, but also most importantly to understand and mitigate its effects on a blockchain ecosystem. It is realistic to assume that at one point in the not too distant future, MEV will significantly outpace block rewards, making it the most important incentive for block proposers. This development would shift a proposer's primary priority, from providing a stable service to the network, to optimizing for their own gain, potentially at the cost of others. Their behavior might go as far as reorganizing blocks as part of a history rewrite.

We have come to understand that how competition for MEV opportunities is organized is essential. It could lead to centralization and the death of entire blockchains. For example, joining mining or validator pools might become even more advantageous, as these pools have more resources that they can use more effectively to improve their MEV extraction. As such, figuring out how to organize competition for MEV fairly, and effectively democratize MEV in the process, is a big priority of MEV-focused research groups and organizations, such as Flashbots.

MEV remains a continued topic of debate in the whole decentralized finance community and beyond, as it poses a centralization risk that every smart contract-enabled blockchain is susceptible to. In the following, we explore different forms of MEV in greater detail and shine some light on the future of MEV-aware blockchain development. To this end, we first look at different forms of MEV. Once we have defined what MEV is, we expand on its emergence in Ethereum, and how it was dealt with over time. Then, we take a step back from Ethereum and discuss the existence of MEV in Bitcoin, before coming to a close with some concluding remarks and a look to the near future of MEV.

MEV FORMS

MEV emerges as a result of a state transition on a blockchain. Although not every state transition exposes MEV, such as a simple Ether transfer between two addresses, transactions that interact with smart contracts, especially decentralized finance (DeFi) contracts, create leverageable opportunities. These opportunities are usually discovered and captured by users, called searchers, who have scripts monitoring the Ethereum memory pool (mempool).[2] The most common MEV forms captured by searchers are arbitrages, liquidations, and sandwiches. More secretive forms of MEV that yield more significant profits compared to the common forms also exist. Such MEV opportunities are known as MEV long tail.

Arbitrages

The most common form of MEV is arbitrage, where one tries to exploit the listing price difference of an asset on different exchanges by the simultaneous purchase and sale of the asset. An arbitrage is a win–win situation for both the arbitrageur and the utilized exchanges, as the arbitrageur balances the prices across them while capturing profits. If arbitrage MEV is not captured, price discrepancies will occur among exchanges, and the DeFi market space will be disrupted. Hence, arbitrage MEV is contributing to the existence of DeFi. Moreover, as arbitrages do not pose any damage to another actor on the network, they are classified as good/benign MEV.

Compared to executing an arbitrage trade on a traditional marketplace, doing arbitrage on Ethereum is significantly less risky due to the sequential and atomic execution properties of the Ethereum Virtual Machine (EVM). In a traditional marketplace, when someone tries to leverage an arbitrage opportunity, the market price may move against them during the execution of the trade, thus, making them earn less money than planned or, sometimes, lose money. In Ethereum, transactions are executed sequentially, based on their order in a block. Thus, the market cannot move against an arbitrageur while their arbitrage transaction is being executed.

Moreover, in Ethereum, a transaction either gets fully executed or not at all. Let us imagine a transaction that calls a smart contract, which then triggers a sequence of calls to other contracts. During this sequence of interactions, if one of the interacted contracts throws an error, maybe because a condition check failed, the whole execution will be reverted. For the execution to be successful, every interaction triggered by the initial call must be accomplished without errors.

The sequential and atomic execution properties of Ethereum transactions open the door for many profitable DeFi strategies, including atomic arbitrages. An atomic arbitrage executes every hop of the arbitrage in a single transaction, and it is only realized under user-favored conditions and reverted otherwise. In layman's terms, the arbitrageur can say that they only want to execute this transaction if their end balance is greater than their starting balance. In this way, they can guarantee that the arbitrage will only be performed if they make a profit.

Figure 12.1 shows the details of an atomic arbitrage transaction. The arbitrageur first swaps 139.09 ETH for 5.76 wrapped Bitcoin (WBTC) on Sushiswap. Then, he swaps 5.76 WBTC for 2 269 314 USDT stablecoins on 0x Protocol. Finally, he swaps the USDT for 1352.12 ETH on Uniswap V2. The net profit of the arbitrageur from this triangular arbitrage is US$2 124 457:

α: Starting Balance = 139.09 ETH
β: Ending Balance = 1,352.12 ETH
γ: Transaction Fee = 0.044 ETH

$$(\beta - \alpha - \gamma) \cdot 1{,}752 \ (\textit{ETH/USD price when the transaction took place}) = \$\ 2{,}124{,}457$$

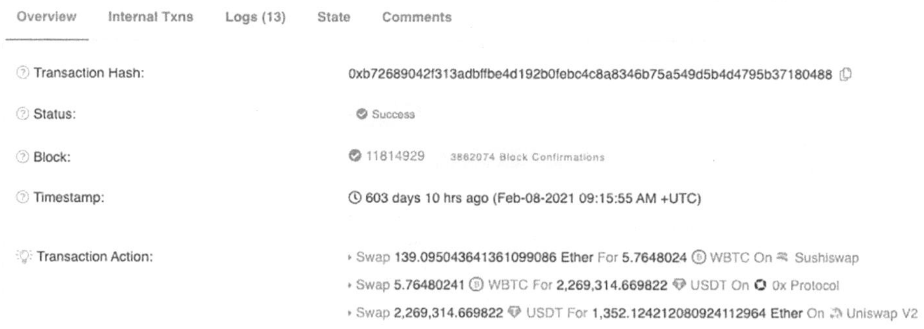

Source: Screenshot from Etherscan.io.

Figure 12.1 *Details of an atomic arbitrage transaction*

Every arbitrage opportunity has an optimal input amount, and investing less than the optimal amount means leaving profits on the table. On the other hand, investing excessively will cause giving up on the profits. While the latter presents a problem that traders can solve by themselves, to solve the former, they need loans.

Flash loans, one of the most convenient forms of loans on DeFi, refers to a DeFi exclusive instrument in which the lending protocol lends money to a borrower without asking for any collateral, but under a single condition: the loan is paid back in the same transaction that it was borrowed. Lending protocols usually have a specific loan fee percentage (for example, Aave, 0.09 percent) that is applied to the borrowed amount to make this deal profitable for themselves. The fee must also be paid when the loan is paid back.

A smart contract of the lending protocol runs condition checks to ensure that the issued flash loan plus the fee is paid back. If any of the conditions fail, an error occurs in the contract, which causes the borrower's transaction to revert (remember that Ethereum transactions are atomic). Thus, the exchange goes back to the pre-transaction state where the lending protocol has not yet issued the loan. However, when the borrower pays back their loan, they can profit from an arbitrage opportunity to its full extent, as they can borrow the necessary amount of Ether. Currently, lending protocols issue flash loans worth millions of dollars.

In Figure 12.2, an atomic arbitrage that uses a flash loan to exploit an opportunity between Uniswap V2 and Sushiswap is shown. The arbitrageur initially takes a 681.63 ETH flash loan from the dYdX protocol. Then, he swaps the ETH for 1 148 464 USDT on Uniswap V2. Finally, he exchanges the USDT for 693.18 ETH on SushiSwap. After paying back his loan to dYdX, the arbitrageur is left with 11.55 ETH.

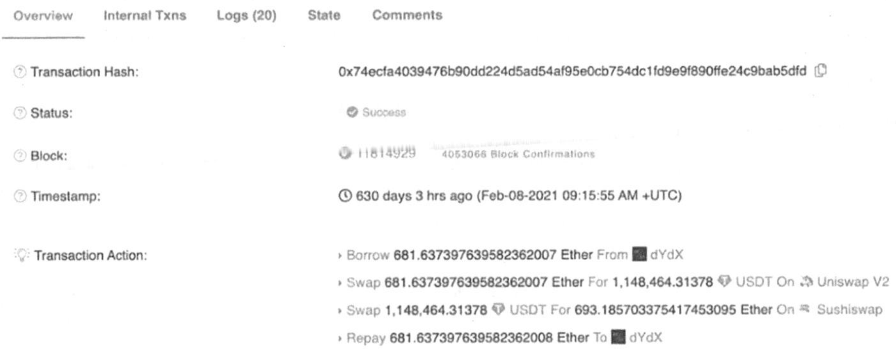

Source: Screenshot from Etherscan.io.

Figure 12.2 Details of an atomic arbitrage transaction that uses a flash loan

According to MEV-Explore,[3] a public dashboard that displays metrics about MEV extracted on Ethereum, more than 3 million arbitrage transactions have been issued through different DeFi protocols on Ethereum since January 2020. These transactions have extracted around US$650 million MEV in total. Although already a significant amount, it covers only some of the arbitrage MEV space. Currently, MEV-Explore only covers atomic arbitrages and not any CEX–DEX hybrid arbitrages, as CEX transactions are held off-chain and thus not publicly available.

Liquidations

Like in traditional finance, loans also exist in DeFi. A user can take out a loan from a lending protocol by depositing an asset as collateral. However, in DeFi, lending protocols usually require the collateral to have a value higher than the borrowed amount, known as overcollateralization. This requirement is necessary for DeFi, as the borrower would otherwise have no incentive to pay back his loan.

As the prices fluctuate, the value of collateral often drops below a certain threshold determined by the protocol. When that happens, protocols often look out for users to liquidate the loan position in return for the collateralized asset plus a liquidation fee. Since liquidations enable lending protocols to keep their solvency, they are critical for DeFi, like arbitrages.

Qin et al. (2022) analyze the liquidations on four popular lending protocols (Aave, Compound, dYdX, and MakerDAO) until April 2021. They detected a total profit of US$63.59 million through 28 138 liquidations. Qin et al. identify 2011 unique addresses capturing liquidation MEV, with each address making US$31 620 profit on average. To capture the profits, liquidators take flash loans and track oracle price updates to foresee a liquidation position opening.

Sandwiches

Ethereum nodes store validated but unconfirmed transactions into a public memory pool until they are included in a block. As transactions are transparent, anyone running a node can simulate them and observe their state changes. By simulating a transaction that executes a swap on a DEX such as Uniswap or SushiSwap, one can understand its price impact and profit from it. It is similar to insider trading, where one knows non-public information beforehand and takes action according to it. However, in this case, everyone has access to the same information. For example, suppose one knows that a particular swap transaction will increase the price of the XYZ token on a DEX. In that case, one can profit from it by buying XYZ tokens right before the swap gets executed (frontrunning) and then selling them immediately afterward (backrunning). This move is called sandwiching, as the initial swap transaction is sandwiched between two other transactions (that is, the buy and sell orders).

At first glance, sandwich MEV seems harmful, as the frontrunning buy order of the MEV searcher causes the sandwiched trade to take place with the worst price possible for the victim (depending on the set price slippage or maximum willingness to pay). However, from an economic perspective, sandwiches can also be considered beneficial, as they increase the system efficiency by forcing the sandwiched users to pay their maximum willingness for that trade. If the MEV searchers do not execute sandwiches, there will be a consumer surplus, and the system will not be in equilibrium.

MEV Long Tail

Although arbitrages, liquidations, and sandwiches are the most common forms of MEV, the real profit lies in the long tail, as there is less competition than in standard forms. Compared to detecting an arbitrage, looking out for an undiscovered MEV form is much more time-consuming and complex. Some strategies that long-tail MEV searchers adopt include exploring newly launched protocols, and developing complex call sequences that interact with multiple protocols.

MEV TIMELINE

The Emergence of MEV in Ethereum, 2019–2020

Official Ethereum developer documents define MEV as the maximum value that can be extracted from block production by including, reordering, and censoring transactions in a block.[4] Although PoW-Ethereum miners always had these capabilities, MEV extraction only became prominent once DeFi protocols became popular in 2020. Until then, Ethereum blocks were mostly filled with simple money transfer transactions that did not expose any extractable value. With the growing DeFi ecosystem such as DEXs, lending protocols, and automated market makers (AMMs), more ways for users to interact on Ethereum emerged.

"Flashboys 2.0" and the dark forest

In the seminal paper "Flashboys 2.0," Daian et al. (2019) analyze the security threats exposed on Ethereum by DEX design flaws. Namely, they study the emerging bot community to capitalize on the arbitrage opportunities. They identify destructive actions such as frontrunning, initially explored by Eskandari et al. (2019), demonstrated by these bots to exploit the market. Furthermore, Daian et al. show that, for the miners, there is an extra value on top of the existing block reward and transaction fees that can be earned from the protocol by manipulating transactions in a block. They coined the term "miner extractable value" (MEV) to represent this value.

When Daian et al. identified MEV, the threats it posed for Ethereum were mostly theoretical, since not much activity occurred on the application layer. In the summer of 2020, MEV became a reality when DEXs gained traction. During this period, arbitrage bots became highly active as many opportunities were exposed.

While arbitrage bots competed with each other to be the first to execute an arbitrage, as uncovered by Robinson and Konstantopoulos (2020) and Escaping the Dark Forest (Samczsun 2020), there was yet another type of bot monitoring the mempool and frontrunning any profitable transaction. A profitable transaction is any transaction that makes the ending balance of the issuer higher than the starting balance. These profit-seeking bots are called generalized frontrunners. Until private mempool solutions such as Flashbots RPC were implemented, the bots were a real threat to any profit-leveraging transaction in the Ethereum public mempool. Since getting detected by a generalized frontrunner meant getting frontrun, thus losing profits, the Ethereum public mempool was compared to the dark forest from the famous science fiction author Liu Cixin's (2015) book *The Dark Forest*, in which getting detected in the forest meant instant death by the predators (Robinson and Konstantopoulos 2020).

Priority gas auctions

In PoW-Ethereum, a rational, utility-maximizing miner is expected to build their block based on the fee per gas transactions in the mempool offer.[5] Knowing this incentive, when MEV bots race against each other to be the first to capture a specific opportunity, they use the gas fee as a bidding mechanism to prioritize their transactions. As the mempool is public, each bot can monitor the bids (transactions) submitted by others, and repetitively try to outbid everyone until the block is mined. These bidding interactions for block space are known as "priority gas auctions" (PGAs) (Daian et al. 2019).

PGAs have negative externalities for everyone except the winner, and in some cases, even for the winner. As PGAs resolve while the bidding is ongoing, losing parties usually do not get a window to submit a 0 gas fee transaction that would cancel their competitive transaction. Hence, they pay fees for profitless transactions, as the winner already captures MEV.[6] Sometimes, the gas fees are driven up so much that the revenue of the winner is eaten by the transaction cost, leading to negative-sum outcomes (Daian et al. 2019). Furthermore, as PGAs congest the network traffic with spam transactions that fill up the block space, they lead to a bad user experience, such as longer waiting times and volatile gas prices for Ethereum users.

The impact on the consensus stability

MEV is an incentive that can, in value, exceed the block reward and transaction fees for the miners or, more generally, block proposers. However, block proposers are mainly hesitant to capture MEV directly due to reputation concerns. Nevertheless, they can issue any MEV-capturing transaction and censor the original one. For example, a miner can duplicate the transaction that wins a PGA while still claiming all the fees.

According to Daian et al. (2019), sufficient incentives can motivate the miners to attempt forking attacks, impacting the consensus stability of Ethereum. One example of such an attack is undercutting attacks, which occur when a miner ignores the latest block and forks the longest chain, capturing some of the MEV available while leaving a significant amount to incentivize the next miner to build on top of their block instead of the existing head of the chain which left less MEV to be captured.

Another MEV-incentivized attack on consensus stability is time bandit attacks. These attacks exploit MEV available on past blocks (not only the latest block, like undercutting attacks do) by reorganizing the chain history. To execute such an attack, a miner needs to hold 51 percent of the hashing rate of the network, which can be remarkably expensive depending on the duration of the attack. For example, rewriting the last ten blocks would be cheaper than rewriting the last 1000 blocks. Miners can subsidize these attacks by retroactively organizing the transactions in the past blocks to realize as much of MEV as possible.

Enter Flashbots, 2020–September 2022

In the summer of 2020, the MEV crisis reached its peak since the launch of Ethereum. Increasing numbers of MEV bots, frequently occurring priority gas auctions, complex smart contract interactions, and generalized frontrunning activities, were all indicators that the MEV game was drifting Ethereum towards a dystopia where network congestion, limited block space, and unstable consensus were the reality. Flashbots emerged from the darkness during those days to "frontrun the MEV crisis."[7] It is a research group consisting of blockchain researchers, white hat hackers, and developers to produce solutions to create a transparent, democratized, and fairly distributed MEV ecosystem. Although their work is mainly focused on Ethereum, as it is the most prominent stateful, smart contract blockchain, the solutions they develop can also be applied to other stateful chains.

MEV market design and the Flashbots Auction

While MEV represents an existential threat for blockchains, how this value is extracted determines its broader impact on the network. If block proposers decide to extract all the value and vertically integrate with trading firms, it leads to private transaction flows and centralization, undermining the core properties of a blockchain such as Ethereum: decentralization, permissionlessness, and transparency. As in PGAs, if MEV extraction takes place publicly in a repetitive bidding format, it leads to network congestion and an inefficient block space allocation. Thus, there must be a market design that enables democratic access to MEV by all types of participants, not only the powerful ones, while not imposing any drawbacks to the user experience of the rest of the network.

Perhaps the first market design to come to mind consists of ordering transactions based on their arrival time, known as "first come, first served" (FCFS). Although FCFS will mitigate the adverse effects of PGAs, such as volatile gas prices or network congestion through transaction spamming, it is not a silver bullet. FCFS can introduce similar detrimental impacts to blockchains as high-frequency trading (HFT) does on traditional finance marketplaces; namely, latency wars. To have the most negligible latency, MEV searchers will be incentivized to invest in robust server racks, much like PoW miners investing in mining hardware. Moreover, searchers will be interested in co-locating with the most powerful block proposer and submitting their transactions directly to them. Thus, FCFS can easily lead to the compromise of decentralization.

Another way to realize MEV extraction can be by ordering transactions based on their hash values. While this can mitigate volatile prices, as paying higher gas fees will not impact a transaction's priority, it will also incentivize MEV searchers to spam the network until they land a transaction with the desired hash value. As block space will be filled up with spam transactions, the user experience will suffer from long waiting times.

While PGAs signify one way to implement block space auctions for MEV extraction where searchers bid for order priority, better designs are also possible. Flashbots developed one such design for Ethereum called the Flashbots Auction, a sealed-bid auction mechanism for block space realized through a private memory pool. The Flashbots Auction shifts the block space auction from on-chain, like PGAs do, to off-chain to avoid affecting everyday users with volatile gas prices and block space allocation by spam transactions. It enables MEV searchers to submit nondisclosed valuations for their preferred transaction order while preserving the privacy of the transactions against frontrunning attacks.

The Flashbots Auction introduces an option for MEV searchers to express their strategies in a more fine-grained manner compared to regular transactions, called bundles. A bundle is a set of transactions executed in the order in which they are placed in the bundle. Transactions in a bundle can be a mix of new searcher transactions and existing transactions from the public transaction pool. Bundles are useful for MEV searchers, as they can ensure their MEV extracting transactions are executed before or after their target transaction(s). For example, suppose a searcher aims to sandwich a swap transaction. In that case, they can include their frontrunning transaction (A), the swap transaction (B), and their backrunning transaction (C) in a bundle, and guarantee that the transactions will be executed in the order *A->B->C*, given that the searcher wins the auction.

A bundle submitted to the Flashbots Auction only gets revealed to the public once its bid wins the auction and lands in a block. Bundles submitted by losing bidders are never revealed with this mechanism, as they are not included in block building. As a result, no payment is required for them, unlike PGAs. Moreover, as bids are submitted to a private pool, congestion on the public network caused by MEV bots is partially overcome.

In the initial design of the Flashbots Auction, which was used in PoW-Ethereum, Flashbots operates a relay that controls the private transaction pool to which MEV searchers submit their bundles. Although each miner could have run its endpoint to receive bundles, this may have led to denial-of-service (DoS) attacks executed directly on the miner side. The Flashbots relay mitigates these problems by handling DoS attempts and checking the submitted bundles' validity as a first line of defense against spam. It also prevents private relay centralization, as searchers can be incentivized to work with miners with more hashing power.

To receive bundles from the Flashbots relay, PoW-Ethereum miners run a modified version of the Go Ethereum (Geth) client called mev-geth. The modified client enables miners to effectively calculate a value for each submitted bundle and compute the most profitable block through the block space auction. Miners running mev-geth earn extra profits from the block space auction through direct payments by the searchers on top of the block reward and transaction fees. Figure 12.3 gives an overview of the Flashbots Auction architecture.

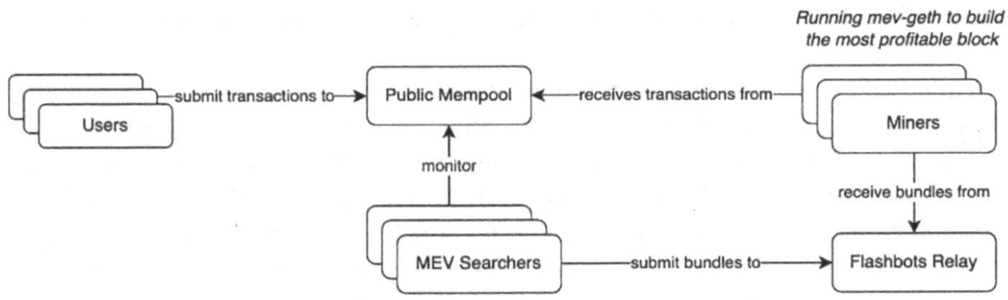

Figure 12.3 An overview of the Flashbots Auction architecture

The Flashbots Auction design inherently introduces trust assumptions to both the Flashbots relay and the miners, as they have access to the bundles' content and can potentially censor them. In a worst-case scenario, Flashbots can duplicate profitable bundles submitted to the relay and forward only their bundles to the miners while censoring the original searcher bundles. If miners act maliciously, they can also steal the MEV that Flashbots attempted to steal from the searchers.

However, defecting from honest strategies is not beneficial in the long run for any parties, perhaps even more for the miners than Flashbots. In the case of Flashbots, one can argue that the game is played on their premises, under surveillance. Thus they are already defecting from honest/decentralized strategies. However, more aggressive strategies such as censoring or MEV stealing can lead to users losing trust in Flashbots products. For the miners, acting maliciously would cause them to lose access to the Flashbots relay, thus abandoning MEV profits.

Before Ethereum stopped running proof-of-work, around 90 percent of the miners utilized the mev-geth software. This adoption rate indicates how prominent of an incentive MEV is and why enabling democratic access to it is critical. Without a mechanism such as the Flashbots Auction, MEV could have been an even more centralizing factor in Ethereum, where few dominant players extract all the value since they have access to private transaction flows, resulting in economies of scale, incentivizing history rewriting attacks.

Flashbots Protect

The primary enabler of MEV strategies such as frontrunning or sandwiching is that the target transaction is publicly visible. If the MEV-exposing transaction is submitted to a block proposer directly, assuming the user has an agreement with the block proposer, it will bypass the public memory pool. Thus it can no longer be detected by MEV searchers. However, this is only a feasible option for some users, as there is no existing market for users to make deals with block proposers.

Flashbots Protect[8] is a private transaction pool offered by Flashbots to protect Ethereum users against frontrunning and other similar MEV strategies. Users can configure their wallets to submit their transactions to the Flashbots Protect endpoint and avoid getting exposed. Compared to the Flashbots Auction, this is a more straightforward way for users to bypass the public transaction pool, as no bidding logic is required.

Flashbots Protect provides failed transaction protection by only including transactions that do not revert. An Ethereum transaction can revert for various reasons, including insufficient gas. In that case, as the block proposer has to execute the failing transaction until it runs out of gas, which consumes his energy, the transaction issuer is still required to pay the transaction fee (used gas amount * fee per unit of gas). Flashbots Protect saves costs for users by not making them pay for failing transactions.

The main reason why a solution such as Flashbots Protect works lies in the reputation of Flashbots, and the trust users have in it. Without such a trust assumption, it would be too risky for a user to submit their transaction to a private transaction pool, as there is no guarantee that the pool operator will not abuse the information the transaction exposes or censor it. Hence, the usefulness of such centrally controlled products directly depends on the operating party's reputation, which, in a sense, contradicts the trust-freeness of a public, permissionless blockchain such as Ethereum.

MEV detection and quantification

Detection and quantification of MEV are critical for analyzing its impact. It can help us to understand the following:

- What kind of protocol design leads to more MEV exposure?
- Which MEV strategies are most prominent?
- What percentage of the block proposer profits are provided through MEV extracting transactions?
- How profitable is it to run MEV bots?
- What are the costs incurred on targets of MEV strategies such as sandwiching?

However, quantifying MEV is a complex task. Known MEV forms such as arbitrages, sandwiches, and liquidations can be detected to an extent through scripts running pattern-detection algorithms on transaction traces. Nonetheless, detecting every MEV-extracting transaction is not a trivial task as there is a long tail of MEV strategies. Besides the extracted MEV, a theoretically extractable value that was not realized, such as manipulating transactions in a block by the block producer, also exists. Hence, any attempt at quantification can only constitute a lower bound to the actual maximal extractable value.

MEV-Inspect[9] is a script offered by Flashbots to detect and quantify arbitrages and liquidations that occurred on Ethereum. Although it has certain limitations, such as not handling multi-transaction MEV extraction opportunities such as sandwiches or non-atomic arbitrages, or not covering all protocols, it still achieves a lower bound for the total extracted value on Ethereum. This script is also the backend for the MEV metrics dashboard of Flashbots, MEV-Explore.

According to MEV-Explore, between January 1, 2020, and September 15, 2022 (the last day of the PoW-Ethereum), a cumulative sum of US$675.52 million gross profit has been made by MEV searchers through atomic arbitrages and liquidations on nine prominent DeFi protocols.[10] During this period, 3 037 218 MEV transactions were successfully executed (99.11 percent arbitrages, 0.89 percent liquidations), which paid around US$240 million (36 percent of the searcher profits) to the miners in the form of transaction fees or direct payments through the Flashbots Auction. Miners also earned US$1.42 million from the gas fees paid by failing MEV transactions, such as any MEV transaction that reverted because it ran out of gas, or deliberately stopped execution because the MEV opportunity vanished.

Although MEV-Explore only captures part of the picture of maximally extractable value available on Ethereum, it still succeeds in determining a lower bound for the extracted value on specific protocols. Using this information, everyday Ethereum users can understand which protocols lead to more MEV exposure. Furthermore, by looking at the searcher and miner profits, one can understand how profitable it is to run an MEV bot, how much of the extracted MEV stays with the searchers, and how prominent an incentive MEV is compared to block reward and transaction fees.

MEV-influenced supply chain

In Ethereum or any other blockchain, a chain of operations is undertaken when a user attempts to express their will. A simple example can be Alice wanting to swap her WETH tokens for USDC on Uniswap. To realize her intention, Alice must first interact with a wallet that would provide her with an interface to submit a transaction. Once the transaction is issued, it will be delivered to a public or private transaction pool, depending on the wallet, where it will await to be included in a block. During this period, the transaction will be spotted by an MEV searcher and placed in a bundle that extracts all the MEV it exposes. The searcher will submit this bundle to a block builder, who will then construct a block, including the bundle, and offer it to a validator, who will finally propose the block and reach a consensus over it with the rest of the validators.[11] This network of components which are included until Alice's transaction is confirmed, or in other words, until her will is accomplished, constitute a supply chain that operates under the influence of MEV.

The MEV-influenced supply chain is a framework to better understand the different components included in transaction processing, and how the value flows from users to validators. An overview of this network can give hints about the centralizing effects of MEV on a blockchain. In a dystopian world, components such as wallets, searchers, builders, and validators are vertically integrated to capture most of the value. For example, a highly skilled searcher can make an off-chain deal with a wallet to get its transaction load in return for some percentage of the MEV those transactions expose. In another case, the searcher can integrate with certain builders and validators to guarantee preferred execution order in return for some profits again.

Vertical integration on the MEV supply chain leads to economies of scale in extracting/controlling MEV, which drives off the competition and creates centralized entities that dictate the user experience. Blockchains with such non-modular, centralized supply chains trade off transparency, censorship resistance, and being permissionless for opacity, exclusiveness, and non-democratic/permissioned access to MEV.

In a utopian world, an open market exists for each separate role in the supply chain, where individual entities compete. In such a world, fair competition drives off centralization and leads to a modular supply chain that is necessary for preserving a permissionless, uncensored, transparent blockchain. Furthermore, in a utopia, MEV does not only accumulate on the searchers or validators, but also flows back to the users.

As MEV is exposed after a particular state transition occurs—let us call this an order—the user that triggers this transition is the owner of the order flow. Without access to order flow, neither searchers nor builders can extract MEV. Thus, each order has a value depending on the MEV opportunity it exposes. Users can profit from the extractable value their orders expose by auctioning off the execution rights to searchers and builders. In this way, MEV will benefit originators—that is, users—as well as extractors.

MEV Post-Ethereum Merge (September 2022–Today)

In September 2022, Ethereum stopped running proof-of-work (PoW) and longest-chain-based consensus (that is, Nakamoto consensus) and merged with the Beacon Chain, launched in December 2020, which runs a proof-of-stake (PoS)-based consensus mechanism. The merge imposed a new architecture on Ethereum that separates the consensus layer (CL) and the execution layer (EL). While previously both CL and EL were baked into the same network, two separate networks exist for them after the merger.

Post-merge, the PoW-Ethereum network became the execution layer of Ethereum. The responsibilities of the EL include collecting and executing transactions, running the EVM, and preparing block payloads for the validators. Ethereum separated EL from CL in order to become a more modular protocol, as opposed to being a monolith. The modularity allows Ethereum to switch the current EL with another protocol, such as a Layer-2 rollup network, if desired.

The Beacon Chain is Ethereum's new consensus engine, where block proposers, called validators, are running PoS. While PoS determines who can be included in block production, validators are also running LMD GHOST (Latest Message Driven Greediest Heaviest Observed SubTree) and Casper FFG (Friendly Finality Gadget) to decide on the correct state of the chain.

LMD GHOST is a weight/vote-based fork choice tool for finding the head of the chain. Casper FFG is a finality gadget which requires more than two-thirds of the total stake to vote on a block for it to be finalized eventually.

In PoW-Ethereum, the block time depended on how fast the miners could solve the mining puzzle with its current difficulty. Hence, it was a non-deterministic, random process with a constant average block production rate (that is, a Poisson process). The new Ethereum protocol divides time into epochs and slots, where each epoch contains 32 slots, and every slot lasts 12 seconds. All validators have a role in a slot of an epoch, determined two epochs beforehand.[12] For each slot, a validator is selected to propose a block, and a set of validators, called a committee, is assigned to attest to the proposed block. Since there is a predetermined block proposer for each slot in an epoch, there is no need for a random process such as solving a mining puzzle as in PoW-Ethereum. Therefore, PoS-Ethereum achieves a deterministic block time of 12 seconds.

In the new consensus mechanism, if an epoch can gather a total number of votes (attestations) cast by validators holding more than two-thirds of the available stake on Ethereum, it becomes justified with Casper FFG. If the attestations given during the next epoch also address the justified epoch as the parent epoch, and the epoch itself also collects more than two-thirds of the total stake's votes, then the justified epoch becomes finalized with every block in it. Hence, it takes two epochs (12.8 minutes) after the merge for a block to become final in Ethereum.[13]

Besides the changes in block production and finality, the transition to PoS also changed the security model of Ethereum. More specifically, it allowed the introduction of in-protocol penalties and slashing in cases of misbehavior; while penalties only reduce the staked amount of a validator (for example, for non-timely attestations), slashing leads to loss of the stake and ejection from the protocol. Slashable offenses include proposing multiple blocks in the same slot, or submitting contradicting attestations. This mechanism also makes 51 percent attacks more expensive for the attacker, as their stake, which they used to conduct the attack, will be slashed and ejected. In PoW-Ethereum, there was no way to remove the attacker's hardware from the system without harming others.

Block building and proposer–builder separation

The separation of execution and consensus layers imposes several changes to the node implementations in Ethereum. Previously, miners were running a single node client to build a block and reach a consensus with the rest of the network. Although protocols such as the Flashbots Auction took over some of the overhead of block building, miner clients were still responsible for proposing the prepared block and achieving an agreement over it with the rest of the network.

After the merge on Ethereum, validators run two separate nodes for consensus[14] and execution.[15] While the consensus node is in charge of proposing blocks and reaching a shared world state on the Beacon Chain, the execution node is responsible for running EVM and delivering an execution payload, including transaction content, to the consensus node. The communication between these two nodes, or more generally between execution and consensus layers, is realized through a new protocol developed for PoS-Ethereum called the Engine API.

When it is the turn for a validator to propose a block, his consensus node contacts his execution node via the Engine API and requests an execution payload. Upon receiving the request, the execution node prepares the most profitable block and delivers it back to the consensus node. The consensus node places the execution payload into the body of the block it is constructing alongside other mandatory fields, such as the proposer index, hash of the parent block, and hash of the current state, and proposes it to the rest of the network. Figure 12.4 displays an overview of this structure.

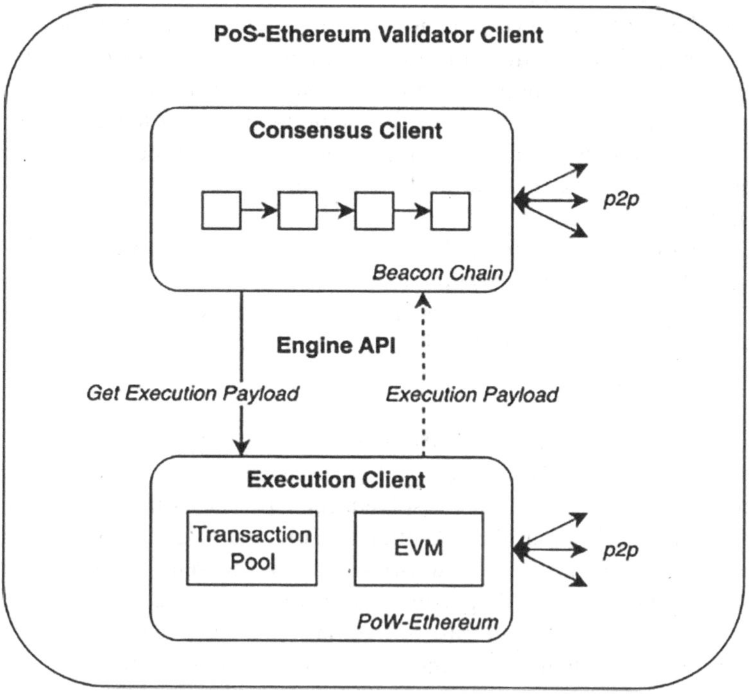

Figure 12.4 An overview of a validator client on the PoS-Ethereum network

When MEV extraction was not as prominent an incentive as it is today, block building was a more straightforward task. It did not require block proposers to be exceptionally skilled at extracting all the value available in the mempool, as the block reward was already a significant subsidy. In PoS-Ethereum, any validator not extracting MEV will be left behind in the game as the in-protocol, fixed block reward is remarkably reduced with the transition from PoW to PoS.[16] The PoS-Ethereum validators who can realize MEV will become centralized forces, as MEV promotes economies of scale.

To avoid incentivizing validators to become sophisticated in block building, proposer–builder separation (PBS) is proposed on Ethereum. PBS divides the tasks of a block producer into two separate roles: proposing and building. In this model, a block proposer is only concerned about reaching a consensus, as he can outsource the block building to a specialized group of builders. When PBS is enshrined into the core protocol of PoS-Ethereum, a validator can just run a consensus node and get the execution payload from the builders market on the execution layer. In this way, he can still profit from MEV available in the mempool while not directly being concerned about extracting it.

In PBS, block builders compete with each other to offer the most value to the validators, and their bidding power depends on the amount of MEV that they can extract from their order flow. Finding the most optimal set of transactions/bundles that provide the most value requires running complex algorithms, which can consume significant energy. The only incentive for the builders to bear this cost is to earn the right to be a monopoly for a single slot. In other words, through this competition, a builder buys the block space of an Ethereum block without doing any staking or mining in PoW-Ethereum.

To avoid validators stealing the MEV that the builder aims to capture for himself, PBS protocol makes an execution payload available only after the proposer accepts the bid and signs the payload header. PBS can also make validators stateless as it delegates the block-building task to builders. Thus validators would no longer have to store the entire Ethereum state.

Flashbots' PBS implementation: MEV-Boost

There remains some time before PBS gets enshrined into the core Ethereum protocol due to complexities that need to be resolved, such as trust assumptions between proposers and builders. The Flashbots Auction was the first stage towards realizing PBS. It enabled more democratic access to MEV in PoW-Ethereum while helping miners to outsource some block-building. However, it was not a silver bullet; mev-geth still required the MEV searchers to trust in the Flashbots relay and miners, as they can see the transaction content and potentially frontrun or censor it to keep the MEV for themselves.

Flashbots developed a new MEV market design to run on PoS-Ethereum, called MEV-Boost,[17] to mitigate some of the trust assumptions required by mev-geth. MEV-Boost can be described as a PBS stopgap implementation where validators can sell their block space to specialized block builders under the surveillance of relays. In MEV-Boost, the complete execution payload of a builder becomes available to the validator of the allocated slot only after they accept the builder's bid and sign the payload header. Thus, a validator cannot attempt to steal the MEV before fully committing to the builder's payload. At that point, they can try to build a new block, but there is no guarantee that the consensus participants will accept this block as the canonical head over the initially signed block. Moreover, their stake will be slashed for proposing multiple blocks in a single slot.

Although MEV-Boost improves the trust model of mev-geth, it is not a complete solution for the trust assumptions between the validators and builders. The MEV-Boost architecture still requires the existence of mutually trusted relays sitting between the validators and builders. These relays are responsible for collecting execution payloads from the builders, simulating them, and finally submitting them to a relay aggregator, called mev-boost, which works as a middleware between the consensus and the execution clients. Moreover, relays are also needed to ensure data availability and DoS protection for the validators.

MEV-Boost aims to push the centralization effects of MEV to the builder level instead of the validator level to mitigate the risk of MEV becoming a threat to the consensus stability of Ethereum. However, this comes with the threat of censorship posed by the relays. A relay can:

- see the content of an execution payload submitted by a builder and attempt to steal the MEV in it;
- censor blocks of certain builders; and
- censor specific validators' access to MEV by not forwarding the builder blocks it received.

The mev-boost middleware allows validators to connect to as many relays as possible to mitigate the risk of censorship. Besides, a validator can always use their execution client for local block construction if there is no trusted relay. Moreover, builders are free to submit their execution payload to multiple relays. By creating a competition on the relay level, MEV-Boost aims to force relays to behave honestly, as relay activity is publicly auditable. As long as there are other options, malicious behavior will cause relays to lose their reputation alongside validators and builders.

MEV-Boost architecture

In the MEV-Boost architecture, a validator has to register with the relays they want to work with. This process is required for validators to inform the relays about the address where they want to get paid, the gas limit of their blocks, and their public key. When the allocated slot of a validator arrives, they contact their mev-boost middleware to get a payload header. The middleware collects the headers with associated bids from the relays that the validator has registered with, and responds to the validator with the header that offers the most value. In a sense, the mev-boost middleware can be thought of as a multiplexer that gets block headers as inputs from various relays and outputs the most valuable one. The validator blindly signs (that is, without seeing the content) this header and submits it to mev-boost, forwarding it to the respective relay. The relay finally verifies the signature of the validator on the signed header and responds back to the validator with the full execution payload.

On the block-building side of MEV-Boost, builders first check whether the validator for the current slot is registered with a relay that they work with. In cases where it is, they start preparing their execution payload by collecting transactions from the public mempool and, if it exists, from their private order flow, such as a private mempool. After constructing the most valuable block possible, builders submit their full block, alongside a bid that they offer to the validator, to the relay(s) they work with. Relays check the validity of the submitted payloads, ensuring that the prepared block pays the validator the promised amount and does not consume more gas than the limit set by the validator during registration. Then, they pick the most valuable, valid payload submitted by their connected builders and offer its header to the mev-boost middleware upon request. Finally, the middleware proposes the header which offers the most value to the validator.

Figure 12.5 shows an example block production scenario for a validator that works with MEV-Boost. In this scenario, there are two relays, Relay X and Relay Y, which the validator works with. While Builder A and Builder B submit their blocks to Relay X, Builder C submits to Relay Y. Across all builders, only Builder C has access to an exclusive order flow through their private mempool. Hence, while the other two builders submit blocks with a value of less than 1 ETH each, Builder C can build a block that offers 10 ETH to the validator. As mev-boost middleware does profit switching, it forwards the block header with the most value to the validator, which is, in this case, from Relay Y. The validator's execution client also prepares an execution payload, but it can only accumulate 0.001 ETH value, even though it builds on the same order flow as Builders A and B.[18] Assuming the validator is rational, they accept the payload by mev-boost.

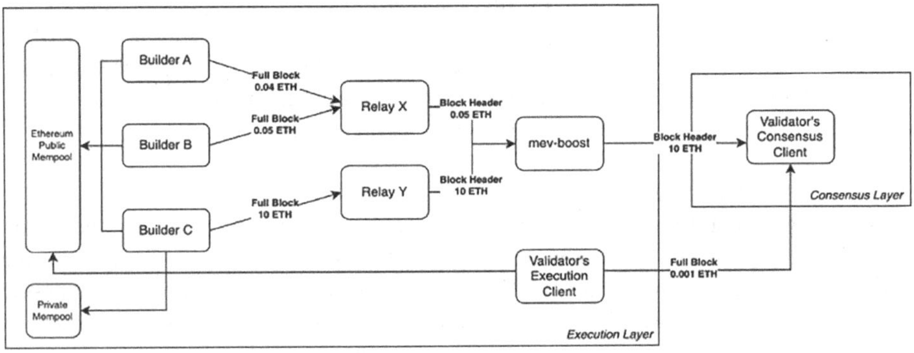

Figure 12.5 An example block production scenario with MEV-Boost and a local execution client

The impact of MEV-Boost

The numbers shared in this section are based on the network activity between September 15, 2022 (Merge Day) and October 31, 2022 on Ethereum. The resources used are: ChainsightAnalytics MEV-Boost dashboard,[19] mevboost.org,[20] and boost-relay.flashbots.net.[21]

MEV-Boost has been actively used since Ethereum transitioned to proof-of-stake. According to the numbers by ChainsightAnalytics, more than 160 000 blocks (45 percent of all PoS-Ethereum blocks) have been proposed by validators using MEV-Boost. These validators have received close to US$34 million payment from the block builders. The builder group that delivered the highest number of blocks (76 463) and made the most validator payment (US$17 million) is Flashbots' builder group. After that, an anonymous builder known as "builder 0x69" has been the most successful one. So far, this builder has delivered 25 426 blocks and paid around US$6 million to the validators.

Currently, seven active relays are operating on MEV-Boost. Based on the data gathered from the Data API of each relay, an open application programming interface

(API) that provides data about delivered payloads and received builder blocks,[22] 136 200 blocks have been proposed by the Flashbots relay. Flashbots is followed by BloXroute Max Profit (11 396 blocks) and Eden (5142). The least number of blocks have been relayed by Manifold (2629).

The current status in the MEV-Boost supply chain points to a centralization around Flashbots, both on the builder and the relay side. On the builder side, this is not a surprise as the Flashbots builders have access to an exclusive order flow from MEV searchers via the Flashbots Auction, which the other builders do not have. Thus, they can usually accumulate more value from the transactions than other builders and, as a result, offer the highest payment to the validators.

On the relay side, the stats show that the Flashbots relay is not only used by the Flashbots' builders but also by other builders. We argue that this is due to both quantitative and qualitative reasons. The quantitative reason is the adoption of the Flashbots relay by the validators. Out of 457 727 active validators on Ethereum, 320 695 are registered with the Flashbots relay. Thus, there is a 70 percent probability that the block proposer of the next slot will have the Flashbots relay configured in their mev-boost middleware. Since block builders depend on the relays for reaching out to the validators, a relay included in the mev-boost configuration of most validators is highly preferable. Hence, the use of the Flashbots relay becomes justified.

As for the qualitative reason, builders prefer the Flashbots relay due to the reputation of Flashbots. The main risks relays pose to builders are censorship and MEV manipulation. Since Flashbots has been the leading research group working on solutions to democratize the MEV scene on Ethereum, any malicious behavior could negatively impact their reputation and potentially the credibility of their products (Flashbots Auction, Flashbots Protect, MEV-Boost). Block builders are also aware of this and know that it is not an affordable risk for Flashbots to censor blocks or steal the MEV in them.[23] Therefore, they do not see a risk in submitting their blocks to the Flashbots relay.

The decentralization of MEV-Boost is only possible with more trustworthy relays and fairer access to order flow on the builder side. As the current numbers show, builders who do not have access to exclusive order flow cannot compete with the ones who do. Although Flashbots currently dominates the MEV-Boost supply chain, it is not aiming to become a monopoly. On the contrary, Flashbots is working towards a more decentralized MEV scene by maximizing the competition. It is encouraging more relays to join MEV-Boost by open-sourcing its relay.[24] Moreover, it is currently working on a mechanism called SUAVE (Single Unifying Auction for Value Expression), which is a decentralized block builder that preserves the privacy of users and wallets and provides optimal, MEV-aware execution for them. SUAVE will be an open-source product that the competitors of Flashbots can also utilize.

MEV IN BITCOIN

Although most of the MEV discussion revolves around Ethereum, as it is the most popular and highly used smart contract blockchain, MEV also exists in other protocols. Theoretically, Bitcoin also includes MEV, which can be extracted, for example, by ordering transactions from the Lightning protocol or fee sniping by reorganizing the chain history. However, compared to Ethereum, the amount of extractable value exposed by Bitcoin transactions is significantly less due to the difference in the complexity of the application layer and the programmability of the two protocols. In Bitcoin, most of the transactions are simple money transfers, and there is close to no value exposed by state transitions; whereas in Ethereum there exist various ways for users to interact with the protocol via smart contracts that can generate extractable value.

On Ethereum, the MEV surface is immense due to the existence of smart contracts that enable countless ways for interaction. Since MEV occurs as a result of state transition, the protocol with more ways for users to interact naturally has more MEV in it. On Bitcoin, if the Lightning protocol starts to create harmful MEV opportunities, its capability can be limited by removing some operations from the Bitcoin Script. However, on Ethereum, it would only be possible to restrict all possible implementations of specific applications, such as DeFi protocols, by constraining the general behavior of permissionless smart contracts. Thus, Ethereum's programmability, which enables an extensive application ecosystem, also acts as its "curse" against MEV. On the other hand, Bitcoin's more restrictive use case space revolving around money transfers is its "remedy" for minimizing the exposed MEV.

CONCLUSION

In this chapter, we first introduced how MEV emerged as an incentive and then we presented different forms of it. We made an extensive analysis of the evolution of MEV in Ethereum. First, we looked at the initial MEV extracting activities on Ethereum, such as bot activities leading to priority gas auctions. We also presented the consensus-level threats that MEV poses. Next, we introduced the MEV market design of Flashbots, The Flashbots Auction, and shared statistics regarding the impact that MEV had on the Ethereum protocol between January 2020 and September 2022. We also discussed the MEV-influenced supply chain framework and why it is critical to achieving modularity. Then, we explained the new architecture of the Ethereum protocol after the transition to proof-of-stake (PoS) and discussed why a solution such as proposer–builder separation (PBS) is needed. Here, we introduced Flashbots' solution for achieving partial PBS, MEV-Boost, until full PBS is enshrined into the Ethereum protocol. We also analyzed the use of MEV-Boost in PoS-Ethereum and pointed out the centralization around Flashbots' solutions. Finally, we discussed the existence of MEV in Bitcoin and argued why it is not as prominent a threat as it is for Ethereum.

The phenomena of MEV has gradually increased its impact surface since its formal recognition by Daian et al. (2019) in "Flashboys 2.0." In the early days, it only posed a theoretical level threat to the consensus stability and decentralization of Ethereum, as users were not heavily active in the DeFi space. Since 2019, MEV has shaped the incentive mechanism design of Ethereum and the decentralized applications built on it. Currently, MEV incentivizes private order flows and vertical integration with other actors of the value supply chain, such as trading firms or wallets, to extract the most value out of the protocol and, potentially, become a monopoly.

Research groups such as Flashbots are continuously working on new products to illuminate and democratize the MEV scene on Ethereum, as uncontrolled MEV can lead to centralization. To avoid Ethereum becoming a censored, opaque, permissioned network, it is critical to ensure that MEV not only accumulates on certain players, but also flows back to the protocol and the end-users.

NOTES

1. https://www.sec.gov/news/press/2009/2009-201-factsheet.htm.
2. Memory pool, or mempool for short, refers to the area where unconfirmed Ethereum transactions wait to be included in a block.
3. https://explore.flashbots.net/.
4. https://ethereum.org/en/developers/docs/mev/.
5. Gas is the unit to measure the computational work done to execute a transaction.
6. PGAs are a mix of English and all-pay auctions in which the price ascends through repetitive bids, finally resolving to one winning bidder, while all participants are paying a cost (not only the winner).
7. https://medium.com/flashbots/frontrunning-the-mev-crisis-40629a613752.
8. https://docs.flashbots.net/flashbots-protect/overview.
9. https://github.com/flashbots/mev-inspect-py.
10. Aave, Balancer, Bancor, Compound, Cream, Curve, Uniswap V2, Uniswap v3, and 0x.
11. In most blockchains, builders and validators are the same entity (for example, miners in PoW-Ethereum). However, there are also designs where these roles are separated (for example, sequencers in Layer-2 solutions, proposer–builder-separation in Ethereum).
12. Validators are allocated to a slot using a random number-generating mechanism called RANDAO.
13. The genesis block is justified and finalized by default.
14. Consensus node clients: Lighthouse, Lodestar, Nimbus, Prysm, Teku.
15. Execution node clients: Geth, Nethermind, Besu, Erigon, Akula.
16. Ethereum has already started the process of becoming deflationary with EIP-1559 transactions, where the BASEFEE part of a transaction fee is burnt instead of given to the block producer. Visit https://ultrasound.money for statistics regarding the burnt amount and the supply change.
17. https://boost.flashbots.net/.

18. This could be due to the fact that builders are more advanced in block building than a validator's local execution client.
19. https://dune.com/ChainsightAnalytics/mev-after-ethereum-merge.
20. https://www.mevboost.org/.
21. https://boost-relay.flashbots.net/.
22. https://flashbots.notion.site/Relay-API-Documentation-5fb0819366954962bc02e81cb33840f5.
23. At the time of writing in October 2022, Flashbots is censoring any transactions interacting with the smart contracts of the transaction mixer application Tornado Cash, to comply with the sanctions of the United States Department of the Treasury's Office of Foreign Assets Control (OFAC).
24. https://github.com/flashbots/mev-boost-relay.

REFERENCES

Daian, P., Goldfeder, S., Kell, T., Li, Y., Zhao, X., Bentov, I., Breidenbach, L., and Juels, A. (2019). Flash Boys 2.0: Frontrunning, Transaction Reordering, and Consensus Instability in Decentralized Exchanges. ArXiv, abs/1904.05234.

Eskandari, S., Moosavi, S., and Clark, J. (2019). SoK: Transparent Dishonesty: Front-Running Attacks on Blockchain. In R. Pass and A. Shelat (eds), *International Conference on Financial Cryptography and Data Security* (pp. 170–189). Springer.

Lewis, M. (2014). *Flash Boys: A Wall Street Revolt*. W.W. Norton & Company.

Liu, C. (2015). *The Dark Forest*, 1st edition. Tor, A Tom Doherty Associates Book.

Qin, K., Zhou, L., and Gervais, A. (2022). Quantifying Blockchain Extractable Value: How Dark is the Forest? *2022 IEEE Symposium on Security and Privacy (SP)*. https://doi.org/10.1109/sp46214.2022.9833734.

Robinson, D., and Konstantopoulos, G. (2020, August 28). Ethereum is a Dark Forest. Paradigm. Retrieved October 16, 2022, from https://www.paradigm.xyz/2020/08/ethereum-is-a-dark-forest.

Samczsun (2020, October 7). Escaping the Dark Forest. Retrieved October 16, 2022, from https://samczsun.com/escaping-the-dark-forest/.

13. From scalability to cross-chain DeFi

Marcel Kaiser

INTRODUCTION

This chapter's purpose is twofold: (1) to elaborate on the role of interoperable ecosystems in general and for the decentralized financial sector; and (2) to provide a simple but systematic overview of the current state of interoperability. As an introduction, I elaborate on the relationship between scalability solutions and interoperability solutions. I clarify the dependence of both topics on their respective trust assumptions and analyze the entire context from the point of view of decentralized finance. Finally, a potential outlook for the future of cross-chain decentralized finance (DeFi) is given. The chapter is written from the point of view of a practitioner, and should serve as an entry point for the vast topic of blockchain interoperability and an orientation for cross-chain DeFi.

Motivation

Distributed ledger technology (DLT) is the basis for cryptoassets such as Bitcoin, but has also been identified as a potentially disruptive topic in different fields, for example in finance, gaming, and art. However, today's blockchain landscape is not continuous, with different, incompatible ecosystems being available to potential users (Schulte et al. 2019). Interoperability between different blockchains is usually not featured in existing protocols and standards. Transferring tokens or invoking and executing contracts can mostly not be carried out outside of a single ledger. There are blockchains which create interoperability between their subchains (for example, Cosmos, Polkadot), and even a few which can effectively act as bridges to other ecosystems. One reason to use decentralized infrastructure lies in its open character. This trait is limited once blockchain ecosystems can only effectively interact using centralized gateways. The vision is a technology in which users, devices, and algorithms can communicate and interact seamlessly across the boundaries of ecosystems and contexts. Blockchain interoperability will vastly simplify a paradigm shift from today's closed systems to open decentralized space.

Trust

In Web3, trust assumptions are broadly discussed in the literature but often overlooked in practice. They are, potentially, on par with protocol design in terms of importance for a truly disruptive change in how digital interactions will be performed in the future. Recent years, particularly 2021 and 2022, have proven that disregarding the corresponding counter-party risk can be detrimental to entire ecosystems. It is worthwhile to briefly define trust. Classically, trust is the relationship between a trustor and a trustee. The trustor is an entity that assumes trust or faith in either the benevolence or the truthfulness of the trustee. The trustee can be an institution, person, technology, convention, or other entity. To quote Becker and Bodó (2021): "Trust is the instrument with which the trustor manages the contingencies that relate to trusting the trustee to act competently, in the interest of the trustor in concrete given contexts."

In the context of blockchain, trust is mostly referred to as a means to switch trustees from individual and institutional middlemen to software. Jacobs (2021) defined a framework for different layers of trust, differentiating the types of trust involved in the usage of distributed ledger technology.

The inability to discriminate against individual transactions based on arbitrary decisions, halting the continuation of entire ecosystems or manipulating the ledger's state, are examples of the many ways in which individuals, institutions, and other groups can manipulate infrastructure that are not trust-free. While broadly applied consensus mechanisms are the subject of debate, the absence of consensus requirements is sometimes disregarded in practice. This is especially true if technology adoption by large entities and corporations leads to centralized blockchain systems which create the impression of being decentralized technology.

THE STATE OF INTEROPERABILITY AND SCALABILITY

A Brief Definition of Scalability

Across the literature, the term "scalability" has been attached to several properties: latency, ecological impact, cost, and most often, transaction throughput or speed. In this chapter, for simplicity, transaction throughput is considered synonymous with scalability. For an overview of the different dimensions of scalability, articles such as Nasir et al. (2022) and Chauhan and Patel (2022) can be considered. I also mention the blockchain trilemma as a motivation and precursor of blockchain scalability: "We prove a Blockchain Trilemma: any method of consensus, be it centralized or decentralized, must give up (i) fault-tolerance, (ii) resource-efficiency, or (iii) full transferability" (Abadi and Brunnermeier 2018).

This quotation outlines the trilemma faced by blockchains, stating that they can only possess two out of these three qualities at any given time: security, speed (and thus cost-efficiency), or decentralization. This trilemma has been discussed in a plethora of literature: Khan et al. (2021) have analyzed 122 primary papers dealing with the scalability problem. This problem still poses a major challenge today. Mogavero et al. (2021) have named it a "quadrilemma" due to considering computational efficiency as well. This chapter, for simplicity, remains focused on the trilemma.

Generation 1 and 2 blockchains that are still alive and used today went with decentralization and security as their two properties and therefore sacrificed scalability to differing degrees. This was not as prevalent in discussion outside of research until adoption massively increased with the dawn of DeFi in the summer of 2020. The skyrocketing gas prices (see Amler et al. 2021) caused minor investors and business models based on small transactions to move away from the Ethereum mainnet. Thus, scalability solutions became more popular and newer protocols focused on this property more strongly (to name a few: Solana 2022; Cardano 2022; Avalanche 2022).

The scalability issue has mostly been tackled either by these new blockchains or by pushing transactions and computations off-chain. The new blockchains attempt to resolve the scalability challenge by using on-chain mechanisms which help to increase transaction throughput. Because they rarely play into cross-chain solutions, they are therefore not the main focus of this chapter.

The question as to how off-chain solutions circumvent the blockchain trilemma (or not) is a matter of debate for practitioners. Table 13.1 gives an overview on how the blockchain trilemma aspects are interpretable in some solutions.

The general rule for scalability solutions outside the realm of blockchain configuration changes is that a good portion of computation and transactions need to be taken off-chain (Eberhardt and Heiss 2018). In a more centralized realm, or at least not in a fully decentralized but relatively trust-free or trusted area, interactions can occur without the same public consensus (strictly speaking, the blockchain trilemma is still valid). This is useful for microtransactions which will later be aggregated or confidential computations. The advantages of these solutions manifest themselves because they either aggregate many (micro) transactions or simply increase the speed of transactions for some use cases. Moreover, off-chain solutions can go along with additional privacy and confidentiality features which cannot be realized in regular open blockchains (Sguanci et al. 2021). This makes them particularly relevant for use cases dealing with sensitive data.

Off-chain solutions can be classified as either hybrid systems (partly confidential or closed access, for example channel frameworks) or public connectors such as open subsystems (that is, rollups) (Lohachab et al. 2021). Table 13.1 gives an overview of the solutions for scalability, off- and on-chain, and their eligibility for cross-chain activity.

In terms of the off-chain ecosystems for the purpose of scalability, one approach in particular sticks out. The usage of a secure hardware element or trusted execution environment (TEE) makes up a new anchor of trust. In Erwig et al. (2020), the possibility of running a plasma system within a TEE (for example, an ARM TrustZone, Intel Software Guard Extension, or AMD Platform Security Processor) is theorized. Furthermore, Andreina et al. (2020) published a secure proof of TEE stake for permissionless blockchains: IEEE Transactions on Services Computing. This approach rests on the assumption that either multiple different TEEs can execute the plasma in parallel, or that the respective creators of the systems are trustworthy and have not built in a backdoor. Further, it rests on the assumption that the systems in place are kept up-to-date in order to avoid the possibility of an attack based on entirely new technology, as currently, research and development of attack vectors and security features are racing against each other (Fei et al. 2021; Lou et al. 2021).

Table 13.1 An overview of existing scalability solutions differentiated by transaction execution layer

Layer	Classification	Trust Assumption	Scalability Mechanism	Examples	Cross-Chain Capability?
Off-Chain (Layer 2)	(Payment) Channel Technology	No, Adjudication Process	P2P-Channels with Hubs	Perun Network, Raiden Network	Yes
	Side Chain	Not always	Two-way pegs, different consensus mechanisms, ...	Plasma, Pegged Side Chains	Yes
	Zk Rollups	No	Validity proven state updates instead of full tx documentation		Potentially
	Optimistic Rollups	Yes, potentially untrusted transactions have to be challenged in time	State commitments	Arbitrium, Optimism	Potentially
	TEE Solutions	Assuming it has no backdoor or scalable attack vectors	Centralized Computation on secured hardware elements.	Erdstall, Oasis Sapphire Paratime, IntegriTEE	Yes
	Hash Time Locked Contract	No	None	Lightning Network	Yes
	Notarized Hash Time Locked Contract	Yes	None	Kraken	Yes
	Decentralized Oracle Networks	Trusting the node operators	None,	Chainlink Cross-chain Interoperability Protocol (CCIP)	Yes, only messaging
On-Chain (Layer 1 Design)	Block Data	No	Expanding blocks or changing global block properties	-	No
	Consensus Mechanisms	Depends on the mechanism	Change of consensus mechanism		No
	Sharding	No	Database partitioning		No
	Directed Acyclical Graphs	No	Architectural change	IOTA, Nano, OByte	No
	Block Expansions	No		-	No

To bridge the gap to the next section, the implications of the facts which have been outlined have to be summarized: blockchain scalability remains a major challenge, inspiring a number of different ecosystems dealing with the issue. As a consequence, subspaces emerged for specialized use cases. Many of these subspaces compete for the existing user base, promising better user experience and lower fees. As a consequence, the fragmentation of the ecosystem progressed.

Connors and Sarkar (2022) have categorized the different generations of blockchains according to their functionality: Generation 1 blockchains cover the basic DLT with payment functionality. As Bitcoin has been the first well-adopted system, it is the archetypical example for a first-generation blockchain. Generation 2 blockchains add the capability of development such as smart contracts to the set of functions of a DLT. The most prominent example in terms of adoption, developer activity and market capitalization is Ethereum. A third-generation blockchain, in this framework, is defined as a blockchain solution aiming to support enterprise applications, interpreted (in this chapter) as a blockchain having subchains (or as Lohachab et al. 2021 phrased it: a blockchain of blockchains) and scalability due to novel consensus mechanisms.[1]

A Brief Definition of Interoperability

Interoperability describes the capacity of one blockchain ecosystem to interact with another. This can entail the exchange of value and information or the invocation of a smart contract located on a different blockchain. The transfer of information using correct corresponding encodings is often referred to as messaging. Interoperability between ecosystems can increase the mobility of users between ecosystems and thus increase the potential user base. Notably, interoperability and scalability solutions often go hand in hand, as both regularly have to bring transactions off-chain (that is, away from the current distributed ledger system) and later bring them back onto trustless infrastructure. Therefore, an overview of blockchain scalability solutions supplements the understanding of the readers when dealing with interoperability solutions.

The possibility of swapping tokens from different ecosystems as such is already useful. Without centralized institutions and many steps, this process has not been feasible. Interconnected ecosystems make it possible to minimize trust and transaction costs while maximizing efficiency. One use case of special relevance to this chapter is to extend the use of decentralized financial protocols across more ecosystems. This extension, to use a popular analogy, would be adding bricks to the set of available money LEGO parts. Users can create more complex financial mechanisms by combining a larger variety of services.

Also, the connection between companies using applications from one blockchain or the other now has the possibility to engage with each other without having to adopt a new system. Thus, businesses can become freer in their choice of their ecosystem.

Interoperability has its own trilemma. Bhuptani (2021) summarizes that creating interoperability between Ethereum Virtual Machine (EVM) or Ethereum-like ecosystems lets developers always only fulfill two out of the following three properties:

- Trustlessness: having equivalent trust models in the underlying ecosystems.
- Extensibility: able to be supported on any system.
- Generalizability: capable of handling arbitrary cross-domain data.

This trilemma implicitly resurfaces throughout this chapter as well. It is useful when reflecting upon the developments throughout the entire interoperability scene. It will become evident that this trilemma also often applies to non-EVM systems.

As an example for trustless and extensible interoperability, we can take a look at so-called hash time locked contracts (HTLCs) on different blockchains. HTLC transactions are transactions which use contracts on both sides of the chain. Funds are redeemed in two ways on both sides: hashlock and timelock. Hashlock is performed through a hash function: the sender locks the transaction by a hash value, while the recipient needs to provide the corresponding value to the hash value. This value is often referred to as a seed. It can be considered as the key to the lock. Timelock does not require extra information to solve. It will be unlocked when the predefined time expires. The destination of the timelock is usually the sender, which triggers the refund process (rolling back the transaction) (DINNGO 2019). These mechanisms enable an automated mechanism which ensures that either the sender gets their funds back, or the receiver proved they obtained them. An exemplary and well-known application of HTLCs is the Lightning Network, a Layer 2 payment network on the Bitcoin blockchain (Poon and Dryja 2016).

Status quo

Interoperability between blockchain networks is motivated to reduce the breaking up of decentral infrastructure into siloes. This effect creates dependence of users on exchanges to manage their funds and applications. These centralized gateways disrupt the chain of trust-free interactions between the users and their applications. Recent examples (PolyNetwork hack, Thorchain hacks, Nomads bridge hack; a combined loss of close to US$1 billion) have shown the disadvantages of dependency on centralized services and exchanges, or swiftly created solutions without security. The requirement of trust-free gateways and applications plays an important role in the technological and scientific challenge that interoperability currently poses. In a later section, I discuss the topic of trust. Further, increased interoperability can sharpen the profile of smart contract platforms, specialized chains for IoT, gaming or NFTs, and payment solutions by reducing the requirement to enable other services as well. This makes it easier for ecosystem builders but also regulators to classify the respective blockchains. As a consequence, less generalization in regulation might occur. This is especially important as blockchain regulation is in its infancy. With the first regulatory frameworks in emergence and heated political debates about the disruptive technology going on, it is possible that blockchain interoperability itself might be a regulated (or at least standardized) topic until 2029.

The landscape of solutions is complex. It can be subdivided into the solutions within blockchain types, that is, EVM compatible, non-EVM compatible, and cross-type compatibility. Another dimension of the solutions at hand can be three degrees of trust: is it centralized (like a permissioned or mono-node blockchain), mostly trust-free (like multi-TEE systems, special committees/watchtower institutions, or shared databases) or fully decentralized (that is, Bitcoin, Ethereum Layer 1).

The following section briefly deals with the existing solutions for cross-chain transactions. A more thorough discussion of them can be found in Zamyatin et al. (2021). There are solutions which aim to solve the interoperability problem. According to Lohachab et al. (2021), the current research scope focuses on developing solutions relying on trusted brokers, hash-locking, and relays with the result that obfuscation ecosystems emerge that are unable to communicate with each other. In order to avoid further complexity, interoperability solutions need to empower the notion of trustless interoperability. They recommend the implementation of a holistic approach to bridge disparate blockchain solutions. Belchior et al. (2021) systematically analyzed and categorized interoperability into three different categories: public connectors, blockchain of blockchains, and hybrid connectors.

Public connectors include sidechains (Loom network, Polygon), hashed timelock contracts (Connext), and notary schemes which include centralized (Coinbase, Kraken) and decentralized exchanges (Anyswap, Wanswap).

Blockchain of blockchains such as Polkadot, Cosmos, or ARK can achieve a high degree of interoperability. A relay chain in Polkadot, for example, can connect different subchains over which transactions are routed. However, interoperability is only possible with subchains within a particular ecosystem, hence interoperability with other blockchains or other ecosystems is not easily possible. This process can be compared to L2-to-L2 interoperability despite subsystems not being Layer 2 solutions.

Hybrid connectors include trusted relays and agnostic protocols. Trusted relays operate as gateways (that is, pNetwork) where interoperability is realized by having a trusted component (hardware module, single entity, or consortium) that locks a token on one blockchain (1 BTC locked) and mints a wrapped token on the receiving blockchain (1 wBTC minted). Gateways are especially useful for connecting blockchains not able to execute arbitrary smart contracts. To my knowledge, native token swaps are not easy to implement with gateways, which is a downside of this solution next to the lower trust assumption.

Agnostic protocols can orchestrate transfer between arbitrary DLT-based and possibly even non-DLT-based systems. Users connect to a dedicated (trustless) hub-node that is connected to multiple blockchain networks and is able to initiate the exchange of tokens through liquidity pools. Compared to gateways, solutions such as state channels can be completely trustless. Further, native token transfers are possible with the use of liquidity pools. Lastly, channels can be used on any blockchain that can execute smart contracts.

Compared to other solutions, channel-based solutions can execute arbitrary smart contracts within a channel that go far beyond simple value transfers. The modular architecture of bridge solutions might turn out to be the key to success. It means that, for example, blockchain connectors can be added without touching the core protocols. This is especially useful for adding non-EVM compatible blockchains such as Tezor or Hyperledger Fabric. Core protocols should be provably secure and peer-reviewed (or even audited).

DECENTRALIZED FINANCE

Definition and Potential Impact

Decentralized finance (DeFi) is the umbrella term for protocols and applications that enable investors to utilize their cryptoassets in financial applications that mimic conventional capital markets. The interaction of individual products can create complex, and new, financial products on the basis of cryptoassets. This sector enables the unbanked with access to the internet to participate in finance. It is estimated that there are currently 1.7 billion people with access to a smartphone and the internet but no bank account (Diem Association 2019).

At the end of 2022, a value of over US$50 billion is locked in DeFi protocols (DefiLlama 2022). This number is remarkable considering the generally still low adoption of cryptoassets (Feyen et al. 2022 estimate that there are 220 million global users) and their rate of utilization on-chain. In Amler et al. (2021), an overview of the different aspects of DeFi as well as a proper introduction to the topic is given. The authors also hint at the potentially disruptive potential of the open, yet highly functional and relatively capital-dense sector. In fully programmable blockchain ecosystems, any financial asset can, in theory, be replicated on-chain. Thus, blockchain technology can be considered a decentralized alternative to the financial infrastructure if it and the protocols built on it adhere to security, trust, and economic requirements of its users.

Cross-Chain DeFi

One of the main topics of this chapter is the introduction and formal definition of cross-chain DeFi. Therefore, this section defines and discusses this phenomenon.

Cross-chain DeFi (or multi-chain DeFi) describes the usage of decentralized financial protocols, services, or products which effectively operate on or with different blockchain ecosystems, leveraging technology to create interoperability (Figure 13.1). The composability of protocols across different blockchains plays an integral role in the exploitation of properties of individual chains or layers and their provision of financial or asset-related products.

Decentralized finance in particular is a field which can benefit from a greater degree of interoperability and scalability. Currently, light interoperability between

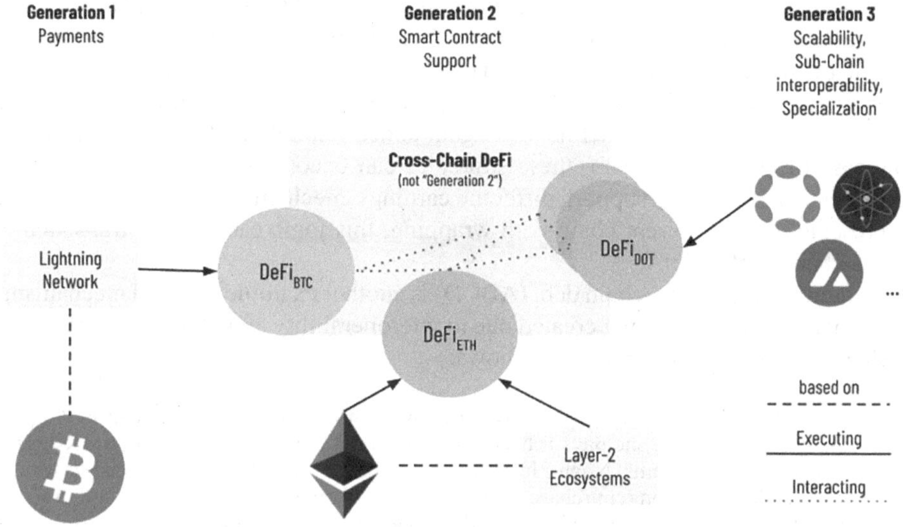

Figure 13.1 *Cross-chain DeFi as the interplay of local DeFi ecosystems of different blockchain generations and the incentive structure for bridges*

different Layer 2 solutions such as rollups and the main ledger is used for arbitrage between DEXs. An example is the difference in prices between Uniswap pools on the Optimism rollup and Arbitrum, or between the Metis rollup and the Ethereum ledger: price movements are not automatically synchronized between these pools despite using the equal protocol/contracts. Users balance differences by performing arbitrage. This scenario occurs because the Uniswap smart contracts can be easily redeployed on any EVM-compatible infrastructure and are deployed in several.

In these cases, efficient bridges can play a major role as the regular off-boarding of funds, for example on optimistic rollups, can take multiple days, up to two weeks. As a consequence, infrastructure scaling these processes is therefore highly valuable.

To name another elementary example, consider an investor whose strategy entails swapping one native token that they hold on-chain for another one (on a different chain). They mostly depend on centralized exchanges and engage in the corresponding counter-party risk and potential regulatory hurdles. While using a centralized exchange theoretically scales well, it does so because the infrastructure is highly centralized (see the scalability trilemma above). While most centralized exchanges support the payout of funds to personal wallets, this is neither a matter of course nor a legal certainty. Further, anti-money-laundering regulation requires proof-of-funds in the European Union before funds which are onboarded to an institution can be used. If the planned strategy involves DeFi protocols on the second chain and a potential swap back to the original ledger, massive manual efforts for the exchange and the investor are created, rendering this hypothetical scenario likely unfeasible.

So-called nested strategies involve the sequential interaction of DeFi protocols. These strategies take the shape of complex financial products. An exemplary practice would be to deposit a pair of tokens to a decentralized exchange (DEX) (for example, Curve; Egorov and Finance 2021), earning governance tokens which are swapped for the underlying asset which is then again added (cumulatively) to the deposit. In the case of cross-chain DeFi, these strategies can become much more layered. As different chains might support different earnings mechanisms and tokens can be represented on a different chain with wrapping, this logic can well be translated to cross-chain applications.

Atomic bonded cross-chain debt (ABCD) is another example of novel mechanisms and financial products being created due to interoperability and DeFi in combination. Tefagh et al. (2020) describe it as follows:

> The idea behind ABCD is inspired by flash swaps. In a flash swap, the loan is not paid to the borrower unless she pays it back immediately at the same block as borrowed (Dan Robinson Hayden Adams, Noah Zinsmeister (2020)). In ABCD this is extended to several blocks i.e. the issuer can repurchase the bond in more than one block but it contains a secret and the bondholder's signature is required everywhere the capital is being utilized.

ABCDs can therefore serve as credit infrastructure for investors and institutions active on different blockchains. This can serve as a primitive building block of financial applications between protocols and ecosystems, and give an indication of what is possible once DeFi can reliably be implemented across multiple ecosystems simultaneously.

The role of decentralized exchanges might further adapt once interoperability exists and cross-chain contracts can be reliably used: decentralized exchanges can be natively built into the cross-chain solution, taking a fee for swaps and forwarding it to those providing liquidity on both respective blockchains. The risks for impermanent loss are equivalent to those of contemporary decentralized exchanges.

The communication between different ledgers can usually be elegantly enabled if chains share a common type (that is, EVM-compatible chains). This vastly simplifies interoperability due to shared encoding and block design.

Cross-chain DEXs

A special role in the context of cross-chain DeFi will be played by cross-chain decentralized exchanges (DEXs). Their role will be twofold: by enabling the possibility to swap assets from one chain to another, they fulfill a role in DeFi (swapping tokens) and in cross-chain applications (moving value from one chain to the other); at the same time, these services can be performed in a clear-cut and well-proven mode of operation (or business model, if you will, for decentralized autonomous organizations). The arbitrage opportunities (for example, price imbalances) resulting from different DeFi ecosystems can be more easily tackled with the use of cross-chain DEXs, as neither intermediaries nor multiple different contracts are necessarily required for the swaps. Furthermore, cross-chain DEXs, if completely decentral, will implement an own pricing mechanism for swaps or will rely on a decentralized oracle network.

The current state of cross-chain DEXs is usually limited in ecosystem support (see ecosystem-specific protocols such as SOLA-X with a dependency on the wormhole bridge) or somewhat centralized/notarized services. In a later section, the dependence on respective bridges and the consequential exposure to technical risk is analyzed in the face of cross-chain DEXs.

The possibility of multi-chain rollups is also worth noting. These rollups can work as DEX and an additional execution layer for generalized DeFi protocols, and offer the possibility to remain off-chain for an extended period of time.

CBDCs and wrapped tokens in interoperable DeFi systems

By 2026, CBDCs of the major currencies (Ghosh 2021) may exist, though this estimate is not conclusive. Independent of CBDCs being blockchain-based or not, they can likely be brought on-chain by tokenization, backing a stablecoin. Once officially accepted currencies are in the space of smart contracts, their movement from one contract to another and from one chain to another will be expected as a requirement by users. The concentration and velocity of CBDCs on different blockchain ecosystems will be a relevant metric for analysts of various disciplines. An analysis of future economies might be done not only on a national basis, but also with an ecosystemic perspective, giving economists true insights on the impact of distributed ledger technologies on the economy. By then, centralized exchanges might become obsolete for some users if blockchain interoperability is mature and systems scale well.

In terms of the implementation of CBDCs across multiple systems, they might be locked and wrapped decentrally with the help of cross-chain contracts (defined in the next section). Currently, wrapped tokens often require trust in a consortium, as demonstrated by wBTC on Ethereum. This solution as a basis for various financial applications is lackluster. Therefore, the cross-chain interconnectivity depends on decentral or at least somewhat trustless mechanisms. Once CBDCs are available in the described manner, they can be used for DeFi, likely even across ecosystems as well. Thereby, the disruptive potential of the decentralized financial sector will be significantly increased.

REQUIREMENTS FOR CROSS-CHAIN DEFI APPLICATIONS AND RISKS

Programmability: Arbitrary Logic Execution in Cross-Chain Contracts?

Cross-chain contracts are smart contracts executed on both chains (Nazarov 2021). They can be considered the next generation of smart contracts, and do not work on only one chain, but across multiple ecosystems. An example could be an offline payment triggering a process in two different ecosystems, or an insurance payment that is triggered by an event observed by an oracle, paying out parties on several different blockchain ecosystems.

To make use of such contracts, several conditions need to be fulfilled. Due to smart contracts not sharing a common language, a different kind of compilation needs to be taken on every end of the interconnecting structure. It highly depends on the layer on which the smart contract is supposed to work: if transactions should directly be triggered on Layer 1, smart contract translation is required. If a Layer 2 protocol is used and accepted, then the transfers can only be made using one protocol. This can, for example, be the case in channel technology which allows arbitrary logic to be executed. The second layer holds the resulting funds and can be withdrawn by owners.

Additional Challenges

Liquidity provision

Liquidity provision is already a challenge for single-chain DEXs. It must be well incentivized by fee models and pool rewards (Egorov and Finance 2021). For cross-chain protocols, the provision of different assets on different chains is even more challenging. While incentivization can work similarly, the liquidity provision itself is nontrivial: funds need to be supplied on different ecosystems (possibly even more than two) and linked by the different contracts in order to map pools correctly. The hard requirement of fund security on all sides heightens the complexity of this issue.

Technical risk

Technical risk is likely the first factor to consider for users and developers. Security and trust issues with bridges have been prevalent and caused massive economic damage in recent years. Chainalysis (2022) estimates that US$2 billion in cryptocurrency has been stolen in cross-chain bridge hacks, the majority of which was stolen in 2022. Attacks on bridges account for more than two-thirds of total funds stolen in the crypto industry up to August 2022.

This theft activity is partly due to the increased demand for bridge solutions, which gave rise to swiftly built solutions that lacked validation in the form of audits and security proofs. This validation should, in theory, be more thorough since each contract on different types of chains needs to be audited instead of a single protocol.

The economic design of a protocol forms another relevant factor in the space of Web3. While the prominent project Terra/Luna did not fail because of security or counterparty risk or even any cross-chain activity, it serves as a showcase for the importance of economically sound DeFi protocols (see Briola et al. 2022 for more details). The Luna blockchain had a native, algorithmically balanced stablecoin which lost its peg when the native token of the ecosystem lost valuation. Because of a lack of collateralization for the stablecoin, while the entire project was attempting to balance itself algorithmically (by automatically trying to regain the peg), the ecosystem essentially lost all value. While technically the blockchain did not fail (it still operates today), the project was rebooted entirely. Complex interactions need to be considered early in the design of protocols, especially if multiple ecosystems might be affected. Thus, simulations and multi-chain audits might gain weight in the Web3 sector with the emergence of novel cross-chain (and DeFi) projects.

Financial risk

The intricacy of potential additional protocols for the transfer of funds, the additional multi-chain tokens, their prices, and ecosystem-dependent dynamics, can play into investment decisions of retailers and institutions. Therefore, increased attention to financial risk mitigation and risk management is important. Novel tools and platforms which focus on the optimization of risk and stabilization of growth rates (for example, Defiria) will gain relevance in the ever more complex evolution of DeFi. The hidden risk for multi-chain analyses may not be disregarded due to higher dependency as well as the potentially higher impact of extreme events affecting different ecosystems.

CONCLUSION AND OUTLOOK

Cross-chain DeFi and cross-chain contracts as a domain will grow in importance due to the demand for decentralized gateways from one blockchain to another. The current state of fragmentation of ecosystems created the opportunity for novel products: different Layer 2 solutions are still competing for the most usable infrastructure types with no clear indication of which will prevail for which problem. Cross-chain DeFi is in a nascent phase and will be a topic of future research in the space. Trust, security, and economic design are primary factors to consider in the analysis of projects involved in blockchain interoperability.

NOTE

1. These new consensus mechanisms, revolving around proof-of-stake, are deemed not fully decentralized by some, for example Saad et al. (2021).

REFERENCES

Abadi, J., and Brunnermeier, M. (2018). Blockchain economics (No. w25407). National Bureau of Economic Research.

Amler, H., Eckey, L., Faust, S., Kaiser, M., Sandner, P., and Schlosser, B. (2021, September). DeFi-ning DeFi: challenges and pathway. In *3rd Conference on Blockchain Research and Applications for Innovative Networks and Services (BRAINS)* (pp. 181–184). IEEE.

Andreina, S., Bohli, J.M., Karame, G., Li, W., and Marson, G.A. (2020). Pots: a secure proof of tee-stake for permissionless blockchains. IEEE Transactions on Services Computing.

Avalanche Foundation (2022). https://www.avax.network/ (accessed: October 25, 2022).

Becker, M., and Bodó, B. (2021). Trust in blockchain-based systems. *Internet Policy Review*, 10(2), 1–10.

Belchior, R., Vasconcelos, A., Guerreiro, S., and Correia, M. (2021). A survey on blockchain interoperability: past, present, and future trends. *ACM Computing Surveys (CSUR)*, 54(8), 1–41.

Bhuptani, A. (2021, October 1). The interoperability trilemma. Connext. https://medium.com/connext/the-interoperability-trilemma-657c2cf69f17.

Briola, A., Vidal-Tomás, D., Wang, Y., and Aste, T. (2022). Anatomy of a Stablecoin's failure: the Terra-Luna case. *Finance Research Letters*, 103358.

Cardano Foundation (2022). https://cardano.org/ (accessed: October 25, 2022).

Chainalysis Inc. (2022). Vulnerabilities in cross-chain bridge protocols emerge as top security risk. https://blog.chainalysis.com/reports/cross-chain-bridge-hacks-2022/ (accessed: October 25, 2022).

Chauhan, B.K., and Patel, D.B. (2022). A systematic review of blockchain technology to find current scalability issues and solutions. In *Proceedings of Second Doctoral Symposium on Computational Intelligence* (pp. 15–29). Springer, Singapore.

Connors, C., and Sarkar, D. (2022). Comparative study of blockchain development platforms: features and applications. *arXiv preprint. arXiv:2210.01913.*

DeFiLlama Data (2022). https://defillama.com/ (accessed: October 30, 2022).

Diem Association (2019). Libra cryptocurrency will increase financial inclusion. https://www.diem.com/en-us/updates/libra-cryptocurrency-will-increase-financial-inclusion/ (accessed: October 29, 2022).

DINNGO Pte Ltd (2019). Cross-chain explained: technical challenge. Medium.com.

Eberhardt, J., and Heiss, J. (2018, December). Off-chaining models and approaches to off-chain computations. In *Proceedings of the 2nd Workshop on Scalable and Resilient Infrastructures for Distributed Ledgers* (pp. 7–12).

Egorov, M., and Finance, C. (2021). Automatic market-making with dynamic peg. Technical report, Curve Finance.

Erwig, A., Faust, S., Riahi, S., and Stöckert, T. (2020). CommitTEE: an efficient and secure commit-chain protocol using TEEs. Cryptology ePrint Archive. https://eprint.iacr.org/2020/1486.

Fei, S., Yan, Z., Ding, W., and Xie, H. (2021). Security vulnerabilities of SGX and countermeasures: A survey. *ACM Computing Surveys (CSUR)*, 54(6), 1–36.

Feyen, E.H., Kawashima, Y., and Mittal, R. (2022). Crypto-assets activity around the world. https://worldbank.org.

Ghosh (2021). ECB will introduce digital EUR by 2026; the future of Crypto as an alternative digital currency may be at stake due to trusted CBDC. Iforex.

Jacobs, M. (2021). How implicit assumptions on the nature of trust shape the understanding of the Blockchain technology. *Philosophy and Technology*, 34(3), 573–587.

Khan, D., Jung, L.T., and Hashmani, M.A. (2021). Systematic literature review of challenges in blockchain scalability. *Applied Sciences*, 11(20), 9372.

Lohachab, A., Garg, S., Kang, B., Amin, M.B., Lee, J., Chen, S., and Xu, X. (2021). Towards interconnected blockchains: a comprehensive review of the role of interoperability among disparate blockchains. *ACM Computing Surveys (CSUR)*, 54(7), 1–39.

Lou, X., Zhang, T., Jiang, J., and Zhang, Y. (2021). A survey of microarchitectural side-channel vulnerabilities, attacks, and defenses in cryptography. *ACM Computing Surveys (CSUR)*, 54(6), 1–37.

Mogavero, F., Visconti, I., Vitaletti, A., and Zecchini, M. (2021, September). The blockchain quadrilemma: when also computational effectiveness matters. In *2021 IEEE Symposium on Computers and Communications (ISCC)* (pp. 1–6). IEEE.

Nasir, M.H., Arshad, J., Khan, M.M., Fatima, M., Salah, K., and Jayaraman, R. (2022). Scalable blockchains—a systematic review. *Future Generation Computer Systems*, 126, 136–162.

Nazarov, S. (2021). *Keynote on the Future of Hybrid Smart Contracts*. YouTube.

Poon, J., and Dryja, T. (2016). The bitcoin lightning network: scalable off-chain instant payments.
Saad, M., Z. Qin, Ren, K., Nyang, D., Mohaisen, D. (2021). e-PoS: making proof-of-stake decentralized and fair. In *IEEE Transactions on Parallel and Distributed Systems*, 32(8), 1961–1973. doi: 10.1109/TPDS.2020.3048853.
Schulte, S., Sigwart, M., Frauenthaler, P., and Borkowski, M. (2019, September). Towards blockchain interoperability. In *International Conference on Business Process Management* (pp. 3–10). Springer, Cham.
Sguanci, C., Spatafora, R., and Vergani, A.M. (2021). Layer 2 blockchain scaling: a survey. *arXiv preprint. arXiv:2107.10881.*
Solana Foundation (2022). https://solana.com/ (accessed: October 25, 2022).
Tefagh, M., Bagheri, F., Khajehpour, A., and Abdi, M. (2020, December). Atomic bonded cross-chain debt. In *3rd International Conference on Blockchain Technology and Applications* (pp. 50–54).
Zamyatin, Alexei, Al-Bassam, M., Zindros, D., Kokoris-Kogias, E., Moreno-Sanchez, P., Kiayias, A., and Knottenbelt, W.J. (2021). Sok: communication across distributed ledgers. In *Financial Cryptography and Data Security: 25th International Conference, FC 2021, Virtual Event, March 1–5, Revised Selected Papers, Part II*, 25 (pp. 3–36).

14. Non-fungible tokens (NFTs)

Mieszko Mazur and Efstathios Polyzos

INTRODUCTION

Contrary to popular belief, a non-fungible token (NFT) is not an image. NFTs emerged as a way of recording the ownership of a unique asset in a database called blockchain, which refers to a tamper-proof, auditable, and globally decentralized ledger uncontrolled by any individual, group, or authority. Because blockchains are made to operate in perpetuity—run by powerful machines and a computer code—the data recorded on the blockchain should be readily accessible at any point in time, forever. This characteristic implies that the ownership of any unique asset that exists, be it digital or real, can be represented by the NFT and easily verified.

Historically, proving ownership and provenance of an asset has not always been effective. To do so, people have relied on authority and trust. Yet, trust erodes and authorities may favor the wealthy and powerful. The NFT solves this problem, as it records the ownership on the blockchain without relying on the intermediary (authority). Moreover, if desired, the holder of the NFT is able to prove the ownership directly, at any time. Also, NFT ownership can be easily transferred at a near-zero cost, instantaneously, circumventing the slow, costly, and inefficient traditional financial infrastructure.

Despite its novelty, NFTs immediately attracted a large number of creators, organizations, and investors. Some of the most established global corporations including McDonald's, Nike, Coca-Cola, Tiffany, LVMH, and Warner Bros launched numerous NFT collections. Accomplished artists (for example, Damien Hirst) began experimenting with NFTs. Moreover, various sports clubs around the globe now issue NFTs to their loyal supporters. In crypto finance, NFTs are used extensively as a proof of liquidity provision in decentralized cryptocurrency exchanges (for example, Uniswap). Interestingly, each such NFT is also graphically unique.

What are the potential applications of NFTs? They are countless. NFT can serve as the underlying technology for fundraising, issuance of financial assets (for example, derivatives, special shares of stock, bonds), issuance of legal instruments (for example, deeds, contracts, certificates). Real estate, art, music, collectibles, brands, luxury items, identity, and much more. Every unique item could be represented by an NFT.

This chapter offers key insights into the NFT functionality and architecture from the perspective of decentralized finance. We start off with an introduction of the primary and secondary NFT markets, including different types of NFT exchanges, minting, and trading. Next, we move on to the NFT liquidity provision, staking, borrowing and lending, as well as fundraising. Further, based on a large dataset of roughly 2 million NFT trades from the leading blue-chip NFT collections, we examine NFT investability from the perspective of raw and market-adjusted returns, during both the bull and bear market periods.

Throughout the chapter we refer to various decentralized finance (DeFi) protocols and NFT collections. Because of their multitude, it is not feasible to cover them all. Specifically, they are selected based on market activity, relevance, and time since inception (protocols that have survived longest are given a priority). It must be emphasized that we, the authors, are not invested in any of these protocols or NFTs, either directly or indirectly.

RELEASING NFTs TO THE PUBLIC: NFT PRIMARY MARKETS

In this section, we discuss mechanisms used to create and disseminate NFTs to the public in primary NFT offerings that take the form of either a sale or a giveaway. The process can be thought of as a decentralized counterpart of the public placement of stocks and bonds in financial markets, although it is much more simplified and cost efficient.

NFT Offer (Mint) Price

Almost each new NFT collection is sold to the public at a price that is set at a relatively low level, with the objective to enable greater participation in the offer. Some NFT collections are distributed free of charge. The offer price is called the mint price, as the price reflects the creation of a token, which can be used as money (traditionally manufactured in a mint). For example, the mint price for Bored Ape Yacht Club was 0.08 ETH, CrypToadz was 0.069 ETH, and CryptoPunks were given away free.

Because the NFT mint prices are usually low, in both absolute and relative terms, the mint price itself is not a success indicator for the NFT collection. More useful as a success predictor is the speed at which the collection sells at launch. Most successful collections, in terms of both market valuation and artistic crafting, sell out in the primary market in several minutes (for example, Azuki, Doodles).

NFT Mint (Drop)

"NFT drop" and "NFT mint" are used interchangeably to indicate the process of NFT production and transfer of ownership from the NFT smart contract to the blockchain address of the NFT holder in the primary sale: direct NFT sale by the NFT creator. As mentioned above, the buyer pays the mint price and the transaction (gas) fee. The NFT drop takes place on a specific date and hour.

Distribution of NFTs to the wallet addresses of the buyers is purely random. Therefore, one is unable to control the rarity characteristics of the NFT purchased on the primary market. Obviously, rare traits should make the NFT more desirable and thus more valuable as compared to characteristics that are more common. However, the match between the identity of the NFT and the identity of the buyer is beyond the control of both the buyer and the NFT creator, and therefore cannot be easily manipulated.

The graphic representation of the NFT can be instant or delayed. Instant NFT "reveal" by the NFT creators lends more credibility to the entire NFT project.

Whitelisting

Whitelisting (also referred to as "allowlist") is an activity performed ahead of the NFT mint, during which the NFT project creator registers the wallet address of the potential NFT buyers. Whitelisting allows the NFT creator to estimate the demand for the collection. Because whitelisting may also verify the monetary balance of the wallet, the creators register only the interested buyers with minimum liquidity.

In exchange for early registration, the NFT buyers are offered lower mint price vis-à-vis the price set for public sale scheduled later on. From this perspective, whitelisting can be seen as a pre-sale for the self-selected buyers. Marketing is another important aspect of whitelisting. Buyers are often asked to advertise the project by disseminating key information about it from their own private social media accounts (for example, Discord, Twitter).

Another important dimension of whitelisting is the avoidance of "gas wars" on the mint date. "Gas" refers to the unit of blockchain capacity, whose price varies depending on the demand for the blockchain space per unit of time. Blockchain architecture allows blockchain users to pay higher transaction fees in order to transact faster, ahead of those who decide to pay a standard fee. If the anticipated demand for the NFT is high, buyers with high net worth may outbid ordinary retail investors and capture the bulk of the new NFT collection. For this reason, whitelisting has become a standard for the NFT communities that value economic fairness.

SECONDARY NFT MARKETS

The majority of NFT exchanges are decentralized,[1] meaning that the exchange is effectively a nexus of smart contracts and that the trade occurs between the blockchain addresses of the buyer and seller via a smart contract that registers the change in the NFT ownership. Consequently, the exchange itself does not hold the NFT inventory. The exchange, however, provides the pricing mechanism, also a smart contract, that interacts directly with the blockchain.

Decentralized NFT exchanges can be broadly classified into those that use an order book and those that use an automated market maker (AMM). The latter rely on NFT liquidity pools.

Another category of NFT exchanges are those that are built around a particular NFT collection and are embedded in official websites linked to a specific NFT project. Typically, these exchanges trade NFTs from a single collection only.

Traditional auction houses, which ventured into the NFT universe early on, exploring new markets and new directions for growth, form the last category of NFT exchanges. For example, Christie's sold the most expensive NFT to date *Everydays: The First 5000 Days* by Beeple, for over $69 million. The same company auctioned several CryptoPunks, as well as NFTs from other collections and creators. Recently, Christie's announced the launch of the NFT exchange akin to OpenSea, where trading takes place directly on the blockchain.

Order Book NFT Exchanges

The largest and most successful NFT exchange to date is OpenSea, which can be thought of as an order book exchange. As of October 31, 2022, the lifetime volume on OpenSea amounted to $32.3 billion. OpenSea displays the graphic representation (image) of NFTs together with the history of ownership as recorded on the blockchain. However, not all displayed NFTs are made available for purchase.

Because the exchange is effectively permissionless, anyone can put up an NFT for sale. The seller selects the price (fixed or auction) and the duration of the listing. Typically, there are two types of auctions. In the English auction, the NFT is sold to the highest bidder. In the Dutch auction, the price falls over time during the duration of the auction according to the predefined schedule and the NFT is sold to the quickest bidder. The seller may set the reserve price and has the right to abstain from the sale to the winning bidder (either highest or lowest).

OpenSea provides a communication platform for potential buyers and sellers. This allows for a seller to quietly sell to a specific buyer, and for the buyer to make a direct, unsolicited offer to the particular seller. OpenSea also serves as an aggregator. It sources the publicly available blockchain data to display NFTs together with a transaction history, NFT rarity properties, and other metadata.

Automated Market Maker (AMM) NFT Exchanges

NFT AMM exchanges rely on NFT liquidity pools and allow for direct swaps between the NFTs and the fungible cryptocurrency (for example, ETH). Liquidity pools are created by users of the NFT exchange in a permissionless manner: unlike in the traditional financial system, anyone who owns an NFT may provide liquidity to the NFT exchange. The liquidity provision is rewarded with fees paid by the users of the exchange. Fee level is determined by the liquidity provider and may vary quite considerably even among very similar NFT pools.

The price relationship (bonding curve) between the NFT and the cryptocurrency is selected by the liquidity provider and can be either exponential or linear. In any case, each bonding curve can be customized (unique), so that it reflects the varying degree of curvature. This curvature is defined by the price change or delta. For linear (exponential) pools, delta is defined as an absolute value (percentage). It follows that, in absolute terms, delta can be either fixed or variable.

Typically, the NFT delta is positive, meaning that a sale of the NFT from the pool will increase the price of the remaining NFTs in the pool, *ceteris paribus*. However, the delta can also be set to zero, in which case each single NFT in a given pool sells for exactly the same price, regardless of the NFT current supply in the pool.

How can one create a pool of NFTs, knowing that each NFT is unique and therefore must be valued differently? Arguably, the NFTs provided in a pool belong to a cluster, implying that they are part of the same collection and their market valuations do not differ significantly from one another. Furthermore, it seems safe to say that the price level of the NFTs in the same liquidity pool is close to the minimum price level within a specific NFT collection (floor price).

Needless to say, the NFT buyer is able to choose a particular NFT from the pool, unlike in a classic decentralized exchange where all cryptocurrencies are indistinguishable from one another.

NFT Aggregators

An NFT aggregator refers to the NFT marketplace that sources NFT listing information from other existing NFT marketplaces. The aggregator provides a broad view of the current state of the market (NFT discovery), facilitates price comparisons, and most importantly, offers positive and substantial savings on transaction costs (for example, 40 percent) that may reach relatively high levels during hot NFT market periods.

More specifically, the aggregator allows for making the transactions in bulk (buying, selling, or listing), despite the fact that NFTs are simultaneously put up for sale in different markets, and some of the NFTs may be listed more than once at different ask prices. In short, aggregators route all existing decentralized NFT supply and demand into one compact venue.

Aggregators continuously expand their scope of operations by rolling out new attractive features. Some of them allow for a “floor sweep” functionality, which is a single transaction of a batch purchase of the lowest-priced NFTs within the same NFT collection. *Ex post*, floor sweeps may substantially increase the entry price for investors within the specific NFT collection. Somewhat related to this point is the indicator of “floor depth,” which shows the number of NFT listings per price range starting from the floor price. Typically, the increment is one unit of the cryptocurrency (for example, 1 ETH).

Aggregators integrate not only varying decentralized markets but also other DeFi protocols. Some of them offer NFT appraisals based on machine-learning technology and flag NFTs that are considered overvalued or undervalued, and assess the magnitude of the misvaluation.

NFT Borrowing and Lending

There are decentralized platforms that specialize only in NFT borrowing and lending. NFT owners are able to take loans in fungible tokens by pledging their NFTs. The loans are overcollateralized, meaning that the market value of the NFT at the time of the loan initiation is greater than the value of the loan by a safe margin (typically 20 percent). However, the level of collateral is unique each time, as it depends on the NFT characteristics and the individual preferences of the lender.

Loan terms are negotiated off-chain. Borrowers set loan terms including the choice of borrowing currency, interest rate, and duration. Lenders may either accept the loan terms, or alternatively make counter-offers. Once the terms are accepted by both parties and the loan is matched, the settlement of the loan occurs on-chain and is recorded on the blockchain.

The reference value for the NFT collateral is usually the lowest list price of the NFT from a specific collection at a point in time (that is, floor price). Needless to say, the floor price is subject to price volatility.

Because the loan terms are typically non-standard (unique), the claim to the pledged asset (NFT), takes the form of the NFT as well. Upon loan initiation, both borrower and lender receive one NFT that represents the claim to the pledged asset. The asset is transferred to the borrower (or lender) once the loan is repaid (or defaults). Unlike in most decentralized lending protocols, loan defaults do not rely on arbitrageurs.

The analysis of the data retrieved from Dune Analytics on Arcade platform reveals that in October 2022 the typical NFT loan was a short-term contract (53 days), average loan size was about $120 000, the default rate was 6 percent, and the average annual percenage rate (APR) hovered around 86 percent per month.

NFT Staking

NFTs can be staked in the processes known as liquidity staking and inventory staking with a number of important differences between the two types. Upon staking, the protocol turns an NFT into a fungible token that can be instantly cashed in on the NFT exchange. In that way, NFT staking generates liquidity by adding NFTs to the market supply, and provides the option to the NFT holder to exit the investment at any time. In other words, the staker may exit without reclaiming the NFT, but the monetary equivalent of it. If the staker chooses to exit with the NFT, the protocol does not guarantee that it will be exactly the same NFT that was originally staked.

In inventory staking, the staker locks the NFT in the smart contract and receives a yield. Yield is variable and financed with the transaction fees paid by exchange participants. The fraction of the fees that accrue to the staker depends on the relative value of the staked NFTs to the aggregate value of all NFTs staked in the inventory. It may also depend on the type of staking. Typically, liquidity staking yields higher return than inventory staking.

In liquidity staking, NFT gets locked in a smart contract together with some amount of ETH. Unlike inventory staking, the rewards to the staker (accrued fees) are not compounded and can be cashed in at any time. Upon exit, the staker may redeem less NFTs and more ETH depending on the supply and demand. For example, if the demand for NFTs is high, the staker will receive back a significantly lower number of

NFTs versus ETH. In the extreme case, the staker may not be able to redeem NFTs. Conversely, in inventory staking, the staker is always guaranteed to get back the same number of NFTs as originally staked.

Staking in-game NFTs including land NFTs can be regarded as another category of NFT staking. Land staking resembles renting out property in the traditional economy. Staking in-game NFTs means effectively lending NFTs to active players (through smart contracts) who cannot afford pricey game items.

Numerous NFT collections offer direct staking opportunities. NFT staking infrastructure exists separately on the official websites of the NFT collections, similar to secondary NFT markets hosted by the collections themselves (for example, Creepz, Jungle Freaks, Sneaky Vampire Syndicate). Staking rewards are paid out in a native token of the collection (for example, $LOOMI, $JUNGLE, $BLOOD). The tokens can be cashed out for other cryptocurrencies or fiat currencies. Equally important, these tokens can be used to receive discounts on the mint price of the forthcoming derivative NFT collections that are released following the NFT genesis (first ever) collection. For example, the holders of $BLOOD can receive up to 50 percent discount for Sneaky Vampiress Syndicate NFTs, a derivative collection of the Sneaky Vampire Syndicate. Certain collections prioritize holders of their genesis NFTs who also own NFT staking tokens.

NFT Fundraising

NFTs are a highly effective charity tool. Funds can be raised quickly in a cost-efficient way, while the disbursement of donations together with the treasury can be actively monitored by the public through the blockchain. This attribute is generally not the case within the existing framework of charitable giving, where financial transactions are informationally opaque.

The nexus of incentives embedded in the NFT allows for the collaborative equilibrium between parties in the fundraising activity that did not exist in the economy before. For example, a nonprofit launches a fundraising campaign by selling NFT artwork by an independent creator, directly finances the beneficiary, and monitors the use of funds in real time. The benefits accrue for each of the participating parties: the nonprofit reaches its statutory objective, the NFT artist receives royalties from the secondary sales of the NFT, and most importantly, the money is spent directly on the cause itself and permanently improves social wellbeing of the beneficiaries.

A recent example of such a charity model is the partnership between the United Nations Children's Fund (UNICEF) Giga project and artist Nadieh Bremer to connect every school in the world to the internet by 2030. Another notable case is the issuance of NFTs by Dallas Symphony Orchestra to help fellow musicians during the COVID-19 pandemic.

DATA, SAMPLE, AND DESCRIPTIVE STATISTICS

Data

Our dataset consists of the leading blue-chip NFT collections including CryptoPunks, Bored Ape Yacht Club, Mutant Ape Yacht Club, Bored Ape Kennel Yacht Club, Axie Infinity, Sorare, Art Blocks, Sandbox, Decentraland, and the Ethereum Name Service (ENS). These collections can be classified into several different groups including NFT Profile Pictures (PFP), NFT Gaming, NFT Art, NFT Metaverse, and NTF "Other."

We derive data from the OpenSea application programming interface (API). The data include information on price, currency, type of sale, token ID, collection ID, timestamp, as well as the buyer and seller by wallet addresses. Due to numerous miniscule transactions at extremely low prices much below 1 ETH, we truncate NFT price distribution in the lower tail at the 0.01 threshold. Also, we remove one transaction in the upper tail of the price distribution that belongs to a CryptoPunk #9998, which sold on October 28, 2021 for 124.45 ETH. This transaction was effectively a self-sale (to the same wallet address) and therefore cannot be considered a real sale.

Table 14.1 presents the NFT breakdown into categories together with the NFT release date, total supply, and market capitalizations of each of these collections as of June 30, 2022, denominated both in ETH and USD. Market capitalization is calculated as the sum of the last transaction price per specific NFT within the collection, identifiable by the ID number. Market Cap in USD is equal to the market price in ETH multiplied by the ETH/USD exchange rate as of June 30, 2022.

Categorizing NFTs

As seen in Table 14.1, CryptoPunks is one of the oldest and most revered NFT collections, launched in June 2017. It belongs to the generative art movement, and NFTs from this series could be claimed free of charge at the time of the mint. At present, the six most valuable NFTs ever belong to CryptoPunks. Moreover, in the ten highest NFT sales, CryptoPunks are listed seven times.[2] The last noteworthy transaction took place in February 2022—CryptoPunk #5822 changed hands for 8000 ETH (the equivalent of over US$23 million at the time of the transaction).

The second most recognizable collection is Bored Ape Yacht Club (BAYC) together with its derivative collections—Mutant Ape Yacht Club (MAYC) and Bored Ape Kennel Club (BAKC) launched throughout 2021. The highest price recorded for a BAYC is for the NFT #3749 which sold for 740 ETH or $2.9 million in September 2021.

Gaming NFTs have an inherent use in video games that use blockchain technology and play-to-earn incentive system for participants. Perhaps the most popular play-to-earn game to date is Axie Infinity, which allows players to earn NFTs that are used as strategic components of the game. For some players, earned NFTs represent

Table 14.1 *NFT collection type, supply, and market capitalization*

NFT Collection (1)	NFT Category (2)	Release Date (3)	Token Supply (4)	Supply Type (5)	Market Cap (ETH) (6)	Market Cap (mil USD) (7)
CryptoPunks	PFP	23.06.2017	10 000	Fixed	481 466	513.9
Bored Ape Yacht Club	PFP	30.04.2021	10 000	Fixed	349 738	373.3
Mutant Ape Yacht Club	PFP	28.08.2021	20 000	Fixed	191 291	204.2
Bored Ape Kennel Club	PFP	17.06.2021	10 000	Fixed	36 173	38.6
Axie Infinity	Gaming	14.03.2018	283 764	Exp.	18 953	22.2
Sorare	Gaming	10.05.2020	335 905	Exp.	36 339	38.8
Art Blocks	Art	27.11.2020	206 912	Exp.	23 204	24.8
Sandbox	Metaverse	29.11.2021	166 464	Fixed	52 048	55.6
Decentraland	Metaverse	20.02.2020	90 601	Fixed	453	0.48
Ethereum Name Service (ENS)	Other	04.05.2017	2 558 989	Exp.	25 288	26.9

Note: The table reports ten leading blue-chip NFT collections that can be classified into different categories including NFT Profile Picture (PFP), NFT Gaming, NFT Art, NFT Metaverse, and NFT "Other." Market Cap is the NFT market capitalization calculated as the sum of the most recent transacted prices across all NFTs within the NFT collection. Market Cap denominated in USD is based on ETH/USD exchange rate as of June 30, 2022. Exp. stands for expanding supply. The data are derived from OpenSea API.

an additional source of income in real-life settings. A very different NFT series is Sorare, a collection of digital cards featuring the world's famous footballers.

Another intriguing NFT category is digital land sold in digital universes called metaverses. There are two leading projects in this domain: Sandbox and Decentraland. Many well-known business organizations have already ventured into the virtual property market including fashion houses (Gucci), commercial banks (JP Morgan, HSBC, Standard Chartered), consulting firms (PwC), manufacturers (Adidas), hospitality groups (Regal Hotels), auction houses (Sotheby's), and many more.

The most expensive NFT to date belongs to the category of NFT art. *Everydays: the First 5000 Days* by Beeple sold for 42 329 ETH in March 2021 (the equivalent of US$69.3 million at the time of the transaction). NFT art signifies a very promising arena for artists and creators, as it allows for direct and uncensored access to markets (for example, collectors, investors). Probably the two immediately recognizable NFT art series to date are *Ringers* by Dimitri Cherniak and *Fidenza* by Tyler Hobbs.

Our last category contains NFTs that do not belong to any of the above groups, due to very different characteristics. Ethereum Name Service (ENS), one of the most well-known, is a decentralized naming protocol on the Ethereum blockchain similar to the existing centralized Domain Name System (DNS).

NFT Market Capitalization

We compute market capitalization as the sum of the last transaction prices on a specific NFT at the collection level. Clearly, different NFTs sell at different points in time, so the market capitalization may contain information on transactions from the recent or more distant past. More importantly, many NFTs in any given collection never sell. This fact understates the true market value of the NFT series.

As seen in Table 14.1, CryptoPunks is the most valuable NFT collection to date worth close to 0.5 million ETH, which is the equivalent of US$0.5 billion at the June 30, 2022 exchange rate. It should be noted, however, that on June 30, 2022 the ETH/USD rate was close to its local minimum after the peak in November 2021. When we recalculate market capitalization of CryptoPunks at the November 3, 2021 peak exchange rate (US$4607.19), we obtain the value of over US$2.2 billion.

The next most valuable NFT collection is Bored Ape Yacht Club (349,738 ETH or US$370 million). Together with its two follow-up derivative collections, its market capitalization amounts to 570,202 ETH (US$616 million). The remaining NFT collections in our sample are an order of magnitude smaller. Among them, two stand out: Sandbox (NFT Metaverse) (US$56 million) and Sorare (NFT Game) (US$39 million). Somewhat surprising is the relatively low valuation of Axie Infinity (US$22 million), especially given that it was created in 2018, long before other NFT collections.

Overall, CryptoPunks and BAYC dominate the entire NFT secondary market, with market capitalization dominance levels of 40 percent and 29 percent, respectively. CryptoPunks has the historical advantage of being the first NFT collection of its kind, launched in 2017. BAYC has a strong community and focuses on developing high-quality, follow-up collections and ultimately a metaverse.

NFT Supply

Most NFT PFP collections have a fixed supply. The supply level is typically equal to 10 000 distinct NFTs. These NFTs differ from one another by certain predefined characteristics in a way that each NFT is created visibly unique. It seems that the number 10 000 was determined historically: the first full-fledged NFT collection of CryptoPunks in 2017 featured 10 000 distinct NFTs. Other creators followed suit. For example, BAYC, Azuki, Moonbirds, Doodles, World of Women, and many others chose the 10 000 standard. Theoretically, the limited supply should have a positive impact on the NFT price.

On the other hand, there are collections without any supply limit. For instance, Sorare will continue issuing NFTs representing the world's best football players. Since every season and every tournament introduces new high-performing players, the total number of Sorare NFTs will keep rising. Similarly for Ethereum Name Service, the number of NFTs will continue to increase with the number of new domain creations.

It should be noted that, by choice of the collectors and investors, many NFTs obtained in the primary market are not traded in the secondary market. This is another important factor that limits the circulating supply and should therefore have a positive impact on the NFT price.

EMPIRICAL RESULTS

NFT Market Activity

As shown in Table 14.2, the median NFT turnover for most PFP collections is 2.00 (CryptoPunks, BAYC, MAYC), implying that a typical PFP NFT is traded twice during the sample period. However, this picture changes somewhat when we take into account the duration of the collection: knowing that CryptoPunks launched in 2017, its turnover per unit of time is significantly lower compared to BAYC, for example, which launched in 2021.

We confirm the above observation by noting the total NFT turnover (Table 14.2, column 7). For CryptoPunks, it is 18 719 NFTs traded since June 2017 (without distinguishing their ID), whereas for BAYC the total turnover is 42 percent higher ("hard" supply for both collections is identical and is equal to 10 000).

When we take into account the value of the traded NFTs (NFT volume in Panel B), we notice that the total trading volume on CryptoPunks (column 7) is 30 percent higher than BAYC, and is equal to 816 549 ETH. The median price of an NFT from the CryptoPunks collection is 27 ETH, whereas the median BAYC transacted for 3.9 ETH. In other words, a typical CryptoPunk is about seven times more valuable than a typical BAYC. The same result is true for maximums of both distributions. The most valuable CryptoPunk to date sold for 8000 ETH, whereas the highest price ever paid for BAYC is 1024 ETH. Here again the difference is almost eightfold (column 6). Overall, the above statistics provide more detailed information that helps explain the dominance of CryptoPunks in the NFT market.

The remaining NFT collections follow different market activity patterns. First, quite surprisingly, they are less frequently traded. For example, the in-game items (Axie Infinity), football cards (Sorare), land plots (Sandbox and Decentraland), and NFT art (Art Blocks) trade, at the median, only once (Table 14.2, column 3). Their total turnover is significantly higher than PFP NFTs, however, their total supply is substantially higher as well. By way of example, only about 49 percent of all Axies are transacted (139 276 / 283 764), whereas the relative turnover ratio for CryptoPunks is equal to 270 percent (26 535 / 10 000). In other words, since the collection's release in 2017, a CryptoPunk NFT traded almost three times, as compared to the total supply. A similar example concerns NFT land plots. In the Sandbox metaverse 41 104 digital land NFTs have been turned over, out of the total supply of 166 464 (about 25 percent of all).

Significantly lower turnover for NFTs from categories other than PFP is followed by their substantially lower NFT volume. This is mainly due to relatively low

Table 14.2 NFT turnover and trading volume

NFT Collection (1)	Mean (2)	Median (3)	S.D. (4)	Min (5)	Max (6)	Total (7)
Panel A: NFT Turnover						
CryptoPunks	2.85	2.00	2.07	1.00	15.00	18 719
Bored Ape Yacht Club	3.03	2.00	2.04	1.00	16.00	26 535
Mutant Ape Yacht Club	2.61	2.00	1.68	1.00	16.00	33 061
Bored Ape Kennel Club	3.43	3.00	2.41	1.00	19.00	21 861
Axie Infinity	1.26	1.00	0.59	1.00	28.00	139 276
Sorare	1.68	1.00	1.04	1.00	15.00	437 980
Art Blocks	1.62	1.00	0.96	1.00	7.00	3 734
Sandbox	1.56	1.00	0.89	1.00	10.00	41 104
Decentraland	1.71	1.00	1.14	1.00	6.00	3 306
ENS	1.22	1.00	0.58	1.00	10.00	91 036
Panel B: NFT volume						
CryptoPunks	46.95	26.99	100.68	0.02	8 000	816 549
Bored Ape Yacht Club	23.51	3.90	40.13	0.02	1 024	622 973
Mutant Ape Yacht Club	12.86	8.25	10.09	0.01	350	424 422
Bored Ape Kennel Club	4.64	3.50	3.63	0.07	89	101 279
Axie Infinity	0.18	0.09	1.81	0.01	300	25 078
Sorare	0.14	0.05	0.59	0.01	116.2	49 885
Art Blocks	8.23	4.50	28.73	0.15	945	30 713
Sandbox	1.94	1.60	1.84	0.02	120	79 473
Decentraland	5.41	3.29	111.15	0.09	6 388	17 871
ENS	0.43	0.06	2.37	0.01	420	35 809

Note: The table presents NFT turnover and NFT volume in the NFT secondary market. NFT turnover (volume) is the number (value) of NFTs traded since the release of the NFT collection. NFT volume is based on all available prices per NFT since the NFT collection launch. We omit the last recorded transaction on CryptoPunk #9989 that sold for 124 457.1 ETH, as this transaction has been documented to be a wash-trade. The data are derived from OpenSea API.

average values of NFTs that belong to, for instance, NFT Gaming or NFT Metaverse vis-à-vis NFT PFP, whose nominal values are much larger. For example, the median NFT in Sandbox (Decentraland) metaverse trades for 1.60 (3.29) ETH, whereas CryptoPunks (MAYC) sell for 26.99 (8.25) ETH. It must be emphasized that the price of the NFT in the primary market is equally low for all NFT collections, regardless of the category.

Return to NFTs

Table 14.3 presents returns to NFTs. We estimate the returns in two different ways: on a trade-by-trade basis (short-term), and as buy-and-hold returns (long-term). In both approaches, NFTs within each collection are matched by NFT ID and are used for the return calculation on the condition that they have been traded at least twice.

Buy-and-hold return is computed as the ratio of the last available sale price divided by the first price minus one. Therefore, the holding period in buy-and-hold returns may vary depending on the specific NFT. A buy-and-hold return can be thought of as the geometric return based on the intermediate trade-by-trade returns.

As shown in Table 14.3, Panel A, the average returns of CryptoPunks and BAYC are spectacular and amount to roughly 1600 percent and 1300 percent per trade, respectively (column 2). Among other NFT collections, Art Blocks, ENS, and Sandbox yield the average return ranging from 220 percent to 160 percent per trade. Nevertheless, average returns are sensitive to outsized returns in the upper tail of the distribution, particularly for CryptoPunks and BAYC (column 6).

The median is more informative about typical NFT returns (column 3). As expected, medians paint a different picture as compared to the means. Returns of NFT PFP are still high; however, the return differences between different NFT categories are not exceedingly large. For example, BAYC yields 83 percent at the median, whereas Art Blocks and Sandbox yield 47 percent and 37 percent, respectively. The latter collections outperform CryptoPunks (31 percent). The worst-performing NFT collection is Axie Infinity that generates -3 percent per NFT sale. Decentraland performs only slightly better (3 percent).

On the buy-and-hold basis, BAYC outperforms CryptoPunks at both the mean and median, and both NFT collections outpace other NFT categories by at least the order of magnitude. The median return from holding BAYC is roughly 2000 percent. CryptoPunks generate 270 percent, whereas the two derivative collections of BAYC (BACK and MAYC) deliver 152 percent and 93 percent, respectively.

NFTs that belong to other categories do not perform as well as NFT PFPs; nevertheless, they deliver returns that are quite substantial. For example, Art Blocks and Sandbox yield a buy-and-hold return of 95 percent and 83 percent at the median, respectively. The worst performers are gaming NFTs: Sorare earns 11 percent, and Axie Infinity generates -6 percent.

Return to NFTs in the Bull and Bear Markets

In the following analysis, we split the sample into bull and bear market periods. We are particularly interested in the NFT performance during the bear market. We select the week of May 9, 2022 as the start date of the bear market. This point in time is related to the Terra stablecoin de-peg from USD, which caused a contagion effect between various cryptocurrency firms, and ultimately led to the cryptocurrency market crash. In that week, the NFT volume stood at $857 643 295, a drop from $1 836 994 002 the week before (or 47 percent).[3] The weekly volume continued to decline thereafter until the end of the sample period. We partition our time-frame into the period prior to May 9, 2022 (bull market) and the period commencing on May 9, 2022 (bear market).

As reported in Table 14.3 (Panel C), the returns measured on the trade-by-trade basis during the bull market period are quite similar to those displayed in Panel A. For the bear market, the best-performing NFT collection is BAYC that generates

Table 14.3 Raw returns to NFTs

NFT Collection (1)	Mean (2)	Median (3)	S.D. (4)	Min (5)	Max (6)	Total (7)
Panel A: Trade-by-trade return (x 100%)						
CryptoPunks	16.31	0.31	114.5	-0.99	5 999	11 252
Bored Ape Yacht Club	12.79	0.83	63.86	-0.99	4 899	17 783
Mutant Ape Yacht Club	0.69	0.19	10.10	-0.99	1 399	20 451
Bored Ape Kennel Club	0.59	0.24	1.32	-0.99	43	15 573
Axie Infinity	0.27	-0.03	2.25	-0.99	99	28 955
Sorare	0.41	0.11	3.48	-0.99	570	126 253
Art Blocks	2.17	0.45	5.79	-0.77	59	1 429
Sandbox	1.61	0.37	3.41	-0.99	69	15 284
Decentraland	0.11	0.03	0.51	-0.92	6.52	1 670
ENS	1.99	0.33	10.73	-0.99	550	16 234
Panel B: Buy-and-hold return (x 100%)						
CryptoPunks	82.12	2.67	243.96	-0.99	3 249	3 711
Bored Ape Yacht Club	94.85	19.84	180.35	-0.99	3 224	6 206
Mutant Ape Yacht Club	1.80	0.93	17.32	-0.99	1 443	8 058
Bored Ape Kennel Club	2.75	1.52	3.85	-0.99	92	4 450
Axie Infinity	0.27	-0.06	2.41	-0.98	179	23 218
Sorare	0.61	0.14	4.96	-0.99	726	78 852
Art Blocks	4.58	0.95	9.57	-0.64	79	910
Sandbox	3.29	0.83	5.27	-0.99	55	8 137
Decentraland	0.86	0.52	1.16	-0.55	3.45	16
ENS	3.54	0.52	32.26	-0.99	2 777	9 637
Panel C: NFT bull market						
CryptoPunks	16.72	0.32	116.78	-0.99	5 999	10 742
Bored Ape Yacht Club	11.89	0.83	61.90	-0.99	4 899	17 190
Mutant Ape Yacht Club	0.70	0.20	10.40	-0.99	1 399	18 929
Bored Ape Kennel Club	0.60	0.25	1.33	-0.99	43.00	14 947
Axie Infinity	0.27	-0.03	2.25	-0.99	99.00	28 955
Sorare	0.41	0.11	3.48	-0.99	570.43	126 231
Art Blocks	2.17	0.45	5.79	-0.77	59.00	1 429
Sandbox	1.69	0.39	3.48	-0.99	69.00	14 522
Decentraland	0.12	0.03	0.48	-0.88	6.06	1 520
ENS	2.43	0.50	12.09	-0.99	550.27	10 163
Panel D: NFT bear market						
CryptoPunks	7.56	0.08	43.17	-0.69	494	515
Bored Ape Yacht Club	39.07	0.73	103.05	-0.99	1 227.57	615
Mutant Ape Yacht Club	0.63	0.06	4.82	-0.97	189	1 628
Bored Ape Kennel Club	0.39	0.04	1.13	-0.68	9.95	673
Axie Infinity	-	-	-	-	-	-
Sorare	0.28	0.00	1.26	-0.74	5.00	22
Art Blocks	-	-	-	-	-	-
Sandbox	0.14	0.14	0.69	-0.81	7.99	800

NFT Collection (1)	Mean (2)	Median (3)	S.D. (4)	Min (5)	Max (6)	Total (7)
Decentraland	0.08	0.00	0.72	-0.92	6.52	156
ENS	1.24	0.12	7.74	-0.96	311.5	6 380

Note: The table presents returns to NFTs. Trades are matched by NFT ID. Two is the minimum number of sales necessary to calculate the return. Values in the table can be converted to percentages when multiplying by 100 percent. Trade-by-trade return is the return per NFT sale. Buy-and-hold return is the return calculated by dividing the price of the last sale by the price of the first sale minus one. We omit the last recorded transaction on CryptoPunk #9989 that sold for 124 457.1 ETH, as this transaction has been documented to be a wash-trade. Period prior to (commencing on) May 9, 2022 is referred to as the NFT bull (bear) market. Values in Panels C–D are based on trade-by-trade returns. The data are derived from OpenSea API.

a return of 73 percent at the median, which compares to the median return of 83 percent during the bull market (Panel D). The second-best-performing NFT collection in the bear market is Sandbox that delivers 14 percent on the per trade basis. The third-highest is ENS with 12 percent median return. CryptoPunks yield 8 percent. OpenSea did not record any sale for neither Art Blocks nor Axie Infinity during that period.

Market-Adjusted Returns to NFTs

In this section, we estimate returns to NFTs on a market-adjusted basis. Returns are benchmarked against returns to bitcoin (BTC) using the daily close price of BTC denominated in ETH (recall that the prices of all NFTs in our sample are denominated in ETH). The results are presented in Table 14.4, Panels A–D.

Panel A reports short-term market-adjusted returns estimated on a trade-by-trade basis. Generally, the market-adjusted returns are somewhat higher both at the mean and at the median for virtually every NFT collection in the sample. The differences, however, are in the order of a few percentage points. This implies that NFTs deliver higher returns than the cryptocurrency market in general as proxied by BTC. In other words, NFTs across different categories seem to represent a more valuable investment opportunity than other cryptocurrencies on the ex-post basis.

A similar picture emerges from buy-and-hold returns (Panel B). Here again, both market-adjusted mean and median returns are higher for almost all analyzed NFT collections by a few percentage points (except ENS).

When we split the sample into bull and bear market periods, we find that market-adjusted returns during the bull market are negligibly larger compared to the raw returns displayed in Table 14.3 (Panel C), whereas during the recent bear market the market-adjusted returns to NFTs are somewhat smaller. For example, the median market-adjusted returns to CryptoPunks, MAYC, and BAKC are zero, whereas the raw returns to the aforementioned collections are 8 percent, 6 percent, and 4 percent, respectively. The best-performing NFT collection on the market-adjusted basis is

Table 14.4 Market-adjusted returns to NFTs

NFT Collection (1)	Mean (2)	Median (3)	S.D. (4)	Min (5)	Max (6)	Total (7)
Panel A: Market-adjusted trade-by-trade return (x 100%)						
CryptoPunks	16.33	0.39	114.5	-2.77	5 999	11 252
Bored Ape Yacht Club	12.83	0.85	63.88	-1.18	4 899	17 783
Mutant Ape Yacht Club	0.70	0.20	10.10	-1.08	1 399	20 451
Bored Ape Kennel Club	0.62	0.26	1.33	-1.04	43	15 573
Axie Infinity	0.28	-0.03	2.25	-1.60	99	28 955
Sorare	0.48	0.17	3.47	-1.31	570	126 253
Art Blocks	2.21	0.47	5.81	-0.89	59	1 429
Sandbox	1.70	0.41	3.50	-1.22	69	15 284
Decentraland	0.12	0.03	0.53	-1.39	6.53	1 670
ENS	1.97	0.32	10.77	-1.33	550	16 234
Panel B: Market-adjusted buy-and-hold return (x 100%)						
CryptoPunks	82.12	2.91	243.87	-2.66	3 250	3 711
Bored Ape Yacht Club	94.95	19.99	180.40	-1.07	3 224	6 206
Mutant Ape Yacht Club	1.81	0.97	17.32	-1.03	1 443	8 058
Bored Ape Kennel Club	2.83	1.63	3.88	-0.91	92	4 450
Axie Infinity	0.29	-0.05	2.41	-1.49	179	23 218
Sorare	0.73	0.24	4.96	-1.24	726	78 852
Art Blocks	4.64	0.99	9.60	-0.49	79	910
Sandbox	3.42	0.93	5.39	-1.03	55	8 137
Decentraland	1.27	1.00	1.14	-0.46	3.43	16
ENS	3.53	0.51	32.29	-1.27	2 777	9 637
Panel C: Market-adjusted returns in NFT bull market						
CryptoPunks	16.75	0.41	116.73	-2.77	5,999	10,742
Bored Ape Yacht Club	11.93	0.86	61.92	-1.07	4 899	17 190
Mutant Ape Yacht Club	0.71	0.21	10.40	-1.08	1 399	18 929
Bored Ape Kennel Club	0.63	0.27	1.34	-0.98	43.10	14 947
Axie Infinity	0.28	-0.03	2.25	-1.60	99.22	28 955
Sorare	0.48	0.17	3.47	-1.31	570.4	126 231
Art Blocks	2.21	0.47	5.81	-0.89	58.95	1 429
Sandbox	1.78	0.44	3.57	-1.03	69.02	14 522
Decentraland	0.13	0.03	0.50	-1.39	6.05	1 520
ENS	2.47	0.52	12.12	-1.13	550.4	10 163
Panel D: Market-adjusted returns in NFT bear market						
CryptoPunks	7.49	0.00	43.16	-1.06	494	515
Bored Ape Yacht Club	38.95	0.43	103.10	-1.18	1 228	615
Mutant Ape Yacht Club	0.49	0.00	4.83	-1.06	189	1 628
Bored Ape Kennel Club	0.28	0.00	1.16	-1.04	9.83	673
Axie Infinity	-	-	-	-	-	-
Sorare	0.36	0.02	1.18	-0.97	4.66	22
Art Blocks	-	-	-	-	-	-
Sandbox	0.03	0.05	0.72	-1.23	8.48	800

NFT Collection (1)	Mean (2)	Median (3)	S.D. (4)	Min (5)	Max (6)	Total (7)
Decentraland	0.03	-0.04	0.75	-1.12	6.53	156
ENS	1.13	0.02	7.78	-1.33	312	6 380

Note: The table presents market-adjusted returns to NFTs. Trades are matched by NFT ID. Two is the minimum number of sales necessary to calculate the return. Returns to NFTs are benchmarked against the return to bitcoin (BTC) denominated in ETH that proxies for the cryptocurrency market. Values in the table can be converted to percentages when multiplying by 100 percent. Trade-by-trade return is the return per NFT sale. Buy-and-hold return is the return calculated by dividing the price of the last sale by the price of the first sale minus one. We omit the last recorded transaction on CryptoPunk #9989 that sold for 124 457.1 ETH, as this transaction has been documented to be a wash-trade. Period prior to (commencing on) May 9, 2022 is referred to as the NFT bull (bear) market. Values in Panels C–D are based on trade-by-trade returns. The data are derived from OpenSea API.

BAYC, with the mean and median market-adjusted returns of 3900 percent and 43 percent, respectively.

CONCLUSION

This study consists of two major parts. It first introduces the reader to the NFT infrastructure—NFT primary and secondary markets, different types of NFT exchanges, NFT aggregators, NFT borrowing and landing, NFT staking, and finally NFT fundraising. The second part is empirical and attempts to answer the question about the level of the market performance of NFTs. To this end, we analyze close to 2 million transactions from various leading blue-chip NFT collections including CryptoPunks, Bored Ape Yacht Club, Mutant Ape Yacht Club, Bored Ape Kennel Club, Axie Infinity, Sorare, Art Blocks, Sandbox, Decentaland, and Ethereum Name Service.

Our results speak in favor of NFTs as liquid and high-performing investment assets. First, we find that the category of profile picture (PFP) NFTs dominate the market in terms of market capitalization, volume, and returns. For example, buy-and-hold returns to Bored Ape Yacht Club and CryptoPunk NFTs are close to 2000 percent and 270 percent, respectively (at the median). Returns to other NFT categories (art, gaming, metaverse) are markedly lower but remain substantial. For instance, buy-and-hold returns to Art Blocks and Sandbox are about 460 percent and 330 percent at the mean, and 95 percent and 83 percent at the median. It is worth emphasizing that the returns are better on the market-adjusted basis, implying that investments in NFTs beat the cryptocurrency market benchmark. Further, during the bear market, raw returns to NFTs remain generally positive, whereas market-adjusted returns are either positive (mean) or zero (median), with the notable exception of Bored Ape Yacht Club and Sandbox that yield 43 percent and 5 percent, respectively (at the median).

NOTES

1. For simplicity, we assume that a decentralized exchange is the exchange where assets are held directly by transacting parties under their own custody.
2. https://dappradar.com/nft/sales.
3. https://dune.com/browse/dashboards.

WEBSITES CONSULTED IN THE WRITING OF THIS CHAPTER

Arcade, https://docs.arcade.xyz/docs.
Axie Infinity, https://stake.axieinfinity.com/.
Bored Ape Yacht Club, https://boredapeyachtclub.com/#/home.
Christie's 3.0, https://nft.christies.com/.
Cryptopunks, https://cryptopunks.app/.
DappRadar, https://dappradar.com/nft.
Dune NFT Market Overview, https://dune.com/hildobby/NFTs.
HeyMint, https://heymint.xyz/.
Indelible Labs, https://indelible.xyz/.
NFTX, https://academy.nftx.io/.
OpenSea, https://docs.opensea.io/.
Premint, https://www.premint.xyz/.
RaritySniper, https://raritysniper.com/nft-price-stats.
SudoSwap, AMM https://docs.sudoswap.xyz/.
Upshot, https://upshot.xyz/.
Wenmint, https://wenmint.io/.

15. The environmental, social, and governance (ESG) aspects of Bitcoin

Andrew Urquhart

INTRODUCTION

Cryptocurrencies are a new asset class increasingly gaining attention due to their unique features and large price appreciation. Bitcoin was the first cryptocurrency which went live in early 2009 after the white paper published by "Satoshi Nakamoto" in the autumn of 2008. Since then, there has been an explosion in the number of cryptocurrencies created, with www.coinmarketcap.com listing nearly 17 000 coins on February 28, 2022.[1] The likely driver for this explosion in new cryptocurrencies is the large price appreciation experienced, with Bitcoin reaching $1 in April 2011 and then experiencing large bubbles during late 2017 and late 2021, finally reaching an all-time high of over $68 000 in November 2021. With the increase in interest of these cryptocurrencies, financial markets have started to accept Bitcoin into their system. Bitcoin futures became listed on the Chicago Mercantile Exchange (CME) in December 2017 and the first Bitcoin ETF debuted on the New York Stock Exchange (NYSE) in October 2021. A recent study conducted by Fidelity Digital Assets found that seven in ten institutional investors expect to buy or invest in cryptocurrencies in the near future, while around 90 percent of those interested in investing in the future said they expected their company's or clients' portfolios to include digital asset investments within the next five years.[2] A separate survey conducted by Nickel Digital Asset Management found similar results with 82 percent of respondents expecting to increase their cryptocurrency allocation in the next two years.[3]

At the same time as interest and size of the cryptocurrency market has grown, financial markets have been giving increased attention to the types of investments that they make. One key criterion that investment managers start to consider is the environmental, social, and corporate governance (ESG) concerns of their investments. Short-term gains are given lower priority than investments that promote ESG goods and a recent survey found that 96 percent of investors in the United States expect their firm to increase prioritization of ESG as an investment criterion while 93 percent expect the companies they invest in to increase their prioritization of ESG initiatives.[4]

However, the ESG impact of cryptocurrencies, and especially Bitcoin, is a hotly debated subject with a number of media outlets reporting their concerns with the environmental impact of the use of the proof-of-work mining (PoW) consensus protocol. This chapter first explores the E, S, and G elements of Bitcoin in order to provide an overview of the investability of these new assets for ESG-conscious investors. It systematically goes through each element of E, S, and G from a traditional viewpoint for Bitcoin, providing the key characteristics of Bitcoin and how it performs in terms of these important metrics.

ESG is an acronym developed in a 2004 report by 20 financial institutions in response to a call from the Secretary-General of the United Nations, Kofi Annan. ESG refers to how corporations and investors integrate environmental, social, and governance concerns into their business models. A similar term is corporate social responsibility (CSR), which has traditionally referred to a corporation's activities with regards to being more socially responsible, a better corporate citizen, while ESG refers to how corporations and investors integrate ESG concerns into their business models (Gillan et al. 2021). ESG, contrary to CSR, explicitly includes governance and therefore is more wide-ranging than CSR. Hence, this chapter examines ESG rather than CSR. There is a large and ever-expanding amount of literature on ESG in the areas of corporate finance and asset pricing.[5] The main findings in the literature show that a firm's ESG rating and activities are strongly related to the firm's market, leadership, and owner characteristics, as well as its risk, performance, and value, while ESG investing appears to be rewarding for investors since 2014, but not prior to this period.[6] Morningstar reports that global sustainable fund assets doubled in the six months prior to September 2021 to reach $3.9 trillion, while the global sustainable universe attracted $134 billion in net inflows in the third quarter of 2021.[7] Therefore there is a large demand for these types of funds in the financial sector, and an increased interest in the types of funds that firms and investors participate in.

Since its introduction in 2009, Bitcoin has attracted much attention from both Wall Street and Main Street, as well as from the academic sphere. Nascent literature has begun to consider the market efficiency of Bitcoin (Urquhart 2016; Khuntia and Pattanayak 2018; Tiwari et al. 2018), the potential of Bitcoin as a hedging instrument, its role in portfolio diversification (Brière et al. 2015; Baur et al. 2018; Platanakis and Urquhart 2020), its role as a currency (Yermack 2015; Weber 2016), and the asset pricing of these cryptocurrencies (Shen et al. 2020; Liu and Tsyvinski 2021; Liu et al. 2022). Although there have been a number of papers documenting various issues with cryptocurrencies, such as the illegal activity (Foley et al. 2019), price manipulation (Gandal et al. 2018; Griffin and Shams 2020), and wash trading (Cong et al. 2022), an investigation into the ESG elements of cryptocurrencies remains needed. This is surprising given the amount of media attention attracted by Bitcoin and the vast number of academic studies that examine the impact of Bitcoin on the financial system.

In related literature, Böhme et al. (2015) provide an overview of Bitcoin and highlight some of the key risks, including market risks, counterparty risks, operational risks, privacy risks, as well as criminality and consumer protection issues. Dierksmeier and Seele (2018) provide the first study examining the ethical significance of blockchain technology on financial transactions from a business ethics perspective, and split the issues into micro, meso, and macro levels, showing that the ethical impact of cryptocurrencies can be beneficial, detrimental, and ambiguous. Scharding (2019) investigates the ethical questions of Bitcoin through the lens of a Fichtean account and argues that Bitcoin undermines the monetary power of nations and therefore threatens their ability to provide access to necessary material goods. Given that Bitcoin offers citizens a means of defending themselves against corrupt regimes, Scharding (2019) concludes that Bitcoin forsakes general welfare and therefore is unethical by Fichtean lights. Bagus and de la Horra (2021) argue that, were cryptocurrencies to become a widespread medium of exchange, the government's capacity to undertake monetary, fiscal, and drug policy would be undermined, representing an ethically desirable outcome from both a private property rights and a utilitarian perspective since it would force governments to reduce their size and scope in these three areas. Recently, Larue et al. (2022) examine the ethics of alternative currencies and how they tackle social and environmental issues. The authors argue that although alternative currencies can contribute to improving social cohesion and mitigating environmental harm, there are challenges such as environmental concerns, and their impact should not come at the expense of people in the Global South who are already worse off than counterparts in the North.

This chapter examines the environmental, social, and governance characteristics of Bitcoin. In turn, it studies the main areas of interest for Bitcoin in respect to ESG, within the environment. It explains the impact Bitcoin has in terms of mining and the proof-of-work consensus mechanism, as well as transaction and other concerns. The social impact of Bitcoin is split into a number of sections which explore the influence Bitcoin has on diversity, financial inclusion, privacy, and consumer protection. Finally, the chapter studies the governance of Bitcoin and shows that Bitcoin may not be as decentralized as "Satoshi Nakamoto" intended. In this way, the chapter adds to two main strands of literature, namely the ever-growing literature studying cryptocurrencies and their impact on financial markets and society, as well as the literature on ESG investing. It marries these two large areas of research and provides guidelines for investors and policy makers on the ESG characteristics of Bitcoin.

The remainder of the chapter is organized as follows. It first investigates the environmental issues, then explores the social issues, and the governance aspect. The final section summarizes and concludes.

ENVIRONMENT

In this section, we examine the main impacts that Bitcoin has on the environment, from mining new coins to the actual Bitcoin transactions themselves.

Mining and Proof-of-Work

Bitcoin and other cryptocurrencies have made headlines on mainstream news networks due to their environmental impact. The main impact that Bitcoin has on the environment is through its proof-of-work (PoW) consensus mechanism. Bitcoin is a digital currency/asset underpinned by a public blockchain that records all transactions which are arranged in sequential "blocks" so that no user is allowed to spend any of their holdings twice. The ledger is public and distributed so that if transactions were tampered with, the altered version would be quickly rejected by other users. To propose the next set of transactions to be added to the blockchain, miners compete against each other to solve an arbitrary mathematical puzzle. Since the Bitcoin blockchain was set up to ensure a block is mined approximately every ten minutes, the difficulty of the puzzle adjusts over time so that blocks are not mined too frequently, or too slowly.[8]

The process of mining accounts for the vast majority of the environmental impact by Bitcoin. The process of trying to solve the puzzle, through a trial-and-error basis, can take trillions of attempts, and with thousands of miners trying to solve the puzzle every ten minutes, there is a lot of wasted energy in terms of the electricity used by the mining computers and the coolers required to stop them from overheating. While it is impossible to know exactly how much electricity Bitcoin uses, as different computers use different amounts of energy, and it is impossible to know how many miners are taking this task seriously, the University of Cambridge Electricity Consumption Index (CBECI) estimates that Bitcoin mining consumes 121.36 TWh a year, which is more than that used by some whole nations, such as Argentina, Norway, and Sweden.[9]

However, by its own admission, CBECI makes some crude assumptions in terms of its figures, though it still remains the most popular source of mining energy usage estimates. Also noted by a CBECI survey,[10] 39 percent of PoW mining is powered by renewable energy, mostly hydroelectric energy. Faced with increased competition and tightening profit margins, miners have had to adjust their activities to make mining financially worthwhile. In June 2021, China banned Bitcoin mining. At its peak, China accounted for over three-quarters of all Bitcoin mining, and since two-thirds of China's energy comes from coal, Bitcoin mining has a huge impact on the environment. Therefore, these miners have relocated to locations where energy costs are low, such as in Texas, which has some of the cheapest energy prices in the world due to its deregulated power grid.[11] Consumers in Texas enjoy huge choices in terms of electricity providers, which encourage providers to lower prices to stay competitive. Another argument is that the move to renewable energy by Bitcoin miners could act as an incentive to develop more environmental forms of energy production; however, this argument could be made for any activity that uses energy. Therefore the process of mining, through PoW, uses a substantial amount of energy, which is damaging for the environment. However, proponents of the PoW consensus mechanism note that mining is essential for the security and smooth workings of the blockchain. The popular alternative among other cryptocurrencies, proof-of-stake (PoS), has a number of security issues which makes it more vulnerable to attacks (see Vashchuk and Shuwar 2018 for a detailed comparison of PoW and PoS).

Transactions and Other Concerns

Bitcoin's environmental issues do not end with mining. Statista[12] reports that one Bitcoin transaction uses over 2264 kWh, while 100 000 VISA transactions use a mere

148.6 kWh; while the Digiconomist reports that a single Bitcoin transaction uses 1029.54 kgCO_2, which is equivalent to over 2 million VISA transactions or 171 000 hours of watching YouTube.[13] Forbes reports that the average transaction consumes over 1700 kWh of electricity, which is almost twice the monthly amount used by the average United States (US) home.[14] Hence transactions on the Bitcoin network are very inefficient compared to VISA and other providers. In terms of carbon footprint, academic studies have shown that annual emissions from Bitcoin are around 22 MtCO_2 (Stoll et al. 2019); while Foteinis (2018) estimates the combined footprint of Bitcoin and Ethereum to be 43.0 MtCO_2. A recent study by de Vries and Stoll (2021) reports that Bitcoin's e-waste is on average 272g per transaction processed on the blockchain, and its annual e-waste generates 30.7 metric kilotons as of May 2021. There are even figures suggesting that Bitcoin transactions could pose a serious threat to the global commitment to mitigate greenhouse gas emission under the Paris Agreement, with one study suggesting that Bitcoin emissions could push global warming to about 2°C (Mora et al. 2018). Additional energy used includes the energy to cool the mining equipment to stop the mining rigs from overheating, and although this energy usage may be small compared to the total environmental impact of Bitcoin, it is still a use of energy that should be noted.

However, we also note that estimates vary considerably depending on several factors, including hardware efficiency and electricity prices used in the process. Miners who are more interested in profits (de Vries and Stoll 2021) than anything else will adapt to using the most efficient and cheapest form of fuelling for their mining enterprises. Nevertheless, Bitcoin is not a global currency used to conduct day-to-day transactions and has been shown to be a speculative asset by the vast majority of investors (Baur et al. 2018; Hackethal et al. 2022), and one can hence argue that we should not be comparing it to VISA or other payment mechanisms.

Some studies (e.g., Rybarczyk et al. 2021) have compared Bitcoin's energy usage to that of the whole banking system, and show that Bitcoin actually uses less than half of the energy consumed by the whole banking system. But this example compares one speculative cryptocurrency to a worldwide banking system, and is similar to comparing one diesel-powered car to the whole electric car network. Further, when comparing the system using Bitcoin with the banking system, one must take into account the fact that the offered services are not identical, and the fact that unlike fiat money, Bitcoin requires special conditions to be used, meaning that its existence is conditioned by the operating of technology such as a laptop and a good internet connection.

Although this chapter is mainly focussed on Bitcoin, we should note here that the environmental impact of other cryptocurrencies is somewhat less than that of Bitcoin.[15] These cryptocurrencies typically do not use the PoW, but use the PoS consensus mechanism, which dramatically reduces the environmental impact of these new assets. Ethereum, the second-largest cryptocurrency in terms of market capitalization, upgraded to PoS in September 2022 and has seen a dramatic fall in the amount of energy used.

SOCIAL

The social part of ESG includes many areas related to societal impact, which can cover an endless number of topics. In this chapter, we focus on four key areas, namely diversity, financial inclusion, privacy, and consumer protection.

Diversity

Bitcoin is a completely decentralized network and offers users the opportunity to participate in a network without any barriers to entry or formal approval. Therefore, the ability to interact in this public blockchain clearly accords with the Universal Declaration of Human Rights Article 19 definition, which states: "everyone has the right to freedom of opinion and expression; this right includes freedom to hold opinions without interference and to seek, receive and impart information and ideas through any media and regardless of frontiers." Bitcoin enables users to evade any form of repression by authorities or oppressive regimes that control an asset. In this respect, Bitcoin can be seen as the Twitter of financial assets. With this ability to interact freely comes the benefits of privacy. Although public blockchains (such as Bitcoin) enable users to track all transactions and see the transaction history of individuals and coins, users can only see the public addresses of participants in the network, and therefore as long as your public address is not publicly known, users have anonymity. This trait forms an especially important consideration for individuals living in developing nations with oppressive governments and hyperinflation. No matter your age, gender, faith, ethnicity, Bitcoin does not discriminate.

However, a recent study by Hackethal et al. (2022) shows that cryptocurrency investors are maybe not as diverse as we may think. In their study, they find that 90 percent of their cryptocurrency investors are male, while 76 percent of their sample of all investors are male. Further, they show that cryptocurrency investors are over 30 percent wealthier than non-cryptocurrency investors, and their incomes are significantly higher. These findings are consistent with those of Pelster et al. (2019), who also show that cryptocurrency investors are generally younger (less than 35 years old), more tech-savvy (Benetton and Compiani 2020), and invest in Bitcoin directly, while older investors find it more convenient to invest in cryptocurrencies indirectly. Therefore although Bitcoin may carry the ability to be as diverse as possible, it seems only a subset of the population are using and investing in Bitcoin. However, this could change if and when Bitcoin becomes more mainstream among investors.

Financial Inclusion

A positive societal impact of Bitcoin is the opportunity to bring banking to the unbanked. According to the World Bank, 1.7 billion adults around the world remain unbanked[16] and without access to basic banking facilities. Often these individuals live within extremely poor and rural regions, without the infrastructure to support a physical bank location, or provide the electricity or internet access to facilitate online banking. Also, individuals from these regions may lack the necessary identification to pass know your customer (KYC) requirements. These individuals lack the basic financial service to send and receive funds and some cannot even access a banking system, such as migrant workers in the US; they rely on money wire services that are often very expensive. Bitcoin enables anyone with a smartphone and an internet connection to participate and have access to this ever-growing network. Individuals can send and receive large or small amounts of Bitcoin very quickly for much smaller transaction fees than using traditional cross-border methods. Beyond Bitcoin, there are other cryptocurrencies, such as Aave and Compound, that provide decentralized borrowing and lending services which do not require KYC or credit scores, but instead use automated smart contracts.

Although criticized and warned by the International Monetary Fund (IMF) and World Bank, in September 2021, El Salvador's governmental leaders officially made Bitcoin legal tender and provided each citizen with $30 worth of Bitcoin. El Salvador President Nayib Bukele argued that 70 percent of his citizens are unbanked yet most have mobile phones and now they can use a mobile Bitcoin wallet and be plugged into a worldwide monetary system. Venezuela has also embraced cryptocurrencies due to the impact that US sanctions have had on the country, with many citizens blocked from accessing the international banking system and the Venezuelan currency being left virtually worthless. Many Venezuelan citizens have converted their wages into cryptocurrencies and use the blockchain to transfer their money and make payments (Cifuentes 2019).

However, these benefits come with some real risks, such as the lack of KYC, which may lead to these individuals lacking access to the world's financial system that requires KYC identification. Although KYC identification may seem to be a barrier, it is in place to ensure the safety and identity of individuals in the system and is very much related to the privacy issues discussed in this chapter.

Privacy

Cryptography, which is used within the Bitcoin blockchain, enables privacy by allowing users to interact anonymously within the Bitcoin network. This characteristic means that Bitcoin does not discriminate against users, unlike the banking system: there are countless studies documenting the gender, age, ethnicity and faith discrimination within the banking industry (see Asiedu et al. 2012; Chatterji and Seamans 2012; Agier and Szafarz 2013 for example). Therefore, privacy can be seen as a moral good.

However, with such privacy comes concerns. The main concern is regarding the use of cryptocurrencies for illegal or illicit activities. Providing a digital and anonymous payment mechanism, Bitcoin has facilitated the growth of online darknet marketplaces in which illegal goods and services are traded. One of the largest and most famous dark web marketplaces was Silk Road, which enabled users to purchase anything from drugs to weapons to stolen credit cards to even assassinations. The US Federal Bureau of Investigation (FBI) shut down Silk Road and numerous other marketplaces in 2013 and seized over $4 million worth of Bitcoin, providing some idea of the scale of the problem. Foley et al. (2019) provide a detailed estimate of illegal activity on the Bitcoin blockchain and find that $76 billion of illegal activity a year involve Bitcoin (46 percent of total transactions). Chainalysis, a blockchain analysis company, also estimated cryptocurrency-related crime in 2021 and showed that theft amounts hit $14 billion, up from $7.8 billion in 2020.[17]

Another issue with the privacy of Bitcoin is the potential of individuals to evade tax through using the public blockchain. At the time of this writing, many regulators around the globe are formulating plans on whether, and how, to regulate this space, but in many countries there is very little regulation whatsoever. Most developed countries treat cryptocurrencies the same as stocks, and any gains should be taxed the same way.[18] For instance, in the United Kingdom (UK), cryptocurrencies are under the umbrella of capital gains tax and should be reported in individuals' tax assessment. However, it is difficult for governments to track individuals who hold cryptocurrencies in digital wallets as, by definition, they have no authority or oversight of these wallets. Moreover, individuals can use cryptocurrencies to buy goods from retailers or swap their cryptocurrencies for gift cards. Some cryptocurrency exchanges have been helping authorities, such as Coinbase providing HM Revenue and Customs (HMRC) in 2020 with details of customers with a UK address who "received more than £5,000 worth of crypto assets on the Coinbase platform during the course of the 2019–2020 tax year."[19] Nevertheless, there may be countless cryptocurrency holders out there not declaring their capital gains and not paying the legal requirement of tax. Although privacy provides some positives, it also provides ways in which criminals can easily interact with a monetary system without regulatory or governmental oversight.

Consumer Protection

Unlike centralized finance with large financial institutions protecting consumers, Bitcoin is part of the new decentralized finance (DeFi) system in which there is no central authority overseeing the network and ensuring that consumers are protected. Therefore, there is no consumer compensation scheme as there is with banks in the UK. Similarly in Europe, Bitcoin falls outside European Union (EU) financial services legislation and outside investor protection rules. In the US, cryptocurrency brokerages are licensed as money transmitters, but do not carry the same protections as traditional brokers or asset managers.

Cryptocurrency holders are responsible for looking after their unique private keys, and if these are lost there is no way to recover the keys, and the holdings are lost forever. If users send their Bitcoin to an incorrect address or a blockchain that is not compatible with that cryptocurrency, the coins are lost and unrecoverable. A recent study by Jahanshahloo et al. (forthcoming) shows that 18.95 Bitcoins have been officially lost due to miners not claiming the full transaction fee or the full block reward, which shows even miners, who should be some of the most experienced users of the blockchain, make mistakes and lose Bitcoin. Some outlets, such as Chainalysis, have estimated that 23 percent of Bitcoin have been lost since these coins have not moved addresses in five years; while Jahanshahloo et al. (forthcoming) estimate this figure at around 14 percent.

Hacks represent another issue. There are countless examples of hacks of exchanges, such as the Mt. Gox hack in 2014 where approximately 850 000 Bitcoin were stolen, an amount valued at more than $450 million at the time. Victims are now starting to regain some of their lost Bitcoin. Other examples include Liquid Global in 2021, KuCoin in 2020, and Coincheck in 2018. These hacks are a real threat to the trust of holding Bitcoin on these exchanges, and explains why many people advocate for holding their coins on digital wallets or in offline cold storage ledgers.

As we can see, in terms of social benefits, Bitcoin brings financialization to the unbanked, as well as privacy benefits, but these positive aspects come with real concerns for society and the individual users themselves, and are some of the biggest concerns for governments and regulators alike.

GOVERNANCE

Governance is an ever-increasingly important aspect of any organization. In the academic literature, thousands of studies examine the governance structure of firms.[20] Many of these studies examine the diversity of the board, whether a firm has any conflicts of interest and political contributions, the transparency of accounting methods, and the ability of stockholders to vote on important meetings and annual general meetings (AGMs). However, with Bitcoin there is no board; all transactions are placed on a public blockchain for anyone to scrutinize, and every participant in the network is created equally, meaning that a new user has as many rights as a long-term user of the network. In this section, we examine the important governance issues specific to Bitcoin.

Within Bitcoin, all users are equal, with no one user having more power or influence than another. Therefore, a user could be interacting on the blockchain for years and have the exact same influence as a new user to the blockchain. This environment provides an attractive feature for new users of Bitcoin. This key feature was outlined by "Satoshi Nakamoto" (2008) in the now infamous white paper and although it holds today, another aspect of governance is the concentration of Bitcoins. "Whales" is a term used in the cryptocurrency world to describe large holders of a certain cryptocurrency, with most outlets[21] denoting a whale as a user who holds over 1000 BTC. We collected data from Glassnode, and in Figure 15.1 show the number of addresses of Bitcoin holding over 1000 BTC. We can see that the number of whales increases steadily over time, peaking at 2488 on February 7, 2021, indicating that at least 2.488 million Bitcoin (over 13 percent) was held by whales. This number is likely to be much higher given that they can hold much more than 1000 BTC. Indeed, Glassnode provides data on individual addresses, but users can hold many addresses and the concentration of Bitcoin may be much higher than this estimate. Jahanshahloo et al. (forthcoming) study the Herfindahl–Hirschman index (HHI) from individual transactions on the Bitcoin blockchain and show that, although the HHI has fallen over time, it is still reasonably high, indicating the lack of diversity of holders of Bitcoin. This finding is supported by Makarov and Schoar (2022), who show that a cluster of 1000 addresses control 3 million Bitcoins at the end of 2020, and the top 10 000 addresses own more than 5 million Bitcoins, which corresponds to about a quarter of all outstanding Bitcoin. They also note that these numbers underestimate the true numbers, since the large addresses may be held by the same entities.

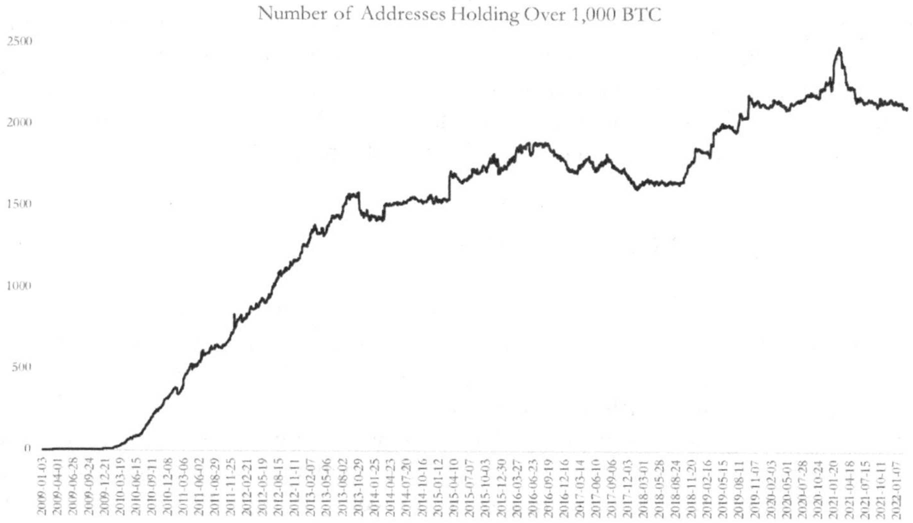

Figure 15.1 *Number of addresses holding over 1000 BTC*

Beyond users, miners generally work within teams to successfully propose the next block to the blockchain, and these teams are called mining pools. Their job is to verify and process transactions by solving a computationally difficult problem, and they are rewarded with newly created Bitcoins and transaction fees. It is important to study the distribution of miners, since if the majority of a colluding set of miners commanded the majority of the mining power in the network, they could control the ledger and result in a 51 percent attack where the group could alter previously verified records. Makarov and Schoar (2022) study mining pools and show a large concentration of miners, with the number of miners on the Bitcoin blockchain falling over time, with the top 50 percent of miners controlling almost all the mining capacity.

Beyond Bitcoin holders and miners, a concentration of elite Bitcoin core developers, who maintain and develop the Bitcoin code, exists. For practical reasons, there is an established hierarchy among them, considered a meritocracy in which those who have been there longest and contributed most of the code have more final decision-making power. The existence of this small group of coders begs the question, how 'decentralized' is Bitcoin if the number of people who can change its rules (or reject proposed changes) is very small? In 2018, Jonas Schnelli, a Bitcoin core maintainer, admitted he was one of only four maintainers of the Bitcoin core code and explained that maintainers have the rights to import changes to the codebase and implied they all knew each other.[22] According to the Bitcoin core's own website, anyone may be a contributor and propose changes to the code, but only project maintainers have commit access.[23]

Therefore, to claim that Bitcoin is decentralized with this sort of structure is similar to arguing that your political party controls the country as they only have 95 percent of the vote. Although Bitcoin is a decentralized network of users with equal power and influence on the blockchain, there is a high concentration of ownerships in a number of large holders of Bitcoin, mining of new Bitcoins is controlled by a few large miners, and the code is maintained by a small group of collaborators.

SUMMARY AND CONCLUSION

Financial markets are at an interesting crossroads. On the one hand, we have the growth and interest in ESG investing: investors are as interested in the impact of their investments as much as they are in the returns that they generate. On the other hand, there is a huge growth in the interest and investment in cryptocurrencies, with Bitcoin receiving the most attention. Bitcoin is well known to have environmental issues. In this chapter, we study in detail the environmental, social, and governance characteristics of the largest and most popular cryptocurrency. We show the various environmental issues faced by Bitcoin and the large impact it is having on the environment, not just in terms of mining, but with transactions, too. We also explore the social characteristics of Bitcoin, outlining some of the positive gains Bitcoin can bring to society. Finally, we explore the governance of Bitcoin, explaining that Bitcoin may not be as decentralized as some make it out to be.

Although we examine Bitcoin in detail in this chapter, we do not examine all cryptocurrencies, since each and every cryptocurrency has different protocols and consensus mechanisms, meaning that their own ESG characteristics will vary. For instance Cardano, a popular and regular top ten cryptocurrency in terms of market capitalization, is based on the proof-of-stake protocol, meaning that the environmental impact of its consensus mechanism is tiny compared to proof-of-work cryptocurrencies, and it is the first ever peer-reviewed blockchain with many developers and academics providing feedback during the development of the blockchain to ensure the quality of the final product.

Therefore, we suggest future areas of research in this area. Future work could study the ESG impact of other cryptocurrencies, especially larger altcoins that are starting to gain the attention of institutional investors. Further research could also look at designing a cryptocurrency, or altering the existing protocol of a blockchain, to improve its ESG characteristics, which in turn will make the cryptocurrency more attractive to investors. Finally, future studies could provide solutions to some of the

ESG issues of Bitcoin and other cryptocurrencies, and highlight the possible ways in which they could improve their image.

NOTES

1. Coinmarketcap has a strict listing criterion for coins to be published on their website which rely on three key principles: credibility, verification, and methodology. For more information on their listing criteria, see https://support.coinmarketcap.com/hc/en-us/articles/360043659351-Listings-Criteria.
2. For the full report, see https://www.forbes.com/sites/lawrencewintermeyer/2021/08/12/institutional-money-is-pouring-into-the-crypto-market-and-its-only-going-to-grow/?sh=1a5424261459.
3. For the full report, see https://www.internationalinvestment.net/news/4034776/most-significant-crypto-hurdle-institutional-investors-revealed-survey.
4. For the full report, see https://www.edelman.com/sites/g/files/aatuss191/files/2020-11/Edelman%202020%20Institutional%20Investor%20Trust_FINAL.pdf.
5. Gillan et al. (2020) provide an excellent review of the literature on ESG in corporate finance; while Hvidkjær (2017) has conducted a review of the ESG investing literature.
6. See Bennani et al. (2019).
7. See https://www.morningstar.co.uk/uk/news/216474/sustainable-assets-are-teetering-on-the-%244-trillion-mark.aspx.
8. For Bitcoin difficulty, see https://www.blockchain.com/charts/difficulty.
9. https://ccaf.io/cbeci/index/comparisons.
10. https://www.jbs.cam.ac.uk/wp-content/uploads/2021/01/2021-ccaf-3rd-global-cryptoasset-benchmarking-study.pdf.
11. https://www.bbc.co.uk/news/world-us-canada-58414555.
12. https://www.statista.com/statistics/881541/bitcoin-energy-consumption-transaction-comparison-visa/.
13. https://digiconomist.net/bitcoin-energy-consumption/.
14. https://www.forbes.com/sites/joshuarhodes/2021/10/08/is-bitcoin-inherently-bad-for-the-environment/?sh=58f5811d3033.
15. See Leafscore for an environmental impact scoring of cryptocurrencies, at https://www.leafscore.com/blog/the-9-most-sustainable-cryptocurrencies-for-2021/.
16. https://globalfindex.worldbank.org/sites/globalfindex/files/chapters/2017%20Findex%20full%20report_chapter2.pdf.
17. See https://blog.chainalysis.com/reports/2022-crypto-crime-report-introduction/.
18. Exceptions to this include Switzerland, Germany, and Portugal.
19. https://www.theblockcrypto.com/post/79722/uk-hmrc-coinbase-tax-data-customers.
20. See Brooks and Oikonomou (2018) for an overview of ESG disclosures and their effects on firms' value.
21. Such as Glassnode, Coinmetrics, and Chainalysis.
22. https://schweizermonat.ch/im-maschinenraum-einer-kryptowaehrung/.
23. https://bitcoincore.org/en/about/.

REFERENCES

Agier, I., Szafarz, A. (2013). Microfinance and gender: is there a glass ceiling on loan size? *World Development*, 42, 165–181.

Asiedu, E., Freeman, J.A., Nti-Addae, A. (2012). Access to credit by small businesses: how relevant are race, ethnicity, and gender? *American Economic Review*, 102(3), 532–537.

Bagus, P., de la Horra, L. (2021). An ethical defense of cryptocurrencies. *Business Ethics, the Environment and Responsibility*, 30(3), 423–431.

Baur, D.G., Hong, K., Lee, A.D. (2018). Bitcoin: medium of exchange or speculative asset? *Journal of International Financial Markets, Institutions and Money*, 54, 177–189.

Benetton, M., Compiani, C. (2020). Investors' beliefs and asset prices: a structural model of cryptocurrency demand. Working Paper No. 2020-107, University of Chicago, Becker Friedman Institute for Economics.

Bennani, L., Le Guenedal, T., Lepetit, F., Ly, L., Mortier, V., Roncalli, T., Sekine, T. (2019). How ESG investing has impacted the asset pricing in the equity market. Available at SSRN: https://ssrn.com/abstract=3316862.

Böhme, R., Christin, N., Edelman, B., Moore, T. (2015). Bitcoin: economics, technology, and governance. *Journal of Economic Perspectives*, 29, 213–238.

Bolt, W., Van Oordt, M.R.C. (2020). On the value of virtual currencies. *Journal of Money, Credit and Banking*, 52, 835–862.

Brière, M., Oosterlinck, K., Szafarz, A. (2015). Virtual currency, tangible return: portfolio diversification with Bitcoin. *Journal of Asset Management*, 16, 365–373.

Brooks, C., Oikonomou, I. (2018). The effects of environmental, social and governance disclosures and performance on firm value: a review of the literature in accounting and finance. *British Accounting Review*, 50(1), 1–15.

Chatterji, A.K., Seamans, R.C. (2012). Entrepreneurial finance, credit cards and race. *Journal of Financial Economics*, 106, 182–195.

Cifuentes, A.F. (2019). Bitcoin in troubled economies: the potential of cryptocurrencies in Argentina and Venezuela. *Latin American Law Review*, 3, 99–116.

Cong, L.W., Li, X., Tang, K., Yang, Y. (2022). Crypto wash trading. Available at https://arxiv.org/abs/2108.10984.

De Vries, A., Stoll, C. (2021). Bitcoin's growing e-waste problem. *Resources, Conservation and Recycling*, 175, 105901.

Dierksmeier, C., Seele, P. (2018). Cryptocurrencies and business ethics. *Journal of Business Ethics*, 152, 1–14.

Foley, S., Karlsen, J.R., Putnins, T.J. (2019). Sex, drugs, and Bitcoin: how much illegal activity is financed through cryptocurrencies? *Review of Financial Studies*, 32(5), 1798–1853.

Foteinis, S. (2018). Bitcoin's alarming carbon footprint. *Nature*, 554, 169.

Gandal, N., Hamrick, J., Moore, T., Oberman, T. (2018). Price manipulation in the Bitcoin ecosystem. *Journal of Monetary Economics*, 95, 86–96.

Gillan, S.L., Koch, A., Starks, L.T. (2021). Firms and social responsibility: a review of ESG and CSR research in corporate finance. *Journal of Corporate Finance*, 66, 101889.

Griffin, J.M., Shams, A. (2020). Is Bitcoin really untethered? *Journal of Finance*, 75, 1913–1964.

Hackethal, A., Hanspal, T., Lammer, D.M., Rink, K. (2022). The characteristics and portfolio behavior of Bitcoin investors: evidence from indirect cryptocurrency investments. *Review of Finance*, 26, 855–898.

Hvidkjær, S. (2017). ESG investing: a literature review. Available at https://dansif.dk/wp-content/uploads/2019/01/Litterature-review-UK-Sep-2017.pdf.
Jahanshahloo, H., Irresberger, F., Urquhart, A. (forthcoming). Bitcoin under the microscope. *Accounting Review*.
Khuntia, S., Pattanayak, J. (2018). Adaptive market hypothesis and evolving predictability of bitcoin. *Economics Letters*, 167, 26–28.
Larue, L., Meyer, C., Hudon, M., Sandberg, J. (2022). The ethics of alternative currencies. *Business Ethics Quarterly*, 32, 299–321.
Liu, Y., Tsyvinski, A. (2021). Risk and returns of cryptocurrency. *Review of Financial Studies*, 34, 2689–2727.
Liu, Y., Tsyvinski, A., Wu, X. (2022). Common factors in cryptocurrency. *Journal of Finance*, 77, 1133–1177.
Makarov, I., Schoar, A. (2022). Blockchain analysis of the Bitcoin market. National Bureau of Economic Research Working Paper Series 29396.
Mora, C., Rollins, R.L., Taladat, K., Kantar, M.B., Chock, M.K., Shimada, M., Franklin, E.C. (2018). Bitcoin emissions along could push global warming above 2°C. *Nature Climate Change*, 8(11), 931–933.
Nakamoto, S. (2008). Bitcoin: a peer-to-peer electronic cash system. https://www.ussc.gov/sites/default/files/pdf/training/annual-national-training-seminar/2018/Emerging_Tech_Bitcoin_Crypto.pdf
Parkin, J. (2019). The senatorial governance of Bitcoin: making (de)centralized money. *Economy and Society*, 48(4), 463–487.
Pelster, M., Breitmayer, B., Hasso, T. (2019). Who trades cryptocurrencies, how do they trade it, and how do they perform? Evidence from brokerage accounts. *Journal of Behavioral and Experimental Finance*, 23, 1–21.
Platanakis, E., Urquhart, A. (2020). Should investors include Bitcoin in their portfolios? A portfolio theory approach. *British Accounting Review*, 52, 100837.
Ren, B., Lucey, B. (2022). A clean, green haven? Examining the relationship between clean energy, clean and dirty cryptocurrencies. *SSRN*. Available at SSRN: https://ssrn.com/abstract=3963957.
Rybarczyk, R., Armstrong, D., Fabiano, A. (2021). On Bitcoin's energy consumption: a quantitative approach to a subjective question. *Galaxy Digital*. Available at https://docsend.com/view/adwmdeeyfvqwecj2.
Scharding, T. (2019). National currency, world currency, cryptocurrency: a Fichtean approach to the ethics of Bitcoin. *Business and Society Review*, 124, 219–238.
Shen, D., Urquhart, A., Wang, P. (2020). A three-factor pricing model for cryptocurrencies. *Finance Research Letters*, 34, 101248.
Stoll, C., Klaaßen, L., Gallersdörfer, U. (2019). The carbon footprint of Bitcoin. *Joule*, 3, 1647–1661.
Tiwari, A.K., Jana, R.K., Das, D., Roubaud, D. (2018). Informational efficiency of Bitcoin – an extension. *Economics Letters*, 163, 106–109.
Urquhart, A. (2016). The inefficiency of Bitcoin. *Economics Letters*, 148, 80–92.
Vashchuk, O., Shuwar, R. (2018). Pros and cons of consensus algorithm proof of stake. Difference in the network safety in proof of work and proof of stake. *Electronics and Information Technologies*, 9, 106–112.
Weber, B. (2016). Bitcoin and the legitimacy crisis in money. *Cambridge Journal of Economics*, 40, 17–41.

Yermack. D. (2015). Is Bitcoin a real currency? An economic appraisal. In: D.L.K. Chuen (ed.), *Handbook of Digital Currency: Bitcoin, Innovation, Financial Instruments, and Big Data*. Elsevier, Amsterdam, pp. 31–43.

16. Regenerative finance: a crypto-based approach for a sustainable future

Eva Meyer, Isabell Welpe, Philipp Sandner, and Mathias Ponte

INTRODUCTION

The blockchain sector has developed into a considerable industry, impacting various areas of society. At its peak in November 2021, the overall cryptocurrency market capitalization exceeded US$3 trillion (CoinGecko 2022) and that of the German stock market "only" US$2.3 trillion in 2020 (World Bank 2022). Renowned brands such as Nike, Gucci, and Tiffany have entered the world of NFTs; the largest bank by market capitalization (CompaniesMarketCap.com 2022), JP Morgan, has executed its first decentralized finance (DeFi) trade on a public blockchain; and the opportunity to build a decentralized, crypto-based Web3 is widely discussed. On the contrary, recent events in 2022, such as the failure of Terra-Luna (cf. Briola et al. 2022) or the implosion of the crypto exchange FTX with an associated loss of several billion USD in customer funds, have reinsured crypto critiques that the crypto space is to be taken with caution, and that it constitutes a risky, gambling-dominated sphere with no positive long-term value.[1]

A growing crypto-based development called regenerative finance (ReFi) has set out to maximize the positive contribution that it can make: to positively add to real-world societal matters. Such matters might include decarbonization (for example, through reforestation and carbon offsetting), ocean conservation, or the improvement of soil and water quality. Concrete ReFi projects include, for instance, the KlimaDAO (KlimaDAO 2022), the Toucan protocol (Toucan 2022), and the Regen Network (Regen Network 2022). In other words, the ReFi community refocuses on the very roots of the crypto space; that is, to use blockchain technology to create (financial) service solutions that serve society better than legacy systems. For 2023, a *Forbes* article projects ReFi as a key Web3 trend (Marr 2022).

To the best of our knowledge, there is no former paper which has used the term "ReFi" under which the field of blockchain- and token-based projects for environmental and societal purposes is currently gaining new traction. However, previous research exists on ReFi-related themes which evaluate how blockchain-based projects can facilitate sustainability endeavors. While most authors conclude that, in theory, the technology has the potential to provide a transparent, trust- and borderless coordination mechanism for regenerative projects, they warn of a scenario in which crypto projects self-enrich under the guise of sustainable pursuits: Howson (2019) and Howson et al. (2019) introduce first blockchain projects related to carbon offsetting and deforestation, and critically review their accomplishments in generating a surplus to climate change mitigation and to fairly involve local communities. Howson (2020) warns of so-called "crypto-colonialism," referring to blockchain platforms that extract economic benefits from already disadvantaged people and further increase the power asymmetry between the Global North and South under climate change mitigation credentials.

Similarly, through the investigation of 27 blockchain-based environmental and conservation initiatives, Stuit et al. (2022) critically claim that the drivers for these projects have so far rather stemmed from blockchain entrepreneurs' motivation to invent new crypto services than from a sustainability mission, and that the environmental success is lacking. To ensure that blockchain-based projects with a regenerative imperative succeed in a positive societal contribution, they propose to more closely involve on-the-ground stakeholders in the projects' design processes. Manski and Bauwens (2020), Thomason et al. (2018), and Chapron (2017) support this call to action for blockchain entrepreneurs to connect with the development and sustainability community to design true regenerative social and economic systems. This also includes a fair and equitable co-involvement of the affected communities in the design and decision process (Pschetz et al. 2020). In doing so, blockchain technology could offer a means to address both climate change and growing levels of poverty (Thomason et al. 2018). If not done properly, the opportunities emerging from blockchain technology might perish to the foreclosing of blockchains' material agency by a small powerful elite (Manski and Bauwens 2020).

The research related to ReFi so far mainly builds upon outside-in commentaries and case studies. However, we are not aware of any research that has interviewed ReFi entrepreneurs and supporters to structurally gather their views on ReFi; research that also Stuit et al. (2022) propose to better understand the mentalities, rationale, and motivation of ReFi project creators. Moreover, to the best of our knowledge, there is no scientific work so far which has systematically defined and conceptualized, nor used, the term "regenerative finance." This chapter fills these gaps. In synthesizing the perspectives from 11 semi-structured interviews with ReFi experts, we derive an understanding of the umbrella term "ReFi" and what its prospects look like.

More concretely, our contributions are fourfold. First, we define the term "regenerative finance" as: any form of business models or activities which employ economic incentive systems, constructed and enforced through DeFi tools, to positively contribute towards environmental and/or other societal matters.

Second, we derive hypotheses for three driving forces leading to the emergence of ReFi: (1) the urgency to combat climate change; (2) the dissatisfaction with how legacy systems contribute to environmental protection; and (3) the failure to date of DeFi to deliver on its promises of presenting a better financial system for society. In combination with DeFi reaching a level of technological maturity able to enter real-world territories, ReFi is aiming to develop solutions addressing those three motive forces.

Our third contribution is to structure common building blocks of ReFi. Leveraging the property of composability—that is, similarly as in DeFi to seamlessly integrate various projects with each other—our interviewees argue that ReFi is better understood along the building blocks of the entire value chain than in individual projects. As the key differentiator to DeFi, the ReFi value chain will always start with some real-world project which presents the means to implement a regenerative mission. Each step of the value chain has its own technological enablers. While the governance form of decentralized autonomous organizations (DAOs) facilitates globally distributed co-involvement and community building, it reaches its limits when it comes to cooperating with real-world legal entities.

Fourth, we take a look forward and derive the overarching goals of the community (increasing both the regenerative project supply and demand), respective enablers to reach those goals (for example, ReFi regulation), as well as the main risks for the ReFi space (for example, a loss of integrity due to ReFi scam projects).

Our results are relevant for both academia and practitioners. We offer the first academic work to structurally derive an understanding of the term "ReFi" from members of the ReFi community, and to synthesize both required actions and risks to be mitigated to grow ReFi's positive impact. We thereby provide the basis for future academic efforts in the field; for example, to support the development of enhanced blockchain-based solutions with a regenerative impact, to facilitate dialogue among required ReFi stakeholders, or to independently assess the actual societal impact of ReFi projects and prevent potential risks from misconduct. In fact, our interviewees identified such academic support as an important enabler to increase ReFi's adaption.

The chapter proceeds as follows. We start by outlining the applied methodology for our research. Subsequently, we present the results from the interview inputs, before discussing the results and concluding.[2]

DATA AND METHODOLOGY

We initiated our research with two objectives: to conceptualize the ReFi community's current understanding, driving motives, and functionalities of ReFi, and to derive its potential pathway. As the field of ReFi is only emerging, there is no extensive research to build on to address these two research objectives. When a (new) phenomenon is poorly understood, explorative studies provide a means to inductively derive generalizations about it (Stebbins 2001). Hence, to approach our research objectives, we pursued an explorative research design leveraging the expertise of early ReFi pioneers. A suitable means to obtain in-depth information on experts' experiences and viewpoints on a particular topic is to conduct interviews (Turner 2010). One of the most widely applied interview methods is the use of open-ended questions in semi-structured interviews, allowing experts to fully elaborate on their viewpoints and provide an extended reflection in comparison to yes or no questions (Knott et al. 2022; Turner 2010). Researchers can hence ensure they address specific dimensions of a research question while still leaving opportunities for interviewees to offer new meaning to the topic of study (Galletta 2013).

In line with the guidance of Creswell and Poth (2007), we developed the interview questions to be a narrowing of the central research questions in our study. The interview guide was hence organized around four broad topics, which were refined through a pilot testing. The first two aimed at answering our first research objective, namely, to conceptualize ReFi, asking participants about: (1) their understanding of ReFi; and (2) a common denominator of building blocks that ReFi projects usually entail. The latter two topics aimed at deriving future avenues for ReFi, asking ReFi experts about: (1) their view on the future of ReFi; and (2) potential risks for a scaling of ReFi. All interviews were conducted by either one or two researchers, audio-taped with the authorization of the participants, transcribed, and if required, translated into English for further processing. To analyze the information input, we applied the coding guidelines for building grounded theory dating back to Glaser and Strauss (1967), allowing us to systematically and inductively develop a theory around the phenomenon under study (Creswell and Poth 2007).

To identify an appropriate set of experts with a background in ReFi, we searched for experts via Google and LinkedIn using the keywords "regenerative finance" and "ReFi" as well as leveraged conference and social network information on people with ReFi content coverage. Overall, we identified and contacted 49 potential interview candidates of which 13 agreed to speak with us. Eventually, two interviews were omitted from the coding analysis due to the poor insights they provided on the posed questions. The participants from the remaining 11 interviews engaged with ReFi related topics from various professional angles, including founders of (multiple) ReFi projects, project engineers, venture capital (VC) investors, journalists and podcast producers, and academic researchers at the intersection of sustainability and blockchain applications, sometimes combining multiple angles in one person. Geographically, the interview participants were based in the United States, India, and Germany. All interviews stayed approximately within the targeted length of 30 minutes.

RESULTS

The coding analysis revealed common patterns in the interviewees' responses towards both of our research objectives. This section starts with the conceptualization of ReFi and continues with the prospects of the space. All results and statements proposed in the following are solely based on the input from the 11 expert interviews.

Conceptualization of Regenerative Finance

The conceptualization of ReFi is divided into three subsections. First, we derive a common definition of the term "ReFi." Second, we explain how the interviewees explain the emergence of ReFi. Third, we present common building blocks which characterize ReFi-related projects or activities.

Definition of regenerative finance

Three common threads emerged for defining the term "ReFi." The first surrounds the ultimate purpose of ReFi projects. While environmental topics are dominating the ReFi ecosystem, the interviewees largely agreed that ReFi projects may relate to any outcome which is not only non-extracting but even beneficial to real-world societal matters, spanning environment, social, and governance topics. Some interviewees specified ReFi projects as aiming to contribute to the Sustainable Development Goals.

The other two common threads can be categorized into means of establishing these goals: (1) the deployment of common capitalistic incentives to steer behaviors which ultimately pay back to the aforementioned societal goals; and (2) the usage of DeFi tools (for example, tokenization and smart contract-based protocols) to implement and enforce these incentive structures. The form of implementation can vary, such as representing a whole business model, a financial application as part of a larger value chain, or even an event. Taken together, we propose the following definition of ReFi emerging from the expert interviewees: regenerative finance describes any form of business models or activities which employ economic incentive systems, constructed and enforced through DeFi tools, to positively contribute towards environmental and/or societal matters.

Drivers for the emergence of regenerative finance

As the definition shows, ReFi projects use smart contract implementation and enforcement mechanisms from the longer-existing DeFi space. A delineation between these can be drawn along two criteria. The first relates to the purpose of the respective projects. While a positive contribution to the aforementioned societal matters is the core of ReFi projects, DeFi projects are rather mission-neutral, or often driven by financial-based success. The second criterion refers to the nature of the underlying assets that DeFi and ReFi are built on. DeFi protocols are often projects which exist fully on-chain; that is, the underlying assets that are traded were constructed solely with the help of a blockchain and can exist detached from real-world, non-blockchain-based phenomena.[3] ReFi projects, on the other hand, are always based on off-chain projects (for example, a reforestation venture) which provide the means to positively add back to society. In other words, while DeFi can exist on virtual assets only, ReFi projects always rely on real-world (that is, off-chain) assets.

Most interviewees hence do not see ReFi as a subcategory of DeFi, but rather as an offshoot. Some of the interviewed experts even described ReFi as a response to DeFi, constituting one of the motive forces for establishing the ReFi space: while DeFi proponents have often praised the technology to enable financial inclusion by only requiring an internet connection and being permissionless, in fact, DeFi has not yet lived up to its promises. The congestion on the Ethereum blockchain has made simple transactions a costly, high-barrier endeavor and so far, the beneficiaries of DeFi have not been the unbanked people in developing countries, but crypto-native protocol developers and investors. The ReFi community aims to return to the early goals of crypto and DeFi pioneers in using the technology to solve societal issues.

As a trailblazer for ReFi, the decrease of blockchains' own energy consumption is put forward, namely the transition from power-intensive proof-of-work (PoW) to energy-friendly proof-of-stake (PoS) block validation mechanisms. While this change reduces the environmental impact of blockchains themselves, ReFi strives for more: building business models that not only cause no harm, but also even positively add to societal interests. Most ReFi stakeholders thereby view the combat of climate change as one of the most urgent issues of our time. Legacy systems of carbon offsetting systems are perceived as not being able to scale their climate protection measures to the required value: they involve too many intermediaries and are processed over cumbersome processes and over-the-counter (OTC) deals, resulting in illiquidity, high transaction costs, and inefficient price building of natural assets. ReFi proponents see DeFi tools as a means to overcome these issues, making them one of the key building blocks in ReFi-related projects, as outlined in the next subsection. A summarizing illustration of the driving forces and proposed definition of ReFi is depicted in Figure 16.1.

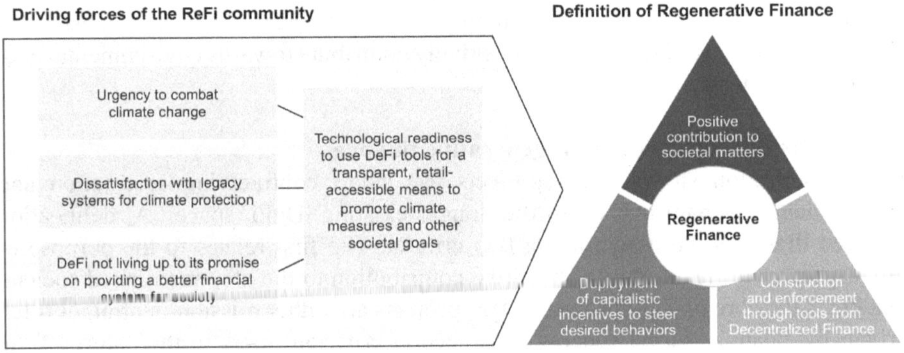

Figure 16.1 *Driving forces for the ReFi community and proposed definition of ReFi*

Building blocks of ReFi projects

As derived from the definition of ReFi and elaborated previously, the common building block across ReFi projects is their underlying mission to positively contribute to societal matters. The characterization of the remaining building blocks differs as a result of the most often stated advantage of using DeFi tools: composability. The possibility to integrate and interoperate different DeFi protocols (for example, exchanges, marketplaces) and tokens due to commonly used standards, allows the emergence of what some of our interviewees call "Nature Lego." As a founder of a ReFi protocol says, "it is very easy to pick up somewhere and build on something and just work on a part of the puzzle, not work on everything."[4] Consequently, the discussion of common building blocks surrounded the typical value chain of ReFi and the various technological and governance enablers leveraged in each of its steps. A graphical overview is depicted in Figure 16.2.

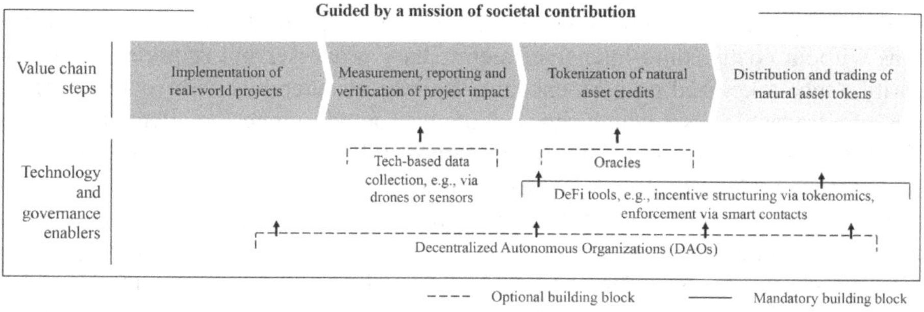

Figure 16.2 *The value chain and technological and governance enablers in regenerative finance*

The starting point of the value chain is the implementation of a real-world project that is positively adding to a societal matter. No common technological enablers emerged in this step, as the nature of the project and hence implementation enablers might differ along with the project's purpose. Currently dominating are carbon credit projects. As a co-founder of a ReFi project explains: "Carbon credits is, I want to call it, almost the low-hanging fruit of ReFi." The interviewee explains that their digital nativeness (that is, existing solely in database entries) and international nature combined with an illiquid OTC-based market, makes carbon credits a perfect use case for ReFi.

The second value chain step is the measurement, reporting, and verification of the projects' impact. In the carbon credit market, organizations such as Verra or the Gold Standard facilitate this process and present an independent, trusted third party to certify the quality of issued carbon credits. Some ReFi projects relied on these standards and provided a bridge to transfer these off-chain registries on-chain. This step, also called tokenization, referring to the representation of an off-chain as an on-chain asset, presents the third part of the value chain. However, with the advancements of DeFi, the interviewees propose these steps to be implemented in a technology-based, trustless way. As one interviewee points out, "the verification process through Verra and Gold Standard is very costly and takes a long time." As she further outlines, the chance of ReFi is to build a bottom-up approach in which also small projects, for example, involving any land stewards, can produce carbon credits. Such an approach would not only further scale the carbon credit market but also include a larger community in this.

The combination of two technological steps paves the way for such a bottom-up approach. First, advanced tools automatically collect and measure project impact data (for example, drones or soil sensors). Second, so-called oracles provide a technological, trustless bridge to transfer this off-chain information onto a blockchain where

DeFi tools can convert a nature-based tokenized asset out of the information. The connection of off-chain and on-chain events through oracles further facilitates a fair participation of contributing off-chain communities on the generated asset value, for example via royalties. Such an interface that maps real-world assets on-chain, functions without costly, time-intensive intermediary processes but requires regulatory clarity. Once tokenized on a blockchain, the project outcomes with societal impact present a tradeable asset which can now be distributed to investors, depicted here as the fourth value chain step. The distribution of tokens may use the full toolbox of DeFi (for example, incentive structuring via tokenomics, and enforcement via smart contacts) such that the same advantages which have been praised in DeFi, now also unfold for ReFi assets: data and transaction transparency, retail accessibility, minimized transaction costs, and trustless real-time trading; resulting in system-embedded trust, enhanced liquidity, and "true" price discovery. To ensure sufficient demand, end-user-faced projects such as marketplaces specialize in aggregating ReFi token registries to provide palatable end-user products for both retail and institutional clients. Given the simple composability of tokenized assets, customized ReFi funds can easily be constructed, for example, with varying asset quality or environmental impact requirements. Tokenomics thereby provides the means to construct any economic models to incentive potential investors to contribute to the societal mission.

Moreover, tokenomics enables simply implemented co-ownership models, which incentivize not only investment but also co-creation. The possibility to create such incentive structures for active participation are one of the most often named advantages of organizing ReFi projects via the governance form of DAOs. Leveraging DAO tokenomics, teams can quickly build a global community of supporters for their regenerative mission, which is particularly important in consumer-facing projects. On the other hand, governance through DAOs also brings some pitfalls. The decentralized nature of DAOs and hence their decision-making processes might hinder effectiveness. This setback becomes especially prevalent in early-stage phases when many important directional decisions are to be taken quickly. Referring back to the value chain, DAOs especially reach their limits in the very beginning and at the end, when it comes to collaborations with non-crypto native entities. As one interviewee explains the issues of implementing real-world projects via DAOs: "A DAO is not a legal entity. A DAO cannot sign contracts; a DAO cannot buy a piece of forest; a DAO cannot even sign a loan agreement." Similarly, for projects with business-to-business (B2B) models, in which a community is less important and the counterpart is a legal entity as well, a non-DAO governance form is better suited.

Having conceptualized the current picture of ReFi, the next section looks forward and outlines ReFi's future pathway.

The Prospects of Regenerative Finance

Considering that legacy systems regularly fail on their climate targets, all interviewees argued in favor of a long-term and impactful perspective of ReFi. To make such a long-term perspective realistic, all of them identified required actions to drive

ReFi's large-scale adaption and impact as well as risks which could threaten this endeavor. A structured overview of the answers is depicted in Box 16.1.

BOX 16.1 DETERMINANTS OF THE FUTURE OF REFI

Conditions and actions to be taken to achieve the overarching goals:

- Creation of more ReFi awareness through cooperations with prestigious legacy institutions, education on ReFi, and academic research.
- Integration of a broader range of stakeholder interests in ReFi business models, that is, regulators, legacy institutions, project suppliers, customers.
- Improvements along the ReFi value chain, that is, more on-site involvement in real-world projects, better integration of off-chain and on-chain steps through oracles, enhanced user friendliness of ReFi applications, closer collaboration among projects.
- Regulation of ReFi-related aspects (DeFi tools, natural assets, DAOs) to provide certainty to all stakeholders.
- Attracting more talent to the ReFi ecosystem.
- Change of narrative in projects towards regenerative benefits via ReFi rather than a crypto focus.

Overarching goals:

- Increase in supply of projects with a regenerative impact.
- Attainment of a larger customer base (institutional and retail demand) for more investments and liquidity.

Risks to be mitigated:

- Reputation issues through bad-quality or scam ReFi projects.
- Reputation issues and market spillover effects from DeFi space.
- Regulatory bans and resistance from legacy institutions.

Two overarching goals emerged for the ReFi community. On the one hand, an increase in supply of regenerative projects and thereby in the regenerative impact from the space is desired. On the other hand, an attainment of a larger customer base is required to provide the demand for the assets generated from regenerative projects. An increase in investments would provide more liquidity in the ReFi market and hence make it more efficient. Both retail and, especially, institutional investments should be targeted to achieve this goal.

Overall, six broad categories of required conditions and actions emerged to enable these goals. The first main vehicle to scale ReFi lies in creating more awareness about it. The most often mentioned means to enhance awareness and subsequent adaption of ReFi is to increase the cooperation with, ideally, well-known and impactful legacy stakeholders, such as through, as one interviewee explains, "collaborations with the federal governments, the UN [United Nations], the EU [European Union], with some NGOs [non-governmental organizations] that are not Web3 native, to begin with, and thus build trust. Identify these 'early adopters,' create this journey with them, and take that as an example for many, many other potential stakeholders." An important accompanying measure, as with all new technologies, rests on educating people about the purpose and functionalities of ReFi more broadly. The education should thereby translate ReFi aspects into an easy-to-understand language for non-crypto natives and span the exact spheres that motivated early adopters to start and join the ReFi community in the first place (see Figure 16.1): (1) means to support the combat of climate change such as carbon credit markets; (2) flaws in the current, non-ReFi processes for environmental protection; and (3) the functionalities of DeFi mechanisms and how they can build the basis for an efficient ReFi market. Objective research about measurable associated regenerative effects, limitations, and potential improvements of ReFi processes is demanded as academic support from the interviewees.

Second, a common thread emerged around the importance of better integrating various stakeholders in ReFi business models. ReFi solutions and projects should hence not only be developed within and for crypto-native spheres, but should be also built to be suitable to a wider community, entailing regulators, legacy institutions such as Verra or the Gold Standard, project suppliers and communities, as well as a broad institutional and retail customer base. One interviewee explains: "as soon as you have this institutional buy-in and this legitimization from the established markets, such as the carbon markets, I believe that this will simply take the topic of ReFi to another level." Another interviewee concretizes his vision for empowered local communities via ReFi: "Because once you give all of this financial tooling and tooling that allows communities to define their own types of green assets, ecological assets or natural capital, they will latch on to that, I think. This means that you will have a network of communities all around the globe that are operating and producing green assets in a sovereign way."

Third, different aspects were mentioned on how to improve different parts of the value chain (see Figure 16.2). Starting with the beginning of the value chain, more on-site involvement from ReFi-related projects is required to ensure a supply of high-quality and equitable regenerative projects. One interviewee explains the strength of the ReFi project MossDAO as regionally engaging on-site in the Amazon region, and that this on-site involvement marks the point where the possibility for ReFi to scale would need to be proven, that is, "whether you then bring the manpower onto the street or into the forest is the exciting question." Further, some interviewees put forward the need for a smooth integration of real-world off-chain components and on-chain token distribution. To do so, reliable oracles are required. Eventually, to ensure an increase in demand, ReFi applications need to become more user-friendly. This aspect is especially crucial to attract more non-DeFi native customers. All these improvements of the value chain would be better attained if projects entered into more partnerships with each other and further realized the composability potential. One interviewee even proposed a consolidation of projects.

A mandatory base for better collaboration among ReFi stakeholders, and for an accomplishment of improvements along ReFi's value chain, also requires regulatory certainty on ReFi-related aspects as well as ReFi's compliance with existing regulations. As the fourth category of required conditions, regulation is thereby needed regarding the usage of DeFi tools (for example, smart contract-based platforms or oracles), the rights and obligations coming with the possession and trading of natural assets such as carbon credits, and the legal status of DAOs.

Fifth, to drive these actions, more talent needs to be steered towards the ReFi ecosystem. Developers currently signify the largest bottleneck. Yet founders and other skilled talent such as designers or people familiar with business development are also in demand.

Sixth, ReFi participants should try to change the overall narrative of their space away from a blockchain and crypto focus. The focus should rather lie on the regenerative benefit which ReFi solutions provide compared to other non-crypto solutions. The change in narrative will also help in mitigating some of the crypto-immersing reputation risks as outlined below.

Three main risks have emerged that might threaten a quick, wide-scale adoption of ReFi. Two of these risks concern reputation issues for the space, stemming either from bad-quality or scam projects within the ReFi space itself, or from spillover effects from DeFi projects. A common example of the former is the KlimaDAO project, in which short-term financial incentives were built upon bad-quality carbon certificates. One interviewee explains the consequences of "projects that virtually bring the bad guys from DeFi to ReFi" as follows: "That such things as Terra Luna happen with natural assets and people feel not only this financial loss, but perhaps also an emotional loss, because it is now perhaps links to forests, or to animals, or to people and accordingly communities." To mitigate this risk of integrity loss and greenwashing accusations, the community needs to make sure that the quality of underlying ReFi assets is high, and that long-term benefits instead of short-term financial incentives are set.

The reputation issues from the DeFi space are accompanied by potential market spillover effects, given the interdependencies between them. One ReFi entrepreneur explains the reputation effects from first-hand experience: "What we have now felt very strongly … in discussions with investors, for example, is the fiasco around Terra Luna. That didn't necessarily help us because it gave the term 'stablecoin' a lot of disrepute." Apart from reputation issues, risks stemming from the underlying technological structure might spill over from DeFi (for example, smart contract issues), and some interviewees outline the investment traction to be generally lower in DeFi bear markets. While regulation is appreciated to provide certainty in ReFi-related endeavors, a regulatory ban of any associated building blocks would threaten ReFi's future. Similarly, headwind and non-cooperation from legacy bodies in the space of regenerative economics would impede ReFi's ambitions.

DISCUSSION AND CONCLUSION

Our work shows that the ReFi community is aware of the critique and risks that former scholars have pointed out. In line with concerns by Howson (2020) and Stuit et al. (2022), the interviewees have named badly designed ReFi projects, which do not positively contribute to societal matters but only benefit their developers, as the main risk of and for ReFi. Similarly, the experts join the call to action of Manski and Bauwens (2020) and Thomason et al. (2018) for a closer collaboration with non-crypto native sustainability stakeholders, to jointly design well-rounded and effective regenerative solutions. To ensure an equitable involvement of communities' needs and concerns in project designs, the interviewees argue for more on-site involvement from ReFi contributors. In the collaboration with other non-crypto native legacy stakeholders, however, the interviewees hold all parties responsible to enable a value-adding cooperation, and name resistance from possible collaboration partners as a main concern.

By providing an independent consolidation of ReFi pioneers' perspectives, driving forces, visions, and concerns, our chapter supports the dialogue between those stakeholders. Further, our chapter contributes to creating awareness on ReFi's goals, and explains the technological and economic means to attain these goals. The synthesization of our interviewees' views on deficiencies and improvement potential in current processes, as well as risks to be mitigated, present actionable measures to be addressed by the ReFi community and support from scholars.

The integration of ReFi-native views, as in our chapter, is only one side of the story. We agree with Stuit et al. (2022) that to assess the actual impact of ReFi, associated project outcomes should be measured on the ground, and in collaboration with the local communities that the project involves. A transparent analysis of both accomplishments as well as limitations and pitfalls would enable an objective record of lessons learned, and in turn an improvement in the future design of impactful ReFi business models. While academic support as demanded from the interviewees thus supports educating people about ReFi and facilitating dialogue among all stakeholders, we agree with Manski and Bauwens (2020) that, eventually, it is the responsibility of ReFi entrepreneurs and investors to design true regenerative social and economic systems beyond capitalism.

NOTES

1. Ironically, the misusage and subsequent loss of customer funds by central intermediaries such as FTX is exactly one of the incidents which Nakamoto (2008) aimed to prevent by inventing the blockchain.

2. For a better understanding of crypto-native terminologies used here, we refer to the following works: Meyer et al. (2022) present the current academic understanding of DeFi; Morrow and Zarrebini (2019) outline how tokenization works, its societal applications, and potential use cases; Kampakis (2018) provides an overview of how tokenomics can be used for various forms of incentive-setting via the analysis of three case studies; Ziegler and Welpe (2022) define and derive a taxonomy of DAOs. For a more in-depth background on regenerative economics, we refer to Fullterton (2015).
3. In some cases, DeFi protocols are attached to a real-world asset; for example, some stablecoins are backed by the real currency which they are pegged to.
4. Where necessary, interview quotations have been translated into English by the authors.

REFERENCES

Briola, A., Vidal-Tomás, D., Wang, Y., and Aste, T. (2022). Anatomy of a Stablecoin's Failure: The Terra-Luna Case. *Finance Research Letters*, 103358.

Chapron, G. (2017). The Environment Needs Cryptogovernance. *Nature*, *545*(7655), 403–405.

CoinGecko. (2022). *Charts zur Krypto-Marktkapitalisierung | CoinGecko*. https://www.coingecko.com/de/global-charts, accessed October 31, 2022.

CompaniesMarketCap.com. (2022). *Largest Banks and Bank Holding Companies by Market Cap*. https://companiesmarketcap.com/banks/largest-banks-by-market-cap/, accessed November 16, 2022.

Creswell, J.W., and Poth, C.N. (2007). *Qualitative Inquiry and Research Design: Choosing Among Five Approaches*. SAGE Publications.

Fullterton, J. (2015). *Regenerative Capitalism: How Universal Principles and Patterns Will Shape Our New Economy*. Whitepaper. Capital Institute.

Galletta, A. (2013). *Mastering the Semi-Structured Interview and Beyond: From Research Design to Analysis and Publication*. NYU Press.

Glaser, B.G., and Strauss, A.L. (1967). *The Discovery of Grounded Theory: Strategies for Qualitative Research*. Aldine.

Howson, P. (2019). Tackling Climate Change with Blockchain. *Nature Climate Change*, *9*(9), 644–645.

Howson, P. (2020). Climate Crises and Crypto-Colonialism: Conjuring Value on the Blockchain Frontiers of the Global South. *Frontiers in Blockchain*, *3*, Article 22.

Howson, P., Oakes, S., Baynham-Herd, Z., and Swords, J. (2019). Cryptocarbon: The Promises and Pitfalls of Forest Protection on a Blockchain. *Geoforum*, *100*, 1–9.

Kampakis, S. (2018). Three Case Studies in Tokenomics. *Journal of the British Blockchain Association*, *1*(2), 1–4.

KlimaDAO. (2022). *ReFi and the Realization of a Regenerative Economy*. https://www.klimadao.finance/blog/refi-and-the-realization-of-a-regenerative-economy, accessed November 23, 2022.

Knott, E., Rao, A.H., Summers, K., and Teeger, C. (2022). Interviews in the Social Sciences. *Nature Reviews Methods Primers*, *2*(1), 1–15.

Manski, S., and Bauwens, M. (2020). Reimagining New Socio-Technical Economics Through the Application of Distributed Ledger Technologies. *Frontiers in Blockchain*, *2*, Article 29.

Marr, B. (2022). The Top Five Web3 Trends in 2023. *Forbes*. https://www.forbes.com/sites/bernardmarr/2022/10/18/the-top-five-web3-trends-in-2023/?sh=4a7a97a3b3f2, accessed October 18, 2022.

Meyer, E., Welpe, I.M., and Sandner, P. (2022). Decentralized Finance—A Systematic Literature Review and Research Directions. *ECIS 2022 Research Papers*, Article 25.

Morrow, M.J., and Zarrebini, M. (2019). Blockchain and the Tokenization of the Individual: Societal Implications. *Future Internet*, *11*(10), 220.

Nakamoto, S. (2008). Bitcoin: A Peer-to-Peer Electronic Cash System. *SSRN Electronic Journal.*

Pschetz, L., Dixon, B., Pothong, K., Bailey, A., Glean, A., Soares, L.L., and Enright, J.A. (2020). Designing Distributed Ledger Technologies for Social Change. In *Proceedings of the 2020 CHI Conference on Human Factors in Computing Systems.* ACM.

Regen Network. (2022). *Regen Network.* https://www.regen.network/, accessed November 23, 2022.

Stebbins, R.A. (2001). *Exploratory Research in the Social Sciences. Qualitative Research Methods: V. 48*. SAGE.

Stuit, A., Brockington, D., and Corbera, E. (2022). Smart, Commodified and Encoded. *Conservation and Society*, *20*(1), 12–23.

Thomason, J., Ahmad, M., Bronder, P., Hoyt, E., Pocock, S., Bouteloupe, J., Donaghy, K., Huysman, D., Willenberg, T., Joakim, B., Joseph, L., Martin, D., and Shrier, D. (2018). Blockchain—Powering and Empowering the Poor in Developing Countries. In A. Marke (ed.), *Transforming Climate Finance and Green Investment with Blockchains* (pp. 137–152). Academic Press.

Toucan. (2022). *DeFi ReFi: Technology for a New Economy that's Regenerative by Design.* https://docs.toucan.earth/toucan/introduction/readme, accessed November 23, 2022.

Turner, D. (2010). Qualitative Interview Design: A Practical Guide for Novice Investigators. *The Qualitative Report*, *15*(3), 754–760.

World Bank. (2022). *Market Capitalization of Listed Domestic Companies (Current US$)—Germany | Data.* https://data.worldbank.org/indicator/CM.MKT.LCAP.CD?end=2020&locations=DE&start=2009, accessed November 23, 2022.

Ziegler, C., and Welpe, I.M. (2022). A Taxonomy of Decentralized Autonomous Organizations. *ICIS 2022 Proceedings*, Article 1.

17. Decentralized finance in the developing world: the end of the financial inclusion gap?

Mariana Carmona and Paz Gomez

INTRODUCTION

Seventy-three percent of the unbanked live in developing economies. The majority reside in rural or peri-urban areas, subsisting in poverty conditions and underemployment. Sociodemographically, the financially excluded are foremostly the youth, women, disabled, and elderly (Ifrim 2022). At the same time, the technological progress made by the financial industry in recent decades has incorporated into the financial system more than 300 million people between 2017 and 2021 (World Bank 2022b). There is a paradox: high technological development and persistent financial exclusion. The devil is in the details. Digital innovation is not the sole ingredient for financial inclusion.

Through a comparative analysis, this chapter examines how to better attain financial inclusion, focusing on decentralized finance (DeFi). Although DeFi is in early adoption stages, multiple actors are already resorting to it under the argument of financial inclusion.

The chapter is organized as follows. It first presents an overview of Web3 and blockchain technology. Next, it reports on financial inclusion in the DeFi era with fresh insights on how decentralized applications enhance and empower users to build, choose, and govern their financial reality. The following section examines historic cases in which financial inclusion macro-policies in massive top-down executions failed to achieve the expected results, showing that the same risk is present with cryptocurrencies and DeFi. We analyze in depth the case of El Salvador, where the authorities set Bitcoin as legal tender, but citizens are rejecting it. In contrast, the next section addresses the case of Brazil, where the authorities successfully established flexible and open rules allowing the flourishing of neobanks, and speculate whether this is the preamble to the deployment of a powerful Brazilian DeFi ecosystem. The final section concludes.

DIGITAL FINANCE ON THE WEB3

The digital economy has gained so much prominence in the 21st century that it has become an influential driving force worldwide. By bringing higher social and economic benefits, its global adoption has accelerated in recent years. Companies, governments, and multilateral agencies have invested significant time and financial resources into it. As a result, new information technologies such as cloud computing, big data, and artificial intelligence have not only boosted the digital economy, but also enabled out-of-the-box solutions in troubled industries and societies (Chen et al. 2022: 1).

As an example, digital finance has made financial products available to a broader population. Technological innovation has reduced costs and time associated with providing financial services, and financial products have lower fees and higher risk resistance. As the number of users and the amount of money has increased in online financial services, concerns about security, privacy, and control have arisen too. In consequence, distributed ledger technologies (DLTs) have gained relevance, due to their potential to create a decentralized Internet (Chen et al. 2022: 2).

DLTs are data storage systems that record and share information across a network of participants. Rather than storing records in unique servers, DLTs save identical copies of information in multiple points of the network, to improve security and make it more difficult to change, remove, or lose the stored data (World Bank 2017: vii). Blockchain is a type of DLT in which data collected during a particular time span is transmitted in information blocks to the rest of the network participants, known as nodes. Then these blocks are concatenated in a sequential manner, deriving into an easy flow of information (Chen et al. 2022: 3).

Blockchains are more difficult to attack because there is no single point of failure. A successful attack needs to target all identical copies of the ledger, or more than half of the nodes need to collude in dishonest behavior. To avoid the latter, blockchain includes computational elements such as cryptography and consensus mechanisms. While cryptography is applied to hash records and provides digital signatures with unique access, consensus mechanisms are predefined algorithmic validation methods that nodes use to verify data before storing it in a decentralized manner. Blockchains transfer trust from service providers to a trustless network system (Chen et al. 2022: 4). Therefore, blockchains are append-only distributed databases with tamper-proof, immutable, time-stamped, pseudo-anonymous transactions with real-time traceability, auditability, and security of transaction records.[1]

With its characteristics, blockchain has become the cornerstone technology of digital finance in which the power of information is far more distributed than before, and transactions can be done in a peer-to-peer manner. In terms of individual behavior and societal organization, unlike current social networks and platform-based economic activities, blockchains create networks that enhance interaction and collective action of digital communities, entailing the next iteration and construction of social communication and economic networking, one in which digital communities can acquire governance attributions over protocols. As a result, new forms of financial intermediation are emerging based on decentralized technologies, open socioeconomic systems, and data (Sigova et al. 2021: 2).

Distributed ledgers shape the new Web3; that is, the internet of value, an immersive experience where users are not only content producers and consumers, but also owners of their data, content, and money (Westermeier 2020: 2048). Predecessors of Web3 moved in the "only reading," unidirectional internet, Web1; while Web2 refers to the internet experience mostly enabled by social networks, where users can browse the web, create content, and upload media to share (Chen et al. 2022: 1). At this stage, the network became more democratic and interactive; however, service providers remain the owners of users' data and custodians of their money. Additionally, Web2 networks are more vulnerable to data loss, manipulation, and leakage due to their centralized storage systems.

On the other hand, Web3 incorporates blockchain along with other disruptive technologies such as artificial intelligence, marking the newest stage of the Internet by decentralization and autonomy (Chen et al. 2022: 2), granting digital sovereignty to users, and enhancing itself without going through centralized platforms. Figure 17.1 illustrates the evolution of the Web.

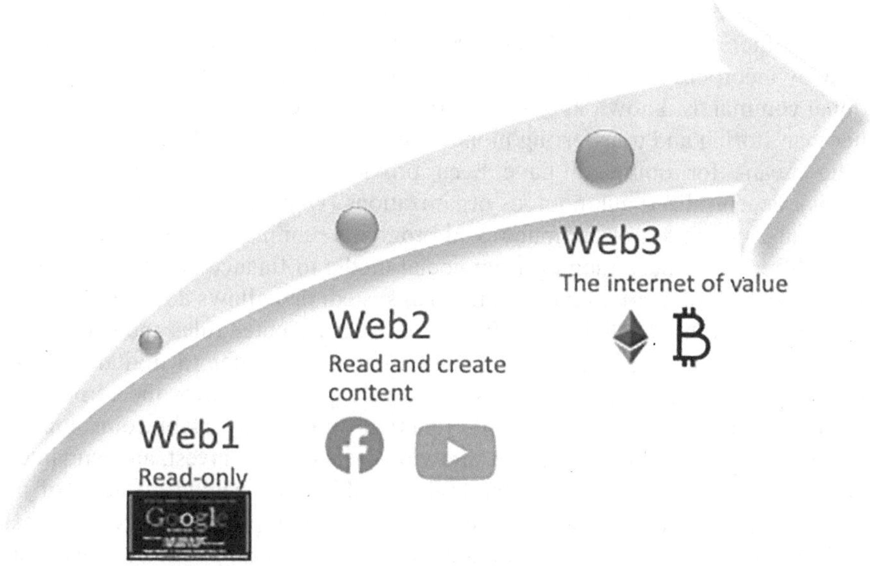

Figure 17.1 *The evolution of the Web*

Enter Decentralized Finance

In 2008, when the world was going through a great depression and policymakers were using taxpayer dollars to rescue "too-big-to-fail" firms and banks, the first blockchain emerged. It was Bitcoin, the first peer-to-peer (P2P) electronic cash system offering an alternative to the traditional financial system. Bitcoin—which was the result of decades of research and piloting in the fields of mathematics, economics, and computer science—not only underlies the Web3 inception, but is also a disruptive innovation in finance.

By acknowledging private property on the Web3, interactions turn into transactions. These transactions need to be recorded and paid, and here is where blockchain gains relevance. Firstly, a transaction's data is stored in the chain of blocks; and secondly, blockchain represents the technology behind most cryptocurrencies, occurring as peer-to-peer electronic cash systems and private forms of digital money.

Bitcoin was novel because it was the first network protocol setting the monetary policy of a digital currency where no central authority was needed. Bitcoin has no censorship, no borders, and no barriers to entry. Therefore, when people started adopting Bitcoin, the paradigm around financial access changed: people acquire sovereignty over the course of their monies, hold it in electronic wallets, and transfer it globally on a permanent operational basis. The ongoing innovation of blockchain continued to challenge the traditional paradigm. Ethereum, launched in 2015, came out as a new generation of blockchains that opened the gateway to a decentralized internet. Ethereum allows P2P transactions in the native currency (Ether) but primarily by incorporating a virtual machine that enables the blockchain to run computational commands, known as smart contracts, in which complex financial services other than storing and transferring money are possible (World Bank 2017: 20–22).

The means for doing so have been provided by decentralized applications (dApps), decentralized autonomous organizations (DAOs), and stablecoins. DApps are digital applications or computational programs running on the blockchain, each with a different purpose ranging from social media to finance (Frankenfield 2022). DAOs are a blockchain-based computational system that allows a group of people to coordinate throughout a digital ecosystem with self-executed rules and decentralized governance (Chen et al. 2022: 9). Finally, stablecoins refer to digital currencies with their value pegged to another asset—namely gold, the dollar, the euro, or other cryptocurrencies—or to an algorithmic function. In this way, stablecoins cope with volatility and maintain a steady price, allowing users to save, invest, and lend in cryptocurrency (Hayes 2022). The technological architecture behind all three of these elements is smart contracts, which also enable a digital representation of physical or real-world assets such as real estate and stocks (Chen et al. 2022: 8). This process is known as tokenization, and blockchain-based digital identifiers are known as non-fungible tokens (NFTs). The ensemble constitutes a moldable stack for financial services, called decentralized finance (DeFi).

DeFi is an open, permissionless, highly interoperable stack, free from centralized intermediaries (for example, brokers, banks, or exchanges) where transactions are executed in a secure, predictable, verifiable way, with legitimate state changes traceable on the public, tamper-proof blockchains (Strüker et al. 2022: 15). DeFi creates new possibilities unlike anything in traditional finance, given its core basis: composability.

Composability refers to the ability to use financial dApps in different combinations. Also known as "Money Lego," DeFi's composability eliminates the need to ask anyone to integrate an element of another protocol, carrying out complex financial strategies and transactions without leaving an ecosystem. For instance, one can borrow a digital currency in DeFi protocol A, to deposit it into DeFi protocol B to back the issuance of a new token, and use the new token to trade in protocol C. Endless combinations can be performed with no third parties involved, which makes a difference compared to Web2 in which, for instance, someone using a digital payments platform X to buy in platform Y needs to log in on both, or use an email or social network Z to do so. In Web2, the user is the composability lever for each application. Moreover, the user has to trust all the applications where they are signing in (Monolith 2021).

The first set of DeFi products replicated those in traditional finance, for example borrowing, liquidity provision, insurance, or derivatives. Nonetheless, new financial products, non-replicable in the traditional world, emerged with DeFi. These include, among others:

1. Flash loans: uncollateralized loans in which the funds are borrowed and paid within the same transaction; otherwise the smart contract reverses the operation as if the loan had never existed.
2. Decentralized exchanges (DEXs): unlike centralized order books that match bid/ask offers, where exchanges are custodians and trusted parties, DEXs are trustless platforms running on smart contracts that use a liquidity pool as counterparty. The asset exchange is done via automated market makers (AMMs), an algorithm that determines the price in which an order is executed based on the ratio of assets in the liquidity pool (Strüker et al. 2022, 21).
3. NFT finance: non-fungible tokens with non-financial use cases are financialized for investment purposes.
4. Prediction markets: decentralized platforms where specific real-life events can be predicted using crowd wisdom with financial incentives (Strüker et al. 2022: 25).
5. Yield farming: high-risk strategies from a combination of lending, borrowing, and liquidity provision, moving the funds at a high speed between DeFi protocols to maximize yields.
6. Staking or passive income generation: locking digital assets into a smart contract allowing nodes in the network to validate transactions[2] in which a share of the transaction fees is passive income for the depositor.

FINANCIAL INCLUSION IN THE ERA OF DEFI

Financial inclusion is the state in which individuals and businesses have access to useful and affordable financial products and services that meet their needs (transactions, transfers, payments, savings, credit, financial planning, account statements, and insurance), delivered in a responsible and sustainable way (World Bank 2022a). Likewise, digital financial inclusion refers to the deployment of digital means such as e-money, whether online or on a mobile phone, cards, wallets, or other means, to reach financially excluded and underserved populations with financial products and services delivered responsibly, at an affordable cost to customers, and sustainable for providers (GPFI 2016: 3).

Financial inclusion policies usually target people living in poverty (Ozili 2020: 3), the majority of whom are less educated, rural, outside the labor market, self-employed, or working in the informal economy.[3] In addition, people in impoverished conditions often lack financial records and documents to identify and prove incomes. The target population is mainly composed of women, the elderly, indigenous, migrants, disabled, and young people (World Bank 2022b: 33); that is, societal groups that experience more social and economic inequalities compared to the rest of the society. As of 2021, the former target population (that is, the unbanked) reached 1.4 billion individuals (World Bank 2022b: 33). The Universal Financial Access Initiative 2020 focuses on 25 developing countries[4] where 73 percent live (World Bank n.d.).

The reasons for financial exclusion are manifold.[5] The lack of physical bank branches was a reason for exclusion in the pre-digital finance era; however, today it is not the pre-eminent barrier. In fact, the cost and time reduction that digital solutions offer are insurmountable by previous branch-banking models. Therefore, what is behind financial exclusion in developing countries?

Given the characteristics of the target population, there is a higher degree of complexity in financially serving them because the dynamics are not purely financial, but also social. In contrast, banking[6] business is designed to serve urban, salaried, middle-upper-income classes; that is, predictable clients for whom risk assessment and one-size-fit-all products are profitable, as well as affordable to customers. The unbanked cannot fit into homogeneous customer categories, therefore creating a dissociation between the supply and the needs. For banks, this target population is risky, costly, and unprofitable. For the excluded, banks offer costly and unattractive products not suited to them.

The Dissociation between Traditional Banks and the Unbanked

Savings offers one of the most straightforward ways to present this dissociation. The unbanked use informal savings products, for instance by keeping money under the mattress. Savings help them to manage basic needs and smooth consumption during the year. Also, unbanked populations seek to raise lump sums for housing, wedding, education, or food security. Given their income instability, liquidity requirements also vary during the year, with high peaks in seasons of high income shortages, when vulnerable populations dip into their savings. The unbanked need savings products adapted to their daily changing conditions, so that they are able to make tiny deposits,[7] and free from paying onerous fees.

Banks fail to offer savings products to this target population. For instance, a bank account with full liquidity demands average balances; otherwise, the bank charges management commissions, something that disadvantages the poor because, in a given month, they might need to withdraw and possibly deplete the account. The next month, the commissions can exceed the deposits, discouraging the use of bank accounts. On the other hand, long-term investments demand initial amounts and lock-up periods that are unaffordable to the poor.

A second dissociation emerges in credit. A disparity in incentives exists between the banks and the financially excluded. On the one hand, banks do not have business incentives to provide loans to the unbanked, much less to finance their economic activities, unless banks are made part of public policies that try to fix the market failure. According to bank standards and business structure, there are multiple information asymmetries in lending money to individuals without financial records: lack of identification documents, and lack of collateral or stable incomes. As such, the interest rates for them are higher. On their side, the target population self-excludes from taking loans, and in the case of qualifying for it, the product does not serve them in an adequate and affordable manner.

Paradoxically, in developing countries, bank revenues come mainly from consumer credit. If banks or microfinance institutions (MFIs) ever approach the poor or vulnerable, it will be by allocating consumption credit (that is, credit to purchase non-durable and small durable goods). Banks offer consumer credit to the poor because small businesses are riskier, and analyzing productive credit for small businesses or peasants has elevated transaction and information costs that commercial banks find unprofitable, debunking the myth that these intermediaries are willing to open the faucet of productive credit if asked to do so. At the same time, the financially excluded are not especially interested in getting loans. Empirical studies have shown that many unbanked do not want microloans even if they qualify. Also, demand for microcredit is neither constant nor necessarily increasing among the poor (CGAP 2008). Banerjee et al. (in Carmona et al. 2018: 97) studied microcredit programs in developing countries and found that two-thirds of the microcredit target population was not asking for a loan. Morvant and Crucifix (in Carmona et al. 2018: 97) analyzed that credit allocation mainly responds to business goals where intermediaries create demand for credit via marketing strategies, rather than a genuine interest to fulfill financial needs. Other reasons that decouple the unbanked and the banks include reciprocal lack of trust, discrimination of customers for instance with indigenous traits, adult women or the disabled; and inescapably, the digital and financial educational gap.

DeFi Features to Potentially Close the Financial Inclusion Gap

At its inception, DeFi could be branded a "crypto *degenerate* camp," where self-described gamblers are willing to put in large amounts of capital, take high risks, and insanely increase their financial gains just as they could also face substantial losses (Raghuveera 2021: 7). DeFi 1.0 is predominantly serving those with access to the financial system, and predominantly institutions. Nonetheless, in emerging markets, people are driving adoption of cryptocurrencies to bypass hyperinflation and currency depreciation, or to avoid the control of authoritarian regimes (Raghuveera 2021: 1). Likewise, DeFi could be a leapfrog technology (WEF 2022) to assist the

Table 17.1 Attributes in DeFi that foster financial inclusion

Traditional financial intermediaries	DeFi
Censorship (possible)	Censorship resistant
Entry is granted and can be banned anytime	Open, no barriers of entry
Operates with schedules	24/7 operations
Geographically constrained	Borderless
Inflationary monetary systems	Monetary systems can be deflationary
Users trust in the custodians of their funds	Users transact in a trustless environment

poor and the unbanked. Among the reasons driving DeFi as a lever for financial inclusion are those displayed in Table 17.1.

DeFi has no barriers to entry; it is borderless, not geographically constrained, and has no operation schedules. In this environment, the unbanked, who have suffered discrimination, mistreatment, or rejection, can certainly benefit. Nonetheless, these advantages do not mean that the financial product automatically fulfills their needs. DeFi 2.0 for financial inclusion should be the moment when the technology provides comprehensive financial tools for savings, loans, payments, insurance, and remittances, and serves as means to build financial health and financial wealth. DeFi can accomplish these goals, and we highlight a few reasons behind this hypothesis.

First, the composability of DeFi allows for designing and developing financial products that users can customize, and moreover individualize every parameter; for example, enable savings and investment amounts according to their changing needs, choose among different liquidity options and perhaps not a lock-up period at all, and still get yields or rewards for their deposits.

Second, DeFi eliminates the credit bias of banks, because DeFi has other revenue streams such as network fees or staking fees. In this case, low-income populations do not need to get undesired loans.

Third, DeFi improves financial intermediation because those wanting to borrow money and those wanting to save concur with the same protocol. In this case, there are no bureaucratic procedures to assess the applications of borrowers and depositors. Funds flow in the way that the users need, and capital flows efficiently.

Fourth, DeFi wallets function as "accounts" and represent unique gateways to execute a large set of financial services; for example, to send and receive money, save, or invest. Moreover, wallets allow the storage and exchange of different cryptocurrencies, stablecoins, tokens, and fiat currencies; that is, all-in-one monetary and financial solutions are feasible, offering better options to cover against inflation, depreciation, or authoritarian regimes that harm every citizen, but more deeply affect the poor.

Fifth, perhaps one of the most relevant characteristics of DeFi and blockchain technology is the opening to savings and loans with community-based approaches (WEF 2022). As happens in the legacy financial world, there are social responses to financial exclusion, such as rotating savings-credit associations, credit co-operatives, partner hands, *susus* in Argentina, or *tandas* in Mexico. As previously mentioned,

Web3 technologies drive collective action and align peers' interests in a way that allows for cooperation and governance as a result of trustless programmed environments, suggesting that these attributes could be extended to decentralized microfinance, in which community funds can be invested, transacted, and moved seamlessly (WEF 2022). An example is Nexus Mutual,[8] a decentralized insurance mutuality where members subscribe through the utility token, and not by an insurmountable pile of paperwork and requirements (claims are also expeditiously executed). Similar insurance models can cover small peasant communities, small and medium-sized enterprises, and health and life insurance for the most vulnerable populations.

Through a financial inclusion lens, DeFi has some caveats for future developments. For instance, closing the literacy gap in the digital and financial realms is inescapable for any application approaching this population. Fortunately, there are novel ways to build financial education programs in Web3; for instance, learn-to-earn models, in which the tokenization of education that allows students to get passive income while learning new topics makes education for adults more attractive as it incorporates economic incentives. The next caveat is the need for friendly, intuitive, and easy-to-use DeFi applications where the user has customer support. More importantly, no DeFi product will lead to financial inclusion if the user is not capable of choosing the risk level and is fully aware of it, underscoring that the unbanked are disadvantaged populations that juggle with multiple risks on a daily basis.

THE FAILURE OF FINANCIAL INCLUSION MACRO-POLICIES IN THE DEVELOPING WORLD

The development of DeFi solutions for the unbanked is a necessary but not a sufficient condition in which the following challenge is adoption and utilization. DeFi deploys its potential in ample ecosystems where multiple dApps and digital tokens coexist. In the absence of competition, friendly regulation, and an organically grown ecosystem fulfilling multiple financial needs, it is likely that DeFi would hardly reach the unbanked. Thus, in this section we refer to three cases of financial inclusion policies where elite-led, massive, top-down solutions have led to poor or opposite results. Such policies generally assume a homogeneous *Homo economicus* response to economic stimuli, tend to disregard socioeconomic intricacies that increase social tensions, or disregard an individual's financial needs, among other unexpected results.

The first example is the Grameen Bank's innovative methodology that has sought to provide loans to unbanked poor populations in developing countries. Its massive standardized reproduction resulted in a world microfinance crisis. The second case shows the global crusade on financial inclusion via social-transfers financing and digitization, where studies in two countries provide evidence of the users' rejection of the sudden delivery of bank accounts and debit cards. The third example is El Salvador's adoption of Bitcoin as legal tender, where a unilateral decision regarding the use of the cryptocurrency by the country's government came in contradiction to the trustless-decentralized nature of Bitcoin, and led to the abandonment and deception of the users.

The Unfortunate Reproduction of Grameen's Group Lending

The Grameen experience dates back to 1976, when Professor Muhamad Yunus demonstrated to banks, governments, and not a few skeptics that the extremely poor could be credited with a microcredit and pay it back. The microcredit with joint guarantee in self-organized, non-family groups became Grameen's flagship lending model. The expansion over forty countries was firstly carried out by the Grameen Bank Replication Program (GBRP) via MFIs and non-profit organizations. The program reached more than 106.6 million clients by 2006 (Greenberg n.d.: xi) with repayment rates exceeding 98 percent (Mainsah et al. 2004: 11). The expansion program demanded an immersive training and adoption of the ethical principles and social lens of the methodology. In 2006, Muhamad Yunus was awarded the Nobel Peace Prize for his contribution to the expansion of microfinance and poverty alleviation.

Group credit products where repayment and collection costs are borne by its members represented a "*eureka*" moment for private sector, for-profit financial intermediaries owned by shareholders and financed by commercial banks or international investors to downscale credit to the masses, making profits at negligible operational costs. Allegedly serving an unmet demand, a "good-natured" credit expansion would allow the disenfranchised to self-lift above poverty line by using credit funds to start up a microenterprise. The expansion was sponsored by the World Bank, which saw in the massive reproduction of group lending, a magic bullet to end financial exclusion in the developing world.

What started as a non-profit provision of credit to purposeful entrepreneurs excluded from the formal financial system, rapidly underwent a state-driven effort and a race to monopolize the poor (Rai 2010). What followed was an unprecedented increase in credit allocation that ended up with households' overindebtedness and the Indian microfinance crisis of 2010,[9] covered by multiple outlets including the *New York Times* (Bajaj and Polgreen 2010) and *The Economist*. Default, client suicides, and increased intrahousehold violence unveiled a series of predatory practices coupled with the reworking of existing relationships of debt predicated upon an underlying constellation of class, caste, and gender relations. In doing so, microcredit intermeshed with prevailing power relations surrounding capital accumulation and social distress reproduction among severe dislocations (Taylor 2011: 485). The crisis spread out to West Africa and Central America. These events overshadowed the potential of microcredit in poverty reduction and financial inclusion.

Financial Inclusion by Financializing Social Aid

Another effort towards massive financial inclusion in the developing world was promoted by the G20 Financial Inclusion Action Plan (GPFI), a coordinated platform launched at the Pittsburgh Summit in 2009 (OECD n.d.). GPFI embarked on a crusade to bank the unbanked via financialization of social programs. New actors entered onto the scene including public and private banks, non-banking intermediaries, and FinTech companies (Carmona and Morvant-Roux 2019: 71). Participating financial institutions provided savings accounts with debit cards to disperse social funds. The G2P strategy would kill several birds with one stone. For instance, fostering a cashless society, banks would install ATMs[10] and point-of-sale terminals to serve the new clientele expanding the financial infrastructure; governments would save operational costs, and the beneficiaries would become financially included. Today, 167 million adults have access to a savings account via G2P strategies. These numbers, however, are not free from a few pitfalls.

The study of Gronbach (in Carmona and Morvant-Roux 2019: 71) about the Sassa program in South Africa brought to the surface new social tensions among the poorest in a post-apartheid context after unauthorized bulk sampling coupled with the uncontrolled use of personal information for commercial purposes. Carmona and Morvant-Roux (2019) studied the Mexican case. With 60 percent financial exclusion in 2012, the target was the conditional cash transfer program "Oportunidades"[11] that benefited 6.8 million households. The financial inclusion attempt stalled at the distribution stage. Beneficiaries withdrew the whole amount and left the account dormant until the next funds release. Predicaments for beneficiaries appeared when the program was transferred to a public bank that used the aid as collateral for credit and compulsory savings, causing the poor to lose track of their balances and their liquidity management. Foremostly, the social policy goals were slashed by transforming social aid into a financial product. Moreover, the National Financial Inclusion Survey 2015 showed that only 6.8 percent of the savings accounts were actively used; that is, a simulated financial inclusion contrasting with reported success figures. Carmona et al. (2018) previously examined the causes behind not using debit cards among beneficiaries of Oportunidades, finding lack of knowledge, lack of trust towards financial institutions, and the fact that nearby merchants did not accept digital payments.

Recentralization of Bitcoin by El Salvador's Government

On June 9, 2021, the Legislative Assembly passed the Bitcoin Law—after a three-hour parliamentary debate—establishing Bitcoin as legal tender alongside the US dollar.[12] In September 2021, the law entered into force. Bitcoin's adoption portrayed El Salvador as being at the forefront of innovative countries, with a warm reception from crypto communities across the world. The dissenting voice came from the International Monetary fund (IMF), arguing about the macroeconomic risks that the country would encounter and eventually suffer from the interruption of credit from the agency (BBC 2022).

According to Salvadoran economist Ricardo Castaneda (2022), the Bitcoin policy was pure improvization, with increased opacity in the use of public funds. For instance, to operate the law, the Legislative Assembly authorized a US$225.3 million budget with the elevated opportunity cost in a country that has compelling needs in health, education, and infrastructure. Castaneda signals that the measure increased the risk profile of El Salvador by 200 percent, and mentions that if Bitcoin continues to be part of public balances, the interest rate for the public debt could rise to 25 percent, labeling it "a financial suicide." This chapter does not analyze the macroeconomic risks. Instead, we focus on the inconsistencies between the decentralized and trustless nature of Bitcoin vis-à-vis its recentralization, trusted-based public policy, failing to serve the financially excluded.

Bitcoin law

The law points to high-profile objectives. For instance, it mentions that Bitcoin can function as a gateway to boost foreign investment, become a financial lever to diversify investment portfolios and investor profiles, push forward national development, and insert the country into the Fourth Digital Revolution. The law establishes that the state is committed to guarantee financial inclusion to the 75 percent of Salvadorans currently excluded from the formal financial system (Asamblea Legislativa 2021).

According to the law, Bitcoin can be used to pay taxes. Also, people can exchange US dollars and Bitcoin based on automatic and instantaneous convertibility at the market exchange rate. Every economic agent must accept Bitcoin payments. The capital gains of Bitcoin investments are tax-free, and the law relieves the use of Bitcoin whenever the customer lacks access to the required technology (for example, smartphone or internet connectivity).

To operationalize the law, the government developed and deployed a centralized wallet named Chivo and installed more than 200 cash machines (exchanging USD/Bitcoin) across the country. To encourage adoption, US$30 in Bitcoin was granted after downloading the wallet and filling the know your customer (KYC) requirements. Exchange is performed by a public trust fund in Bandesal, the Salvadoran development bank. Additionally, the government announced the building of Bitcoin City by issuing US$1 billion in public bonds backed by the cryptocurrency, where a volcano near the futuristic city would provide enough energy for Bitcoin mining. Bonds were not issued, and the Bitcoin City remains a concept.

A year later ...

Bitcoin changed the international narrative of El Salvador. A small country in Central America appeared in the financial headlines of international media outlets, and for good reasons. Salvadoran President Nayib Bukele became a crypto influencer and Twitter celebrity with over 4.3 million followers at the time of writing in 2022.[13] However, a deeper look can disenchant. Today, very few households have joined early movers, and more than 60 percent have not made a transaction after spending the free Bitcoin. Among the small group of consumers actively using the app are banked, educated, young males (NBER 2022). A national survey[14] carried out by Universidad Centroamericana showed that 66 percent of Salvadorans consider the Bitcoin policy a "national failure." More results showed that 76 percent have never used Bitcoin as a means of payment, 77 percent are dissatisfied and consider that the government must stop using the public budget to buy Bitcoin, and 77 percent mentioned that their economic situation has not improved (Universidad Centroamericana 2022).

Perception about Bitcoin policy

Two interlocutors in El Salvador provided testimony to us: “Van” is a woman with an e-commerce business; “Ish” is a Bitcoin evangelist and programmer. Their testimonies provide a detailed landscape on the overall national sentiment.

Ish mentioned:

> President Bukele is not talking to the Salvadorans; he is talking to the international community. The government used bitcoin to build the country’s brand, but policymakers did not construct a long term strategy where you have infrastructure, education, and a crypto ecosystem to effectively boost economic growth. You can verify there is no long term view since there is no roadmap and no indicators to measure policy goals. The law creates a monopoly for bitcoin and although there is no ban to use other cryptocurrencies, the government did not create incentives for other exchanges and other digital currencies to circulate in El Salvador.

Van commented: “My husband explained to me how blockchain works, so now I understand that this is an open and decentralized technology. Therefore, why do we need a law to use a cryptocurrency that is out there, available for everybody?”

When we asked Van what she dislikes the most, she answered: “I did not like the invasion of privacy. Chivo wallet belongs to the government, and for the KYC registry, we provided a picture and ID documents. The fact that the government can track my financial activity linked to my personal data is something that bothers me. I prefer not to use the Chivo wallet anymore.”

Traction

Both interlocutors agree that, at the beginning, there was a euphoric atmosphere. Long queues formed at the cash machines and cashier lines to pay with Bitcoin. There was a fever to download the Chivo wallet, mostly driven by the $30 grant. As days went by, the queues became shorter. Today, cash machines are empty, and no merchant accepts Bitcoin payments.

Van says: “At the beginning, I thought bitcoin would bring me more wealth because the price was increasing. Today, I acknowledge that the price of cryptocurrencies fluctuates, and holdings are for the long term.”

Ish confirms that Bitcoin lost traction: “When its price began dropping, people got rid of it and kept transactions in US dollars.”

Knowledge

The two interviewees agree that the introduction of Bitcoin should have incorporated a literacy program for the population, including digital and financial education. Prior knowledge about Bitcoin was non-existent. Financial literacy is also absent, and people did not know the mechanics behind the cryptocurrency.

Ish pointed out that the awareness of cryptocurrencies is concentrated in a small group of young people, predominantly men, and the rest are not really gaining more knowledge about decentralized cryptocurrencies and Web3. Ish mentioned: "Perhaps the next bull market will bring back interest and the need to learn more." Nonetheless, in his view, educating the public should be a national policy, such that El Salvador effectively harnesses the benefits of cryptocurrencies, stablecoins, and decentralized finance. He stated: "The good side of all this disastrous situation is that we have more awakened minds, especially the young who are eager to learn about cryptocurrencies. We must prepare them for the next bull market so that they can benefit from its advantages."

NEOBANKS: THE PRELUDE TO GREATER FINANCIAL DECENTRALIZATION IN BRAZIL

While top-down policies designed to encourage financial inclusion most likely fail, policies that are bottom-up, flexible, and open to competitiveness have borne fruit. Rather than taking over absolute control of the policy execution, these policies set simple, clear rules that allow the market and beneficiaries to participate and develop their own solutions. This is the case of Brazil, where policymakers started introducing reforms on the financial legislation back in 2013 (Gómez 2020). After a hyperinflation period in the 1990s that reached a peak of 80 percent, banks were unable to weather the storm. The three largest private banks in the country went bankrupt, and more than 38 banks merged to create five large banks. During the next two decades, these banks created an oligopolistic environment that strengthened after the 2008 global financial crisis, since governments tightened regulations to avoid future bank collapses. Five Brazilian banks controlled over 80 percent of all financial assets (Vicente 2020: 9). In Latin American countries, bank concentration translates into financial exclusion: by 2010, around 40 percent of Brazilian adults did not have a bank account. To promote financial innovation and inclusion, in 2013, policymakers enacted new rules to modernize the payment system, encompassing electronic payments. The rules came into force in 2014, regulating mobile payments, prepaid cards, and electronic currencies. Other policies related to removing barriers in the offering of other financial services such as digital loans and crowdfunding, as well as open banking, have followed (Gómez 2020).

In 2013, officials granted a bank license to an emergent, digital-only financial institution (neobank). It was the Sao Paulo-based Nubank. Neobanks are a new generation of lean institutions with banking licenses that operate exclusively online and offer streamlined, low-cost services. By leveraging cutting-edge technology such as artificial intelligence, they offer tailored finances and better user experiences (Gómez 2020).

Today, with over 50 million active accounts across Latin America, Nubank has served 5.6 million previously unbanked people (Cárdenas 2022). At least nine other neobanks and a dozen challenger banks—those lacking a bank license—were created afterwards (Gómez 2020). New players have made banking in Brazil more competitive and inclusive, becoming drivers of financial and socioeconomic development in the country by targeting those who are historically unbanked (Vicente 2020: 1). As of mid-2022, almost 85 percent of the population have access to financial services (Cárdenas 2022).

The same conditions that led neobanks to flourish might operate similarly in DeFi expansion as a lever to fill the pending gap in financial inclusion, and financial wealth improvement for those already served. For instance, in January 2022, a cryptoasset manager launched the first Latin American DeFi exchange traded fund (ETF) tracking a basket of DeFi projects, deepening the industry's foray into virtual assets (Johnson 2022: para. 1); whereas among non-institutional investors, Brazil appeared in the Chainalysis Global DeFi Adoption Index 2022, occupying the 7th position on a worldwide level. It is worth noting that the index quantifies and locates countries where DeFi has penetrated the most, and where cryptocurrency markets are well developed (Bitcoin News 2021).

CONCLUSION

The chapter has presented the case for DeFi as a lever for financial inclusion in the developing world by highlighting how the technology behind it enhances the power of users to build, govern, customize, and fulfill their financial needs. To do so, the analysis compares DeFi against traditional banking systems that have failed to fully incorporate the disenfranchised populations. In addition to the former, the chapter contributes to the literature from a little-explored perspective that deromanticizes the assumption that with the sole introduction of financial technology, the society will automatically harness its benefits. The chapter shows that policy matters, and that socioeconomic considerations are important, through contrasting cases in history. For instance, in El Salvador, top-down monopolistic policies risk extending the pathologies of financial globalization (Campbell-Verduyn and Goguen 2018); whereas in Brazil, a more comprehensive regulation created conditions for the emergence of digital banks that effectively increased the financial inclusion indicators. Finally, we discuss some DeFi challenges ahead, such as the unavoidable financial and digital education program in which the same technology offers novel mechanisms to attract large populations into learning new topics, the need for friendly and easy mobile applications with intuitive walkthrough, and the design of financial products where the risk tolerance is a choice and not an imposition of the DeFi protocols.

NOTES

1. These characteristics refer to public open source blockchains. Records of transactions become less traceable and more private in permissioned distributed ledgers.

2. The token delegation process to validate transactions and make staking profits occurs in blockchains whose consensus mechanism is precisely the proof-of-stake.
3. Informal economic activities are businesses or employment conditions that are outside the fiscal and regulatory framework. Latin America and Sub-Saharan Africa have the highest levels of informality.
4. Bangladesh, Brazil, China, Colombia, Côte d'Ivoire, Democratic Republic of the Congo (DRC), Egypt, Ethiopia, India, Indonesia, Kenya, Mexico, Morocco, Mozambique, Myanmar, Nigeria, Pakistan, Peru, the Philippines, Rwanda, South Africa, Vietnam, Tanzania, Turkey, and Zambia.
5. The last mile problem: the lack of access to information and communication technologies is a barrier to financial inclusion (as well as for other Sustainable Development Goals). As of 2021, 2.9 billion people remain offline, of whom 96 percent live in developing countries (ITU 2021). This issue is beyond the scope of this chapter.
6. In this section the analysis of banks encompasses MFIs and FinTech platforms.
7. For example $5 per month is what an indigenous family among the poorest of the poor in the Highlands of Southern Mexico can save.
8. Nexus Mutual provides insurance against hacking and other security vulnerabilities in DeFi protocols. However the relevant aspect for this chapter is that the same model can be extended to other coverage.
9. Crisis initiated in Andhra Pradesh and Krishna.
10. ATMs are automated teller machines that in the Mexican program allowed for simple financial operations such as cash withdrawal, checking balances, and paying for credits.
11. *Oportunidades* means opportunities.
12. The US dollar has been legal tender in El Salvador since November 2000.
13. @nayibbukele has 4.3 million followers as of October 24, 2022.
14. The surveys were levied on September 9 27, 2022 in a national representative sample of 1269 interviews, with 95 percent confidence level, 2.75 percent error.

REFERENCES

Asamblea Legislativa. (2021). *Ley Bitcoin*. Asamblea. Retrieved October 25, 2022, from https://www.asamblea.gob.sv/taxonomy/term/933.

Bajaj, V., and Polgreen, L. (2010). India Microcredit Sector Faces Collapse From Defaults. *New York Times*. https://www.nytimes.com/2010/11/18/world/asia/18micro.html.

BBC. (2022). *IMF Urges El Salvador to Remove Bitcoin as Legal Tender*. BBC. https://www.bbc.com/news/world-latin-america-60135552.

Bitcoin News. (2021). *Brazil and Argentina Present in Chainalysis Defi Adoption Index – Bitcoin News*. Bitcoin.com News. https://news.bitcoin.com/brazil-and-argentina-present-in-chainalysis-defi-adoption-index/.

Campbell-Verduyn, M., and Goguen, M. (2018). Blockchains, Trust, and Action Nets: Extending the Pathologies of Financial Globalization. *Global Networks*.

Cárdenas, A. (2022). Brasil líder en inclusión: 85% de la población accede a servicios financieros. *Economy*. https://www.economy.com.bo/articulo/banca-finanzas/brasil-lider-inclusion-85-poblacion-accede-servicios-financieros/20220610131046006391.html.

Carmona, M., Crucifix, C., Morvant-Roux, S., Angulo, L., and González Quintero, J.C. (2018). *Inclusión financiera y transferencias condicionadas: ¿desafiar o reproducir relaciones de género?* Universidad de Guadalajara.

Carmona, M., and Morvant-Roux, S. (2019). La Financiarisation des politiques sociales au Mexique: la laborieuse conversion des transferts monétaires en produits financiers. *Mondes en Développement*, *4*(188), 69–84.

Castaneda, R. (2022). *La Ley Bitcoin debe derogarse*. ICEFI. https://mail.icefi.org/blog/la-ley-bitcoin-debe-derogarse-0.

CGAP. (2008). *Are We Overestimating Demand for Microloans?* CGAP. https://www.cgap.org/sites/default/files/CGAP-Brief-Are-We-Overestimating-Demand-for-Microloans-Apr-2008.pdf.

Chen, C., Zhang, L., Li, Y., Liao, T., Zhao, S., Zheng, Z., and Huang, H. (2022). When Digital Economy Meets Web 3.0: Applications and Challenges. *ArXiv*, *abs/2210.08993*, 1–14. Semantic Scholar. arXiv:2210.08993v1.

Frankenfield, J. (2022). *Decentralized Applications (dApps): Definition, Uses, Pros and Cons*. Investopedia. https://www.investopedia.com/terms/d/decentralized-applications-dapps.asp.

Gómez, P. (2020). *Neobanks a Game-Changer for Unbanked in Brazil*. Econ Americas. https://econamericas.com/2020/09/neobanks-a-game-changer-for-unbanked-in-brazil/.

GPFI. (2016). *G20 High-Level Principles for Digital Financial Inclusion*. Global Partnership for Financial Inclusion. https://www.gpfi.org/sites/gpfi/files/G20%20High%20Level%20Principles%20for%20Digital%20Financial%20Inclusion.pdf.

Greenberg, L. (n.d.). *Guidelines for Establishing and Operating Grameen-Style Microcredit Programs*. Grameen Foundation. https://grameenfoundation.org/documents/GrameenGuidelines.pdf.

Hayes, A. (2022). *Stablecoins: Definition, How They Work, and Types*. Investopedia. https://www.investopedia.com/terms/s/stablecoin.asp.

Ifrim, O. (2022). *The Many Faces of Financial Exclusion in the Developed Markets and Who is at Risk*. The Paypers. https://thepaypers.com/expert-opinion/the-many-faces-of-financial-exclusion-in-the-developed-markets-and-who-is-at-risk--1257545.

ITU. (2021). *Facts and Figures 2021*. https://www.itu.int/itu-d/reports/statistics/2021/11/15/internet-use/.

Johnson, S. (2022). World's First DeFi ETF to Launch in Brazil Next Month. *Financial Times*. https://www.ft.com/content/2d00d0e4-0297-484d-aaa5-069bf4df64b7.

Mainsah, E., Heuer, S.R., Aprajita, K., and Zhang, Q. (2004). *Grameen Bank: Taking Capitalism to the Poor*. Columbia Business School. https://www0.gsb.columbia.edu/mygsb/faculty/research/pubfiles/848/Grameen_Bank_v04.pdf.

Monolith. (2021). *Understanding DeFi: Composability Explained | by Monolith | Monolith*. Medium. https://medium.com/monolith/understanding-defi-composability-explained-70f93d9c0f01.

NBER. (2022). *El Salvador's Experiment with Bitcoin as Legal Tender*. National Bureau of Economic Research. https://www.nber.org/digest/202207/el-salvadors-experiment-bitcoin-legal-tender.

OECD. (n.d.). *Leaders' Statement The Pittsburgh Summit*. https://www.oecd.org/g20/summits/pittsburgh/G20-Pittsburgh-Leaders-Declaration.pdf.

Ozili, P. (2020). Theories of financial inclusion. *Munich Personal RePEc Archive*, 1–22. https://mpra.ub.uni-muenchen.de/109579.

Raghuveera, N. (2021). *Designing Decentralized Finance for Financial Inclusion*. Atlantic Council. https://www.atlanticcouncil.org/wp-content/uploads/2021/10/Designing-decentralized-finance-for-financial-inclusion.pdf.

Rai, V. (2010). India's Microfinance Crisis is a Battle to Monopolize the Poor. *Harvard Business Review*. https://hbr.org/2010/11/indias-microfinance-crisis-is.

Sigova, M., Vasiliev, S., and Kliuchnikov, O. (2021). Financial Inclusions in Social Networks. *Globalization and its Socio-Economic Consequences*, *92*. https://doi.org/10.1051/shsconf/20219206034.

Strüker, J., Urbach, N., Gramlich, V., Principato, M., Schellinger, B., Sedlmeir, J., Amend, J., Stramm, J., and Zwede, T. (2022). *Decentralized Finance—Foundations, Applications, Potentials and Challenges*. Branch Business and Information Systems Engineering of Fraunhofer FIT.
Taylor, M. (2011). Freedom from Poverty is Not for Free: Rural Development and the Microfinance Crisis in Andhra Pradesh, India. *Journal of Agrarian Change*, *11*(4), 484–504.
Universidad Centroamericana. (2022). *Boletín bitcoin y Régimen de Excepción*. UCA. https://uca.edu.sv/iudop/wp-content/uploads/Boletin-de-Regimen-de-Excepcion.pdf.
Vicente, J. (2020). Fintech Disruption in Brazil: A Study on the Impact of Open Banking and Instant Payments in the Brazilian Financial Landscape. *Social Impact Research Experience (SIRE)*, *86*. ScholarlyCommons.
WEF. (2022). *Why Decentralized Finance is Good News for the Unbanked*. World Economic Forum. https://www.weforum.org/agenda/2022/09/decentralized-finance-a-leapfrog-technology-for-the-unbanked/.
Westermeier, C. (2020). Money is Data—The Platformization of Financial Transactions. *Information, Communication and Society*, *23*(14), 2047–2063.
World Bank. (n.d.). *Country Progress*. Universal Financial Access. Retrieved October 23, 2022, from https://ufa.worldbank.org/en/country-progress.
World Bank. (2017). *Distributed Ledger Technology (DLT) and Blockchain*. World Bank. https://openknowledge.worldbank.org/bitstream/handle/10986/29053/WP-PUBLIC-Distributed-Ledger-Technology-and-Blockchain-Fintech-Notes.pdf?sequence=5&isAllowed=y.
World Bank. (2022a). *Financial Inclusion Overview*. World Bank. https://www.worldbank.org/en/topic/financialinclusion/overview.
World Bank. (2022b). *The Global Findex Database 2021*. World Bank. https://www.worldbank.org/en/publication/globalfindex/Report.

Index